BUSINESS CYCLES, PART II

F. A. HAYEK

THE COLLECTED WORKS OF

F. A. Hayek

BUSINESS CYCLES
PART II

Edited by Hansjoerg Klausinger

Liberty Fund

This book is published by Liberty Fund, Inc., a foundation established to encourage study of the ideal of a society of free and responsible individuals.

𒀀𒈠𒄄

The cuneiform inscription that serves as our logo and as the design motif for our endpapers is the earliest-known written appearance of the word "freedom" (*amagi*), or "liberty." It is taken from a clay document written about 2300 B.C. in the Sumerian city-state of Lagash.

Business Cycles, Part II is volume 8 of The Collected Works of F. A. Hayek, published by The University of Chicago Press.

This Liberty Fund paperback edition of *Business Cycles, Part II* is published by arrangement with The University of Chicago Press and Taylor & Francis Books, Ltd., a member of the Taylor & Francis Group.

17   18   19   20   21   P   5   4   3   2   1

Frontispiece: Friedrich Hayek © Bettmann/CORBIS
Cover photo: Friedrich August von Hayek © Hulton-Deutsch Collection/CORBIS

Library of Congress Cataloging-in-Publication Data

Names: Hayek, Friedrich A. von (Friedrich August), 1899–1992, author. |
    Klausinger, Hansjörg, editor.
Title: Business cycles / edited by Hansjörg Klausinger.
Description: Indianapolis : Liberty Fund, 2017. | Series: The collected works of
    F.A. Hayek ; volumes 7–8 | Originally issued as a 2 volume hardback set in 2012.
    | Contents: Part I – Part II. | Includes bibliographical references and index.
Identifiers: LCCN 2016020043 | ISBN 9780865979031 (part 1 : pbk. : alk. paper)
    | ISBN 9780865979048 (part 2 : pbk. : alk. paper)
Subjects: LCSH: Business cycles. | Prices. | Money.
Classification: LCC HB3711 .H349 2017 | DDC 338.5/42–dc23
LC record available at https://lccn.loc.gov/2016020043

Liberty Fund, Inc.
11301 North Meridian Street
Carmel, Indiana 46032-4564

This book is printed on paper that is acid-free and meets the requirements of the American National Standard for Permanence of Paper for Printed Library Materials, Z39.48-1992. ♾

Cover design by Erin Kirk New, Watkinsville, Georgia
Printed and bound by Thomson-Shore, Dexter, Michigan

THE COLLECTED WORKS OF F. A. HAYEK

Founding Editor: W. W. Bartley III
General Editor: Bruce Caldwell

*The University of Chicago Press edition
was published with the support of*

The Hoover Institution on War, Revolution,
and Peace, Stanford University

The Cato Institute

The Earhart Foundation

The Pierre F. and Enid Goodrich Foundation

The Heritage Foundation

The Morris Foundation, Little Rock

CONTENTS

EDITORIAL FOREWORD

This volume complements the first part of *Business Cycles*, which contains Hayek's two major monographs on money and the cycle, with a series of shorter papers, stretching from the 1920s to his final word on these matters in 1981. In particular, this volume includes four hitherto unpublished contributions: The first, and possibly most important, results from a book project that Hayek pursued between 1924 and 1929, the "Geldtheoretische Untersuchungen", of which an unfinished typescript of eight chapters has survived in the Friedrich A. von Hayek Papers at the Hoover Institution Archives; this fragment is published here for the first time, translated as "Investigations into Monetary Theory" (chapter 1). Two of the unpublished contributions relate to Hayek's London School of Economics (LSE) lectures in January 1931 that gave rise to *Prices and Production* (1931): one is a lecture given at the University of Cambridge on his way to London ("The Purchasing Power of the Consumer and the Depression", chapter 2); the other lecture was presented in 1981, on the fiftieth anniversary of these LSE lectures ("The Flow of Goods and Services", chapter 12). Finally, a short typescript prepared for a London publisher ("Restoring the Price-Level?") is also reproduced here for the first time. My hope is that the availability of these hitherto unpublished materials will serve to deepen our understanding of Hayek's thought on money and the cycle.

With regard to the presentation of the text this edition keeps to the standard established for the *Collected Works*. Specifically, the full reference of a source is always given at the first quotation and abbreviated references when there are further quotations; however, the Editor's Introduction and each of the chapters are treated as self-contained parts to which this rule applies separately. Inaccurate quotations have been left as in Hayek's original, yet these inaccuracies will be corrected: in the text these are pointed out in accompanying editorial notes, and in the footnotes inaccurate quotations are supplemented by corrections in brackets. Incomplete references by Hayek will be silently supplemented, yet brackets are used for correcting references that are definitely wrong, e.g., as regards the author's name, title, or pagination. Finally, the translations from German-language sources are principally by the editor, if no other source is indicated.

This volume would not have been produced had it not been for help and support from various persons and institutions. Papers relating to my editorial work on Hayek's *Business Cycles* have been presented at numerous conferences and seminars throughout Europe, in the United States, and in Japan, and the final result has indeed much profited from the suggestions and queries received on these occasions. Of the persons to whom I feel most indebted, I would like to mention—without any claim to completeness—Roger Garrison, Susan Howson, Robert Leonard, Larry White, Günter Chaloupek, Harald Hagemann, Heinz D. Kurz, Hans-Michael Trautwein and Arash Molavi Vasséi, and among my colleages at the WU (Wirtschaftsuniversität) Vienna, J. Hanns Pichler, Alfred Sitz, and Herbert Walther. The comments by two anonymous readers of the original typescript proved invaluable for improving the final outcome. I have also to acknowledge with many thanks the hospitality I experienced at the University of Stuttgart-Hohenheim, the Walter Eucken-Institute (Freiburg im Breisgau), Hitotsubashi University (Tachikawa), and Yokohama National University, and in particular the stimulating atmosphere during my stay as a senior research fellow of the Duke Center for the History of Political Economy, with special thanks to Craufurd Goodwin, Kevin D. Hoover, Neil de Marchi, E. Roy Weintraub, and in particular to Bruce Caldwell, also in his capacity as the most helpful and patient general editor of this series. Having made heavy use of these facilities, I also want to thank the staff of all the libraries and archives I visited in the course of my research on Hayek.

I am grateful to Anthony Courakis, the literary executor of Sir John Hicks, for permission to quote from the unpublished correspondence of Sir John Hicks; to the Hoover Institution Archives (copyright Stanford University), the repository of the Machlup papers, for the unpublished correspondence of Fritz Machlup; and of course to the Estate of F. A. Hayek for his unpublished papers and correspondence. Furthermore, I would like to thank Mary Kaldor as well as John Wiley and Sons, Ltd., for permission to reprint Nicholas Kaldor's "Professor Hayek and the Concertina-Effect" and "Postscript". I have also to thank Murray Milgate for generously making his correspondence with Hayek available to me. Finally, work on these volumes has been much facilitated by financial assistance from the WU-Jubiläumsstiftung, which provided the financial means for a one-year sabbatical (*Forschungsvertrag*), and the Austrian National Bank for awarding its *Internationalisierungspreis*, which I gratefully acknowledge.

Hansjoerg Klausinger

INTRODUCTION

The contributions to the theory of the cycle collected in this volume encompass a period of more than fifty years—from an early hitherto unpublished typescript to a paper that Hayek presented at the fiftieth anniversary of his famous LSE lectures. Thus it also documents the evolution of Hayek's thought, and concomitantly the rise, transient decline, and ultimate restoration of Hayek's reputation as an economic theorist.

After a short biographical sketch, this introduction will concentrate on two issues: first, on Hayek's attempts to cope with the problem of deflation and his final and vain effort to provide a dynamic foundation for his theory of the cycle, the two areas of Hayek's approach most vulnerable to criticism, and second, on the continuity and change that may be seen in Hayek's system of thought during his long struggle to free himself from the suppositions of the equilibrium framework in which his early writings were embedded.

Hayek in London, 1931–42

In the introduction to the companion volume[1] we left off at the point at which Hayek had arrived at the London School of Economics (LSE) in 1931 and on the eve of the controversies in which he, together with other members of the faculty, was soon to be embroiled. These included, for example, Lionel Robbins's clash in the Macmillan Committee with John Maynard Keynes, in particular on the issue of free trade, and Hayek's early confrontation with Keynes and Cambridge, highlighted by the mutual reviews of Keynes's *A Treatise on Money* by Hayek and of Hayek's *Prices and Production* by Keynes and Piero Sraffa.[2] With regard to economic policy the challenge of the Great Depression

---

[1] *Business Cycles, Part I*, ed. Hansjoerg Klausinger, vol. 7 (2012) of *The Collected Works of F. A. Hayek* (Chicago: University of Chicago Press).

[2] John Maynard Keynes, *A Treatise on Money*, 2 vols. (London: Macmillan, 1930), reprinted as vols. 5 and 6 (1971) of *The Collected Writings of John Maynard Keynes*, ed. Austin Robinson and Donald Moggridge (London: Macmillan; Cambridge: Cambridge University Press); and F. A. Hayek, *Prices and Production* (London: Routledge, 1931; 2nd ed. rev., 1935), reprinted in F. A.

initiated a series of public debates on the question of reflation,[3] on saving versus spending,[4] and on stable prices versus neutral money.[5] Outside the domain of money and the cycle the other battles fought by Hayek and the Austrians ought not to be forgotten, that is, the controversies on the nature of capital, on economic calculation under socialism, and generally on the trend of recent economic thinking. As these battles took place during the 1930s Hayek and the liberal camp he represented were repeatedly seen to be on the losing side,[6] and consequently his influence on economic policy-making as well as his reputation as a first-rate economic theorist began to wane.

A similar evolution can be discerned with regard to the circle of Hayek's students at LSE. Although Hayek had never attempted to transform this circle of disciples into a 'school', as time went by the attraction of being regarded a follower of Hayek was fading. To give but a few examples, John R. Hicks's leaving London in 1935 for a lectureship at Cambridge was widely considered a serious loss, although he collaborated there more closely with Dennis Robertson than with Keynes and the Cambridge circus; others like Abba P. Lerner and G. L. S. Shackle after a spell under Hayek's influence converted to Keynesianism. Lerner after spending six months at Cambridge in 1934–35 immigrated to the United States in 1937; at the same time Shackle, who had started his thesis under Hayek's supervision, changed the topic to a Keynesian theme. Whereas many of Hayek's former disciples, like those just mentioned, affirmed their continuing high esteem for Hayek's achievements as a theorist,[7]

Hayek, *Business Cycles, Part I*. On the debate cf. the editor's introduction and the respective chapters in *Contra Keynes and Cambridge: Essays, Correspondence*, ed. Bruce Caldwell, vol. 9 (1995) of *The Collected Works of F. A. Hayek*.

[3] Cf. in particular Lionel Robbins, "Letters to the Editor: Monetary Policy", *Economist*, May 14 and 28, June 11, 1932, pp. 1081, 1188–89 and 1295, and Roy F. Harrod, "Letters to the Editor: Monetary Policy", *Economist*, June 4 and 18, 1932, pp. 1242–43 and 1358.

[4] Cf. in particular the letters to the editor signed by Harrod et al. in the *Times*, July 5, 1932, p. 10, and March 10, 1933, p. 15. Another letter ("Private Spending—Money for Productive Investment. A Comment by Economists") by D. H. Macgregor, Arthur Cecil Pigou, John Maynard Keynes, Walter Layton, Arthur Salter, and Josiah C. Stamp appeared in the *Times*, October 17, 1932, p. 13, and was followed by a critical comment ("Spending and Saving—Public Works from Rates") by Theodore E. Gregory, F. A. Hayek, Arnold Plant, and Lionel Robbins (October 17, 1932, p. 13), and a reply by the former ("Spending and Saving—What Are National Resources? The Economists' Reply", October 21, 1932, p. 15).

[5] On this debate see the editor's introduction to F. A. Hayek, *Business Cycles, Part I*, p. 36.

[6] Cf. Mark Blaug, "Commentary", in *Austrian Economics: Tensions and New Directions*, ed. Bruce J. Caldwell and Stephan Boehm (Boston, Dordrecht and London: Kluwer, 1992), pp. 31–34.

[7] Cf., e.g., John Hicks, "The Hayek Story", in *Critical Essays in Monetary Theory* (Oxford: Oxford University Press, 1967), pp. 203–15; and George L. S. Shackle, "F. A. Hayek, 1899–", in *Pioneers of Modern Economics in Britain*, ed. D. P. O'Brien and John R. Presley (London: Macmillan; Totowa, NJ: Barnes and Noble, 1981), pp. 234–62. Indeed, Shackle in his specific brand of Keynesianism combined a Hayekian concern with the role of knowledge in economic affairs with Keynes's emphasis on uncertainty.

the case of Nicholas Kaldor was different, and paradigmatic for the turning from disciple to foe. As Kaldor also played a vital role in the controversy that for nearly three decades ended Hayek's endeavours in the theories of money and the cycle, the relationship between Hayek and Kaldor in the 1930s shall be addressed here more thoroughly.[8]

In 1930 Kaldor had just graduated from LSE and been awarded a two-year research studentship which he used to embark on a research project on the economic problems of the Danubian succession states. The geographical focus of this project provided the first contacts with the Austrian school and in particular with Hayek. Possibly at the initiative of Robbins, Kaldor in 1930 had translated Hayek's habilitation lecture[9] and was offering to translate *Geldtheorie und Konjunkturtheorie*,[10] and from May to July 1931 Kaldor visited Vienna to enrol for the summer term at the university. Thus, when he and Hayek met again in London, at the beginning of Kaldor's career as a professional economist, all his contemporaneous writings, whether on the economics of the Danubian states, the origins of the Austrian banking crisis, free trade and exchange restrictions, or the possibility of technological unemployment, were firmly rooted in the specifically Austrian version of liberal thought. In this regard, it might then have been difficult to decide if he considered himself more a disciple of Hayek or of Robbins.

Just as Hayek was becoming entangled in his famous controversies with Keynes and Sraffa, however, Kaldor began to dissociate himself from his teachers, possibly due to Hicks and Brinley Thomas disseminating the novel approach of the Swedish economists, in particular of Gunnar Myrdal.[11] Consequently, in the controversy (between Harrod and Hayek) on stable prices versus neutral money Kaldor adopted an intermediate position, and he remained conspicuously silent on the themes of reflation and public spending. Furthermore, he actively participated in the imperfect competition revolution of Edward Chamberlin and Joan Robinson, and his view of excess capacity as a po-

---

[8] The following draws on Hansjoerg Klausinger, "Hayek and Kaldor: Close Encounter at LSE", *History of Economic Ideas*, vol. 19, no. 2 (2011).

[9] Jointly with Georg Tugendhat, published as "The 'Paradox' of Saving", *Economica*, no. 32, May 1931, pp. 125–69, reprinted as chapter 2 of F. A. Hayek, *Contra Keynes and Cambridge*.

[10] Cf. Hayek to Kaldor, December 1, 1930, in the Nicholas Kaldor Papers, section 3, box 4, King's College Archive Centre, Cambridge. Eventually the translation became a joint effort by Kaldor and Honoria Croome, another of Robbins's students (see *Monetary Theory and the Trade Cycle* [London: Cape, 1933], reprinted in F. A. Hayek, *Business Cycles, Part I*).

[11] Cf. Gunnar Myrdal, "Der Gleichgewichtsbegriff als Instrument der geldtheoretischen Analyse", in *Beiträge zur Geldtheorie*, ed. F. A. Hayek (Vienna: Springer, 1933; reprinted, Berlin, Heidelberg, and New York: Springer, 2007), pp. 361–487; see for an English translation *Monetary Equilibrium* (London: Hodge, 1939; reprinted, New York: Kelley, 1965). On the Swedish influence see Nadim Shehadi, "The London School of Economics and the Stockholm School in the 1930s", in *The Stockholm School of Economics Revisited*, ed. Lars Jonung (Cambridge: Cambridge University Press, 1991), pp. 382–83.

tential justification for government regulation for the first time drew explicit protest from Hayek's side (albeit only in private correspondence).[12]

If by then Kaldor's distancing from Hayek's position was already becoming evident, things changed dramatically with the appearance of Keynes's *General Theory*[13] and Kaldor's rapid conversion. At first, Kaldor's thought evolved in two directions; he contributed to the development of the Keynesian approach, yet also continued in his attempt at a synthesis of capital and business cycle theory. As a by-product of this endeavour he severely criticised Hayek's attempts directed at a similar aim. Typical examples of Kaldor's critique are his survey on capital theory and, in particular, two companion papers on capital intensity and the cycle, the one conceived as a logical and empirical criticism of Hayek's *Prices and Production*, the other dealing more generally with structural obstacles to the sustainability of full employment.[14] When Hayek published his final venture into the theory of the trade cycle, introducing the notion of the Ricardo effect, this gave rise to the ultimate showdown. First, Tom Wilson, whose thesis was supervised by Kaldor, called into question the microeconomic foundation and thus the logical validity of the Ricardo effect, to which Hayek responded with another attempt at clarification.[15] Yet, it was Kaldor himself who in a devastating critique dealt the final blow (or so it appeared to contemporaries) to the Hayekian edifice.[16] In any case, apart from a short reply, Hayek remained silent on matters of money and the cycle for more than twenty years.[17] This

[12] Cf. Nicholas Kaldor, "Market Imperfection and Excess Capacity", *Economica*, n.s., vol. 2, February 1935, pp. 33–50, reprinted as chapter 4 of *Essays on Value and Distribution*, vol. 1 of *Collected Economic Essays* (London: Duckworth, 1960; 2nd ed., 1980), and the correspondence between Hayek ("A Note on Kaldor", typescript [1935?]) and Kaldor ("Reply to Hayek", typescript [1935?], both in the Friedrich A. von Hayek Papers, box 105, folder 18, Hoover Institution Archives, Stanford University).

[13] John Maynard Keynes, *The General Theory of Employment, Interest and Money* (London: Macmillan, 1936), reprinted as vol. 7 (1971) of *The Collected Writings of John Maynard Keynes*.

[14] Cf., respectively, Nicholas Kaldor, "Annual Survey of Economic Theory: The Recent Controversy on the Theory of Capital", *Econometrica*, vol. 5, July 1937, pp. 201–33, reprinted as chapter 9 of his *Essays on Value and Distribution*; "Capital Intensity and the Trade Cycle", *Economica*, n.s., vol. 6, February 1939, pp. 40–66, and "Stability and Full Employment", *Economic Journal*, vol. 48, December 1938, pp. 642–57, reprinted as chapters 6 and 5, respectively, of his *Essays on Economic Stability and Growth*, vol. 2 of *Collected Economic Essays*.

[15] Cf., respectively, F. A. Hayek, "Profits, Interest and Investment", chapter 1 of *Profits, Interest and Investment. And Other Essays on the Theory of Industrial Fluctuations* (London: Routledge and Sons, 1939), reprinted as chapter 8 of this volume; Tom Wilson, "Capital Theory and the Trade Cycle", *Review of Economic Studies*, vol. 7, June 1940, pp. 169–79; and F. A. Hayek, "The Ricardo Effect", *Economica*, n.s., vol. 9, May 1942, pp. 127–52, reprinted as chapter 9 of this volume.

[16] Nicholas Kaldor, "Professor Hayek and the Concertina-Effect", *Economica*, n.s., vol. 9, November 1942, pp. 359–82, reprinted as chapter 10 of this volume.

[17] F. A. Hayek, "A Comment", *Economica*, n.s., vol. 9, November 1942, pp. 383–85, reprinted in this volume, pp. 313–15. He eventually returned to this topic with "Three Elucidations of the

concluded, for a time, the scientific controversy between Hayek and Kaldor, yet animosities between them were to persist for the rest of their lives.

Coping with Deflation

Just at the time when Hayek had entered the scene as an economic theorist in Great Britain, the economies of the major industrial countries found themselves in the midst of what came to be known as the Great Depression,[18] characterised by a slump in production, high rates of unemployment, and a fall in prices accompanied by a shrinking circulation of money. As soon as the fall in prices made itself felt, a debate on the proper reaction in terms of monetary policy evolved, in particular on whether the authorities should respond with expansionist policies and reflation. Indeed, policies for preventing and counteracting deflation appeared to follow from Hayek's stance, too, as neutral money to a first approximation corresponded to a policy of stabilising monetary circulation. Yet, as is well known, Hayek—like most of the economists close to the Austrian school—refrained from any such proposals and was extremely cautious with regard to expansionist monetary policies. Therefore a crucial question to be addressed is how Hayek conceived of the phenomenon of deflation and why he remained so hostile to anti-deflation policies.[19]

In order to answer this question it is necessary to reconstruct Hayek's approach to deflation.[20] To recapitulate, according to Hayek's theory the crisis is

---

Ricardo Effect", *Journal of Political Economy*, vol. 77, March/April 1969, pp. 274–85, reprinted as chapter 11 of this volume.

[18] Cf., e.g., Lionel Robbins, *The Great Depression* (London: Macmillan, 1934; reprinted, Auburn, AL: Ludwig von Mises Institute, 2007).

[19] On the related issue of stable prices versus neutral money in the presence of technical progress cf. the editor's introduction to F. A. Hayek, *Business Cycles, Part I*, pp. 34–39.

[20] Hayek's concern with deflation started in 1931, when he began discussing it with Gottfried Haberler, Fritz Machlup, and Wilhelm Röpke in a correspondence of which unfortunately only a single letter survived (Hayek to Haberler, December 20, 1931, Gottfried Haberler Papers, box 65, Hoover Institution Archives, Stanford University; an excerpt is reprinted in this volume as an appendix to chapter 5). He had not dealt before with deflation in his two monographs, *Geldtheorie und Konjunkturtheorie* (Vienna: Springer, 1929; reprinted, Salzburg: Neugebauer, 1976) and *Prices and Production* (1st ed., 1931), yet he added short passages to the prefaces of the respective English and German versions, *Monetary Theory and the Trade Cycle* (1933) and *Preise und Produktion* (Vienna: Springer, 1931; reprinted 1976), both prefaces reprinted in F. A. Hayek, *Business Cycles, Part I*. Next, some reflections on deflation and the policies directed at it are to be found in a contribution to *Der Deutsche Volkswirt* ("Das Schicksal der Goldwährung", vol. 6, February 12 and 19, 1932, translated as "The Fate of the Gold Standard" and reprinted as chapter 3 of *Good Money, Part I: The New World*, ed. Stephen Kresge, vol. 5 (1999) of *The Collected Works of F. A. Hayek*), and in a comment on the current monetary policy of the Federal Reserve System in a Viennese daily ("Die Bedeutung der New-Yorker Börsenhausse. Konjunkturumschwung?", *Neues*

caused by a maladjustment in the structure of production typically initiated by a credit boom, such that the period of production (representing the capitalistic structure of production) is lengthened beyond what can be sustained by the rate of voluntary savings. The necessary reallocation of resources and its consequences give rise to crisis and depression. Thus, the 'primary' cause of the crisis is a kind of 'capital scarcity' while the depression represents an adjustment process by which the capital structure is adapted. This process can, but need not, be accompanied by deflation. It is in this specific meaning that Hayek speaks of deflation as being 'secondary', for example, when referring to "these (in a methodological sense) secondary complications which arise during the depression", or maintains that "the process of deflation represents only a secondary phenomenon".[21] It should also be clear that Hayek was propounding the definition of deflation then prevailing in Austrian circles, that is, deflation as a decrease in (the circulation of) money as opposed to the more common meaning of a decrease in prices (or the price level).[22]

A full understanding of the primary-secondary distinction as well as the policy conclusions drawn from it requires a short glance at the contemporary German debate. The origin of the terms derived most probably from Schumpeter, who in his writings on the business cycle distinguished between two types of liquidation (or depression): 'normal' and 'abnormal', 'primary' and 'secondary', or later on between 'recession' and 'depression'.[23] In this vein,

---

Wiener Tagblatt, August 21, 1932, p. 16). In 1933 Hayek devoted a section of his "Der Stand und die nächste Zukunft der Konjunkturforschung" (in *Festschrift für Arthur Spiethoff*, ed. Gustav Clausing (Munich: Duncker and Humblot, 1933), pp. 110–17, translated as "The Present State and Immediate Prospects of the Study of Industrial Fluctuations" and reprinted as chapter 4 of this volume) to the problem of secondary deflation. He dealt with reflation in a short paper, "Restoring the Price Level?", intended for a London publisher (reprinted as chapter 5 of this volume), but appearing instead the following year in Italian as "Una politica artificiale dei prezzi" (in the biweekly *La Borsa – Quindicinale dei mercati finanziari*, no. 25, March 3, 1934, pp. 3–4). The issue was once again taken up in some detail in "Capital and Industrial Fluctuations" (*Econometrica*, vol. 2, April 1934, pp. 152–67, reprinted as chapter 6 of this volume), later on included as an appendix in the revised second edition of *Prices and Production* (1935), which otherwise contained no modifications of his views on the mechanism of depression. After discussing the limits set for monetary policies within a framework of an international monetary system in *Monetary Nationalism and International Stability* (Geneva: Longmans, 1937; reprinted as chapter 1 of *Good Money, Part II: The Standard*, ed. Stephen Kresge, vol. 6 (1999) of *The Collected Works of F. A. Hayek*), Hayek for a last time returned to the topic of deflation in connection with the Ricardo effect (in "Profits, Interest and Investment").

[21] "The Present State and Immediate Prospects", this volume, p. 175, and "The Fate of the Gold Standard", p. 165. The first use of 'secondary deflation' is in the preface to *Preise und Produktion*, reprinted, p. 184; cf. also *Monetary Theory and the Trade Cycle*, reprinted, p. 54, and "Capital and Industrial Fluctuations", this volume, p. 200–205.

[22] The 'circulation of money' refers to MV, the 'left-hand side' of the quantity equation.

[23] Cf., e.g., Joseph A. Schumpeter, *Theorie der wirtschaftlichen Entwicklung*, 2nd ed. (Munich and Leipzig: Duncker and Humblot, 1926), p. 348, translated as *The Theory of Economic Development*,

Röpke and Haberler used the distinction—often referring to 'depression' and 'deflation' interchangeably—to denote two phases of the cycle.[24] The primary depression is characterised by the reactions to the disproportionalities of the boom, and accordingly an important cleansing function is ascribed to it; thus it is necessary to allow the primary depression to run its course. In contrast, the secondary depression refers to a self-feeding, cumulative process, not causally connected with the disproportionality that the primary depression is designed to correct. Thus the existence of the secondary depression opens up the possibility of a phase of depression dysfunctional to the economic system, where an expansionist policy might be called for.[25] Typical elements of the secondary depression are both deflation as an endogenous shrinkage in the circulation of money and the vicious spiral of reductions in income and expenditure chasing each other. Put into an equilibrium framework, the primary process is akin to an adjustment directed towards equilibrium, the secondary process to its overtaking by a movement away from equilibrium. Consequently, in the secondary depression criteria derived from equilibrium are prone to mislead: with economic activity at an unprecedentedly low level "there will scarcely be any investment that will not turn out to be a 'faulty investment'", and "there will hardly be any wages which are not too high" to ensure profitable production.[26]

---

trans. Redvers Opie (Cambridge, MA: Harvard University Press, 1934), p. 236. Keynes used the terms 'primary' and 'secondary' in *A Treatise on Money* (reprinted, vol. 1, pp. 254–59), and a similar notion had been present in Robertson's distinction between 'appropriate' and 'inappropriate fluctuations in output' (Dennis H. Robertson, *Banking Policy and the Price Level: An Essay in the Theory of the Trade Cycle* [London: King, 1926], reprinted as vol. 3 of *The Development of Monetary Theory, 1920s and 1930s*, ed. Forrest Capie and Geoffrey E. Wood [London: Routledge, 2000], chapters 2 and 4).

[24] Wilhelm Röpke used it in his monograph *Krise und Konjunktur* (Leipzig: Quelle and Meyer, 1932), translated as *Crises and Cycles* (London: Hodge, 1936; reprinted, Auburn, AL: Ludwig von Mises Institute, 2007); cf. also Röpke, "Trends in German Business Cycle Policy", *Economic Journal*, vol. 43, September 1933, pp. 427–41, and for a summary Gottfried Haberler, *Prosperity and Depression: A Theoretical Analysis of Cyclical Movements* (Geneva: League of Nations, 1937), pp. 53–57. Outside Germany, Robertson and Jacob Viner might be listed as prominent adherents. Cf. Dennis H. Robertson, "Industrial Fluctuation and the Natural Rate of Interest", *Economic Journal*, vol. 44, December 1934, pp. 650–56, reprinted in *Essays in Monetary Theory* (London: King, 1940), pp. 85–91; and Jacob Viner, *Balanced Deflation, Inflation, or More Depression* (Minneapolis: University of Minnesota Press, 1933), reprinted in vol. 4 of *The Development of Monetary Theory, 1920s and 1930s*, ed. Capie and Wood.

[25] This passage draws on Hansjoerg Klausinger, "'In the Wilderness': Emigration and the Decline of the Austrian School", *History of Political Economy*, vol. 38, Winter 2006, p. 636.

[26] Röpke, *Crises and Cycles*, p. 130. This idea is similar to the notion of the 'corridor' (around equilibrium, where the system exhibits homeostatic properties) introduced by Axel Leijonhufvud, "Effective Demand Failures", *Swedish Economic Journal*, vol. 73, March 1973, pp. 27–48, reprinted as chapter 6 of his *Information and Coordination: Essays in Macroeconomic Theory* (New York and Oxford: Oxford University Press, 1981).

Hayek's view was fundamentally different. He doubted that deflation was indispensable for the recovery from the depression, and instead linked secondary deflation with the existence of rigidities. He also warned against policies whose goal was to directly combat deflation.

Hayek's doubts on the necessity of deflation as an element of the adjustment process derived primarily from his criticism of the quantity theory. For Hayek the cause of the price declines that typically occur during the early stage of the depression need not be sought in monetary factors, as would follow from adherence to "the mechanistic quantity theory".[27] Rather it could be perfectly explained by 'real' factors alone, that is, by a temporary excess supply of consumers' goods, such as from distress sales, although probably not to the extent experienced in 1931.[28] On another occasion he reiterates that "the deflationary tendencies . . . are not a necessary consequence of any crisis and depression".[29] Furthermore, one might draw on Hayek's distinction, though part of an argument against *reflation*, between the harmful effects stemming from *changes* in the price level (if generated by changes in monetary circulation) and the irrelevance of the *level* itself.[30] Hayek kept to this distinction even when taking into account the distorting effects of an unexpectedly low (or high) price level on the redistribution of wealth between debtors and creditors in the presence of long-term contracts fixed in terms of money. Yet, the evidence on this issue is not wholly clear-cut: for example, when in correspondence discussing Haberler's widely circulated first draft of the survey of business cycle theory, Hayek objected to a passage that attributed to him a purely non-monetary explanation of the depression,[31] and indeed in *Prosperity and Depression* Haberler listed Hayek among those who are "of the opinion that the deflation is a necessary consequence of the boom".[32]

However, even if Hayek might not have considered the coexistence of deflation with crisis and depression a theoretical necessity, he was certainly aware that for some types of monetary systems such a link was inevitable. The vital distinction to be made here is between a commodity-based currency like the gold standard and a managed fiat currency.[33] In the case of a closed economy

---

[27] Preface to *Preise und Produktion*, reprinted, p. 185.

[28] Cf. Hayek to Haberler, December 20, 1931.

[29] "Capital and Industrial Fluctuations", this volume, p. 203. Already in his letter to Haberler, cited above, Hayek insisted that "the required shortening of the roundaboutness of production would also result without deflation" (this volume, p. 185).

[30] Cf. Hayek, "Restoring the Price Level?", this volume, p. 181.

[31] Cf. Gottfried Haberler, *Systematic Analysis of the Theories of the Business Cycle* (Geneva: League of Nations, 1934), p. 17, and Hayek to Haberler, September 4, 1934, Haberler Papers, box 66.

[32] Haberler, *Prosperity and Depression*, p. 56.

[33] Prior to *Monetary Nationalism* Hayek had conducted the analysis without explicitly taking account of the complications of an open economy. For example, when discussing neutral

on the gold standard, the credit inflation that fuels the boom will eventually be stopped by an internal drain due to the increasing cash requirements of the public. As banks in the crisis reduce their deposit-reserve ratio there must be some deflation (a decrease in money broadly defined), and in the aggregate prices will tend towards their pre-inflation level. This is, of course, precisely the mechanism on which for a gold standard regime Hayek bases his view of the inevitability of the breakdown of the boom.[34] In this context of a fixed gold parity, then, it is legitimate to ascribe to Hayek the notion of an 'unsustainable' price level that needs to be adjusted by means of deflation in order to restore equilibrium.[35] The case will be different for a managed currency. Here (or in a pure credit economy), as in principle credit expansion can go on practically without limit, an internal cash drain is no longer sufficient to explain the upper turning point. Indeed Hayek argued that it is accelerating inflation that ultimately will bring an end to the boom, at the latest when inflation threatens to destroy the function of money and therefore must be stopped.[36] Yet, it is here that the belief in the indispensability of deflation as a means to restore equilibrium loses its force, as all the arguments that Hayek assembled against a policy of reflation appear to apply also to the reverse case of deflation. This conclusion may also be supported by Hayek pointing to "the evil effects" of Great Britain's attempt after World War I "to use deflation in order to restore prices to their pre-war level".[37]

Having thus disposed of the *necessity* of deflation, how then did, in Hayek's view, a secondary deflation develop and what would have been an adequate policy response to it? Here the crucial element is the existence of wage and price rigidities:

---

money, he referred to a single closed ('isolated') economy or to the world as a whole; cf., e.g., "Das intertemporale Gleichgewichtssystem der Preise und die Bewegungen des 'Geldwertes'", *Weltwirtschaftliches Archiv*, vol. 28, July 1928, translated as "Intertemporal Price Equilibrium and Movements in the Value of Money" and reprinted in F. A. Hayek, *Good Money, Part I: The New World*, p. 220. In contrast, Lionel Robbins had based his arguments against reflation in Great Britain on his worries about the repercussions on the exchange rate (cf. his "Letter to the Editor: Monetary Policy", p. 1081).

[34] Cf., e.g., *Monetary Theory and the Trade Cycle*, reprinted, pp. 136–37.

[35] Cf. Lawrence H. White, "Did Hayek and Robbins Deepen the Great Depression?", *Journal of Money, Credit and Banking*, vol. 40, June 2008, pp. 753–54. White (p. 757) identified the deflation required by the gold standard as Hayek's 'initial' in contrast to 'secondary deflation' (see the quotation below, p. 10).

[36] See the discussion in Hayek, "Capital and Industrial Fluctuations", this volume, pp. 197–99.

[37] Hayek, "Restoring the Price Level?", this volume, p. 181. Note however that Hayek's Austrian colleague Machlup in 1933 was ready to accept the decrease in U.S. banking deposits to their pre-inflation level of the 1920s as a "necessary consequence" and warned against "deflation hysteria" (Fritz Machlup, "Diagnose des Falls Amerika", *Der Österreichische Volkswirt*, vol. 26, December 23, 1933, p. 317).

There can be little question that these rigidities tend to delay the process of adaptation and that this will cause a 'secondary' deflation which at first will intensify the depression but ultimately will help to overcome these rigidities.[38]

From this passage (and similar ones) we can conclude that the remedying effect of the (primary) depression could be successfully fulfilled, were it not for the obstacle of rigid wages and prices. In turn, it is the delay in this adaptation of the economy due to rigidities that gives rise to secondary deflation. Thus, this deflation "is not a cause but an effect of the unprofitableness of industry".[39] Presumably he considered the stickiness of wages as the most important obstacle in this regard. For in order to adapt the structure of production as inherited from the boom to the structure of demand, a reduction of production costs and of the demand for consumers' goods is required, both to be furthered by wage cuts. Deflation by its effect on demand and unemployment may thus perform a useful function in exerting downward pressure on wages.

Nevertheless, as Hayek notes, the policy conclusions to be derived from this idea depend on the answers to two more queries, namely:

firstly, whether this process of deflation is merely an evil which has to be combated, or whether it does not serve a necessary function in breaking these rigidities, and, secondly, whether the persistence of these deflationary tendencies proves that the fundamental maladjustment of prices still exists, or whether, once that process of deflation has gathered momentum, it may not continue long after it has served its initial function.[40]

On the first point, Hayek rejects any measures directed against deflation unless its function has been fulfilled in eliminating the imbalances that had given rise to the crisis. He expresses this most clearly on one of the first times that he discussed the issue:

If the deflation is induced [by the lack of profitability], then it will stop only after costs of production have decreased stronger than prices, and as long as

[38] Hayek, "The Present State and Immediate Prospects", this volume, p. 176.

[39] Hayek, *Monetary Theory and the Trade Cycle*, reprinted, p. 54. Hayek did not explicitly specify the economic mechanism whereby these rigidities generated a process of deflation. Banning deflationary policies (as Hayek did), endogenous deflation could be attributed to hoarding (which Hayek relegated to the special case of 'induced' deflation) or to a contraction of credit, a process which Schumpeter was to refer to as "autodeflation"; cf. Joseph A. Schumpeter, *Business Cycles: A Theoretical, Historical, and Statistical Analysis of the Capitalist Process* (New York and London: McGraw Hill, 1939), p. 156.

[40] Hayek, "The Present State and Immediate Prospects", this volume, p. 176.

this is not the case any attempt to combat deflation will only delay the attainment of a new equilibrium.[41]

In particular, he thought that the experiments in expansionist monetary policy that he felt had occurred in the United States in 1931–32 had delayed the necessary adjustments and thereby contributed to the length and depth of the depression.[42]

On the second point, Hayek did not take a definite stand, yet as a rule opted in his prescriptions for caution, that is, against expansionist measures that could turn out as ill-timed.[43] The problem with policies directed at stopping deflation lay in their similarity to 'homeopathic' treatments, fighting the disease by a small dose of the means that caused it. The danger was that the alleviation of the current depression might come at the price of an exacerbation of the next one.[44] In a similar vein, in connection with the Ricardo effect Hayek contrasts the unsustainability of full employment to be reached by expansionist policies with the lower but stable level of employment arrived at otherwise, and likens the attempt to aim at short-run maximum employment to "the policy of the desperado"—yet, in special circumstances, like that of pre-Hitler Germany in 1932, even such a policy could be justified.[45] Finally, it is to be acknowledged that Hayek, like most contemporary economists, had to base his policy recommendations on much less reliable empirical data, for example, on monetary aggregates, than are now available, yet there is no conclusive evidence that knowledge of such data would have modified his views.[46]

In any event Hayek never succeeded in integrating his approach to deflation into his framework for explaining money and the cycle, and arguably never even appeared to feel the need to do so. Rather, the pronouncements on defla-

[41] Hayek to Haberler, December 20, 1931, this volume, p. 185. Cf. similar passages in "Die Bedeutung der New-Yorker Börsenhausse", and *Monetary Theory and the Trade Cycle*, reprinted, p. 54.

[42] Cf., e.g., Hayek, "The Fate of the Gold Standard", p. 165, and *Monetary Theory and the Trade Cycle*, reprinted, p. 55. Obviously, Hayek is opposed to the monetarist view of the Great Depression as caused by a 'great contraction' in the money supply, forcefully put forward by Milton Friedman and Anna J. Schwartz, *A Monetary History of the United States, 1867–1960* (Princeton, NJ: Princeton University Press, 1963), chapter 7.

[43] If on the one hand the harmful consequences of a premature implementation shall be avoided and on the other hand such policies make no sense once deflation has stopped on its own, this will leave only a narrow corridor of time anyway.

[44] Cf., e.g., Hayek, "Die Bedeutung der New-Yorker Börsenhausse", and "Capital and Industrial Fluctuations", this volume, p. 200. The metaphor of "economic homeopathy" is due to Robbins, "Letter to the Editor: Monetary Policy", p. 1081.

[45] Hayek, "Profits, Interest and Investment", this volume, p. 250n.64.

[46] Cf. on this Hansjoerg Klausinger, "'Misguided Monetary Messages': The Austrian Case, 1931–34", *European Journal of the History of Economic Thought*, vol. 12, March 2005, pp. 25–45.

tion appeared as a series of afterthoughts. Significantly, he failed to relate his policy recommendations towards deflation to the theoretical concept of neutral money, or to his more general discussions of the goals of monetary policy.[47] The reason might be found in that the notions of neutral money and of a natural rate of interest, by their very nature, could only be legitimately used (or even defined) with respect to a state of equilibrium. Thus, for an economy in depression, with a maladjusted structure of production and price expectations that had lost their base in a firm view of the future, these concepts became equivocal. As Robertson succinctly remarked in this regard,

> Normality, and its symbol the 'natural rate of interest', seem to be like a path which is plain enough to see while you are treading it, but which is exceedingly difficult to rediscover once you have strayed away from it.[48]

Consequently, Hayek would not have denied that starting from a state of equilibrium deflationary developments had to be counteracted, or that deflationary policies should not be actively pursued. Yet, things became much more complicated in the disequilibrium situation of the depression: although deflationary policy on behalf of the monetary authorities was still to be rejected, the existence of a kind of endogenous or secondary deflation appeared to constitute a much more ambiguous case. Hayek's equilibrium-based theory simply did not provide the tools for ascertaining the proper value for the money rate of interest (quite apart from its natural value) to be set in midst of a depression.[49] Faced with these insurmountable obstacles for deriving concrete policy recommendations from the theoretical framework, Hayek eschewed the 'mechanistic' application of constructions like neutral money, and

[47] Hayek was aware of the importance of other aspects besides neutral money, e.g., the stability of the value of money in relation to long-term money contracts, when formulating monetary policy; cf. F. A. Hayek, "Über 'neutrales Geld'", *Zeitschrift für Nationalökonomie*, vol. 4, October 1933, p. 659, translated as "On Neutral Money" and reprinted as chapter 6 of F. A. Hayek, *Good Money, Part I: The New World*, p. 230. In the case of deflation, recognition of these additional aspects should have made policy more, not less, active in combating deflation.

[48] Dennis H. Robertson, "Der Stand und die nächste Zukunft der Konjunkturforschung", in *Festschrift für Arthur Spiethoff*, ed. Clausing, p. 239.

[49] Fritz Machlup (in a letter to Hayek, December 11, 1934, Friedrich Machlup Papers, box 43, folder 15, Hoover Institution Archives, Stanford University) addresses this problem, asking, "Which movements does the 'natural rate' make in the depression? What is the value of the equilibrium rate of interest before costs have been adjusted, that is, when the rate of return on capital is negative?" (my translation). Note that when Hayek speculated about the proper level of the rate of interest in Great Britain in 1934 (Anon. [F. A. Hayek], "The Outlook for Interest Rates", *Economist*, vol. 118, March 17, 1934, pp. 563–64), he argued for raising it to the expected future equilibrium level.

in his policy advice ever preferred to err on the conservative side. Thus, when in doubt, he was inclined to advise against expansionist policy or reflation.[50]

Hayek's caution in this regard probably did not only result from the theoretical model employed, or rather from the lack of it. Equal importance should be attached to his imputing to policy-makers an ever-present susceptibility to inflationism, the harmful consequences of which were all too present in his memory of the hyperinflations that had haunted Central Europe in the 1920s. Moreover, in the face of the onslaught against economic liberalism in so many Western countries, Hayek might not have been ready to sacrifice the adherence to sound money, as a pillar of economic liberalism, to what he must have perceived as mere short-term exigencies.

Summarising the evidence, deflation was probably *not* an essential element of Hayek's theory of the cycle, nor of the cleansing function of the depression, although the eventual reversal of the credit expansion of the boom was inevitable within a gold standard regime. In the presence of rigidities a secondary deflation might develop, which in breaking those rigidities and in re-establishing a sustainable structure of the economy could play a useful role. As long as it did so, and did not degenerate into an induced deflation driven by expectations of falling prices, deflation should not be counteracted. Furthermore, such changes in the nature of deflation were difficult to discern, and thus attempts at combating it were as a rule prone to be premature, or excessive, and thereby to cause new maladjustments. Consequently, the utmost caution was required in advocating anti-deflationary measures, and indeed Hayek never advocated any of them in practice.[51]

What then were the consequences of Hayek's policy recommendations, emanating from his view of deflation, in the face of the Great Depression? As regards actual policy-making, the influence of Hayek, joined by Robbins and other members of the LSE faculty, must not be overrated. Specifically, in Great Britain when Hayek entered the debate, most of the drama—for example, the pound's going off gold—had already happened, and in general the resistance against expansionist measures of fiscal and monetary policy in

---

[50] In marked contrast to Arthur Cecil Pigou, the Keynesian archetype of a 'classical economist', who had recommended, "When in doubt, expand" ("Letter to the Editor: Productive Spending—Confidence through Lower Taxation", *Times*, February 21, 1933, p. 13).

[51] In retrospect Hayek recanted his earlier position on deflation, stating flatly, "Such a 'secondary depression' caused by an induced deflation should of course be prevented by appropriate monetary counter-measures" (F. A. Hayek, "The Campaign against Keynesian Inflation", in *New Studies in Philosophy, Politics, Economics, and the History of Ideas* [London: Routledge and Kegan Paul, 1978], p. 210). Yet, in light of the evidence presented above it is difficult to agree with White ("Did Hayek and Robbins Deepen the Great Depression?", pp. 764–65) that Hayek's views during the 1930s were primarily based on "political considerations".

13

these days owed more to the conservative 'gold standard mentality'[52] of politicians and bureaucrats than to the teachings of economists. Although Hayek was anxious to put his weight behind the liberal agenda in public discussion, there is little evidence of any direct impact on the policies of the 1930s, either in Great Britain or in the United States.

On a different level, however, Hayek's position on deflation and on the policies towards depression had vital consequences indeed. For this became one of those fields where Hayek's view became ever more distant from that of much of the public, as well as other economists. With regard to secondary deflation (or depression), opinions, as voiced for example by Röpke and Haberler, diverged even within the Austrian school. In the public debates on monetary policy and reflation, or on saving versus spending, Hayek and his followers were soon outnumbered by the critics.[53] These critics also included economists friendly to the liberal cause so that, by the end of the decade, although the Keynesian revolution had reopened another cleavage among economists—Keynes's adherents versus those denounced as 'classical economists'—Hayek remained almost alone in defending the Austrian position on money and the cycle.

However, it would be an oversimplification to attribute Hayek's failure only to lack of political expediency, that is, to his unwillingness to offer the public a 'tract for the times' that suited the 'trend of economic thinking'. Rather, the crucial failure was theoretical, namely, the failure to integrate the phenomenon of deflation (and its secondary effects) into a theory of the depression on a par with the explanation of the upper turning point, which many of the critics would have been ready to accept.[54] In his narrow focus on the real maladjustments caused by inflation that were to be remedied by the depression, Hayek neglected the possibility that under special circumstances market processes might lack the supposed tendency towards equilibrium, due to a failure of 'effective demand'.[55] Haberler and Röpke had tried to supplement the Hayekian core of the Austrian approach with a theory of secondary depression, thus incorporating both functional market adjustments (as a rule) and dysfunctional ones (as an exception). In the end, however, for the next

[52] As has been argued by Barry Eichengreen and Peter Temin, "The Gold Standard and the Great Depression", *Contemporary European History*, vol. 9, July 2000, pp. 183–207.

[53] Cf., e.g., the broad support gathering behind a policy of reflation, as in the letters drafted by Harrod and published in the *Times*, referred to above. Similarly, Pigou in a letter in favour of 'wise spending' ("Letter to the Editor: Private Economy—Wise Spending and Wise Saving", *Times*, June 7, 1932, p. 10) was able to maintain that "on this matter, economic opinion is practically unanimous", that is, opposed to Hayek's views.

[54] Cf. Haberler's critical treatment of Hayek's theory of the depression (Haberler, *Systematic Analysis of the Theories of the Business Cycle*, p. 17; *Prosperity and Depression*, pp. 57–61).

[55] Cf. Ludwig Lachmann, "On Crisis and Adjustment", *Review of Economic Statistics*, vol. 21, February 1939, p. 68, for a perceptive contemporary account.

decades the Keynesian approach prevailed, that is, from the Austrian point of view, an approach based on a belief in the generic dysfunction of the market system.

The Ricardo Effect and the Stability of Full Employment

When in 1938 Hayek was busy working on *The Pure Theory of Capital*, he planned to include a sketch of what a dynamic theory in a monetary setting was supposed to look like. Yet, this sketch soon evolved into a separate piece of work on its own. The next year he wrote to Machlup,

> I have worked since Christmas on a great essay on business cycle theory. Originally it should have been the final chapter of my capital book, yet it has grown far beyond that and will now be published in a volume of essays titled *Profits, Interest and Investment.*[56]

This is the origin of the essay, which introduced the Ricardo effect as a novel element into Hayek's theory of the cycle; three years later, Hayek reacted to criticism with a more systematic presentation.[57] These two essays became for a long time Hayek's last words on the subject of the business cycle, and in fact their reception turned into a fiasco.[58] In the following we investigate the conundrum of the Ricardo effect.

Although Hayek occasionally alludes to his objections to the thrust of the recent writings by Kaldor and of Keynes's *General Theory*, the real target of his essays is the view of investment as a derived demand, and thus of increases in consumption bringing forth increases in the demand for investment goods. Evan Durbin, one of Hayek's colleagues at LSE, had referred to this thesis as the 'English view'.[59] Indeed as Durbin's overall approach provides in some respects the background against which Hayek's attempt is to be understood, a

---

[56] Hayek to Machlup, April 4, 1939, Machlup Papers, box 43, folder 15 (my translation).

[57] "Profits, Interest and Investment" (1939), followed by "The Ricardo Effect" (1942).

[58] The most devastating critique came from Kaldor, "Concertina-Effect"; yet cf. also the reserve expressed by Haberler in *Prosperity and Depression*, 3rd ed. (1941), pp. 481–91. Hayek himself appears not to have felt satisfied with his work: He noted that his preoccupation with other topics (his *Abuse of Reason* project and the nucleus of *The Road to Serfdom*) made it "more and more difficult to keep up with current economic literature", and that his task as editor of *Economica* "forced [me] again and again (already with the Ricardo effect) to bring things out before I am really ready" (Hayek to Machlup, July 31, 1941, and August 8, 1942, Machlup Papers, box 43, folder 15).

[59] Evan F. M. Durbin, *Purchasing Power and Trade Depression: A Critique of Under-Consumption Theories* (London: Jonathan Cape, 1933), p. 147. Accordingly, "the demand for capital is derived from the price level of consumption goods" (p. 149).

short sketch of it appears worthwhile.[60] Durbin subscribes to part of Hayek's explanation of the cycle in considering inflationary induced overinvestment as the cause of structural maladjustment, yet he differs from Hayek in two respects: First, conforming to the 'English view' he posits that increases in the price level of consumers' goods positively affect the demand for investment goods, and, secondly, uses as the starting point of the analysis an economy with unused resources. Consequently, he disagrees with Hayek's 1931 view on the upper turning point. According to Durbin, it is not the shift towards consumption—which in his view rather stimulates than stifles the demand for investment goods and is apt to trigger a cumulative process of inflation—but the end of monetary expansion that makes the boom collapse. He characterises the boom by credit creation in the face of considerable surplus capacity in the production of investment goods, though with capacity in the consumption sector rapidly becoming scarce. As long as inflation is permitted to accelerate, there is nothing like a 'natural end' to the boom, yet when sooner or later inflation is stopped, the crisis must set in. For the depression phase Durbin advises against inflation, which would only aggravate the problem of the top-heavy structure of the economy, but sees the solution either in wage cuts (in favour of saving) or in a rebalancing of the sectoral structure, that is, a shift from the production of capital goods to that of consumers' goods. Yet he is doubtful of the practicality of the latter solution in light of the well-known obstacles to the mobility of labour (in Great Britain).[61]

Apparently, when Hayek in 1939 introduced the term 'Ricardo effect'[62] he aimed at a more general explanation of the upper turning point, and of the cycle as a whole, than in his earlier work. Although he retained his crucial idea that the crisis is caused by a relative shift of demand towards consumers' goods, he tried to demonstrate its validity under different conditions and thus by a different mechanism than before. Accordingly, he now assumes[63] a given rate of interest with an elastic supply of credit, unused resources of labour—

[60] During the 1930s Durbin gave a regular course on business cycle theory at LSE (cf. Susan Howson, "Keynes and the LSE Economists", *Journal of the History of Economic Thought*, vol. 31, September 2009, pp. 268 and 271). His 1933 book was followed by *The Problem of Credit Policy* (London: Chapman and Hall, 1935), where he advocated the social control of credit. In the debate on socialist economic calculation he figured as a proponent of 'market socialism' and as Hayek's opponent in this respect; cf. the editor's introduction to *The Road to Serfdom: Text and Documents*, ed. Bruce Caldwell, vol. 2 (2007) of *The Collected Works of F. A. Hayek*, pp. 24–28.

[61] Durbin, *Purchasing Power and Trade Depression*, pp. 180–83.

[62] For a critical evaluation of Hayek's attribution of the effect to Ricardo cf. Harald Hagemann and Hans-Michael Trautwein, "Cantillon and Ricardo Effects: Hayek's Contributions to Business Cycle Theory", *European Journal of the History of Economic Thought*, vol. 5, Summer 1998, pp. 292–316; and Christian Gehrke, "The Ricardo Effect: Its Meaning and Validity", *Economica*, n.s., vol. 70, February 2003, pp. 143–58.

[63] Cf. Hayek, "Profits, Interest and Investment", this volume, pp. 213–14.

immobile between sectors (or stages),[64] such that in the boom the scarcity of labour makes itself felt in the consumption sector well before the investment sector—and a rigid money wage. Finally Hayek stipulates a relation between consumption and investment demand conforming to the 'English view', or what he termed the 'acceleration principle'.[65] All in all, a family resemblance between Hayek's model and Durbin's can hardly be missed. The new features of the model—in comparison to *Prices and Production*—are crucial for the novel explanation of the upper turning point. For without an elastic supply of credit and with the circulation of money ultimately limited, eventually the rate of interest would rise sufficiently to choke off investment demand and the boom. Alternatively, with full employment of resources physical constraints would keep the output of investment goods from growing (except at the expense of consumers' goods), and at the same time wages and prices of investment goods would start rising. Thus in this latter scenario unlimited credit creation would end up in the well-known 'cumulative process' of (accelerating) inflation, and the moment an attempt were made to stop inflation, by raising the interest rate, the boom would come to an end. Yet, what Hayek is now attempting to demonstrate is the inevitability of the breakdown of an inflationary boom, even when both these limiting factors are absent, that is, with unlimited credit creation[66] and with less than full employment, at least in the investment goods industries. In this regard, Hayek's model of the Ricardo effect does not contradict his earlier view, but rather is designed to supplement it.[67]

The core of the model consists of the relationship between consumption and investment demand where Hayek combines the Ricardo effect with the working of the accelerator. On the one hand an increase in consumption demand (which raises prices and profits in the consumption sector) will lead via the mechanism of the accelerator to an increase in investment demand. On

[64] Hayek distinguishes between industries producing consumers' and investment goods and moreover between different stages of production manufacturing investment goods. In the following we will use as a short-cut the terms 'consumption sector' and 'investment sector', and by 'investment demand' denote the demand for the goods produced and the means employed in the various stages within the investment sector. We follow Hayek in denoting stages as 'later' or 'earlier' according to their distance from consumption, the stage producing consumers' goods being the 'last' stage.

[65] Cf. Hayek, "Profits, Interest and Investment", this volume, pp. 222–23. Indeed, neither the 'English view' as described by Durbin nor the 'acceleration principle' according to Hayek corresponds exactly to the (then and now) common notion of the 'accelerator', which posits a relation between the *change* in the demand for consumers' goods and the *level* of the demand for investment goods. See also the editor's note, this volume, p. 194n.16.

[66] The experience of a long period of low and stable interest rates in Great Britain might have convinced him of the new version being more 'realistic'. In fact, with the exception of two months in 1939, from the end of June 1932 until 1951 the Bank Rate remained fixed at 2%.

[67] Thus, Kaldor's allegation ("Concertina-Effect", this volume, p. 288) that Hayek's new view is in contradiction to his earlier one is ill founded.

the other hand, through Hayek's Ricardo effect, the same rise of profits in the production of consumers' goods will induce a less capitalistic structure of production. Thus the aggregate change in the demand for investment depends on the interaction between these two effects, working in opposite directions. Now Hayek argues that inevitably, some time before full employment in the investment sector is reached, the Ricardo effect will come to dominate the accelerator effect, so that in the aggregate the demand for investment decreases and thereby initiates the crisis. However, as we will see, in general the Ricardo effect will not be able to do the work it is supposed to do.

The purpose of the Ricardo effect is to show the reaction of the structure of production to an increase in demand for the final product, consumers' goods. In Hayek's framework, an increase in the demand for consumers' goods raises their price due to an inelastic supply. With the money wage fixed by assumption, in the consumption sector the wage in terms of its product must fall and the profit rate rise. For this case, Hayek shows by means of a numerical example that if goods are produced by simultaneously utilising processes of different capital intensity, then due to the lower product wage the profit rate will rise for all these processes, but will rise the largest in the least capitalistic processes.[68] Thus the less capitalistic the processes, the more profitable they will become through the rise in prices. It is this observation on which Hayek bases the Ricardo effect, that is, the thesis that for a given wage and rate of interest (and, implicitly, given prices of investment goods) a *rise* in the profit rate will induce the transition to a less capitalistic structure of production. Hayek explicitly points out that with the Ricardo effect the profit rate fulfils the task that he in earlier writings had ascribed to the rate of interest.[69] This statement, however, should have been alarming, as it must appear dubious that a firm should respond to a rise in the revenue (and with given costs, the profits) it expects to accrue from a production process (that is, to a rise in the rate of profit) in the same way as to a rise in the costs of financing this process (that is, to a rise in the rate of interest).

In Hayek's earlier writings he had focused on the effects of the rate of interest: a decrease in the rate of interest leads to an excess of the profit rate over the interest rate; with unchanged prices (of products and means of production) all the activities that hitherto had generated zero excess profits now become profitable, which induces an increase in the scale of those activities, and simultaneously a switch to longer processes. Eventually, the increased demand will raise the prices of the means of production, and of wages, and thus

---

[68] Cf. Hayek, "Profits, Interest and Investment", this volume, p. 216. In fact, Hayek distinguishes the processes used by their "rate of turnover of labour invested" (ibid.), which is just inversely related to the capital intensity of the process.

[69] Cf. ibid., p. 235n.40. Cf. also the footnote added in 1939 to "The Present State and Immediate Prospects", this volume, p. 177n.16.

re-establish the zero excess profit condition.[70] The reverse will happen when the interest rate increases: profits turn into losses, and there is an incentive to switch to shorter processes. This is, of course, Hayek's explanation of the upper turning point and of the crisis in *Prices and Production*.

Now applying the same logic to Hayek's new model, would it exhibit a Ricardo effect? An increase in product prices and thereby in the rate of profit will again make all activities profitable (or more profitable than before), and thus increase the demand for all means of production, that is, the demand directed at all the preceding stages of production. Yet, with the wage and the rate of interest—which jointly with the price of investment goods determines the relevant rental price of capital—fixed, and thus the ratios of factor prices unchanged, there is *no* incentive for capital intensity to change.[71] Placing profit maximising firms into the Hayekian economy of 1939 would thus *not* give rise to a Ricardo effect. For, indeed, the numerical example on which Hayek based his argument is deceptive. After the price rise, the profit rates in all (shorter and longer) processes, although to a different extent, exceed the rate of interest. This makes it profitable to increase the scale of activities in all these (shorter *and* longer) processes, and that until the (marginal) rate of profit has been brought down to the rate of interest—which is, of course, how a profit maximum is achieved; and with the rate of interest unchanged, the profit maximum will be arrived at the same structure of production as before. In the contemporary terminology of Hawtrey, the increased demand for consumers' goods will bring forward 'capital widening', but no 'capital enshallowing'.[72]

Thus it seems plain that the Ricardo effect cannot be rescued in the context of Hayek's original model.[73] However, in "The Ricardo Effect", Hayek came

[70] In Hayek's flow-input-point-output model, a permanently lower rate of interest results in a higher real wage made possible by the more productive use of labour in 'longer' processes.

[71] Strictly speaking, this is only true if the underlying production function is homothetic so that for given factor price ratios there is no substitution bias against any of the factors when output is expanded. In any case, this aspect plays no role in Hayek's argument. Cf. the discussion in Mark Blaug, *Economic Theory in Retrospect*, 5th ed. (Cambridge, New York, and Melbourne: Cambridge University Press, 1996), p. 525.

[72] Cf. Ralph G. Hawtrey, *Capital and Employment* (London: Longmans, 1937), p. 36. The above arguments amount, of course, just to a reformulation of the criticisms by Wilson, "Capital Theory and the Trade Cycle", and Kaldor, "Concertina-Effect". In "Three Elucidations", this volume, p. 329, Hayek apparently concedes this point.

[73] A reader suggested that, these criticisms notwithstanding, the Ricardo effect might work as conceived by Hayek when we take into account the multi-stage structure of the economy and the existence of lags in the propagation of derived demand backwards to the early stages. However, as Hayek pointed out already in his description of a money economy in "Investigations" (this volume, pp. 105–6), the demand for investment goods, goods of the early stages, will be financed out of an economy-wide capital market and therefore the lags in question cannot be ascribed to constraints in the transmission of purchasing power across stages, but must result from some other source.

forward with the idea of placing firms in a different setting. He argues that the traditional assumption of perfect competition is unrealistic, in particular with regard to credit markets and the pervading role of risk, and thus that some form of credit rationing must be postulated. Individual firms will face an upward sloping credit supply curve instead of an infinitely elastic one, or in an extreme case might not have any access to credit at all. In the latter case of complete credit rationing, firms can react only by reallocating the capital they already own to different uses. In this case Hayek's numerical example of the Ricardo effect is trivially valid: with an increase in prices it indeed pays to shift capital to shorter processes where they generate on average higher profit until within the firm again a uniform rate of profit higher than before has been reestablished.[74] In the more general case, with an upward sloping credit supply to the individual firm, a redirection of capital to shorter processes will result, too, when at the profit maximum the rate of profit is geared to the higher rate of interest the firm is facing. Yet, as closer inspection shows, with the introduction of credit rationing Hayek salvaged the Ricardo effect at the expense of its intended use for explaining the upper turning point. Turning first to the case of complete credit rationing, it obviously cannot be integrated into Hayek's theory of the cycle: if firms are fully rationed, investment as determined by the interaction of credit demand with a vertical credit supply will always be zero, so there is neither a boom at the outset nor a need to explain its end. Similarly, for the more general case: here credit rationing will only become effective to the extent that investment demand has indeed *increased*, and thus it will be a source for mitigating, but not reversing, such increases.[75] Indeed, what effect there is of credit rationing should be perceived more properly as that of a rise in the *effective* rate of interest paid by the firms than that of a rise in the rate of profit.[76]

[74] For a mathematical proof of the Ricardo effect with complete credit rationing see William J. Baumol, "The Ricardo Effect in the Point Input-Point Output Case", in *Essays in Mathematical Economics in Honour of Oskar Morgenstern*, ed. Martin Shubik (Princeton, NJ: Princeton University Press, 1967), pp. 191–96.

[75] The refutation of the Ricardo effect by Kaldor, "Concertina-Effect", is based on this reasoning.

[76] The same counter-argument prevents the Ricardo effect from being saved by appealing—with credit available in unlimited amount—to rising prices of investment goods. Again, a *rise* (instead of a fall) in the demand for investment goods is needed for such a cumulative process to ensue (cf. Hayek, "The Ricardo Effect", this volume, pp. 272–76). Undeniably, when demand meets the capacity constraints in the various stages of production, the respective prices will rise and thereby redirect production towards less capitalistic methods. In this respect the role of rising prices of investment goods is the same as that of a rising rate of interest. In this case, in particular, it becomes evident that a positive relationship between consumption and investment *demand* (as stipulated by the 'English view') does *not* imply that in the course of the process consumption *output* would be reduced to zero (contra Hayek, cf. ibid., p. 276, and "Three Elucidations", this volume, p. 330).

The error in Hayek's argument becomes most obvious when drawing on the marginal product conditions for a profit maximum.[77] Here, Hayek tries to prove his case by pointing out that in such a profit maximum the higher profit rate, when adjusted to the higher interest rate, will result in a less capitalistic structure of production.[78] However, this is based on the confusion of an *exogenous* increase in the rate of interest—which, indeed, makes production less capitalistic and *reduces* investment demand, with an increase in the rate of interest *induced* by a rise in the profit rate—which makes production less capitalistic, yet must be accompanied by investment demand being *higher* than before.[79]

Belatedly, Hayek put forward an interpretation of the Ricardo effect, perhaps already implicit in his earlier work, which avoids the pitfalls pointed out by his critics. He now associates the extent of credit rationing not with the level of current investment, but with the sum of past investments throughout the boom, as indicated, for example, by "the proportion of the total indebtedness of a borrower to his equity".[80] Then the longer the boom lasts, the greater the risk perceived by the banks and the stronger the rationing of credit will become. Thus during the course of the boom the credit supply curve faced by investing firms will be continuously shifting upwards, the rising rate of interest will induce a switch to shorter processes, and in the end it will even reduce the aggregate of investment demand. This may indeed consistently explain the upper turning point, yet it is a long way from the Ricardo effect induced by a rise in the rate of profit to this type of effect, induced by a rise in the rate of interest due to changes in the perception of risk.[81] Thus, the novel

[77] Hayek refers to this condition in "The Ricardo Effect", this volume, p. 273; a simplified version is depicted graphically in *Prices and Production*, 2nd ed., reprinted, p. 250, and in *The Pure Theory of Capital* (London: Macmillan, 1941), reprinted, ed. Lawrence White, as vol. 12 (2007) of *The Collected Works of F. A. Hayek*, p. 271, fig. 26.

[78] Hayek's position has been seconded by, e.g., Laurence S. Moss and Karen I. Vaughn, "Hayek's Ricardo Effect: A Second Look", *History of Political Economy*, vol. 18, Winter 1986, p. 561. Moss and Vaughn insist that with credit rationing "the scale [i.e., accelerator] effect cannot outweigh the substitution [i.e., Ricardo] effect". Cf. also Jack Birner, "The Place of the Ricardo Effect in Hayek's Economic Research Programme", *Revue d'Économie Politique*, vol. 109, November 1999, pp. 808–9; Birner explicitly denotes the distinction between the profit rate and the interest rate as "immaterial" (p. 810n.12).

[79] Kaldor, in "Concertina-Effect", this volume, pp. 305–6, notes on a similar occasion the necessity of distinguishing movements along a curve (that is, in our example a rise of the interest rate leading to lower investment demand) from shifts of a curve (that is, an upward shift of the demand curve along an upward sloping supply curve leading to a higher interest rate associated with higher investment demand).

[80] Hayek, "Three Elucidations", this volume, p. 328.

[81] Note that this interpretation bears some resemblance to the 'financial instability hypothesis' of Hyman P. Minsky; cf. his *Stabilizing an Unstable Economy* (New Haven, CT: Yale University Press, 1986).

explanation is not only almost indistinguishable from the earlier one, where investment is stopped by a rise in the rate of interest engineered by the central bank, but is also completely divorced from the determination of investment demand by the profits earned in the consumption sector—in fact, any justification for a persistent demand for investment during the boom would do. So in the end the Ricardo effect was salvaged by giving up most of what had distinguished it from alternative explanations of the upper turning point.

In regard to its reception, "The Ricardo Effect" must be considered an exceptional failure. Almost as soon as it was published, it was first criticised by Wilson, then demolished by Kaldor, and in the following years there was little mention of it, as Hayek remained silent for more than two decades. However, in other regards, Hayek's contribution addressed a vital theoretical issue, namely the stability, or sustainability, of full employment.

For at this time Hayek's contribution was still discussed within the context of a structural theory of the business cycle. This was so because the nascent methodological reorientation that in the end was to characterise the success of the Keynesian approach had not yet been completed. Even the Keynesian theses (and the policy conclusions derived from them) were often analysed from the point of view of the business cycle, that is, as a question of stabilising the boom, or of sustaining full employment reached near the end of the boom period. These analyses also took account of the structure of production, whether in basing it on capital theoretic foundations or, more modestly, in keeping to the distinction between two sectors producing, respectively, consumers' and investment goods.[82] In such a setting complications due to the sectoral structure were prone to arise because of the specificity or complementarity of the factors of production used, and therefore, the possibility of stable 'full employment' was not taken for granted.

Hayek, again similar to Durbin, had distinguished for the short run, with given capacities[83] in the consumption and investment sector, between "stable employment" and full employment.[84] Because of the remnant effects of past booms, the investment sector typically will be larger than is compatible with the rate of (voluntary) saving at full employment. Consequently, the level of

---

[82] As is clear from the very first reviews (cf., e.g., John R. Hicks, "Mr. Keynes and the 'Classics': A Suggested Interpretation", *Econometrica*, vol. 5, April 1937, pp. 147–59, and James E. Meade, "A Simplified Model of Mr. Keynes' System", *Review of Economic Studies*, vol. 4, February 1937, pp. 98–107), Keynes's *General Theory* was at the outset also perceived as a two-sector-model. Axel Leijonhufvud's re-interpretation (*On Keynesian Economics and the Economics of Keynes* [New York: Oxford University Press, 1968]) caused a stir when bringing this to light again.

[83] For both authors the cause of the capacity constraint lies in the limited availability of sector-specific labour.

[84] Cf. Hayek, "Profits, Interest and Investment", this volume, p. 247.

employment when the capacity constraint in the consumption sector becomes binding constitutes a kind of barrier beyond which employment cannot be sustainably raised. Hayek ascribed this lack of sustainability to the Ricardo effect. Durbin, as has already been noted, derived from similar assumptions a state of generalised excess demand for goods, driving the economy into inflation that ultimately must be stopped at the price of a crisis. Thus, both pointed to the problem that the preservation of a state of full employment required not only a specific level of (effective) demand but also a proper distribution of demand between sectors.

Kaldor, then well along the way to becoming a full-blown Keynesian, shared these doubts.[85] Although in the short run he considered the proper stimulation of effective demand sufficient for bringing about full employment, problems arise as soon as equipment and labour in the sectors are treated as specific and complementary. In the longer run, when the capacity built up in the consumption sector is taken into account, the economy faces the dangers of either excess saving or excess investment, as the investment determined by the equipment required for keeping pace with the increase in consumption demand must be matched by the saving generated by rising income. Even if this condition is fulfilled, due to the assumed strict complementarity between equipment and labour, another obstacle will turn up as soon as labour specific to the consumption sector becomes the scarce factor. Because of the resulting excess equipment in producing consumption goods, investment demand slumps and again full employment cannot be sustained.[86] Were it not for complementarity, remedies for this problem might be sought in the adjustment of factor prices, for example, a higher wage and a lower interest rate inducing an increase in capital intensity and thus in investment demand. Alternatively, one must foster hope that, as Kaldor put it, "providence decrees that there should be an adequate rate of technical progress".[87] Kaldor's conclusion might sound strange in the ears of latter-day Keynesians in its likening the task of sustaining the boom, and thereby full employment, to a "steeplechase, where the horse is bound to fall at one of [the] obstacles".[88]

As the mechanisms employed by Kaldor were those of the accelerator principle, a lesson to be learnt, relevant for Hayek's approach, is that this mecha-

---

[85] Cf. Kaldor, "Stability and Full Employment".

[86] Kaldor considers this an example of a "temporary exhaustion of investment opportunities" (ibid., p. 653; reprinted, p. 115), an explanation to which Hayek had strongly objected: "Once the cumulative process has been entered upon the end must always come through a rise in profits in the late stages and can never come from a fall in profits or an exhaustion of investment opportunities" (Hayek, "Profits, Interest and Investment", this volume, p. 246).

[87] Cf. Kaldor, "Stability and Full Employment", p. 653, reprinted, p. 115.

[88] Ibid., p. 657, reprinted, p. 119.

nism rightly understood would have been sufficient, without any recourse to the Ricardo effect, of making full employment unstable.[89] The need for providence, to which Kaldor had referred, was of course predicated upon the neglect, due to the assumptions of specificity and complementarity, of flexible factor prices working on factor proportions. With these assumptions discarded, Solow was able to demonstrate the existence of a steady-state equilibrium growth path.[90] His achievement could be judged as the answer not only to the problem of 'knife-edge' equilibrium attributed to Harrod, but also to Kaldor's and Hayek's endeavours with the traverse. The solution was made possible by translating the problem into a framework of a perfect foresight, one-commodity intertemporal equilibrium model.[91] However, by getting rid of the complexities that had beset the theories of Hayek (and Kaldor) and that had left them both interesting and mathematically intractable, something was lost in this translation. In any case, this 'solution' is indicative of the revolution in 'macroeconomic' thought during the years of Hayek's silence on matters of money and the cycle that followed his investigation into the Ricardo effect, an evolution whereby equilibrium replaced a process-oriented approach and aggregates replaced a structural approach.[92]

Hayek on Money, Capital, and the Cycle: Continuity and Change

Most of Hayek's contributions to the theories of money, capital, and the cycle assembled in this volume, in particular those preparing and arguing out *Prices and Production*, belong to the 1920s and 1930s. Towards the end of this time period, Hayek as an economic theorist is now widely regarded to have undergone a 'transformation'[93]; thus it is natural to ask whether in these fields a

[89] The similarity of Kaldor's formulation of the stability problem to the issues discussed by Roy F. Harrod, *The Trade Cycle: An Essay* (Oxford: Clarendon Press, 1936) should be noted. Cf. also Daniele Besomi, *The Making of Harrod's Dynamics* (Houndmills and London: Macmillan, 1999) for an interpretation of Harrod's writings that goes beyond the so-called Harrod-Domar growth model.

[90] Cf. Robert Solow, "A Contribution to the Theory of Economic Growth", *Quarterly Journal of Economics*, vol. 70, February 1956, pp. 65–94.

[91] In contemporary literature this solution also incorporated the idea of the 'neoclassical synthesis' according to which "the achievement of full employment requires Keynesian intervention but . . . neoclassical theory [as represented by Solow's contribution] is valid when full employment is reached", as critically noted by Kenneth J. Arrow, "Samuelson Collected", *Journal of Political Economy*, vol. 75, October 1967, p. 735.

[92] Roger W. Garrison, *Time and Money: The Macroeconomics of Capital Structure* (Abingdon and New York: Routledge, 2001) highlights another aspect of the demise of the structural approach as the transition from "capital-based" to "labor-based macroeconomics".

[93] Cf. Bruce J. Caldwell, "Hayek's Transformation", *History of Political Economy*, vol. 20, Winter 1988, especially pp. 514–15.

similar development can be discerned, too. In answering this question we will also sketch how the significance of the equilibrium concept in relation to his analysis of adjustment processes evolved over Hayek's lifetime career.

The following proposes a periodisation of Hayek's writings that in this regard supplements, extends, and on some occasions revises Caldwell's account. The phases suggested are as follows: (1) An early, preparatory phase, which centred on equilibrium and adjustment and ended when Hayek came to LSE in 1931; (2) the event of *Prices and Production*, as in effect a simplification of Hayek's analysis; (3) the period of the 'capital project' that eventually turned into *The Pure Theory of Capital* (1941), where Hayek abandoned some of the simplifications of *Prices and Production* and re-focused on dynamic aspects, yet without integrating them into a theory of a *monetary* economy; (4) "Economics and Knowledge",[94] which temporally overlapped with the capital project, proved crucial for Hayek's transformation and initiated his novel approach to the coordination problem; and (5) Hayek's 1981 lecture,[95] his final, most radical contribution to this topic.

1. Preparation

Hayek's writings of the first phase, besides *Geldtheorie und Konjunkturtheorie*, encompass the important articles "Intertemporal Price Equilibrium" and "The 'Paradox' of Saving", yet the most interesting insights into his approach towards time, money, and fluctuations are to be found in his unpublished typescript of the first part of "Geldtheoretische Untersuchungen", dealing with price formation in a monetary economy.[96]

The point of departure of all writings of this period is the notion of equilibrium as formulated in what Hayek calls 'static theory'. It refers to an imagined (or fictitious) economy where price formation and the structure of production, that is, in anachronistic terms, the allocation of resources, is fully determined by the economy's real data, that is, tastes, endowments, and tech-

[94] *Economica*, n.s., vol. 4, February 1937, pp. 33–54, reprinted as chapter 2 of *Individualism and Economic Order* (Chicago: University of Chicago Press, 1948; London: Routledge and Kegan Paul, 1949).

[95] F. A. Hayek, "The Flow of Goods and Services", paper read at LSE on January 27, 1981, reprinted as chapter 12 of this volume.

[96] Cf. "Geldtheoretische Untersuchungen", in Hayek Papers, Incremental Material, box 105, folders 1–4, translated as "Investigations into Monetary Theory", chapter 1 of this volume. On the origins of the "Untersuchungen" see the editor's introduction to F. A. Hayek, *Business Cycles, Part I*, p. 8, and Hansjoerg Klausinger, "Hayek's *Geldtheoretische Untersuchungen*: New Insights from a 1925–29 Typescript", *European Journal of the History of Economic Thought*, vol. 18, October 2011, pp. 580–83.

nology.[97] Thereby static theory establishes the norm of "correct prices" and (in response to changes in economic data) of "necessary price changes".[98] The economy in question is conceived as one where money does not play any active role in influencing the outcome of price formation. The paradigm of static theory is the analysis of a stationary economy with constant data, yet, as Hayek is keen to demonstrate, under the assumption of perfect foresight statics may be extended to also cover the analysis of anticipated changes in the economic data, thus replacing stationary by intertemporal equilibrium. Furthermore, the "Investigations" deal both with the state of equilibrium and the reactions to changes, the former as static theory proper and the latter as part of dynamics. The application of this static notion of equilibrium and of the analysis of adjustments to ever more complicated types of economies forms the research programme pursued by Hayek in this early period.

At the outset of the "Investigations", Hayek points out what it is that makes the economy of static theory immune from all influences apart from those exerted by real economic data, which is also why it differs crucially from the actual economies we live in, entrapped in the intricacies of time and money. This crucial property is the simultaneity of decisions.[99] Accordingly, the time period to which 'equilibrium' refers must be defined so that all decisions relevant for this period are taken at the same instant of time and comprehend all possible (anticipated) changes in the data. This implies that within such a period individuals formulate their plans under the condition of a single budget constraint, and then the institution of "central commodity clearing"[100] will render the individual plans mutually compatible. Under this arrangement in particular, the generation of income (from the goods produced) and the use of income (directed at those same goods) will be simultaneous. For the case of a stationary economy, Hayek states the relevant assumptions of static theory as follows.

> It must be assumed that the whole economic process can be split up into closed time periods, so that between periods all economic activities repeat themselves and within periods all acts of exchange take place at a single and as regards time and place homogeneous market.[101]

[97] Cf. "Investigations", this volume, p. 53. In a simple exchange economy these data comprise the individual preferences and the distribution of the endowments of goods.

[98] Ibid., title of chapter 4, p. 46.

[99] In *Monetary Theory and the Trade Cycle*, reprinted, pp. 104 and 161, Hayek makes use of the contrast between simultaneous decisions within the closed system of statics and successive decisions within the open system of (monetary) dynamics.

[100] Cf. Hayek, "Investigations", this volume, p. 76. This assumption is, of course, reminiscent of Walras's famous 'auctioneer'.

[101] Ibid., p. 67.

Moreover, by means of the assumption of correct foresight Hayek extended the domain of statics also to non-stationary data and thus replaced 'stationary' by the more general 'intertemporal' equilibrium.[102]

At this juncture in the argument we may pause and ask if with this application of the static method to equilibrium in time Hayek had indeed anticipated the present-day type of dynamic models of equilibrium with perfect foresight.[103] The answer might be simply that although Hayek proposed the concept of intertemporal equilibrium and associated it with correct foresight, he certainly could not have been aware of all the logical consequences that followed from its consistent use. For example, he did not fully recognise the logical tension between, on the one hand, imposing simultaneity on decisions by restricting them to 'closed' time periods and, on the other hand, extending the analysis to time paths of indefinite (indeed infinite) length. For individual plans the requested type of simultaneity necessitated either the existence of a single budget constraint stretching to the end of a potentially infinite time horizon, or alternatively a perfectly foreseen sequence of budget constraints.[104] Due to these budget constraints actions of the present will be linked to the most distant future and therefore the extent of perfect foresight cannot be restricted to an arbitrary time horizon.[105] Moreover, the kind of foresight to which Hayek referred appears different from perfect foresight (as the term is used today) in that he considered it a property of individual cognition, not as an interactive concept to be determined simultaneously with the equilibrium

---

[102] Indeed, the 1928 article "Intertemporal Price Equilibrium" evolved from the drafts of chapters 6 and 7 of "Investigations". Note that in this connection Hayek also introduced the notion of 'dated commodities', that is, of treating the same sort of commodity at different times as different commodities (cf. "Intertemporal Price Equilibrium", p. 188). On intertemporal equilibrium see also the editor's introduction to F. A. Hayek, *Business Cycles, Part I*, pp. 14–16.

[103] As suggested, e.g., by Murray Milgate, "On the Origin of the Notion of 'Intertemporal Equilibrium'", *Economica*, n.s., vol. 46, February 1979, pp. 1–10.

[104] In general equilibrium analysis this corresponds to the alternatives of either an Arrow-Debreu economy with complete markets, where at the present all future markets are active so that all individual decisions, from now on to eternity, are to be taken at the present, or of a sequence economy, where only current markets and a market for transferring purchasing power between time periods are active, so that individual decisions are taken sequentially, yet under the assumption of temporally unlimited perfect foresight. Cf. Roy Radner, "Existence of Equilibrium of Plans, Prices and Price Expectations in a Sequence of Markets", *Econometrica*, vol. 40, March 1972, pp. 289–303.

[105] Hayek was aware that, strictly speaking, perfect foresight would require that all decisions be made irrevocably at the beginning of a prospective time path, calling these "the most extreme static assumptions imaginable" (F. A. Hayek, "The Mythology of Capital", *Quarterly Journal of Economics*, vol. 50, November 1936, pp. 225 and 226). In his re-evaluation of equilibrium analysis Hayek ("Economics and Knowledge", pp. 41–42, reprinted, p. 42) is explicit that foresight will not extend into the indefinite future; cf. also *The Pure Theory of Capital*, reprinted, p. 327.

time path.[106] In all these regards Hayek's anticipation was rather incomplete, and ultimately his work on expectations did not progress towards the notion of perfect foresight of later coinage.[107]

In "Investigations" Hayek examines a threefold extension of the equilibrium of static theory: first, as already noted, towards intertemporal equilibrium by taking account of anticipated changes; second, towards a money economy; and third towards an economy that incorporates the core Austrian idea of a time structure of production, as exemplified by Böhm-Bawerk's notion of successive stages of production. Although Hayek is aware of the scope of complications introduced by these extensions, he takes it for granted that in all these cases—under reasonable assumptions—the economies in question will exhibit equilibria equivalent to those of static theory. With regard to a money economy this is the role played by the theoretical construct of neutral money, so central to the argument of *Prices and Production* and *Monetary Theory and the Trade Cycle*. With regard to non-stationarity, Hayek already had dealt with the issue in his 1928 article on intertemporal equilibrium, although the model used there was one of only single-stage production,[108] so that it in effect evaded the problem of production in time. Overall, in "Investigations" (and elsewhere) Hayek simply asserted the existence of equilibrium compatible with static theory, even for the most sophisticated case of money and a time structure of production,[109] without demonstrating it in detail.

However, especially in "Investigations", Hayek's main concern is not with the state of equilibrium, but much more so with a detailed account of how those different types of economies are supposed to adjust to changes in the data. The distinction between an analysis within the confines of static theory and the truly dynamic processes, when the assumptions of statics are violated, is crucial. Given the simultaneity assumption, Hayek maintains that within statics

[106] This is crucial when the equilibrium time path, and the corresponding set of self-fulfilling expectations, is not unique, which is a familiar feature of present-day dynamic models of monetary economies.

[107] Cf. the implicit discussion between Morgenstern and Hayek: Oskar Morgenstern, "Vollkommene Voraussicht und wirtschaftliches Gleichgewicht", *Zeitschrift für Nationalökonomie*, vol. 6, no. 3, 1935, pp. 337–57, translated as "Perfect Foresight and Economic Equilibrium", trans. Frank H. Knight, in *Selected Economic Writings of Oskar Morgenstern*, ed. Andrew Schotter (New York: New York University Press, 1976), pp. 169–83; F. A. Hayek, "Preiserwartungen, monetäre Störungen und Fehlinvestitionen", *Nationalökonomisk Tidsskrift*, vol. 73, no. 1, 1935, translated as "Price Expectations, Monetary Disturbances, and Malinvestments", chapter 4 of *Profits, Interest and Investment*, reprinted as chapter 7 of F. A. Hayek, *Good Money, Part I: The New World*; and "Economics and Knowledge". For an evaluation cf., e.g., Nicola Giocoli, *Modeling Rational Agents: From Interwar Economics to Early Modern Game Theory* (Cheltenham and Northampton: Edward Elgar, 2003), chapter 3, and Carlo Zappia, "The Assumption of Perfect Foresight and Hayek's Theory of Knowledge", *Revue d'Économie Politique*, vol. 109, November 1999, pp. 833–46.

[108] Cf. Hayek, "Investigations", this volume, pp. 69 and 91–92.

[109] Cf. also ibid., p. 92; the passage is crossed out in the typescript.

any reaction must be automatic and instantaneous, so that a new equilibrium will be reached virtually at one stroke.[110] In the same vein, *Monetary Theory and the Trade Cycle* ascribes to static theory a "tendency towards equilibrium".[111] Yet, both money and production in time, per se, are thought necessarily to violate the simultaneity condition and, by giving rise to successive adjustments, severely to interfere with this tendency towards equilibrium.[112] In both cases successive reactions over time replace simultaneous adjustments taking place within a closed period. In a money economy the origin of such successive reactions lies in the feature of money to split the direct exchange of goods (as organised by a clearing agency) into the two independent halves of indirect exchange—with the lag between the generation and the use of income a pertinent example of such a split. The same is true, according to Hayek, in an economy where production takes time because the exchange of means of production is conceived as an indirect one whose ultimate aim is indeed the exchange for consumers' goods.[113] Concretely, in such a multi-stage economy the simultaneity of decisions will be disturbed by the passage of time required both for the physical build-up of a new structure of production throughout the stages and for the transmission of purchasing power and price signals across stages.

What then will these divergences from the static assumptions mean for the type of adjustments to be expected? Although the economies examined differ in the degree of abstraction, in principle the adjustment patterns derived by Hayek exhibit much the same properties. First, adjustment to equilibrium will not be instantaneous but at best asymptotic. Even temporary misdirections, in modern terminology overshooting and cyclicality, cannot be ruled out.[114] As in contemporary discourse there existed consensus neither with regard to the terminology nor to the conceptualisation of what today would be recognised as stability analysis, the term 'stability' itself possessed only a vague meaning.[115] Hayek's emphasis that thus in effect equilibrium will never be reached in finite time is apt to cast doubts on whether he would have been willing to impute to these processes a 'tendency towards equilibrium'. Another notable feature is that Hayek in his analysis takes explicit account of actual transactions taking place during the adjustment process. For a multi-stage economy,

---

[110] "Any change in the data will lead to an instantaneous and final adjustment, because there are no carry-overs inherited from the past and the factors determining the new prices will persist in their effects" (ibid., pp. 78–79; cf. also pp. 82 and 85).

[111] Cf., e.g., the reference to "that tendency towards equilibrium which is described in pure analysis" (*Monetary Theory and the Trade Cycle*, reprinted, p. 88).

[112] Cf. Hayek, "Investigations", chapters 5 and 8.

[113] Cf. ibid., p. 101.

[114] Cf. ibid., pp. 84–85, for a money economy; and pp. 101–2, for multi-stage production.

[115] Cf. Roy E. Weintraub, *Stabilizing Dynamics: Constructing Economic Knowledge* (Cambridge: Cambridge University Press, 1991).

in particular, he is aware of the further complications introduced by the effects of disequilibrium prices on the structure of production and thereby on the nature of the adjustment process, and he notices that in this way misdirections of production might affect the end point of the adjustment process, that is, equilibrium itself.[116] On one occasion Hayek even mentions such indeterminacies as making permanent beneficial effects of forced saving a possibility that cannot be excluded on purely logical grounds.[117] In addition, outside equilibrium the static assumption of correct expectations can no longer be justified, so further complications may arise from the disappointment of expectations. In the end, after having pointed to so many possible sources of maladjustment and error, Hayek apparently felt compelled to calm the reader that nevertheless due to the continuity of the economic process such economies will not be completely ruled by chaos.[118]

In contrast to the lessons to be drawn in *Prices and Production*, in the preparatory "Investigations" sustained deviations from the equilibrium of static theory are deemed the rule even before the main culprit of Hayek's monetary theory of the cycle, credit creation or destruction, enters the scene. However, it is the creation and destruction of credit prevalent in a money economy that is considered responsible for such deviations becoming sufficiently significant in order to explain the occurrence of cycles.[119] Whereas in "Investigations" credit creation is considered an additional complication of the introduction of money, in *Monetary Theory and the Trade Cycle*, and still more so in *Prices and Production*, it is treated almost as if this were the only way for a money economy to diverge from the results of statics. Thus, although not in contradiction to the earlier preparatory work, in this regard the focus in Hayek's later monographs has shifted. In comparison to Hayek's published works of this period, the "Investigations" stand out in their emphasis on the obstacles to the eventual attainment of a determinate equilibrium. Outside of statics, "we must in principle regard the economy as an infinite stream"[120] instead of in a state of equilibrium. For an economy shaped by indirect exchange Hayek rejected the

---

[116] Cf. "Investigations", this volume, p. 79: "in the course of the adjustment process the money economy is subject to necessary changes so that the state of equilibrium eventually attained . . . , although it will fulfil the formal theoretical conditions, in substance may differ considerably from the equilibrium derived from static theory, towards which the money economy is supposed to tend." In present-day analysis, these phenomena appear under the heading of 'path dependence'; in contemporary terminology this type of equilibrium was referred to as 'indeterminate' (cf. Nicholas Kaldor, "A Classificatory Note on the Determinateness of Equilibrium", *Review of Economic Studies*, vol. 1, February 1934, pp. 122–36, reprinted as chapter 1 of *Essays on Value and Distribution*).

[117] Cf. "Investigations", this volume, p. 130n.64.

[118] Cf. ibid., p. 83.

[119] Cf. ibid., chapter 6 and p. 130.

[120] Ibid., p. 79.

idea of a regular and unchanging circuit of money (or income) apposite to the synchronised working of an economy in stationary equilibrium in favour of a manifold of interlocking circuits. Accordingly, the proper metaphor for such a circuit is not that of an even flow, but rather of "a river system made up of a main river and many tributaries and branches of different length".[121]

Summarising Hayek's approach prior to *Prices and Production*, we find him convinced of the necessity of taking the equilibrium of static theory as a reference point for any further analysis, yet, with the main focus not on equilibrium or comparative statics, but on the processes triggered by changes in economic data. Although the equilibrium in question is a kind of general equilibrium, the analysis is completely in verbal terms, with just a single reference to a Walras-like system of simultaneous equations,[122] so that its characterisation as "total equilibrium analysis" (Blaug), or still better, "total adjustment analysis" (Rizzo), seems perfectly adequate.[123] In this early phase Hayek appears preoccupied with what Hans Mayer, then the mentor of his habilitation at the University of Vienna, propagated as 'causal-genetic analysis', in contrast to the less fruitful type of 'functional analysis', the former being concerned with a 'theory of the path', the latter only with the conditions of equilibrium.[124] Taking account of money and the time structure of production—irrespective of whether the circulation of money is kept constant or not—makes it impossible to reduce these adjustment processes to cases of an instantaneous or asymptotic return to a predetermined equilibrium. Rather, money becomes a source of dynamics, a "dynamic force".[125] In this sense Hayek's purpose in this first period was to redefine the task of monetary theory as a general theory of a money economy which cannot but focus on such dynamic phenomena, instead of just reproducing the results of statics in monetary garb.[126]

---

[121] Ibid., p. 111.

[122] Cf. ibid., p. 135.

[123] Cf. Mark Blaug, "Comment on O'Brien", in *Carl Menger and His Legacy in Economics*, ed. Bruce Caldwell (Durham, NC: Duke University Press, 1990), p. 185; and for the attribution to Rizzo cf. Bruce Caldwell, "Wieser, Hayek and Equilibrium Theory", *Journal des Economistes et des Etudes Humaines*, vol. 12, March 2002, p. 55n.

[124] Cf. Hans Mayer, "Der Erkenntniswert der funktionellen Preistheorien", in *Die Wirtschaftstheorie der Gegenwart*, ed. Hans Mayer, Frank A. Fetter, and Richard Reisch, vol. 2 (Vienna: Springer, 1932), pp. 147–239, translated as "The Cognitive Value of Functional Theories of Price", in *Classics in Austrian Economics*, vol. 2: *The Interwar Period*, ed. Israel Kirzner (London: Pickering, 1994), pp. 55–168; numerous references to Mayer are to be found in "Investigations"; cf. also Kaldor, "Determinateness of Equilibrium", pp. 127–28.

[125] Cf. "Investigations", table of contents, this volume, p. 47.

[126] Cf. ibid., pp. 134–35, and also the well-known passage from *Prices and Production*, "the task of monetary theory is . . . nothing less than to cover a second time the whole field which is treated by pure theory under the assumption of barter, and to investigate what changes in the conclusions of pure theory are made necessary by the introduction of indirect exchange" (reprinted, pp. 279–80).

2. "These incredibly successful lectures . . ."

Proceeding to the next phase of Hayek's writings, we may note how he remembered the creation of *Prices and Production*:

> The invitation [to the lectures at LSE] reached me when I had for the first time a clear picture of this theory but had not yet gone into all the complicated details. If I had progressed in working out an elaborate treatise, I would have encountered any number of complications . . . Since I was not yet aware of the difficulties, I gave these incredibly successful lectures.[127]

The second phase of Hayek's theories of money, capital, and the cycle, epitomised by *Prices and Production*, is distinguished by his readiness to make use of grave simplifications as compared to the elaborate treatise of the "Investigations". These simplifications show themselves at least at four levels of the argument: First, *Prices and Production* restricts the analysis to an economy in stationary equilibrium although the application to the more general case of intertemporal equilibrium is still kept on the agenda for future research.[128] Second, it postulates the existence of neutral money, thus taking the equilibrium of static theory as a norm that ideally could be arrived at even in a money economy with a time structure of production. Third, there is a neat separation of successful transitions when money is neutral from failed transitions when it is non-neutral. In addition, the non-neutrality resulting from the endogeneity of credit creation is treated as the primary source of dynamic divergences from the outcomes predicted by static theory almost to the neglect of all the other causes mentioned earlier. And fourth, in order to make the analysis concrete it reduces the time structure of production to a Böhm-Bawerkian model of flow-input-point-output stages, so that roundaboutness can be indicated by an average period of production.

The analytical return to this simplification paid off in straightforward results. On the one hand, as long as money is kept neutral—with all the necessary prerequisites including the absence of Cantillon effects, perfect foresight, and flexibility of prices and contracts—the results of static theory apply. In particular an increase in voluntary saving will bring forth a successful transition to a new and more productive equilibrium. On the other hand, with neutrality violated by credit creation and forced saving, the transition thus started will fail and bring forth crisis and depression. Now even in the dynamic case the possibility of path dependence, in particular the permanency of beneficial

---

[127] *Hayek on Hayek: An Autobiographical Dialogue*, ed. Stephen Kresge and Leif Wenar (Chicago: University of Chicago Press; London: Routledge, 1994), pp. 77–78.

[128] Cf. Hayek, *Prices and Production*, reprinted, p. 215.

effects from forced saving, is denied. However, in order to explain the presence of unemployment and idle capacities in the depression, the analysis had to preserve the notion of the specificity and complementarity of capital goods[129] as an element that transcends the simple structure of production utilised elsewhere in the analysis.

3. The Capital Project

It is only a slight exaggeration to characterise *Prices and Production* as the most simplified, and yet the most immediately successful, of Hayek's endeavours in this field. However, it is also true that Hayek soon realised the need to generalise his approach in some regards. One path of inquiry, to be dealt with in the next subsection, led him to question the assumptions underlying the framework of intertemporal equilibrium and perfect foresight, implicit in the stationary state of his simple model. Another concern was with the generalisation and dynamisation of the analysis of the time structure of production in order to provide a sounder basis for an elaborated theory of money and the cycle. This was the subject of the capital project, on which Hayek embarked circa 1934 and which he finished in 1941 with *The Pure Theory of Capital*. It is also this project that Hayek announced as "a later more complete exposition", when he published the revised, yet in its essentials largely unchanged, second edition of *Prices and Production*.[130] For the sake of the proposed periodisation of Hayek's writings the capital project marks the third phase.

One external motive for Hayek to move away from the simplified version of the structure of production lay in the necessity to delineate more precisely the core of Austrian capital theory in his defence against Knight's concept of capital as a fund.[131] Hayek criticised this approach for its association with the erroneous concept of capital as permanent, homogeneous, and completely malleable, and in contrast advocated the Austrian characterisation of capital by a temporal structure. The capital stock by its very nature consists of a variety of heterogeneous capital goods, with a limited diversity of uses in the different branches and stages of production and similarly with a limited range for substitution. The upshot of this conception is that it is not only the stock (conceived as a quantity) of capital that is economically relevant, but its struc-

---

[129] Cf. ibid., reprinted, pp. 243–44 and 256.

[130] Ibid., reprinted, p. 176.

[131] Cf. Avi J. Cohen, "The Hayek/Knight Controversy: The Irrelevance of Roundaboutness, or Purging Processes in Time?", *History of Political Economy*, vol. 35, Fall 2003, pp. 469–90; and the editor's introduction to F. A. Hayek, *The Pure Theory of Capital*. For the following cf. F. A. Hayek, "On the Relationship between Investment and Output", *Economic Journal*, vol. 44, June 1934, pp. 207–31, and "The Mythology of Capital".

ture, that is, its composition of different types of heterogeneous goods. Consequently, a given structure of capital determines the type and the quantity of goods which can be produced with its help. The heterogeneity of capital goods prevents them from being instantaneously rearranged as a reaction to a change in the economy's data.[132]

The emphasis on heterogeneity implies the inadequacy of any attempt to reduce the complexity of the structure of capital to a single scalar measure, such as the average period of production as an index of capital intensity. In retrospect Hayek admitted that the average period was "a beautiful simplification", with problems of which he had not been fully aware when he used it in *Prices and Production*.[133] In his debate with Knight, Hayek was soon to reject the idea of the average period, stating that the complete specification of an investment function "is the only adequate representation . . . and cannot usefully be replaced—except by way of a provisional simplification in an early stage of analysis—by any one-dimensional magnitude such as the 'average period of production'".[134] Two years later he called the average period "hopelessly inadequate".[135] Henceforth Hayek steadfastly clung to this line of argument, and indeed the necessity to discard the average period was pivotal for starting the capital project.[136]

Apart from the fact that the period concept is ill suited for dealing with a heterogeneous structure of capital, there are other shortcomings of the average period, and in fact of any scalar measure of capital, on which a few remarks are in order. First, for calculating such a period the averaging of dated inputs of original means of production requires the discounting of past inputs. Unfortunately, when using compound instead of simple interest for discounting, the length of the average period, computed for one and the same time profile of inputs, will differ with the rate of interest used. Hayek acknowledged this problem, already pointed out by Wicksell, and he repeatedly noticed that due to this deficiency it does not make sense to speak of the rate of interest as being determined by the time structure of production envisioned as a one-

---

[132] Among Austrian economists, Ludwig Lachmann (cf. *Capital and Its Structure*, 2nd ed. [Kansas City: Sheed Andrews and McMeel, 1978]) most strongly emphasised this aspect of the structure of capital.

[133] *Hayek on Hayek*, p. 77.

[134] Hayek, "On the Relationship between Investment and Output", p. 211.

[135] Hayek, "The Mythology of Capital", pp. 220–21.

[136] Similar statements are to be found in Hayek's contribution to a questionnaire circulated by Fritz Machlup, "Zu den Ergebnissen von Machlups Rundfrage über einige begriffliche Unklarheiten in der Kapitalstheorie" ("On the Results of Machlup's Questionnaire on Some Ambiguities in the Theory of Capital"), dated October 26, 1934, in Machlup Papers, box 86, folder 29; in F. A. Hayek, "Investment That Raises the Demand for Capital", *Review of Economic Statistics*, vol. 19, November 1937, reprinted in this volume, p. 211; in "Profits, Interest and Investment", this volume, p. 241n.50; and in *The Pure Theory of Capital*, reprinted, p. 4.

dimensional, scalar variable.[137] Other important issues in this regard were highlighted later on in the so-called Cambridge capital controversy.[138] According to the Cambridge critique, not only will a scalar measure like the average period associate different values with the same chosen technique for different rates of interest, but, worse, it will not be possible in general to construct an average period so that profit maximisation induces entrepreneurs invariably to choose techniques represented by a longer period whenever the rate of interest is lower. For example, the same technique (the same time profile of dated inputs) may turn out as profit maximising at two different values of the interest rate, yet with a different technique maximising profits for intermediate values—the famous phenomenon of 'reswitching'. Evidently, if reswitching is present, a monotonically negative relation between an average period and the rate of interest will become impossible.[139] It appears that although in his capital project Hayek became aware of most of these crucial points on the non-existence of aggregative measures of capital, he persevered in his belief in the relevance of the traditional relationships between the economic variables characterising the structure of production, for example, an inverse relationship between the rate of interest and capital intensity.[140] Moreover, as a final drawback, the possibility to map a capital structure into a finite time profile of dated inputs is predicated upon this structure being linear. In contrast, when fixed capital is taken into account beside circulating capital, the structure will become circular and the corresponding time profile infinite.[141]

[137] Cf. Hayek, "On the Relationship between Investment and Output", pp. 212–13, and "The Mythology of Capital", p. 207. In his response to Machlup's questionnaire Hayek states explicitly that in order to determine a value measure of capital, "we have to take the interest rate as given instead of deriving, as intended, interest from the changes in the time dimension [that is, the average period]". Today this problem is known as the 'price Wicksell effect'; cf. Knut Wicksell, *Lectures on Political Economy*, vol. 1: *General Theory* (London: Routledge, 1934; reprinted, New York: Kelley, 1967; and Auburn, AL: Ludwig von Mises Institute, 2007), p. 184.

[138] For an overview on the controversy cf. Avi J. Cohen and Geoffrey C. Harcourt, "Whatever Happened to the Cambridge Capital Controversies?", *Journal of Economic Perspectives*, vol. 17, Winter 2003, pp. 199–214; a discussion with reference to Böhm-Bawerk's capital theory is Paul A. Samuelson, "A Modern Post-Mortem on Böhm's Capital Theory: Its Vital Normative Flaw Shared by Pre-Sraffian Mainstream Capital Theory", *Journal of the History of Economic Thought*, vol. 23, September 2001, pp. 301–17.

[139] Moreover, although there will always be for any set of investment functions a negative relation (across steady-state equilibria) between the rate of interest and the real wage, such a negative relation is not logically necessary for the rate of interest and consumption per head.

[140] Cf. Ian Steedman, "On *The Pure Theory of Capital* by F. A. Hayek", in *The Economics of F. A. Hayek*, vol. 2: *Capitalism, Socialism and Knowledge*, ed. Marina Colonna, Harald Hagemann, and Omar F. Hamouda (Aldershot: Edward Elgar, 1994), pp. 21–23. Hayek's single attempt to confront the problem of reswitching is in "The Flow of Goods and Services", this volume, p. 340.

[141] Cf. Heinz D. Kurz and Neri Salvadori, *Theory of Production: A Long-Period Analysis* (Cambridge, New York, and Melbourne: Cambridge University Press, 1995), p. 178; circularity im-

Hayek's attempt at a capital theory without the average period culminated in *The Pure Theory of Capital*. As Hayek regularly used the term 'pure theory' to designate the field covered by economic statics, we should not be surprised that it takes equilibrium once more as the starting point. Furthermore, Hayek leaves no doubt about the type of equilibrium used and where to draw the line between statics and dynamics. In this regard, his approach has stayed much the same since his beginnings: "The only relevant distinction is between two methods, that of logical analysis of the different plans existing at one moment ('equilibrium analysis') and that of causal analysis of a process in time",[142] which is equivalent to the distinction between statics and dynamics. The equilibrium analysis of statics can also "be applied to situations which are not stationary and where the same correspondence between plans prevail . . . because [people] correctly foresee what changes will occur in the actions of others",[143] which is the definition of intertemporal equilibrium. Thus, *The Pure Theory of Capital* should be considered as a final attempt at integrating the concepts of intertemporal equilibrium and time-consuming production, without resorting to the simplifications employed before, and as representing rather a continuation of than a break with his earlier work. One may, however, find that Hayek went still more out of his way in stressing the "fictitious character" of equilibrium, such as in his warning that "we must abandon the pretense that it refers to something real".[144]

Inasmuch as it turns to the "causal explanation of the process in time", the analysis must leave the field of statics and enter that of dynamics. The 'causal analysis' to which Hayek refers should again be viewed as evolving from the kind of 'total adjustment analysis' characteristic of his early phase. Similar to the "Investigations", the crucial point is that changes in data and the principally infinite duration of adjustment render the re-establishment of equilibrium, once disturbed, impossible—even, which needs to be emphasised, in the absence of monetary complications. Here the heterogeneity of capital provides the crucial element. As the structure of capital is built up over time, it necessarily reflects a history of past disturbances and adjustments and in turn determines the possibilities of present production: "Once unforeseen changes occur after capital has been invested in a definite form, all further investment will be influenced by the historical accident of the existence of certain capital goods, and the movement towards a state of equilibrium will at best be an

---

plies the existence of a commodity that enters directly or indirectly into the production of all commodities.

[142] Hayek, *The Pure Theory of Capital*, reprinted, p. 43n.7.

[143] Ibid., pp. 43–44.

[144] Ibid., p. 46; cf. also pp. 44 and 47.

asymptotic movement."[145] Indeed, a consistent rethinking of this argument could not justifiably stop short of conceding the indeterminacy of equilibrium, too. In any case, with regard to the processes in real time characterising an actual economy, its capital structure will of necessity be always out of equilibrium: Forward and backward looking measures of the value of capital, that is, discounted future returns and actual production costs, will as a rule not coincide, and so profit maximising decisions will typically not lead to a mere reproduction of the existing structure of capital, and thus the economy will never end up with an equilibrium capital structure.

The Pure Theory of Capital could at best deliver the prolegomena to the dynamic analysis Hayek strived for because it was predominantly conducted in real terms. However, "the crux of the matter is that where analysis aims directly at a causal explanation of the economic process as it proceeds in time, the use of the conception of a money-less exchange economy is misplaced",[146] that is, a truly dynamic analysis—as required for a treatment of the cycle—necessitates the introduction of money. Hayek had for the time being reserved the analysis of such a dynamic theory of capital for a planned second volume of his capital theory, which however never materialised.[147] The only attempt of applying the insights from the pure theory of capital to a monetary setting consisted in the essay "Profits, Interest and Investment", which—as already has been pointed out—turned out as one of the least successful pieces ever written by Hayek.[148]

Hayek's capital project should thus be considered the continuation and conclusion of the ambitious enterprise of the "Investigations", aiming at an integration of the theories of money, capital, and the cycle within a framework which, although starting from the notion of equilibrium, focused on the analysis of adjustment processes.[149] However, Hayek abandoned this project with-

[145] Hayek, "On the Relationship between Investment and Output", p. 227; cf. also *The Pure Theory of Capital*, reprinted, pp. 249–50.

[146] *The Pure Theory of Capital*, reprinted, p. 54.

[147] For example, Hayek (in *Hayek on Hayek*, p. 79) speaks of an "intended monetary or dynamic continuation".

[148] For an alternative perspective that links Hayek's writings on money and the cycle in this phase more closely to his 'transformation', cf. Constatinos Repapis, "Hayek's Business Cycle Theory during the 1930s: A Critical Account of its Development", *History of Political Economy*, vol. 43, Winter 2011, pp. 699–742.

[149] This interpretation is confirmed by Hayek himself, when he remembers the fate of his 1928 article on intertemporal equilibrium: "Though the 'Intertemporale Gleichgewichtssystem' was my first major theoretical effort and had occupied me for several years, I was afterwards so little satisfied with it that I refused to have it translated into English. My plan was then to return to the problems in a second, 'dynamic' part of my work on capital which I also never wrote. The 'new love' which I first articulated in my 1936 paper on 'Economics and Knowledge' led into

out achieving his goal of providing a foundation for a theory of the cycle more satisfactory than in *Prices and Production*.

4. Hayek's Transformation

While to some extent the capital project marked a dead end to one strand in Hayek's thought, another strand, which evolved (at the start in parallel with the capital project) from his stance in the economic calculation debate, stands out as a unique and lasting achievement. This is Hayek's novel approach towards the role of prices and expectations with regard to the dissemination and coordination of dispersed knowledge. It is this new direction in Hayek's thought that is generally considered as the essence of his 'transformation'.

A first hint of this reorientation can be already discerned in Hayek's Copenhagen Lecture of 1935,[150] which besides contributing to the ongoing debate on the meaning of perfect foresight focuses on expectations as driving forces of the economic process. Whereas in intertemporal equilibrium an independent role for expectations is prevented by their endogenous nature, now the emphasis turns on the fact that outside equilibrium fallible expectations become a major autonomous factor of the dynamic process. Then, in "Economics and Knowledge", the *locus classicus* of Hayek's transformation, the analysis of expectations and the market process rests on new foundations, that is, on the notion of subjectively held and dispersed knowledge.[151] In our context this is significant in two regards: First, with idiosyncratic information expectations will typically become heterogeneous, as each individual's expectations are built on a specific set of information. Second, the information subjectively held by the individuals will change over time, due to the modification of prior beliefs in the light of new experience and due to the discovery of new profit opportunities by individuals in their entrepreneurial function. Such changes in individual knowledge and expectations constitute a new element that shapes the market process, and indeed they become a further factor destroying the idea of equilibrium or rather of a smooth transition towards it. It should be acknowledged that some such obstacles to an adjustment towards equilibrium, or more precisely to the description of an existing economic system by means of an equilibrium framework, were already present before Hayek's transformation, early in "Investigations" as well as more thoroughly elaborated as part

---

so many directions that I somewhat had lost interest in the narrow problems of changes in the structure of capital." (Hayek to Murray Milgate, March 15, 1979. I am grateful to Murray Milgate for generously making his correspondence with Hayek available to me.)

[150] Originally published as "Preiserwartungen, monetäre Störungen und Fehlinvestitionen".

[151] Cf., e.g., Caldwell, "Hayek's Transformation", and *Hayek's Challenge: An Intellectual Biography of F. A. Hayek* (Chicago and London: University of Chicago Press, 2004), chapter 10.

of the capital project. Yet, these earlier arguments against equilibrium were mainly based on the enduring effects of past disturbances; the resulting dynamics was in this sense 'backward looking'. In contrast, the character of the market process as derived from these new insights is 'forward looking'; the dynamics follows from the ever-changing view of the future as perceived by the actors from their distinct individual perspectives. Whereas essentially the former processes could still be described as adjustments towards an equilibrium albeit conceived as fictitious, these processes now became open-ended in principle, and the connection with equilibrium a very loose one.

Although not directly pertinent to the study of money and the cycle, Hayek's analysis of the informational role of the price system should also be noticed. The 'marvel' of the price mechanism[152] is that it succeeds in transforming the dispersed information into price signals that efficiently indicate scarcities and thereby effectively coordinate the plans of individual actors. Indeed, it is the aspect of coordination, the compatibility of individual plans based on differing information, that lends a new shade to Hayek's notion of equilibrium as expounded in "Economics and Knowledge". Moreover, taking this compatibility of plans based on idiosyncratic knowledge (and thus heterogeneous expectations) as the point of departure, the successful working of the price system appears to imply a kind of convergence of expectations; beyond the mere compatibility of plans some congruence between plans and perceptions or what the individual actors conceive as 'facts' must be brought about.[153] The crucial issue in this regard is therefore how the price system will establish this kind of congruence. Hayek put his trust in the efficacy of the incentives set by the market system for eliminating perceived disequilibria, but he did not think that this warranted detailed empirical studies nor did he apparently consider the kind of analytical exercises conducted in "Investigations" or in the capital project as helpful for solving this problem—rather he took the resilience of the actual market economies as a kind of empirical confirmation.

It is noteworthy that Hayek's idea of the informational role of the price system has been rediscovered, or so it has been claimed, by modern economic theory, mainly under the heading of 'rational expectations'.[154] From the foregoing it should be evident, however, that Hayek's approach differs radically

[152] F. A. Hayek, "The Use of Knowledge in Society", *American Economic Review*, vol. 35, September 1945, p. 527, reprinted as chapter 4 of *Individualism and Economic Order*, p. 87.

[153] On compatibility versus congruence cf. Meghnad Desai, "Equilibrium, Expectations and Knowledge", in *Hayek, Co-ordination and Evolution: His Legacy in Philosophy, Politics, Economics and the History of Ideas*, ed. Jack Birner and Rudy van Zijp (London: Routledge, 1994), pp. 25–50.

[154] Robert E. Lucas ("Understanding Business Cycles", in *Stabilization of the Domestic and International Economy*, Carnegie-Rochester Conference Series on Public Policy, vol. 5, 1977, ed. Karl Brunner and Allan Meltzer, pp. 7–29) was probably the first to maintain an Austrian connection from Hayek to new classical economics and rational expectations.

from the modern one in vital respects. From a Hayekian perspective the marvel of the price system in transmitting heterogeneous information throughout the economy lies just in relieving the individuals from the burden of information processing: "The most significant fact about this system is the economy of knowledge with which it operates, or how little the individual participants need to know."[155] This is quite distinct from the role attributed to individuals in models based on rational expectations (or, indeed, perfect foresight). True, in such models, a rational-expectations equilibrium might be 'revealing' in that it synthesises all the diverse information and condenses it into a signal that reveals the state of nature to all actors.[156] Yet, this astonishing achievement is accomplished just because the actors are assumed to know beforehand how all possible distributions of information will affect the equilibrium price vector, so that once they know the equilibrium price they can invert this relation and decode the corresponding information structure from it. In remarkable contrast to Hayek's perspective, in the modern re-interpretation the price system works because each individual is supposed to do all the work of the price system 'in his own head'. In this instance modern economic theory has been able to formalise and solve Hayek's problem only at the price of a complete volte-face: instead of relieving individuals, the modern re-interpretation burdens them with the task of calculating all the economy-wide relationships impinging on equilibrium prices, a task resembling the insoluble challenge to central planning and an assumption that completely perverts Hayek's idea of the 'division of knowledge'.[157] We may thus conclude that the modern exercises in formal dynamic equilibrium analysis integrating (rational) expectations, money, and deviations due to misperceptions, valuable as they may be on their own as enquiries into the logic of formal dynamic systems, cannot by the very nature of their construction shed much light on Hayek's knowledge problem.

In the end, how do these developments relate to Hayek's theories of money, capital, and the cycle? First, we realise that the capital project and the writings on the division of knowledge, albeit not in contradiction with one another, pointed to some extent into different directions.[158] The capital project made

---

[155] Hayek, "The Use of Knowledge in Society", pp. 526–27, reprinted, p. 86.

[156] On this concept cf. Roy Radner, "Rational Expectations Equilibrium: Generic Existence and the Information Revealed by Prices", *Econometrica*, vol. 47, May 1979, pp. 655–78.

[157] Hayek, "Economics and Knowledge", p. 49, reprinted, p. 50.

[158] In this regard, opposite positions within the range of interpretations are taken by Ulrich Witt ("The Hayekian Puzzle: Spontaneous Order and the Business Cycle", *Scottish Journal of Political Economy*, vol. 44, February 1997, pp. 44–58), who speaks of "two basically incompatible research programmes", and Peter Boettke ("Introduction: Which Enlightenment, Whose Liberalism? Hayek's Research Program for Understanding the Liberal Society", in *The Legacy of Friedrich von Hayek*, vol. 1: *Politics*, ed. Peter Boettke [Cheltenham and Northampton: Edward Elgar, 1999], p. xxv), who argues that Hayek's technical economics should be read against

no explicit use of the idea of dispersed knowledge but examined the problems of equilibrium and adjustment as referring to an economy with a heterogeneous capital structure. In contrast, when Hayek contemplated market processes in the context of the coordination of plans based on dispersed information, he abstracted from the problems of capital. In addition, both neglected the role of money, thus highlighting that even in a moneyless economy equilibrium is no more than a fiction. As already noted, the decisive step towards a truly dynamic analysis resulted however from the recognition of the knowledge problem, and thus from the emphasis on the information- and expectation-based, forward-looking character of the market process.

5. Beyond Equilibrium?

At last, we may proceed to Hayek's final words on this issue, his lecture "The Flow of Goods and Services". In light of his accomplishments as a theorist, how did Hayek deal at this occasion with the tensions between equilibrium and market process, between logical and causal analysis, in the context of money, capital, and the cycle? We may find a clue in Hayek's own characterisation of his venture:

> Of the direct significance of equilibrium analysis to the explanation of the events we observe, I never had any doubt. I thought it was a very useful concept to explain a type of order towards [which] the process of economics tends without ever reaching it. I'm now trying to formulate some concept of economics as a stream instead of an equilibrating force, as we ought, quite literally, to think in terms of the factors that determine the movement of the flow of water in a very irregular bed. That would give us a much better conception of what it does.[159]

---

the background of his later writings in social philosophy. Cf. also Nicolai Juul Foss, "More on 'Hayek's Transformation'", *History of Political Economy*, vol. 27, Summer 1995, pp. 345–64, for an account that emphasises the continuity of Hayek's thought within the 1930s, although—without recourse to "Investigations"—it possibly underrates Hayek's early scepticism about the notion of equilibrium.

[159] F. A. Hayek, "Nobel Prize–Winning Economist", ed. Armen Alchian (transcript of an interview conducted in 1978 under the auspices of the Oral History Program, University Library, University of California–Los Angeles [transcript 300/224, Department of Special Collections, Charles E. Young Research Library, UCLA]), pp. 187–88. The quotation is from a series of interviews with Hayek conducted in November 1978, when he was actively developing this notion of a flow and planned to include a respective chapter in *The Fatal Conceit: The Errors of Socialism*, which was ultimately edited by W. W. Bartley III and published as vol. 1 (1988) of *The Collected Works of F. A. Hayek* without this chapter. To be sure, what Hayek wanted to express in the first sentence in the quotation is that he had *always doubted* the significance of equilibrium.

The concept of the economy as a flow of goods and services appears to be Hayek's most radical rejection of economic thinking in terms of aggregates or economic circuits, and it has also been interpreted as a final renunciation of the usefulness of an equilibrium framework for economic analysis. In any case it provides a final, if only verbal, synthesis of the studies in the theory of knowledge and of money, capital, and the cycle. The flow to which Hayek refers is not much different from the one he described in "Investigations" and in *The Pure Theory of Capital*—an irregular flow of goods through the stages of production, continuously rendering consumers' goods at the final stage, using up goods of the earlier stages and replacing them by goods of the same or of other types in the light of the variety of knowledge and expectations dispersed throughout the system. The sustained effects of past disturbances and the ongoing adjustments of the capital structure on the one hand, and the expectation of future profit opportunities on the other hand, shape the production possibilities of the present and determine how the capital structure is to be modified to accommodate for changing future needs. The dynamic process is conceived as both backward-looking and forward-looking, and it is crucially indeterminate because of the heterogeneity of capital goods. In stressing the irregularities of this flow, Hayek resorts to the aquatic metaphors he had first used fifty years before: the streams are likened to "rather complex ramified river systems", and to "the ramifications of this flow, or rather countless interlocking and intertwined flows, requiring confluences at determined but variable rates, and each spreading like a tree as well as each branch combining with branches of other streams into a multiplicity of river systems".[160] Consequently, "the achievement of an equilibrium is strictly impossible. Indeed, in a literal sense, *a stream can never be in equilibrium*."[161] Thus, more than ever the fictitious character of equilibrium is asserted, that is, the impossibility of equilibrium ever to be attained by such a system of flows. In this sense, one has to agree with Caldwell's contention that here "Hayek's commitment to equilibrium theory . . . had reached its lowest point".[162] Yet, even in this most radical attempt to get rid of the constraints of equilibrium theorising, the tension between equilibrium and the market process (or the economy conceived as a flow) is, one might argue, still present: how, otherwise, could one make sense of Hayek's remark that the criterion for judging the efficacy of an economy characterised as a system of flows can be only "the *degree* to which the order will ever approach the unattainable ideal of equilibrium . . . the average close-

---

[160] Hayek, "The Flow of Goods and Services", this volume, pp. 335 and 338. Note the similarity to the passage from "Investigations" (this volume, p. 111) quoted above.

[161] Hayek, "The Flow of Goods and Services", this volume, p. 338. Again see "Investigations" (this volume, p. 79) for the characterisation of the economy "as an infinite stream".

[162] Caldwell, *Hayek's Challenge*, p. 227.

ness to the ideal"[163]? Indeed, there is a very thin line separating 'disequilibrium analysis' from 'non-equilibrium analysis' in this regard.

To sum up, the major insight, drawing on Hayek's preparatory work in "Investigations", appears to be a stronger sense for the continuity in Hayek's thought in the fields of money, capital, and the cycle. Considering the development from his beginnings circa 1924 until the 1940s, when his writings on these subjects subsided, we find the main methodological approach unchanged throughout: the fiction of static theory as the point of departure, the extension from stationary to intertemporal equilibrium, and the main focus on what has aptly been called 'total adjustment analysis'. The only changes, or perhaps just vacillations, in Hayek's views concerned the utilisation of a short-cut like the average period of production, giving way to a full account of the heterogeneity of capital, and the role assigned to money as the prime cause of dynamics and thereby of the cycle. This interpretation disjoins the capital project to some extent from the work on the division of knowledge, but confirms "Economics and Knowledge" as crucial for Hayek's transformation and for providing a new (and additional) perspective on the nature of dynamic market processes. According to this reading of the evidence, with the possible exception of his 1981 lecture,[164] this new perspective left fewer traces in Hayek's writings on the business cycle than in other fields. In any case, this continuity in Hayek's thought on money, capital, and the cycle corresponds well with the overall unity of his research programme, especially with regard to economics, as centred on the problem of the coordination of individual actions and the informational (or signaling) role of markets and prices, be it the rate of interest in business cycle theory or be it market prices in an economy characterised by dispersed knowledge.[165]

Hansjoerg Klausinger

[163] Hayek, "The Flow of Goods and Services", this volume, p. 339.

[164] In the field of money, Hayek's radical proposal of *Denationalisation of Money* (London: Institute of Economic Affairs, 1978), reprinted as chapter 4 of F. A. Hayek, *Good Money, Part II: The Standard*, must be mentioned.

[165] This unity is attested by F. A. Hayek, "Foreword: On The Way", to Gerald P. O'Driscoll, jr., *Economics as a Coordination Problem: The Contributions of Friedrich A. Hayek* (Kansas City: Sheed Andrews and Mc Meel, 1977), p.ix: "That it seems in principle possible to recast a great part of economic theory in terms of the approach which I had found useful in dealing with such different problems as those of industrial fluctuations and the running of a socialist economy was the more gratifying to me as what I had done had often seemed to me more to point out barriers to further advance on the path chosen by others than to supply new ideas which opened the path to further development. Professor O'Driscoll has almost persuaded me that I ought to have continued with the work I had been doing in the 1930s and 1940s rather than let myself be drawn away to other problems which I felt to be more important."

ONE

INVESTIGATIONS INTO
MONETARY THEORY[1]

[1] [The following piece by F. A. Hayek is published for the first time. It consists of an incomplete and ultimately abandoned typescript prepared for a grand book project, on which Hayek spent roughly five years, from 1925 to 1929. The text has been preserved in the Friedrich A. von Hayek Papers, Incremental Material, box 105, folders 1–4, Hoover Institution Archives, Stanford University. The translation is by the editor.

The book, to be titled *Geldtheoretische Untersuchungen* (*Investigations into Monetary Theory*), was planned to comprise three parts, to be released in two volumes by the German publisher Gustav Fischer. Of these three parts only the first one, "Price Formation in a Money Economy", came near to completion; the unfinished typescript includes eight of the planned ten chapters. Most of Hayek's writings between 1925 and 1929 were destined to contribute to this book project: his well-known 1928 article "Das intertemporale Gleichgewichtssystem der Preise und die Bewegungen des 'Geldwertes'" (*Weltwirtschaftliches Archiv*, vol. 28, July 1928, pp. 33–76; translated as "Intertemporal Price Equilibrium and Movements in the Value of Money" and reprinted as chapter 5 of *Good Money, Part I: The New World*, ed. Stephen Kresge, vol. 5 (1999) of *The Collected Works of F. A. Hayek* (Chicago: University of Chicago Press; London: Routledge)) made up two chapters of the book, and his habilitation lecture, "Gibt es einen 'Widersinn des Sparens'?" (*Zeitschrift für Nationalökonomie*, vol. 1, November 1929, pp. 387–429; translated as "The 'Paradox' of Saving", *Economica*, no. 32, May 1931, pp. 125–69, reprinted as chapter 2 of *Contra Keynes and Cambridge: Essays, Correspondence*, ed. Bruce Caldwell, vol. 9 (1995) of *The Collected Works of F. A. Hayek*), was intended to be integrated into the final chapters, too. Indeed, we find sections of the printed article cut and pasted into the typescript, which makes it possible to date the final phase of the project to the end of 1929. At this time Hayek abandoned the whole venture and turned to another one, when he was approached to write the missing part on money for the famous *Grundriß der Sozialökonomik* series—this project also came to naught, with the four existing chapters published only in 1991 (in *The Trend of Economic Thinking: Essays on Political Economists and Economic History*, ed. W. W. Bartley III and Stephen Kresge, vol. 3 (1991) of *The Collected Works of F. A. Hayek*).

The existing material of the "Geldtheoretische Untersuchungen" consists of the typescript of the main text (eight chapters), a draft table of contents, incomplete versions of the preface and the introduction (reprinted in the present volume), and besides that numerous notes, which will be occasionally referred to. As regards the typescript, it was apparently written from Hayek's dictation and then corrected by him in handwriting, yet even so it is certain that Hayek would have revised it one more time before considering it ready for publication. It is possibly due to these circumstances that—still more than usual—in this work Hayek's style is characterised by the propensity to express his ideas in long and often convoluted sentences and, moreover, by the excessively repetitive use of terms. The translation by the editor, apart from occasionally splitting up long sentences, has refrained from any attempts to 'improve' on Hayek's style.

For more details cf. the editor's introduction to *Business Cycles, Part I*, ed. Hansjoerg Klausinger,

DRAFT TABLE OF CONTENTS[2]

---

vol. 7 (2012) of *The Collected Works of F. A. Hayek*; and Hansjoerg Klausinger, "Hayek's *Geldtheoretische Untersuchungen*: New Insights from a 1925–29 Typescript", *European Journal of the History of Economic Thought*, vol. 18, October 2011, pp. 579–600.

The title page covering the preserved typescript reads, in translation, "Investigations into Monetary Theory. First Part: Price Formation in a Money Economy. Jena: Gustav Fischer, 1929."—Ed.]

[2] [The preserved table of contents obviously originates from a different phase of the project than the title page. It displays the contents of all three planned parts of the book, and the title for the whole project is given as, "On the Goal of Monetary Policy. A Theoretical Investigation into the Nature of Monetary Disturbances to the Economy, Their Relation to Changes in the 'Price Level', and the Significance of an Artificial Stabilisation of the 'Value of Money'. By Friedrich A. Hayek."—Ed.]

[3] [In the typescript this became a section of chapter 3.—Ed.]

[4] [Up to chapter 8 the table of contents accords with the typescript; no additional chapters have been preserved, although apparently some material destined for later chapters has been included in chapter 8.—Ed.]

---

[5] [In a handwritten note this chapter is just titled: "Velocity of money".—Ed.]
[6] [The numbering of chapters is erroneous.—Ed.]

Preface[1]

I do not foster any hopes that the following theoretical investigations on the various ways in which the use of money may disturb economic life otherwise than by shifts in the creditor-debtor relationship will directly pave the way for eliminating these disturbances. Even if they may contribute to a small degree to a solution of this problem—as far as there is one at all—its main purpose is a negative one. These investigations shall demonstrate that the state of the economy with an unchanged value of money, which is aimed at in order to secure the meaning of monetary calculation with regard to credit transactions, cannot be considered at all as free from monetary disturbances. Rather, the measures necessary for stabilising the value of money not only need not contribute to the elimination of a group of very important disturbances, but may as well have the opposite effect; thus, we must not exclude in advance the possibility that such an attempt may cause more harm than it may prevent.

Awareness of this fact should bring about a thorough revision of all the principles underlying current monetary policy, which has seen its single uncontested goal in the stabilisation of the value of money, and should thus create novel foundations for the doctrine of the possibilities and goals of monetary policy. In particular, the insight of [considering][2] money as an essential and ever effective determinant of the course of an exchange economy opens up new vistas: For consequently the course of the economy will never be influenced solely by the natural determinants of the economy and of the distribution of resources, but always as well by the respective regulation of the monetary system, so that—knowing the type of these influences—it can be altered by changes in monetary policy.

It is not the subject of this work to explicitly formulate the tasks and goals of monetary policy. This would necessitate far more extensive investigations, and possibly our general knowledge of the most important relationships in question is not yet advanced enough to warrant such an attempt. What can be said preliminarily in this direction is, in my view, best put in the context of a criticism of the ruling doctrine. Yet I believe that even if this investigation cannot contribute anything to a reformulation of monetary policy, it will be justified by the fact that those ill-conceived doctrines which it tries to refute have been put forward in recent years in an extremely dogmatic fashion and have requested a far reaching subordination of policy under the goals propagated on the basis of these doctrines. In the current state of the debate the

---

[1] [Untitled in the original, this has been selected as the most elaborate version of a preface to be found in the notes and materials for the "Geldtheoretische Untersuchungen".—Ed.]

[2] [The word in brackets is missing in the typescript and has been inserted as a conjecture.—Ed.]

most important point to be emphasised in this regard would be the demonstration of what small a part of all the shortcomings associated with the use of money can be eliminated by 'stabilising the value of money' and that, in addition, other damages emanating from the same source of money may not only be not remedied, but instead reinforced.

Thereby the idea becomes obsolete that it must be possible to discern by means of a simple criterion whether there are influences from the side of money on the course of the process of distribution and consequently that money could be regulated in such a way as to avoid such influences. We shall have to accept that such influences will always be present and thus have to restrict ourselves to regulate money in this regard so as to make its effects as favourable as possible. With this insight in mind the postulate of leaving the economy to its own becomes obsolete.

Introduction[1]

The main task of this book is a critical evaluation of the doctrine that a constant general level of prices will make possible a course of the economic process free from monetary disturbances. Starting from the fact that any effect of money on the economy must be mediated by its influence on price formation, we will examine the function of the 'correct' price formation, undisturbed by monetary influences, the extent to which the deviations in price formation caused by the introduction of money disturb the economic process, and finally if these disturbances can be prevented by specific ties to the value of money. In order to answer these questions it is necessary first to thoroughly investigate the principal difference between the laws that govern income distribution as usually derived by neglecting the effects of money and those valid in a money economy; this will lead towards a re-examination of the justification and the range of applicability for the rules governing the economic process as derived from the former assumption. [It will turn out that these deviations due to the use of money are not incidentally caused by the particular organisation of the monetary system, but are the necessary consequence of the indispensability of indirect exchange and of the passage of time in any exchange economy. Those irregularities of the economic process in comparison with   which are commonly attributed to the imperfection of the organisation of the monetary system must be recognised as inextricably linked to the nature of the exchange economy, even if not to the economy per se.][2] The analysis of the shifts in the structure of the economy due to the use of money demonstrates that the shifts in the debtor-creditor relationship, commonly considered solely or mainly as damages due to 'changes in the value of money', are but a particular phenomenon among a much greater number of unintended shifts within the economy, which disturb equilibrium of the individual as well as of the social economy and thereby the correspondence among all of its parts necessary for its steady course. Furthermore, these disturbances due to the use of money need not always be caused by prior changes on the side of money, rather, due to the use and the intermediation of a means of payment, changes on the side of goods will often cause shifts in the structure of production that do not approach the state of equilibrium and thus do not conform to the laws of static theory. Analogously, with respect to 'changes in the value of money', as far as after the criticism of the following part this term is still appropriate for denoting price changes not solely caused by the goods situation, we will distinguish between active and passive changes in the value of money. Active changes are those caused by prior changes on the side of money, while passive changes are

---

[1] [The title "Introduction" was inserted in a handwritten marginal note.—Ed.]
[2] [The passage in brackets, inserted into the typescript in handwriting, is incomplete.—Ed.]

those that result from shifts on the side of goods with the volume of money unchanged, but which due to the unchanged money incomes exceed the necessary relative shifts among the prices of individual goods. A failed attempt to construct a causal role for money even for changes of the latter group, by presenting changes in the demand for money as a causal factor, renders the opportunity for criticising the concept of the demand for money. It offers valuable hints with regard to the preconditions for maintaining a constant value of money and the consequences of such a maintenance. Active and passive changes in the value of money may mutually compensate one another, and in the case of commodity money will do so as a rule. As changes in the volume of money are the only cause of active changes in the value of money, such active changes can only be prevented by a constant volume of money. Its effects[3] have hitherto been much too little examined. It is essential for commodity money that any change in the demand for money will be met partly by changes in the value of the commodity in question and thus cannot be fully satisfied. This makes up the crucial difference between money tied to a value base which itself is used as money and thereby is influenced by a change in the demand for money and money tied to a value base where this is not the case; in the latter case the shifts within the economy caused by changes in the demand for money will be much greater.[4]

[3] [That is, the effects of a constant volume of money.—Ed.]
[4] [Here the typescript breaks off unfinished.—Ed.]

I. Original and Organisational Determinants of Prices

All the influence that money can exert on the economic process is by its effect on price formation. Yet, as not merely the prices in the narrower sense, the equivalents of money exchanged for goods, are, by definition, brought about only with the assistance of money, but also the prices in a wider sense, the exchange ratios of goods (their objective exchange value), money will thereby influence *all* economic processes. In the following, it will be demonstrated that such a determinate influence on the course and the structure of the economy actually always exists. However, in the presentations of the driving forces of an exchange economy offered by economic theory this influence has been almost completely neglected. This is due to the fact that a determinate system of exchange ratios can be derived from the original determinants of human economic activity even without taking account of these influences exerted by money. Consequently, whenever a strong influence of money on price formation is perceived, it is considered an abnormal disturbance of the 'normal' formation of prices.

The respective investigations have for good reasons put particular emphasis on those original data, of which it is usually assumed that under normal circumstances they alone will determine the formation of prices, and they have been presented in isolation with great benefit. The needs of the members of an exchange economy, their endowment with goods of all types, and the distribution of these goods among them—these are the 'data' in question.[1] And these data would suffice for completely determining men's activity directed towards the satisfaction of their needs, and also for deriving what the best economic outcome would be that each of them could realise, if all perfectly pursued their interests and if the mechanism of the exchange economy could work without frictions and devoid of other determining influences. These determinants[2] of economic activity are necessary in a specific sense: they are given at once with the causes that compel men to act economically; and they alone, among all the factors that affect prices and thereby direct economic forces, *must* make themselves felt in those prices in order to maintain an exchange economy based on the division of labour, such that it becomes possible for the individual not only to produce for his own needs, but for the market. Since Adam Smith[3] all descriptions of the mechanism of the exchange economy—whether they endorse or condemn it—agree in two respects: the working of these forces is

---

[1] For a complete listing of the economic data see Richard Strigl [cf. *Die ökonomischen Kategorien und die Organisation der Wirtschaft* (Jena: Fischer, 1923), chapter 1—Ed.].

[2] [That is, the *original* determinants.—Ed.]

[3] [Adam Smith (1723–90) was the founder of English classical political economy; his notion of the 'invisible hand' has been widely interpreted as emphasising the coordinating role of the price system and of profit-seeking behaviour within a market economy.—Ed.]

seen, on the one hand, as a necessary consequence of the preconditions on which the exchange economy is built and, on the other hand, as an indispensable precondition for its sustained existence. It is due to these forces that without being guided by an overall plan and without mutually knowing beforehand the activities of others the efforts invested by the individual economic subjects are in accordance one with another. Therefore, every individual may venture to produce things in excess of his own needs and to refrain from producing those goods necessary for the satisfaction of his most urgent needs without ever being punished for this behaviour by starvation. It is the basic assumption both of all theoretical considerations and of every political judgment of the existing economic system that this self-steering of the economy by the price mechanism, as determined by those original economic driving forces, is a prerequisite for the economy's steady course. One may subscribe to the belief of economic liberalism that the free play of economic forces will secure the feasible optimum, or to the contrary that the outcome of the automatic direction of the economy can be improved upon by conscious interventions. In any case there will be consensus that these automatic forces will at least bring about a relative optimum, beyond which the economic outcome may be boosted by authoritarian interventions into the process of exchange, yet, that as long as there are no such interventions, the realisation of this optimum must be safeguarded by eliminating all disturbances.

The significance of this type of price formation, which can be derived from the original economic driving forces, for the steady evolution of the economy, free from disturbances, will be more closely examined in the third chapter. These original determinants have been characterised preliminarily only to the extent necessary to distinguish them from other forces which also affect the formation of prices, yet without having the same function attributed to the original forces. The existing mechanism, which serves the implementation of the relations necessitated by the original data, does not work in such a way that these necessities are realised to the exclusion of modifying influences of other factors. Rather the mechanism itself actively affects the economic process and thereby prevents the pure implementation of those forces which it serves. For within this mechanism intermediate links have been inserted, which although destined to serve the original goals of economic action have risen beyond this subservient role and acquired an independent and decisive influence on the course of the economy often counteracting these original goals.[4]

The very element of the economic mechanism which predominantly has

---

[4] Those determinants of prices that are not already inherent in the original driving forces of economic action, but result from the specific type of mechanism which evolved under the pressure of these original forces, I denote for lack of a better term as 'organisational' determinants. Even though this is not a perfectly fortunate expression, the substantial contrast to which it refers will be sufficiently clear as not to give rise to misunderstandings.

acquired this position is money, the indispensable medium for transferring goods in any developed exchange economy. It has been one of the earliest economic experiences that money may decisively affect the course of the economy and thereby may possibly cause great harm. Money being merely a means for exchanging goods such that it does not serve directly the satisfaction of a need and its increase or decrease will not directly alter the means disposable for the satisfaction of needs, all of the effects exerted by money will not—in contrast to all other events that determine the course of the economy—be subject to the same economic principle that otherwise regulates the adaptation of means to ends. Therefore its effects on prices and on the economic process as a whole are different from those of the original data or 'real' determinants, to which they are usually contrasted and which exclusively serve the purpose of improving the provision of goods. There are movements of single or numerous prices of goods of which it is evidently clear that they have not been conditioned by changes in the original data of the economy and that thus the adjustments in the direction of production to which they give rise will not be justified by those data. The accomplishment of a state of equilibrium, towards which prices only determined by original data would tend, will not be furthered by such movements but disturbed. Such price changes without any function in serving an improved balance in the provision of goods may very gravely interfere with individuals striving for the best results of their activities and introduce an element of permanent uncertainty into economic life as a whole. Although quietly sleeping in times of relatively stable monetary conditions, after heavy upheavals to the monetary system the awareness of this fact invariably has led to questioning whether a change in the monetary constitution might prevent similar harm in the future. In particular, the past decade has vividly demonstrated the dangers pertinent from the side of money to the present generation so that it will take up the question of how to completely eliminate this evil more seriously than any before it.

II. The Dogma of the Stable Price Level as a Prerequisite to a Course of the Economy Devoid of Monetary Disturbances

1.

In the very numerous investigations devoted in more or less recent times to the problem of how to avoid monetary disturbances to the economy as a rule the problem has not been treated in the general form indicated above but taken up much more narrowly. Almost generally the problem of how to avoid all monetary disturbances to the economy has been replaced by the problem of how to maintain a constant value of money, and without further justification both problems have been considered as equivalent. The identification of the two problems usually has gone so far that the first one is treated as accomplished with the solution of the second. Thus typically it has been assumed that with total stability in the value of money there will be no decisive influence of money on the course of the process of production and distribution,[1] but rather that this process would evolve as if money played a completely passive role. Not only is there hardly any doubt about the possibility to eliminate all active influences of money on the course of a money economy, but there is also principal agreement on the conditions of how this desirable goal would be achieved. The view is uncontested that the stability of its value is the crucial quality of perfect money and that this exhausts all the requirements to be fulfilled by a monetary system.[2] Indeed, one of the most distinguished teachers of German economic policy could go so far as to denote the stabilisation of the value of money as the single generally accepted goal of economic policy.[3] Most scholars appear to identify all possible harmful effects of money with the consequences of changes in the value of money. Nothing is more

---

[1] [It should be noted that in contemporary German literature, *Verteilung*, in the following translated as "distribution", did not refer just to the distribution of incomes to the factors of production, but more generally to what later came to be denoted as the 'allocation of resources'.—Ed.]

[2] Cf. Correa Moylan Walsh, *The Fundamental Problem of* [*in*] *Monetary Science* (New York: Macmillan, 1903), p. 1: "The primary quality of [in] good money has therefore almost universally been recognized to be stability of value." See also already David Ricardo, "Proposals for a Secure and Economical Currency", *Essays*, ed. Gonner, p. 400. [Hayek's reference is inaccurate on several accounts: The correct reference of the original is *Proposals for an Economical and Secure Currency* (London: Murray, 1816); in the reprint in *Economic Essays*, ed. E. K. G. Gonner (London: Bell, 1923), the correct page reference is p. 161, whereas it is p. 400 in *The Works of David Ricardo*, ed. John Ramsey McCulloch (London: Murray, 1846). Cf. *The Works and Correspondence of David Ricardo*, ed. Piero Sraffa, vol. 4: *Pamphlets and Papers, 1815–1823* (Cambridge: Cambridge University Press, 1951; reprinted, Indianapolis: Liberty Press, 2004), p. 58: "a currency, to be perfect, should be absolutely invariable in value".—Ed.]

[3] Ludwig Pohle, *Die gegenwärtige Krise* [*Krisis*] *in der deutschen Volkswirtschaftslehre* (Leipzig: Deichert, 1911), p. 74.

characteristic for this approach to the problem than the titles of the three best known books that primarily address the problem of how to eliminate monetary disturbances to the economy: The first is titled *Introduction to the Doctrine of the Stability of the Value of Money*;[4] the second, under the title *The Fundamental Problem of Monetary Science*,[5] deals exclusively with the question which of the various indicators of the value of money should be stabilised; finally, the third with the still more general title *Monetary Stability*[6] contents itself with the question of whether complete stabilisation of the price level is to be desired or if only fluctuations of a too violent or irregular nature should be avoided—yet all these books lack a thorough-going investigation of how far stability of the value of money can be considered the most important goal of monetary policy.[7] However, the apparent consensus of these authorities on the goal of monetary policy disappears on closer inspection, as most visibly demonstrated by Walsh in his book,[8] because opinions differ sharply on the nature of the value of money to be stabilised and in particular on the possibilities and methods how to ascertain its changes.

A series of reasons has contributed to confer to the call for an absolute stability of the value of money the kind of dogmatic validity that it possesses

---

[4] Gerard Marius Verrijn Stuart, *Inleiding tot de leer der waardevastheid van het geld* ('s Gravenhage: Martinus Nijhoff, 1919).

[5] Walsh, *The Fundamental Problem in Monetary Science*.

[6] John Rutherford Bellerby, *Monetary Stability* (London: Macmillan, 1925).

[7] The distinguished Dutch economist Nikolaas Gerard Pierson is a commendable exception in this regard; especially in the field of monetary theory we owe him very valuable critical comments on generally accepted heresies. Cf. in particular *Principles of Economics*, vol. 1, trans. A. A. Wotzel (London: Macmillan, 1902), part 2, chapter 4, paragraph 4, pp. 587ff.: "The Disadvantage of Excess or Scarcity of Money". Here, he states explicitly (p. 588): "If fixity of value were to mean fixity of purchasing power under all circumstances, we should be wrong in requiring that money should exhibit that quality." [Nikolaas Gerard Pierson (1839–1909), Dutch economist and politician, professor of economics at the University of Amsterdam, 1877–85, president of the Dutch central bank, 1885–91, minister of finance, 1891–94 and 1897–1901. His *Principles* introduced Austrian and Marshallian approaches into Dutch economic thought.—Ed.] Furthermore, recent opponents of the dogma of stabilisation to be mentioned are Alfred Müller with his recently published work on *Ökonomische Theorie der Konjunkturpolitik* (Leipzig: Gloeckner, 1926), which sharply attacks the dogma of the stable price level, yet in my view without sufficiently refuting its theoretical foundations, as well as Dennis H. Robertson, *Banking Policy and the Price Level: An Essay in the Theory of the Trade Cycle* (London: King, 1926) [reprinted as vol. 3 of *The Development of Monetary Theory, 1920s and 1930s*, ed. Forrest Capie and Geoffrey E. Wood (London: Routledge, 2000)—Ed.], and finally Joseph Stagg Lawrence, although his book *Stabilization of Prices: A Critical Study of the Various Plans Proposed for Stabilization* (New York: Macmillan, 1928) is theoretically irrelevant.

[8] Cf. Walsh, *The Fundamental Problem in Monetary Science*, p. 2: "Unfortunately, the little word [']value['] is ambiguous. And so it [has] happened that the writers who agree in the words they use have had very different meanings, and the unanimity with regard to the price quality in good money is only apparent."

today and has thereby prevented a thorough examination of the justification for this request. The most important of these reasons will be extensively discussed in the following, thus here a short enumeration shall suffice with the details postponed to the later parts of the book.

2.

The most important reason is that active effects of money on the course of the economy have for the first time caught attention by observing changes in the value of money claims. Quite generally this perspective was the very first from which to look at the influences of money on the economic process and to propose regulations of the monetary system. For many scholars even today it is the only perspective they take into account when dealing with monetary disturbances to economic life. It has necessarily led them to regard the 'stability of value' as the crucial criterion of good money. This view of monetary disturbances to the economy solely from the perspective of the relationship between debtor and creditor nurtured the idea that all harmful effects of money on the economic process could be eliminated if only disturbances of this relationship were to be avoided. Yet, in fact, there cannot be any doubt that there are still other influences from the side of money, beyond those connected with the debtor-creditor relationship, that actively determine and disturb the course of the economy.[9] And, of course, it cannot be excluded from the outset that just regulating money in order not to interfere with the debtor-creditor relationship (if possible at all) might not aggravate these other harmful influences on the economic process. This one-sided view of monetary disturbances to the economy as the harmful consequences of 'changes in the value of money', derived from this perspective, is still ruling today, although often the phenomena dealt with under this topic hardly fit into it.[10]

[9] The increasing acceptance of this fact in the German literature owes primarily to the investigations of Ludwig von Mises, in the Anglo-American literature mainly to the works of Edwin Cannan. We will repeatedly refer to the writings of both authors. [Ludwig von Mises (1881–1973) was widely considered the leader of the Austrian school in the interwar period. He worked as a secretary of the Vienna Chamber of Commerce until 1934 when he left for the Graduate Institute of International Studies in Geneva, and in 1940 he immigrated to the United States, where he taught at New York University (1945–69). Hayek explicitly acknowledged that his monetary theory of the cycle was based on Misesian ideas. Edwin Cannan (1861–1935), professor of economics at LSE, 1895–1926, was to become for a short time a highly appreciated colleague of Hayek.—Ed.]

[10] For example, when the excessive granting of credit or other instances of inflation causes shifts in the structure of production, which by no means are the effects, but at best the causes of changes in the 'general value of money'. The fact that *often* the causes of such dislocations of production and those of the simultaneous changes in the value of money are the same in no

3.

A second reason obviously consists in the deficient conception of the general role and significance of money in the economy. This in turn derives from the common practice of theoretical investigations first to wholly disregard the necessity of a medium of exchange and to describe the process of distribution as if it could be accomplished without the use of money. Only after explanations have been derived in this way, the assumption of the use of money will be introduced, yet without examining in what respect the results of the foregoing investigation have to be modified.[11] As will be shown below, this is related to the problem that the theory of distribution must at the first step abstract from the passage of time and on the contrary must deal with all the processes

---

way justifies the conclusion that the changes in the value of money are to blame for these dislocations. Cf. also my comments in *Geldtheorie und Konjunkturtheorie*. Beiträge zur Konjunkturforschung, vol. 1, ed. Österreichisches Institut für Konjunkturforschung (Vienna: Springer, 1929 [reprinted, Salzburg: Neugebauer, 1976]). [For a translation cf. *Monetary Theory and the Trade Cycle*, trans. Nicholas Kaldor and Honoria Croome (London: Cape, 1933), reprinted in F. A. Hayek, *Business Cycles, Part I*. In the typescript this handwritten reference replaced an earlier one, typed and crossed out, to Hayek's "Einige Bemerkungen über das Verhältnis der Geldtheorie zur Konjunkturtheorie", in *Schriften des Vereins für Sozialpolitik*, vol. 173, part 2: *Beiträge zur Wirtschaftstheorie, Konjunkturforschung und Konjunkturtheorie*, ed. Karl Diehl (Munich and Leipzig: Duncker and Humblot, 1928), pp. 247–94, which is in effect a preprint of the first three chapters of *Geldtheorie und Konjunkturtheorie*. Cf. the translation as "Some Remarks on the Relation of Monetary Theory to Business Cycle Theory", in *Business Cycle Theory: Selected Texts 1860–1939*, vol. 3: *Monetary Theories of the Business Cycle*, ed. Harald Hagemann (London: Pickering and Chatto, 2002), pp. 161–97.—Ed.]

[11] Cf. also Wesley C. Mitchell, *Business Cycles: The Problem and Its Setting* (New York: National Bureau of Economic Research, 1927), p. 106: "Most economists have explicitly subordinated the pecuniary aspect of behavior on the ground that money is merely a symbol the use of which makes no difference save one of convenience, so long as the monetary system is not in disorder", as well as by the same author, "The Role of Money in Economic Theory", *American Economic Review*, vol. 6, Supplement, Papers and Proceedings, March 1916, pp. 140–61. [Wesley Clair Mitchell (1874–1948), American economist, professor at Columbia University (1910–44), and director of the newly founded National Bureau of Economic Research (1920–45), pioneered in his work the statistical analysis of the business cycle. During his stay in the U.S. Hayek in 1923 had participated in Mitchell's class on the history of economic doctrines.—Ed.] For evidence for this argument see the quotation from John Stuart Mill, referred to in the introduction. [There is no quotation from Mill in the preserved introduction apart from a reference contained in a handwritten note. Presumably, Hayek refers to Mill's view of money that "there cannot, in short, be intrinsically a more insignificant thing, in the economy of society, than money . . . like many other kinds of machinery, it only exerts a distinct and independent influence of its own when it gets out of order" (John Stuart Mill, *Principles of Political Economy*, ed. William James Ashley (London: Longmans, Green, 1909; new edition, 1921), book 3, chapter 7, paragraph 3, p. 488; cf. *Principles of Political Economy, Part 2*, ed. John M. Robson, vol. 3 (1965) of the *Collected Works of John Stuart Mill* (Toronto: University of Toronto Press; London: Routledge and Kegan Paul; reprinted, Indianapolis: Liberty Fund, 2006), p. 506).—Ed.]

as if compressed into one point of time because economic theory has up to now hardly faced the problem of integrating time into its analysis. This made it possible to regard money only as a passive medium for facilitating the process of distribution or, as it often has been expressed since David Hume,[12] as the oil in the economic machinery.[13] Accordingly money need—and ideally should—not interfere with the course of the exchange process determined independently of it, whereas in fact it is money that makes this process of exchange possible and thus determines its course in a most active way.

4.

It is also owing to this point of view that the question of the influence of money on prices has been treated as a problem of a general value of money and in this form constituted the central problem of monetary doctrine. Yet the question of prime theoretical interest is not that of the determination of an imaginary general value of money, but the influence exerted from the side of money on individual prices and how these, each one in a specific way, will thus deviate from their value as otherwise determined, and on the shifts thereby resulting in the process of distribution in the economy. This attitude towards the 'problem of the value of money'—as a unified problem instead of as one of the distinct influences of money on the individual prices—has without doubt contributed much to identify the practical problem of eliminat-

---

[12] [Cf. David Hume, "Of Money", in *Political Discourses* (Edinburgh: Kincaid and Donaldson, 1752), p. 41, reprinted in *Essays. Moral, Political and Literary*, ed. Eugene F. Miller (Indianapolis: Liberty Classics, 1985), p. 281: "Money . . . is none of the wheels of trade. It is the oil which renders the motion of the wheels more smooth and easy." David Hume (1711–76), philosopher of the Scottish Enlightenment, significantly contributed to monetary theory.—Ed.]

[13] With regard to this example even such a distinguished monetary theorist as Knut Wicksell emphasises this, in my view, totally fallacious view. In the second volume of his *Vorlesungen über Nationalökonomie: Geld und Kredit* (Jena: Fischer, 1922 [reprinted, Aalen: Scientia, 1969]) he writes: "Among the many *similes* which have been employed to illustrate the nature and function of money that which describes it as *the oil in the machinery* is, from many points of view, the most *appropriate. Oil is not a component part of a machine; it is neither a motive force nor a finishing tool*; and in an absolutely perfect machine a minimum of lubrication would be required. Naturally, however, our simplification is only provisional. Economists frequently go too far when they assume that the economic laws which they have deduced on barter assumptions may be applied without qualification to actual conditions, in which money actually effects practically all exchanges and investments or transfers of capital. *The ideal machine*, running without friction, and therefore without a lubricant, has not yet been invented, even though we have perhaps approached nearer to perfection in the economic field than in the mechanic field." (pp. 4–5, emphasis added). [The quotation is from the English translation, *Lectures on Political Economy*, vol. 2: *Money*, trans. Ernest Classen (London: Routledge, 1935; reprinted, New York: Kelley, 1967, and Auburn, AL: Ludwig von Mises Institute, 2007), pp. 5–6.—Ed.]

ing monetary disturbances to the economy with the problem of 'stabilising the value of money'. The whole field of monetary doctrine has suffered from the uncritical acceptance of a constant purchasing power or a constant value as the property of ideal money. Consequently, many of its most important problems have only been examined from this one-sided and deficient point of view. This is particularly true for the effect of autonomous changes in the volume of money within a tied currency and for the effects of a constant volume of money; when analysed, in both cases the focus has been only on the effects on the 'value of money', yet hardly on its influence on the process of distribution.[14] A doctrine of money to be based on a theory of an economy imagined as money-less first of all would have to examine how the diverse regulations of the monetary system will give rise to deviations from the course of the economy as derived from the former assumptions.[15] The primary object of a monetary theory that can be integrated into the existing system of general economic theory has to be not the movements of the value of money, but the influence of money on the process of the distribution of goods. This influence shows itself in the monetarily caused deviations from the course of the distribution process as theoretically imagined for a money-less economy. The subject of the following first part consists of some attempts in this direction.

5.

Finally we have to take into account that all existing or seriously discussed regulations of the monetary system, in particular those of the free metal curren-

---

[14] This view has also often caused much harm for the investigation of other economic problems. For example, the development of the highly important doctrine of the connection between the rate of interest and the changes in commodity prices, founded by Knut Wicksell, yet since then treated quite unsatisfactorily, was severely impaired by using, instead of changes in individual prices, the abstraction of a 'price level' as an element of this theory (a function for which it, the price level, is totally inadequate). A similar observation applies to the field of business cycle research, which unlike any other has furthered the insights into the true influences of money on the course of the economy. As I have tried to demonstrate in my book referred to above [*Geldtheorie und Konjunkturtheorie*—Ed.], unfortunately this doctrine has ever more succeeded in putting the explanations of the cycle into the straitjacket of the notion of the value of money, and to use the abstraction of the 'value of money' as a tool of analysis instead of pursuing the individual effects of money on prices; thereby, in the end, it has obscured the relevant relationships. In this regard, the book by William Truffant Foster and Wadill Catchings, *Money*, Publications of the Pollak Foundation, no. 2 (Boston and New York: Houghton Mifflin, 1923), strongly influenced by the ideas of Herbert J. Davenport, *The Economics of Enterprise* (New York: Macmillan, 1913) provides, to a large part, an especially fortunate exception. [On Foster and Catchings see below, p. 143.—Ed.]

[15] [That is, from the assumptions of barter.—Ed.]

cies, are regulations with reference to the value of money. For in these systems all tendencies to price changes originating from the function of money will be met by reactions which aim at some type of stability of value. The idea of a different type of stability of money than that of stability of some imagined value of money could not emerge unless purely theoretical deliberations led towards it. To name but an example of a different kind of stable money, we may point here to the possibility of money of a constant volume.

The opinion has been almost uncontested that the primary requirement of perfect money must be the stability of its value and that with the accomplishment of this goal all monetary disturbances will be eliminated from economic life. As a consequence, for a long time proposals have been recurrently worked out how the automatic regulations of the commodity currencies could be replaced by alternative regulations in order to maintain a constant, or otherwise regulated, 'value of money' (whatever the individual authors may have meant by this concept). The most ingenious and formally most perfect proposal of this type has been worked out by Irving Fisher in all its details,[16] although it had been proposed earlier, yet with hardly any serious notice, by other scholars.[17] Fisher's well-known proposal aims at the maintenance of an approximate stability of the 'general price level' and thus of the 'general purchasing power of money'. However, the mechanism he proposed could be used just as well for achieving some definite rise or fall in purchasing power, that is, for any arbitrary regulation of the 'value of money'.

In the United States Fisher's proposal was for some time the subject of intense propaganda aiming at its realisation at short notice and indeed subjected in the form of a fully worked out bill to debate in a committee of the House of Representatives.[18] Yet, even more than Fisher's the writings of

[16] Cf. primarily Irving Fisher, *Stabilizing the Dollar: A Plan to Stabilize the General Price Level without Fixing Individual Prices* (New York: Macmillan, 1920) [reprinted as vol. 6 (1997) of *The Works of Irving Fisher*, ed. William Barber (London: Pickering and Chatto, 1997)—Ed.] and the numerous references given there. [Irving Fisher (1867–1947), American economist, professor at Yale University, was an ardent adherent to the quantity theory and a propagator of price level stabilisation.—Ed.]

[17] Yet, these older proposals, of which Fisher himself in his book mentions no less than six [cf. ibid., pp. 293–294—Ed.], have not been completely overlooked; this is evidenced by the fact that Walsh, in his repeatedly cited important book, *The Fundamental Problem in Monetary Science*, p. 224, as early as 1903 lists the alteration of the quantity of metal into which paper money can be redeemed, besides the regulation of the quantity of irredeemable paper money, among the well-known methods for stabilising the purchasing power of money.

[18] Cf. Hearings before the Committee on Banking and Currency, House of Representatives, Sixty-seventh Congress, Fourth Session, on the bill HR 11788, Washington, 1923, and also Lawrence, *Stabilization of Prices*. [The hearing in question concerned the Goldsborough Bill, incorporating many essential features of Fisher's plan, which failed in committee.—Ed.]

J. M. Keynes, Cassel, and Lehfeldt,[19] all of which suggested a specific method for stabilisation, have made the idea of stabilisation very popular. In a later part of this study devoted to the concrete plans for stabilisation we will have to address these authors more closely.

7.[20]

The plan of this investigation is shaped by the fact that almost all attempts and proposals for monetary stabilisation are based on the idea that a money economy could follow the same course as an economy that does not use money. In particular, the doctrines of the necessity of stabilising the *value of money*, which form the special subject of this investigation, go beyond this view in assuming as self-evident the conditions when this will be the case. This is so although up to now the question has not been faced seriously if this aim can be accomplished at all or what other conditions might be most adequate for the course of the economic process of a money economy. Therefore we will have to examine the relation between monetary disturbances of economic life and changes in the variously defined 'values' of money. For this purpose the first part of these investigations will analyse in detail the influences of money on the economic process. The following second part[21] then will examine the relation between these monetary effects on the economic process and changes in the so-called 'general value of money'. After a preliminary discussion of this notion it will show in which way the monetary determinants of the economic process would be influenced by actual attempts at stabi-

[19] [All three authors mentioned had argued for a policy of price stabilisation as part of a programme of monetary reconstruction after World War I. Cf., e.g., John Maynard Keynes, *A Tract on Monetary Reform* (London: Macmillan, 1923), pp. 201–13, reprinted as vol. 4 (1972) of *The Collected Writings of John Maynard Keynes*, ed. Austin Robinson and Donald Moggridge (London: Macmillan; Cambridge: Cambridge University Press), pp. 147–54; Gustav Cassel, *Money and Foreign Exchange After 1914* (London: Constable, 1922; reprinted, New York: Arno Press, 1972); and Robert Alfred Lehfeldt, *Restoration of the World's Currencies* (London: King, 1923). The Keynes and Lehfeldt plans are extensively quoted in Lawrence, *Stabilization of Prices*, pp. 146–50 and 165–67. John Maynard Keynes (1883–1946), who later on as the founder of the 'Keynesian Revolution' was to become Hayek's most important adversary in the field of economics, then had acquired major fame for his sharp critique of the Versailles Treaty; cf. *The Economic Consequences of the Peace* (London: Macmillan, 1919), reprinted as vol. 2 (1971) of *The Collected Writings of John Maynard Keynes*. Carl Gustav Cassel (1866–1945), Swedish economist, professor at the University of Stockholm from 1903 to 1936, in the 1920s had arrived at the peak of his worldwide reputation. Robert Alfred Lehfeldt (1868–1927), economist and physicist, had become the first professor of economics in South Africa, at the University of Witwatersrand.—Ed.]

[20] [There is no section 6 in the typescript.—Ed.]

[21] [The second part never came to be written.—Ed.]

lising the value of money and, respectively, which consequences such attempts must have on the evolution of the economy. If we succeed in proving that:

1. influences from the side of money will frustrate the intentions of the economic subjects, and thereby defeat the purposes for which they have made their dispositions, in other ways than merely by changing the expected value of future money payments, and
2. specifically a regulation of the monetary system so that the losses of the second type are reduced to a minimum by stabilising the 'value of money' must increase the losses of the first type,

then the absolute validity of the up to now generally accepted goal of monetary policy would be destroyed. A theoretical foundation for monetary policy then could not concentrate on this goal alone, but would have to weigh against each other the relative importance of two competing goals. At best monetary policy could choose a middle course for securing the most beneficial influence of money on the economic process without being able to do full justice to each of the two separate points of view.

III. The Function of Price Formation as Determined by the Goods Situation[1]

1.

Before discussing the relation between changes in the value of money and monetary disturbances of economic life, this chapter attempts a clarification of what is meant at all when speaking of determining influences of money on the price system. More generally, those changes will be discussed which the use of money will bring about compared with the course of the economy as determined by the original data.

As already noted and as will be shown in more detail below, it is imperative to fill at least provisionally a significant gap within economic theory that arose from too extensive a division of labour between general economic theory and monetary theory. It is to a great extent attributable to this gap that the applicability of the insights from general economic theory to the problems of the modern exchange economy appears rather restricted and ever again is prone to be rejected as useless by 'realistically'-minded economists. Starting from the pure economics of the theory of income distribution, which although it cannot wholly abstract from the use of money believes it legitimate to neglect all determining influences that money brings about, we have to examine how far its results must be modified when account is taken of the new determinants necessarily associated with the use of money.

We have already emphasised the fact that all elements which determine the course of the economic process can do this only in a specific way, namely by affecting the prices of the individual goods and services. The same is true for money and its determining influence on the course of the exchange economy. The assumption that the influence of money on prices may change and thereby *disturb* the course of the economic process presupposes that, even without taking account of the use of money, prices will be sufficiently determined and that the prices so determined will *fulfil definite purposes*. Prior to discussing the specific deviations of the course of the economy caused by money we must thus demonstrate the reason and the purpose of the formation of certain exchange ratios which abstracts from the assistance of money. With regard to the original determinants and the necessity of certain prices we can in

---

[1] [Attached to the typescript there is a handwritten note with the section headings planned for this chapter: "III. 1. What is the normal state compared to which we can speak of monetarily caused deviations? 2. The preconditions of pure theory are only fulfilled under the assumption of commodity clearing *in natura*. 3. General conditions of equilibrium with given quantities of goods. 4. Conditions of equilibrium with produced goods. 5. Correct prices and necessary price changes. 6. Illegitimate distinctions between correct and wrong prices. 7. Correct prices are equilibrium prices. 8. The notion of a function only justified within an equilibrium framework. 9. Idea of equilibrium indispensable, the sole criterion reproducibility."—Ed.]

general simply refer to the results of the theory of distribution (pure economics) and content ourselves with just a few remarks on the underlying premises. As the problem has been rarely dealt with in the literature,[2] we will have to treat in more detail the *functions of price formation*, that is, to ask about the significance of those prices necessitated by the assumption of a merely passive behaviour of money and why just these prices will be able to keep the course of the economy devoid of disturbances.

These are then the questions that must be answered before describing the monetarily caused disturbances of economic life: Are the relative prices of goods sufficiently determined if we assume that there are no influences from the side of money; what is the purpose of this assumption; and what is the economic significance of those prices, keeping in mind that deviations of prices caused by money are considered harmful? Only after an answer to this question has been found, can we go further to the *main question* of the first part of this investigation: *Are these deviations* from the course as determined only by the original economic data *of an accidental nature or are they inseparably connected to the function of money?* In addition, is it possible to differentiate in this regard among the various modifying influences, or even to find out which of the avoidable influences should be considered harmful and how these might be prevented? Subsequent to this last point the second part of this work will examine to what extent this result—of preventing harmful influences from the side of money—can be accomplished by a certain control of the so-called value of money.

2.

The description of the determination and the role of the exchange ratios brought about without the assistance of money pose considerable difficulties. Traditional theory as a rule attempts to lift the so-called 'veil of money' by abstracting from the effects exerted by money and concentrating on the effects of the original data.[3] However, it must presuppose the use of money and just assumes—somewhat inconsistently—that it will not exert any determining influence on the course of the distribution process. Yet for our purpose such a procedure is by no means admissible. For the theory of distribution, which centred—and as will be seen for good reason—on the effects of the original determinants of the economy, such a procedure was permissible at least as a first step of the investigation. However, here the focus is on the difference

---

[2] Some remarks are to be found in Franz Eulenburg, in his essay in *Grundriß der Sozialökonomik*, vol. 4, part 1 (Tübingen: Mohr, 1925 [reprinted, Frankfurt: Keip, 1985]). [The essay, on pp. 258–315, was titled, "Die Preisbildung in der modernen Wirtschaft".—Ed.].

[3] [In this sense the metaphor of the 'veil of money' had already been used by the Austrian economists Eugen von Böhm-Bawerk and Joseph A. Schumpeter.—Ed.]

between an economy that actually lacks money and a money economy. Thus it would be illegitimate to use as the basis for comparison, from which to differentiate the processes of a money economy, the conditions of an economic system which although impossible without the assistance of money[4] consciously neglects its effects. For in order to delineate the monetarily caused deviations of the course of the economic process it is obviously necessary to determine first the course taken by the economy without the assistance of money.

Therefore for the purposes of this investigation it does not suffice to assume, as is usually done, that exchange takes place through the medium of money, yet without money exerting any influence on the economic process as a whole. Rather, in order to describe the function of prices determined solely by the situation on the side of goods, it is necessary to construct, if only in imagination, a mechanism which enables money-less exchange. As will be shown, for eliminating the influences of money it is necessary to complement the assumption of the absence of a medium of exchange by a second one, which usually is introduced only tacitly. It must be assumed that the whole economic process can be split up into closed time periods, so that between periods all economic activities repeat themselves and within periods all acts of exchange take place at a single and as regards time and place homogeneous market. Only under this assumption is it conceivable that exchange without using media of exchange can be universal (that is, that all theoretically existing exchange opportunities will be exhausted).

Under this assumption one may imagine that the exchange of all goods destined for the market is accomplished by a kind of commodity clearing *in natura*. The exchange ratios of all goods would then be calculated on the basis of the participants announcing their willingness to exchange (depicted in theory as the demand and supply curves representing the gradual individual evaluations of the various goods) so that all goods coming to the market can be sold.[5] This presupposes that the consumable goods supplied realise just

---

[4] The exhaustion of all theoretically possible exchange opportunities presupposed by pure theory is predicated upon the existence of indirect exchange to an extent in practice possible only with the use of money.

[5] Léon Walras might have had such a procedure in mind when he says: "Perhaps, someday the application of mathematics to economic theory will allow substituting calculation for the mechanical execution of rising and falling prices at the market" (*Mathematische Theorie der Preisbestimmung der wirtschaftlichen Güter: Vier Denkschriften*, trans. L. Winterfeld (Stuttgart: Enke, 1881 [reprinted, Glashütten: Auvermann, 1972]), p. 5). [*Mathematische Theorie* is the German translation of four lectures given by Walras in 1873 and 1874 in Paris and Lausanne, where he presented a condensed version of the first part of his *Éléments d'économie politique pure* of 1874.—Ed.] Similar fictions are used by Adolf Lampe, *Zur Theorie des Sparprozesses und der Kreditschöpfung* (Jena: Fischer, 1926), pp. 66ff., when he feigns a "personification of the market process" for "managing the social product" [p. 67—Ed.], and by Ralph G. Hawtrey, *Currency and Credit*, 3rd ed. (London: Longmans, 1928). [There is no page reference, so it is unclear to which passage Hayek wanted

such prices that for each of them demand corresponds to supply. Furthermore, the exchange ratios between the consumers' goods and the producers' goods[6] used in their manufacturing must be such that everywhere the costs of maintaining production will be covered by the prices[7] of consumers' goods. Yet for the time being, as will be emphasised, we restrict the analysis to a market where only consumers' goods are exchanged one for another. Here the apparatus described above would indeed enable universal exchange as a precondition for the working of an exchange economy. Thereby, it would fulfil the task presently performed by money, yet without interfering in any way with the course of the distribution process so that this process would be solely determined by the relative magnitudes of demand and supply *in natura*.

3.

Now what does the general theory of prices tell us about the conditions where, given these preconditions,[8] a state of equilibrium will be accomplished, that is, a state where all prices are adjusted to the original data and there exists no tendency for a change in prices? The analysis of price theory as a rule starts from the rare but simple case that the quantities of consumers' goods are given and constant. Then the answer to our question is that prices will reduce the potentially infinite demand for every good to the amount that can be satisfied by the existing stock.[9] Thereby the stock will be divided in such a way among the various consumers that with universal free exchange the owners of the exchanged goods can secure for themselves the greatest possible gain. Beyond that, under these assumptions prices have no specific function in determining the economic process. As the consumers' goods of each type are fixed

---

to refer. Note, in any case, Hawtrey's assumption of "a completely organised and civilised society" as the point of departure for discussing "credit without money" (p. 2).—Ed.]

[6] [In general Hayek uses the terms *Produktivgüter* (translated as 'producers' goods') and *Produktionsmittel* ('means of production') synonymously; he adopted the same convention in *Prices and Production* (London: Routledge, 1931; 2nd ed. rev., 1935), lecture 2, section 5 (reprinted in F. A. Hayek, *Business Cycles, Part I*, p. 220). Accordingly, producers' goods comprise both the 'original means of production' (labour and land) and the stock of 'intermediate products'.—Ed.]

[7] [In comparing prices and costs, Hayek often refers to these terms by (the German equivalent of) 'unit price' and 'unit cost', reserving the uncommon term 'total price' for denoting proceeds or revenue. See also p. 94n.7, below.—Ed.]

[8] [That is, the conditions of static analysis as mentioned above.—Ed.]

[9] Cf. Gustav Cassel, *Theoretische Sozialökonomie*, 1st ed. (Leipzig: Winter 1918), paragraph 10, p. 54: "The fixing of prices thus has the social economic task of so restricting the demands for goods that they can be met with the available means." [Emphasised in the original; the quotation is from the translation, *The Theory of Social Economy*, new rev. ed. (London: Benn; New York: Harcourt, Brace and Co., 1932; reprinted, New York: Kelley, 1967), p. 66.—Ed.]

in their quantities by assumption, economic activity is restricted to acts of exchange, and there is no need for any specific economic activity directed at the provision of these quantities of goods.

4.

Things are different, if we get closer to the actual situation by assuming that the goods coming to the market are not wholly given as constants, but at least for the greater part depend for their origin on human activity, so that their quantities coming to the market will depend on the prices to be realised. In an economy where almost all consumable goods result from a shorter or longer process of production prices become the guides for production, the driving force, which decides upon the use made of the existing producers' goods, and thereby upon the direction of all productive activity, that is, which and how many goods will come to the market.

In a mature exchange economy the produced quantities of the various goods will not only be determined by the relative height of the prices of the various *products*. As the production of almost any good can be split up into a series of sub-operations, performed by different economic subjects, there is besides the exchange of consumers' goods an extensive exchange of producers' goods, and the prices thereby realised have no less effect on the direction of production than the prices of final products. However, the prices of producers' goods are in many regards only derived prices, which depend in a special way on the prices of final products and possess no *autonomous* function. Later on (in chapters 8 and 9)[10] we will have to deal in more detail with the significance of these prices for the economic process. For the next chapters, however, it is advisable to abstract from the existence of this special type of price in order not to overly complicate the analysis of the function of price formation. Therefore we take as the starting point of our considerations an economy where although the individual consumers' goods are not given in their finished form, but must be produced, the production of each good occurs within a single economic unit which owns all the required means of production so that only consumers' goods are exchanged.

Price formation fulfils a different task for goods given in fixed quantities and for produced goods, of which the quantities are not fixed. The crucial difference is that in the latter case, preceding the actual act of exchange, some goods which can be used for different purposes must be definitely devoted to one of these purposes, based on the expectation of a specific outcome of this exchange. The ultimate realisation of a certain price is therefore the precondi-

[10] [There is no chapter 9 in the typescript.—Ed.]

tion that the use of producers' goods for a definite purpose achieves the result conforming to the acting individual's intention. The use of existing producers' goods for certain branches of production[11] is based on the assumption that the actual product can be exchanged for certain other goods, and it is for the sake of acquiring these other goods that production has been undertaken. This presupposes in turn that those other goods actually come to the market in just the appropriate quantity, so that each produced good is matched by other goods for which the former can be advantageously exchanged. Therefore within an exchange economy any production, any individual activity directed at the provision of goods presupposes—for this production to be maintained at all or to the same extent—the existence of certain prices of products as well as of means of production. Only in the expectation of a certain product price will a certain amount of producers' goods be purchased at a certain price, and only as long as this product price can be realised will production be maintained at all or to the same extent.

Thus with regard to produced goods as well prices bring about a division of the available goods among the possible uses. However, this division is not only the result of exchange alone, but apart from and preceding the acts of exchange it presupposes a certain economic activity of the individuals in order to achieve the intended result of this exchange. In the exchange economy all economic activity—directed at the provision of goods—is guided by existing or expected prices, and to each system of prices corresponds a certain structure of production—a certain division of the factors of production among various uses. *This direction of production* (production in the widest sense, including retailing, personal services, etc.) *is the ultimate function of prices*. It ensures that *the results of current production at the same time create the current demand for this production, and that thus the extent of the activities of all individual branches of production is arranged so that the products can be sold at the market at a price which covers costs and which secures the maintenance of production*, provided that the original data, needs and available means of production, will not change. If prices fulfil this function completely, every economic activity will achieve just those results for the sake of which it has been undertaken. Consequently, as long as the data remain unchanged as assumed, changes in the current dispositions will accrue

---

[11] [In general, a 'branch of production' (*Produktionszweig*) is characterised by the type of consumers' good finally produced, while a 'stage of production' (*Produktionsstufe*) by the order of the good produced. Goods of higher and lower order are produced at earlier and later stages of production, where consumers' goods are goods of the first order, and accordingly the order of goods is the higher (and the stage of production the earlier) the more distant the goods in question are from the stage of consumption. The terminology of the 'order of goods' dates back to Carl Menger, and the notion of a structure of production represented by a linear sequence of stages of production to Eugen von Böhm-Bawerk. The distinction between 'branches' and 'stages' corresponds to that between the horizontal and the vertical structure of production; see below, p. 92–93.—Ed.]

no advantage, but only a disadvantage, to the individual economic subject. Thus the correct price formation brings about a state of equilibrium of the economy that can be maintained as long as there are no changes in the fundamental data.

5.

The undisturbed maintenance of the direction of production as required by the existing needs and the available means of production is thus predicated, as long as these data do not change, on the permanent existence of certain prices. A temporary change of prices which is not caused by changes in the original data will thus always bring about changes in the structure and direction of production that cannot be maintained and thus must be reversed. Thus correct prices are those which determine a structure of production that can be maintained at these same prices for unchanged original data. Accordingly justified price changes are those which bring about a structure of production that can be maintained at the new prices as long as those data do not change anew (that is, after the change that necessitated the change in prices).

There is congruence among the individual branches of production if the sale of all the finished products is possible and generates for their owners just that result which allows the maintenance of the same production. This congruence, which alone in an exchange economy secures the maintenance of production, is the work of the price mechanism, which under the assumed conditions—if the original data only determine prices and remain unchanged from one market period to the next—will be achieved in an ideal way. It is only due to its working that the money economy, too, exhibits the relative steadiness of the structure of production which under the rule of the division of labour is a prerequisite for each individual's gain in utility. This steadiness results from the fact that each good will be used in just that way that a change in its use will not improve the gain from exchange but rather that any alternative use, or the gains to be realised in exchange for the respective product, will appear less valuable than the chosen ones. Put in other words, in the state of equilibrium, toward which prices tend, the realised prices in all branches of production cover the costs expended so that the maintenance of production to the same extent and in the same structure is possible.[12]

---

[12] Foster and Catchings (in *Money*) characterise the function of prices principally in the same way. Although these authors deserve great praise for having demonstrated the fallacy of the common view that money is irrelevant for the structure of the process of production and distribution, they nevertheless believe that in the money economy prices will fulfil their function perfectly only if the price level remains stable. The relevant passages are quoted in the following:

p. 186 [pp. 186–87]: "*The Economic Function of Price*. The economic function of price is to bring about the production and distribution of goods . . . prices have one major

6.[13]

The point of view underlying the above distinction between 'correct' and 'wrong' prices is not at all the only one conceivable for distinguishing them. Rather these notions are ambiguous to a degree that their use carries the greatest danger of misunderstanding. It is therefore necessary to delineate the sense in which these notions have been used here from other conceivable meanings. This is also true of the essentially similar idea of the 'necessity' of price changes, if necessity is not used in a causal sense of a necessary consequence, but—as is done here—in the sense of a necessary condition for the maintenance of a system. [The justification of the apparent value judgment inherent in these notions affords the opportunity to establish also the methodological validity of the notion of a 'function', as used in the preceding chapter without justifying it there. Eventually it will lead to a more precise characterisation of the methodological position of the state of equilibrium as the reference system that alone lends meaning to all these notions. Thus the purpose of the short critical remarks, which follow, is not only to safeguard the notions arrived at in the preceding positive considerations from misunderstandings, but also to give them more precision so that they can be used in the subsequent parts without further methodological deliberations.][14]

Evidently there is no reason to deal with those distinctions between correct and wrong prices that are not based on socio-economic, but purely ethical grounds. For the latter case take for example the just price of the scholastics, who for each individual price only assessed its effect on the economic subjects participating in the act of exchange while neglecting the significance of prices

interest for society as a whole, prices do or they do not move goods . . . Production cannot long proceed at any given rate unless daily purchases take the goods away at the rate of production. To bring about that movement of goods is the function of price."

p. 210 [pp. 210–11]: "We must conclude that prices serve completely [completely serve] their economic purpose when they are a sufficient incentive to the maximum production that is continuously possible and desirable, and that they continue to be such an incentive as long as the money spent daily on [in] consumption buys this maximum output. In other words, prices serve their purpose when they are in the right relation to the productive capacity of the country, on the one hand, and to the money in circulation, on the other hand. *This relationship is maintained on a stable price-level* as long as buyers are left alone to determine prices and production in free markets, and producers and distributors have sufficient knowledge of what is going on." (Emphasis added.)

The view reproduced in these sentences must be considered the prevailing doctrine.

[13] [The following section 6 has taken the place of chapter 4 ("'Correct' Prices and 'Necessary' Price Changes") of Hayek's original plan, as in the draft table of contents reproduced above (p. 46); the respective chapter heading has been crossed out at the beginning of the typescript. Note that sections 7 to 9, referred to in the handwritten note, are missing, too.—Ed.]

[14] [The passages in brackets are crossed out in the typescript.—Ed.]

for the determination of the economic process as a whole. In contrast, we turn only to those distinctions which in some way refer to the significance of prices for the course of the economic process as a whole and which accept no other criterion for the accomplished result than the mutually incommensurable appraisals of individuals. Thus, in particular all those distinctions are discarded which take as their criterion for the correctness of the whole price system that the economic subjects as a whole realise a utility maximum, that is, that the sum of the individual utilities is maximised. Today it must be regarded as the prevailing doctrine that the intensities of needs and the utilities of different individuals are absolutely incommensurable so that a summation of such utilities is impossible in theory.[15] The only such comparison conceivable must rely on a criterion of ethics and therefore lies outside the framework of theoretical economics.

However, the significance of actual prices for the course of the economy as a whole has been judged from very dissimilar points of view, too. Most notably, however, when using the notions of correct and wrong prices, rarely is the criterion precisely stated on which this distinction is based. As a rule the relevant criterion is just the tacit or even expressly acknowledged interest of groups or strata of the population deemed particularly important. Thus as with all economic policy judgments these distinctions are based on an exterior value system, which is out of the question for a purely theoretical investigation. Our problem is just how it may be possible to distinguish between adequate and inadequate, correct and wrong prices—or however these opposites may be denoted—based only on immanently economic factors and without introducing from outside value judgements into the economy.[16]

---

[15] This is even so although, still most recently, otherwise careful researchers like Laurits V. Birck, *The Theory of Marginal Value* (London: Routledge, 1922), do not hesitate to carry out such interpersonal comparisons of utility. It is more astonishing that even so distinguished a thinker as Enrico Barone, in 1909, bases his deductions on the assumption of the comparability of the utilities of different persons. Cf. Enrico Barone, *Grundzüge der theoretischen Nationalökonomie*, trans. Hans Staehle (Bonn: Schröder, 1927) [the translation of *Principi di economia politica* (Rome: Bertero, 1908)—Ed.] and my book review in *Zeitschrift für die gesamte Staatswissenschaft*, vol. 85, no. 1, 1928, pp. 178–81. [Laurits Vilhelm Birck (1871–1933), a Danish economist, worked in the Walrasian tradition. The Italian economist Enrico Barone (1859–1924) is now best known for his contribution to the debate on economic calculation where he opposed the Austrian view.—Ed.]

[16] [As already noted, chapter 4 is missing, having been replaced by section 6 of chapter 3 above.—Ed.]

V. Exchange among Three, Indirect Exchange, and the Sequence of Time

1.

An adjustment of the supply of goods to demand such that a steady course of the economic process can be secured will only result under certain preconditions. In the preceding chapter these could be considered fulfilled due to the special assumptions introduced. For an actual economy the theorems derived there will remain valid at best if the economy is in such an early stage of its development that the only type of exchange is that of *direct* barter. Yet, for an exchange economy of the degree of development presupposed as the starting point of the theory of general equilibrium—that is, one where all existing exchange opportunities will be exhausted—the preconditions for the direct applicability of this theory are never fulfilled. In the preceding chapter the assumption of a special kind of organisation of exchange has made it possible to fulfil this precondition, as is otherwise only the case with direct exchange, and thereby to secure the permanent matching of demand and supply at the prices determined in the market. In any case this precondition requires that with necessity any two or more acts which together constitute a self-contained exchange must happen simultaneously, so that to each sale of a given quantity of one good corresponds the sale of a quantity of another good the purchase of which made up the motive to sell for the seller of the first good.

If there is only direct exchange in the strict sense, that is, that both partners in the exchange purchase goods for the sake of consuming them themselves, evidently each act of exchange will be self-contained and justified by itself. Therefore such exchanges can be reproduced again and again—as long as there are no changes.[1]

However, the conditions for accomplishing such a state of equilibrium are less clear for an economy where exchange has been extended up to its economic limits and all existing gains have been exhausted. This is so because in such an economy exchange must take place not only directly between two individuals, but also in the form of indirect exchange.

As already pointed out, the price mechanism will work with equal perfection as in the case of direct exchange only if the assumption introduced above[2] holds. Only by resorting to this assumption is it possible to solve a problem that in practice can be overcome only by the kind of universal exchange made possible in a money economy, yet without having to consider the particular in-

---

[1] [That is, no changes in the data.—Ed.]

[2] [That is, the assumption of commodity clearing.—Ed.]

fluences necessarily emanating from the use of a medium of exchange. It is this problem of the exchange among three the significance of which will be commented upon in the following.

2.

It is well known that in an economy with a fully developed division of labour it will not be possible to exhaust all the opportunities to improve the provision of goods to the individuals by the means of direct exchange. Only by chance will the person whose wants are directed towards a specific good happen to offer himself a good which the supplier of the first good intends to purchase. Until a complete coincidence among individuals in the relative grades of the marginal utilities of the various goods has been accomplished, the participating persons' provision of goods can still be improved by further exchanges and thus a motive to exchange persists. Yet such a state of complete coincidence can only be arrived at by involving a third person, or still more persons, into the process of exchange until for each of the commodities supplied by them there will also be a buyer among them so that exchange becomes possible even if in a roundabout way.[3] In the economy under consideration the third person will become involved when a person unable to acquire the desired goods by the way of direct exchange will realise this purpose by purchasing those goods from the third person in question that can be exchanged against the desired

---

[3] It is not just the obvious phenomenon that in certain circumstances direct exchange is impossible at all that makes it indispensable to include a third person, or still more persons, in the process of exchange. Rather, as has been demonstrated, a state of general equilibrium can only be accomplished by means of multilateral exchange, because direct exchange in single pairs would result in different prices for the same goods, which can only be balanced by some kind of arbitrage. This observation follows from Léon Walras, *Élements* [*Éléments d'économie politique pure*, 1st ed. (Lausanne: Corbaz, 1877)—Ed.], leçons 19–21 [cf. the definitive edition (Lausanne: Rouge, 1926), reprinted as a variorum edition in vol. 8 (1988) of *Oeuvres économiques complètes*; translated as *Elements of Pure Economics*, trans. William Jaffé (London: Allen and Unwin, 1954; reprinted, New York: Kelley, 1977), lessons 11 and 12, and the notes on the collation of editions—Ed.], and has repeatedly been noted in the German literature, especially by Knut Wicksell, *Geldzins und Güterpreise: Eine Studie über die den Tauschwert des Geldes bestimmenden Ursachen* (Jena: Fischer, 1898 [reprinted, Aalen: Scientia, 1968]), pp. 19–20 [cf. *Interest and Prices: A Study of the Causes Regulating the Value of Money*, trans. Richard F. Kahn (London: Macmillan, 1936; reprinted, New York: Kelley, 1965, and Auburn, AL: Ludwig von Mises Institute, 2007), pp. 21–22—Ed.], *Vorlesungen über Nationalökonomie*, vol. 1 (Jena: Fischer, 1914 [reprinted, Aalen: Scientia, 1969]), p. 114 [pp. 114–17; cf. *Lectures on Political Economy*, vol. 1: *General Theory*, trans. Ernest Classen (London: Routledge, 1934; reprinted, New York: Kelley, 1967, and Auburn, AL: Ludwig von Mises Institute, 2007), pp. 63–65—Ed.], and Joseph A. Schumpeter, *Das Wesen und der Hauptinhalt der theoretischen Nationalökonomie* (Leipzig: Duncker and Humblot, 1908), p. 173 [pp. 273–75].

ones. In this way by using a medium of exchange the purchase of the desired good and the sale of the good produced oneself, which up to now happened uno actu, are broken up into two successive acts of exchange which are subject to specific, not necessarily identical conditions.

It is true that even under the assumption of central commodity clearing introduced above exchange will be indirect, but without being temporally separated into two autonomous acts of exchange possibly subject to different conditions. This assumption has been indispensable at the present stage of this investigation just because only in this way indirect exchange is conceivable without giving rise to such effects. Under this assumption crucial conditions are fulfilled, the violation of which in an economy where media of exchange are used make the function of price formation diverge significantly from that analysed up to now. These conditions are:

At such a market no supply of goods can become an effective demand unless at the same time it eliminates from this market, by satisfying it, another demand that itself has become effective by means of a supply of goods that in turn (directly or through an arbitrary number of intermediations) *satisfies precisely that demand which has been induced by the very supply of goods which satisfied the demand mentioned in the first place.* Every such market can be dissolved into one or several circles (chains of exchange) which although they may cross, or branches may join, each other in places must all ultimately return to themselves. In this way within the system any effective demand can be matched by a supply satisfying this demand without any demand or supply remaining without a counterpart. Yet this is so although there need not be a single case where an act of direct exchange or any other act of exchange would remain feasible if any element of the chain were omitted. This complete coincidence between demand and aggregate supply is necessitated by the fact that under the conditions assumed each of the chains of exchange brought about by the clearing system will be self-contained. Thus wherever we will start the inspection it will be the final buyer who brought the goods to the market purchased by the first seller.

3.

Under the assumption introduced up to now all exchange is in some sense indirect. For example, the good which person A has put into the clearing will perhaps be purchased by B, who in turn puts in another good, obtained by C, who again puts in another good and so on, until eventually we come to a person who has put in the very good for the purchase of which A had put in his own. Yet, we see that here all the goods that have been interposed between A and the final person do not serve as media of exchange such that, in determining exchange ratios, they replace the goods the exchange of which they ultimately mediate. Any supplier of one of these goods will be able to sell them against a desired object, because the person who demands his good offers another good which is demanded by some person willing to offer the good demanded by the first person, or the same result might be obtained with the help of still more intermediaries. Such a balancing, so that all intended acts of exchange can be realised simultaneously, will only be accomplished in the short term if there exists a central agency, of the type of a clearing-house, which based on the recorded demand and supply can ascertain and realise all the required single movements. However such a clearing agency can only be imagined theoretically; thus, in the absence of such an agency, indirect exchange will just mean that for the good brought to the market every person purchases another good serving as a medium of exchange, possibly exchanging it against still another good and so on, until eventually the desired one is obtained. Thereby two new elements are introduced into the process of exchange, which up to now have not been considered. Yet, once we take them into account, they may change the picture radically by disturbing the necessary coincidence between demand and supply. These elements are, first, the introduction of a good which due to its function as a medium of exchange is now demanded in a greater quantity and which works as an additional determinant of exchange ratios, and second, the splitting up of the process of exchange, hitherto thought as simultaneous, into a temporal sequence. The effects of these two elements, the use of a medium of exchange and the sequence of time, will be considered more closely in this and in the next chapter.

With the introduction of the use of a medium of exchange another abstraction must be discarded, as a rule only tacitly, namely that all the relevant acts of exchange are concentrated in a single point as regards time and place. Indeed, the discarding of this assumption is the most important reason why the theorems derived for a system of universal barter cannot be applied without further emendation to an economy where indirect exchange with the assistance of a medium of exchange is the rule. It is well-known that the time moment, thereby involved into our consideration, constitutes the most difficult problem for economic theory.[4] The gravest deficiencies in existing

---

[4] Cf. Edgeworth II 60; Marshall, "Preface" to *Principles* 3 XV p. 103. [Cf. Marshall's references to "the element of time" as a main source of difficulties in economics in *Principles of Economics*, 1st ed. (London: Macmillan, 1890), "Preface to the First Edition", p. vii, and book 3, chapter 4, paragraph 5, p. 109 of the ninth variorum edition with annotations by C. W. Guillebaud (London: Macmillan, 1961), reprinted in 2 vols. in *The Collected Works of Alfred Marshall*, ed. Peter Groenewegen (Bristol: Overstone Press, 1997). There is no obvious candidate for the Edgeworth reference; for a contribution to the time problem cf. Francis Ysidro Edgeworth, "Distance in Time as an Element of Value", in *Dictionary of Political Economy*, ed. R. H. Inglis Palgrave, vol. 1 (London: Macmillan, 1894), pp. 592–93, reprinted in *Mathematical Psychics and Further Papers on Political Economy*, ed. Peter Newman (Oxford: Oxford University Press, 2003), pp. 442–44.—Ed.]

theoretical analyses must be attributed to the fact that we have not yet come closer to a solution of this problem.[5] Under the assumption of a money-less economy, by means of the auxiliary construction referred to above, demand and supply of goods necessarily coincide. This construction made it possible for the sake of theoretical analysis to cut an arbitrary period out of the economic process and to consider it as sufficiently determined in itself. The acts of exchange within this period could be considered as self-contained and fully determined by the data given for this period. Thus the system within which these acts of exchange occurred was that of a closed period sufficiently determined by the original data given for that period.

In such a closed system no object will be exchanged more than once and only such acts of exchange will take place that assign each object directly to its ultimate economic purpose. The price system established in each period is capable of unlimited repetition, provided the original data, which determine prices, do not change. Yet, any change in the data will lead to an instantaneous and final adjustment, because there are no carry-overs inherited from

[5] Possibly it is not needless to emphasise that here the problem of time is not only conceived in the narrow sense, referring to a special phenomenon, as investigated by Böhm-Bawerk and others in connection with the problem of capital; rather it is conceived in the widest sense, as primarily in the recent investigations by Hans Mayer ("Untersuchungen [Untersuchung] zu dem Grundgesetz der wirtschaftlichen Wertrechnung", *Zeitschrift für Volkswirtschaft und Sozialpolitik*, n.s., vols. 1, 2, and 6 [that is, part 1 in vol. 1, no. 3, 1921, pp. 431–58; and part 2 in vol. 2, no. 1, 1922, pp. 1–23, both reprinted in *Zeitschrift für Nationalökonomie*, vol. 15, June 1955, pp. 265–86, 287–303; the third part, announced in 1922 as "forthcoming" and cited by Hayek, never appeared; the journal having discontinued publication with volume 5 in 1927—Ed.]), Leo Schönfeld, *Grenznutzen und Wirtschaftsrechnung* (Vienna: Manz, 1924 [reprinted, Munich and Vienna: Philosophia, 1982]), and most recently Rosenstein and Morgenstern. [Cf. Paul N. Rosenstein-Rodan, "Das Zeitmoment in der mathematischen Theorie des wirtschaftlichen Gleichgewichtes", *Zeitschrift für Nationalökonomie*, vol. 1, May 1929, pp. 129–42, and Oskar Morgenstern, *Wirtschaftsprognose: Eine Untersuchung ihrer Voraussetzungen und Möglichkeiten* (Vienna: Springer, 1928), especially pp. 61–66. Note Rosenstein's conclusion (ibid., p. 142): "In reality, there is no general interdependence, but only various irreversible dependencies." Hans Mayer (1879–1955), Friedrich Wieser's successor as professor of economics at the University of Vienna, interpreted the Austrian theory of value in terms of his own 'causal-genetic' approach, in contrast to the 'functional' approach of general equilibrium theory. Leo Schönfeld, later Illy (1888–1952), was an Austrian economist whose 1924 book was favourably reviewed by F. A. Hayek in *Archiv für Sozialwissenschaft und Sozialpolitik*, vol. 54, no. 2, 1925, pp. 547–52; cf. for a translation F. A. Hayek, *Money, Capital and Fluctuations: Early Essays*, ed. Roy McCloughry (Chicago: University of Chicago Press; London: Routledge and Kegan Paul, 1984), pp. 183–89. Paul N. Rosenstein-Rodan (1902–85), Austrian economist and in the 1920s a disciple of Mayer, left Vienna in 1930 for Britain and then for the United States, where he taught at the Massachusetts Institute of Technology (MIT); his later contributions turned to the novel field of development economics. Oskar Morgenstern (1902–77) succeeded Hayek in 1931 as the director of the Austrian Institute for Business Cycle Research. Presently, he is best known for his collaboration with John von Neumann (1903–57) in the foundation of the theory of games.—Ed.]

the past and the factors determining the new prices will persist in their effects, as long as the data do not change anew.

4.

All things become different when after discarding the assumption hitherto used we are forced with the use of a medium of exchange to take account of the temporal dimension of the economic process. It is then no longer possible to arbitrarily cut out self-contained periods from the course of the economy; rather we must in principle regard the economy as an infinite stream. Yet, *this provides the room for the influence of new elements which affect the formation of prices, although they have nothing in common with the original driving forces of the economy*. In the following we have to examine the principal significance of these elements; however, we will be able to ascertain their full influence on the economic process only after we have investigated how production must be arranged for its steady maintenance over time.

We start by pointing out quite generally how the prices in an exchange economy where media of exchange are used will differ from those derived under the formerly assumed mechanism of exchange. To jump at once to the result: *The prices determined in the money economy differ from the 'equilibrium prices' of* static theory *insofar as they do not necessarily secure a course of the economy which* ceteris paribus *is capable of unchanged repetition.* Rather prices may be established that even without any external changes cannot be maintained, but over time are subject to shifts inherent to the system, which although weakening over time will persist in their effects and never come to a standstill.

The theorist is often inclined, yet is wrong in doing so, to neglect this circumstance, by ascribing it to the working of 'frictions', and to point out that ultimately the state of equilibrium as derived from the money-less economy must be attained. The theorist is wrong, because on the one hand it is just this process of price changes that is intimately related, and indeed part of the nature, of a money economy. And, on the other hand, in the course of the adjustment process the money economy is subject to necessary changes so that the state of equilibrium eventually attained (which in a strict sense the economy can approach only asymptotically[6]), although it will fulfil the formal theoretical conditions, in substance may differ considerably from the equilibrium derived from static theory, towards which the money economy is supposed to tend.[7]

---

[6] See below, p. [83—Ed.].

[7] Cf. Ludwig von Mises, *Theorie des Geldes und der Umlaufsmittel*, 2nd ed. rev. (Munich and Leipzig: Duncker and Humblot, 1924), p. 126 [translated as *The Theory of Money and Credit*, trans. H. E. Batson (London: Cape, 1934; reprinted, Indianapolis: Liberty Press, 1981), p. 168—Ed.].

5.

The divergences indicated above of price formation in an economy that uses a medium of exchange compared to one without such a medium are of fundamental significance and may alter the nature of the economy in an essential way. This can be convincingly demonstrated by means of a somewhat lengthy but in my view extremely important argument on the crucial difference between these two economic systems. Although perhaps judged as insignificant when viewed superficially, it will be shown that these peculiarities resulting from the use of media of exchange acquire extraordinary importance as they necessarily prevail in a much wider field than just that of the use of media of exchange in a narrower sense.

As we have seen, the money-less economy accomplished the necessary identity of demand and supply in every market because exchange could be completed within a single act and the imagined accounting scheme could offset, in a single moment, all demand and supply positions of the market. In contrast, the use of a medium of exchange and the splitting up of every exchange into two separate acts dissolves the closed circles of exchange of the money-less economy into open-ended chains. A schematic diagram will clarify this procedure (see fig. 1.1):

The top row represents the exchange process as imagined to happen in the case of periodical clearings. As here only the goods brought to the market in the respective period are exchanged to the exclusion of any other demand and supply positions, the circles of exchange are necessarily closed. Things change as soon as due to the use of a medium of exchange the single acts of exchange must happen successively. The bottom row represents the exchange process when a medium of exchange is used. Similar to the case depicted in the top row it is assumed that any good can be sold only once in each of the economic periods. Everyone who has brought a good to the market in one period will use the media of exchange thereby received for the purchase of other goods in the next period, and the respective seller can enter the market as the purchaser of a third good only in the period after he has sold his good, that is, at a still later point in time. It is obvious that in this case the chain of exchange can never return to the *same good* but at best will meet a *good of the same type*. Good A, drawn in the diagram as the last one of the first chain of exchange, may well be a good of the same type as the good A at the beginning of the same chain, yet never can it be the same piece of this good. (Strictly speaking, the second good A cannot even be a good of the same type as the first, because it is exchanged at a different point in time.)[8] Thus when a medium of exchange is used the chains of exchange will no more be closed. The exchange process will no longer be completed for a given supply of goods, but, how long the pe-

---

[8] See chapter 6.

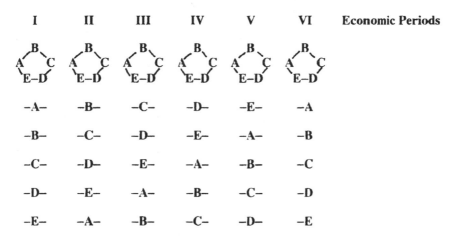

Figure 1.1. Dissolution of the chains of exchange

riods in question may ever last, never will the goods supplied and the supply of goods on which the demand is based be identical. At the beginning of the period in question there will always be a demand resulting from an earlier period which affects the formation of prices,[9] and there will always be a part of the supply of goods sold in this period which will not lead to a demand effected in this period. In other words: With the chains of exchange becoming infinite due to the use of a medium of exchange, for each finite economic period the identity between demand and supply—of crucial importance for the function of prices in the imagined money-less economy—will vanish.[10]

This difference is inconsequential as long as we assume that a state of equilibrium once established can be maintained, because there will be no changes in the fundamental data in the steadily proceeding economy. Then, as can be easily seen, the money economy will follow the same unchanged economic process, too. Yet, the difference becomes crucial if we assume a change in the fundamental data and then ask if and in which way under these circumstances a state of equilibrium will re-establish itself. This problem shows that price formation in an economy which uses a medium of exchange does not fulfil the same function as the exchange ratios derived for an economy where the assistance of a medium of exchange can be neglected.

[9] [That is, the formation of this period's prices.—Ed.]

[10] Cf. Mitchell, *Business Cycles*, p. 115: "The price system has no definable limits in time. No analysis can go back to the earliest term in the endless series of bargains which helped to make the prices of to-day, nor can anyone say how much influence is exerted to-day by the anticipation[s] of what prices will be to-morrow, or how many to-morrow[s] are taken into business reckonings." "Nor has the price system any logical beginning or end. At whatever point analysis may begin tracing the interlocking links of the price chain, to that point it will [will it] come round again if it proceeds far enough . . ."

6.

In a steadily proceeding economy the splitting up of the complete acts of exchange into periods is irrelevant, because the place of that part of each single act of exchange completed in a later period is taken by a similar act of exchange that completes an exchange process started in an earlier period. In this way the coincidence of demand and supply with regard to all acts of exchange carried out at one point in time can be accomplished. In contrast, with any change in the fundamental data the supply and the demand based on it do not change simultaneously. Rather both these reactions give rise to a time period (if ever so short), in which either only the change in demand or in supply affects the market without bringing about the required change of the corresponding item.[11] This difference between demand and supply, consequent upon the use of a medium of exchange, is however crucially distinct from those shifts between demand and supply in the money-less economy that result from changes in the data and give rise to justified price changes. In contrast, the shifts, resulting from the use of media of exchange, are by their very nature temporary and in this transient phase bring about prices which lack any economic function.

In the above case whenever a new goods supply comes into existence or vanishes, it will take some time until it is followed by the corresponding movement of demand based on that change in supply. For example, a new supply of goods must be sold the first time at a market where the income based on this supply does not yet exist (or will be spent by different persons); conversely, if some supply of goods vanishes it will be missing the first time at a market where the demand based on its previous sales is still effective and contributes to the formation of the new price system. If this would only mean that after a change in data the money economy would adjust successively instead of instantaneously, that is, that the price changes succeed each other in time, yet move in the direction required for the ultimate reestablishment of equilibrium, then the significance of the difference to the process typical of a money-less economy would indeed be negligible. However, besides these price changes there are also such that do not, neither in their direction nor in their extent, lead to a new state of equilibrium, but only result from the temporary divergence between aggregate demand and aggregate supply. These price movements, although temporary by their nature, in turn give rise to changes in the structure of the economy that cannot be maintained, *even if there are no further changes in the original data.*

For example, if the supply of a good increases due to improved production conditions, then under some circumstances not to be discussed here in detail a

[11] [That is, of supply or demand, respectively.—Ed.]

temporary curtailing of the consumption of other goods will result. This curtailment will, however, be compensated at least partially the moment that the income earned from the increased production of the favoured good comes to the market. Similarly, in the case of a shortfall in production (or the failure of some production because the good becomes unsaleable due to a change in tastes) the consequent increase in demand for other goods will for a time not be compensated by the shortfall of demand due to the eventual deficiency of income from the lost or failed production. Thus the prices of other goods will rise to an extent that cannot be maintained at all, or at least to some extent.

These effects can be most easily grasped if we consider for a moment the transition from a money-less to a money economy. Let us imagine that at some point in time all the money to be used will be distributed quite arbitrarily among the economic subjects, for example in equal amounts, so that now in the money economy the whole production must be sold against these amounts of money. It is evident that the prices determined in this first period cannot be maintained. Yet the same will be true for next period's prices, which come about by selling the production of this second period against the incomes created by first period sales—these must change, too, as first period prices, and thus incomes, have changed. Thus, prices can only be permanently maintained as equilibrium prices as soon as the incomes spent in the exchange against goods do not change any more; conversely, as in turn the incomes are determined by these prices, they will change as long as prices change. Therefore an absolute state of rest will never be accomplished. Although the required changes will become smaller and smaller, strictly speaking the economy in question will approach a state of equilibrium, if it has not existed from the beginning, only asymptotically.

7.

Indeed, the actually existing continuity of the evolution of the economy reduces the extent to which such fluctuations in prices occur; however, these cannot vanish altogether because with the use of a medium of exchange demand and supply are independent of each other. Here the economy is guided by demand which does not derive from contemporaneous production so that its recurrence cannot be taken for granted even if there are no 'changes in data'. The recurrence of the same demand in the consecutive period and thereby the repetition of an unchanged production will be secured only if production is guided by demand based on completely identical production. In order that a given structure of production can be maintained, in the absence of changes in fundamental data, goods produced contemporaneously must exhibit full mutual saleability at an exchange ratio which in each line makes it worthwhile to continue production to exactly the same extent. Price formation in a market where quantities demanded and supplied meet each other that do not derive from the same economic period, nor even must derive from equally long periods, cannot guarantee the accomplishment of such an inherent state of equilibrium with regard to current production. The money prices so determined do not bring about a coincidence between demand and supply such that all the goods sold at these money prices could also be exchanged in a natural clearing at the corresponding exchange ratios without any leftovers. Yet only such a state guarantees that, without changes in data, the current product will be sold without any disturbances against the proceeds from the sale of the product of the preceding period. For any other configuration of prices the system will inherently necessitate new price changes indicating that a full adjustment of production to the existing conditions has not yet been achieved. Rather in this case production activities guided by previously existing prices cannot be maintained in the same way as before.

8.

The way the changes in various data make themselves felt in the money economy may be best pursued by means of a hypothetical assumption often used to bypass the problem of time. This assumption refers to an intermediary step between, on the one hand, the money-less economy with periodical barter of the type of natural clearing examined at the beginning of our investigation and, on the other hand, a developed money economy with continuous monetary exchange. In this regard, we should not deceive ourselves about the artificiality of any attempt to split up the continuum of the money economy into separate periods. Yet as a justification for temporarily using such a makeshift assumption we may point out that following the method of the decreasing degree of abstraction[12] we shall meticulously examine the differences between the actual economy and our hypothetical one. With this proviso in mind, let us assume that even in an economy in which a medium of exchange is used

[12] [The method of 'decreasing abstraction' had been propagated among Austrian economists by Friedrich Wieser; cf. *Theorie der gesellschaftlichen Wirtschaft* (*Grundriß der Sozialökonomik*, vol. 1, part 2), 2nd ed. (Tübingen: Mohr, 1924), p. 128, translated as *Social Economics* (New York: Adelphi, 1927; reprinted, New York: Kelley, 1967, and London: Routledge, 2003), p. 178. Friedrich von Wieser (1851–1926) was a member of the second generation of the Austrian school, professor at the University of Vienna, 1903–22, and a teacher of Hayek; *Theorie der gesellschaftlichen Wirtschaft* is his major synthesis of Austrian teaching. See in this regard F. A. Hayek's obituary "Friedrich Freiherr von Wieser" (1926), translated and reprinted in *The Fortunes of Liberalism: Essays on Austrian Economics and the Ideal of Freedom*, ed. Peter G. Klein, vol. 4 (1992) of *The Collected Works of F. A. Hayek*, pp. 115–16.—Ed.]

all acts of exchange by which the product of a definite economic period is sold are concentrated with regard to time at a single market. Accordingly, anyone who supplies goods to this market can use the proceeds from the sale only at the next market for the purchase of goods. Thus in such an economy the whole product of the current economic period is confronted with the proceeds from the sale of the product of the preceding period. Therefore, the maintenance of equilibrium is predicated upon the condition that at the end of the period every individual participating in this exchange disposes of the same amount of money as at the beginning of the period. Only then will an unchanged production realise again the same prices in the next period, with preferences unchanged. However, this will only be the case if in the preceding period the same production had also realised the same prices, that is, that equilibrium had already existed. In order to elucidate the problem which interests us most, we must thus assume again a change in the fundamental data and then ask if and in which way a state of equilibrium will be established under these circumstances.

For example, let us consider an improvement in the methods of production so that a product will be brought to the market in greater quantity than before. Then subsequent to this disturbance of equilibrium, after exchange has been finished, the distribution of the aggregate stock of money will be different than before. This change in the distribution of money resulted from the change in prices at the current market due to the increase in supply. Yet, these prices will change in the next period, too, as the same increased supply of goods will confront a differently distributed demand in terms of money. Thus, as already pointed out above, each of these price changes leads to new changes in incomes and therefore again in prices, so that the economy described—and the same will be true for any money economy—will never come to a state of rest, once any change has happened.

Again the essential point is not just that the new state of equilibrium will not be attained instantaneously, but strictly speaking will only be approached slowly and asymptotically. *Rather* it is that among the chain of shifts caused by the one-time change in data there will be some that will not serve the reestablishing of equilibrium but introduce new disturbances into the course of production. For example, under specific conditions not to be discussed here in detail, the increase in the supply of a product may result in a greater sum of money being spent on it than before. This will cause a temporary fall in prices of other products, which may perhaps be reversed partially later on, as part of the increased proceeds for the former product may be used for the purchase of the other products. However, in the meantime the temporary fall in prices will not only have generated a contraction in the respective branches of production, but also a decrease in the demand for still other products in the next period, which will again in the same way feed back to other demands. The

85

same will also happen if instead of a one-time shortfall a one-time, yet temporary, increase in the demand in terms of money[13] takes place. How long ever we will pursue the sequence of periods, there will always be some effect of the one-time shift between the supply of money and of goods. Thus the money economy will never come completely to rest even if it steadily approaches such a state.

The significance of this factor becomes evident when considering an actual economy, where, of course, at any moment a great number of such chains of persisting shifts are operating, each one caused by an earlier one-time change. Then, even if no further changes in data happened, for a long time the ongoing shifts in the structure of the economy would be substantial. In any case, misdirection of production will be inevitable in a money economy because after a change in data production is typically still guided by the supply of a preceding period. Thus in successive periods the goods brought to the market will always be confronted with a money income used for their purchase, which derives from the production of a preceding period totally different in its structure and composition. Indeed, it is only due to the relative continuity of the evolution of the economy that a misdirection of production can be prevented of such an extent that might lead to a total confusion in the economy and the impossibility of production based on the division of labour.

9.

Furthermore, in an economy where the acts of exchange are not concentrated in periodically recurring markets but occur continuously, the danger is greatly mitigated that these influences make themselves felt in such a fatal way. The possibility for individual economic subjects to compensate excessive disturbances by adjusting their budgets, that is, by taking account of an expected future change in their income even before it has happened, may also restrict the extent of such disturbances. Yet, they cannot be completely eliminated in this way. For the temporal shifts brought about in individual budgets by saving or borrowing cannot bring about a temporal balance in the provision of goods for the economy as a whole. Their effect is only to shift the source of the disturbance to a different place in the economy.

Even if, under the assumptions hitherto introduced, the significance of the source of disturbance discussed may appear small, this will not justify its complete neglect, as has been the rule up to now. The justification for the detailed investigation above of seemingly self-evident facts is that these constitute the gap through which influences disturbing the price system intrude into

---

[13] [That is, the demand for goods in terms of money.—Ed.]

the money economy. For it is the self-contained character of the price system of a barter economy which leaves no room for the influence of factors other than those associated with the original driving forces of the economy. Yet, all the changes of individual prices that do not result from changes in the relation between the demand and supply of goods, but in the relation between the supply of goods and the supply of money, constitute an obstacle to the working of the indispensable organising forces of the economy. They inevitably bring about losses due to misguided decisions, which cannot be recognised beforehand, as the existing prices constitute the only guide to the organisation of production.

10.

The extent to which these effects materialise depends, of course, on the length of the time interval between these acts of exchange, originally conceived as simultaneous and now separated by the use of money, and, in particular, on how much the length of these intervals will change, too. The further back in time production on which the demand confronting the results of current production is based, and the more the interval of time varies during which money remains in the hands of the individuals, the greater will be the role played by disturbances of the type considered. And accordingly the greater this role, the less meaningful it is to assume that at every point in time the required coincidence of demand and supply can be secured, and the more often will prices come about which misdirect production.

Before turning to the amplified effects due to the use of money facilitating arbitrary shifts in demand, it is necessary to take account of the significance of time for the economic process in a different respect. Every such shift in demand in the end means an intended exchange between two goods available at different points in time; it thus establishes a relation between the prices of these goods at different points in time, the significance of which must be clarified. With respect to the effect of prices as guiding the temporal sequence in the provision of goods this examination will close a gap. For up to now price formation has been analysed under the fictitious assumption that all exchanges that depend on one another take place simultaneously. However, after introducing a medium of exchange and thereby introducing time among the givens of the analysis, what is then the function of the relative height of prices determined at consecutive points in time? There cannot be any doubt that even in a stationary economy, in which the state of equilibrium is not disturbed by any change in data, prices of the same good at different points in time often need not be identical, but must be graduated in a particular way. In this sense one may speak of an intertemporal price system. After ascertaining the significance of the maintenance of such an intertemporal price system for the undisturbed course of the economic process, it will become possible to find out what the effect of changes in these prices will be as brought about by the influences discussed above for the money economy. In the following we attempt to investigate the up to now wholly neglected significance of the temporal structure of prices and the disturbances of it. Thereby we will be able also to take account of another factor which hitherto has been neglected in this investigation. We shall start by investigating the effect of abnormal delays in the spending of money received in a given period, or specifically the case of money received in the preceding period not spent in the current period. Then we turn to the case of changes in the flow of money, either because money used as a demand for goods does not result from the proceeds of goods sold in earlier periods[14] but enters the economy from outside, or because money vanishes from the economy, as regularly happens with tied currencies. We have seen that in principle—that is quite apart from the cases just referred to—price formation in a money economy may result in prices lacking an economic function and therefore influencing the structure of the economy in a way detrimental to its undisturbed evolution. Yet, it is only by taking account of these cases that we arrive at phenomena where these disturbances attain practical relevance.

The full significance of this idea will only be recognised after another step in the process of decreasing abstraction to which we ascribe in this investigation. In a later chapter we will also take account of another influence deriving from the element of time, that is, the length of time necessary for all processes of production, which we have up to now eliminated by assuming that production consists just of an instantaneous combination of factors of production. However, the analysis of this problem is based on an understanding of the function of the intertemporal price system, which the next chapter will deal with.

In order to avoid the impression that the results of the following chapter are in contradiction to what has been just analysed, the opposite points of view of this and the following chapter shall be briefly indicated. The above concentrated on finding out the source of misguided production with respect to the *direction* of demand at a point in time, which must give rise to the production of the wrong goods or quantities of goods. In contrast, the following will deal with the sources of misguided production with respect to the relative *magnitude* of aggregate demand at different points in time, which must give rise to a wrong structure of the provision of goods among different points in time.

---

[14] [In the German typescript this passage is unintelligible and ungrammatical; a literal translation might read, "because money is used as a demand for goods, the proceeds of goods not sold in earlier periods". The version in the text is my conjecture.—Ed.]

Otherwise than in the first case a relative change in the aggregate supply of goods in the face of an unchanged flow of money here does not mean that this new relation is incapable of being maintained. As now the whole demand will exert its effect on the changed supply, the latter will realise prices that have changed correspondingly, and thus demand will stay the same in the following periods.

VIII.[1] *Time and the Structure of Production*[2]

1.

The preceding two chapters have led us deep into the problems of a money economy. Now, however, in continuing the process of the systematic decrease in the degree of abstraction, we have to return to our previous starting point in order to take into consideration some hitherto neglected relationships. Specifically, we will investigate the consequences of the introduction of money under the relatively simple assumptions to which we have adhered before. It is yet in another sense that the preceding remarks have transcended the system of these investigations, namely in its attempt—within the framework of an investigation directed at the deficiencies of the static approach to a money economy—to extend the scope of application of statics far beyond its usual limits. This extension of the equilibrium approach to the relationship between economic activities at separate points in time was only made possible by resorting to very artificial assumptions. Yet, this proved necessary for demonstrating, even under the simple circumstances considered up to now, the significance of the temporal structure of prices, and the sense in which disturbances, in particular monetarily caused disturbances of price formation, can be identified.

Now the task will be to integrate an extraordinarily important fact into the scheme of our considerations, namely that in a mature exchange economy the production of individual goods will not be carried out, from its beginning to its end, by a single economic subject but rather that almost all goods change hands in the course of their production. Therefore, exchange will not

[1] [Chapters 6 and 7, apart from stylistic modifications and a few footnotes added, are identical to F. A. Hayek, "Das intertemporale Gleichgewichtssystem der Preise", translated as "Intertemporal Price Equilibrium". In particular chapter 6, "The System of Intertemporal Price Equilibrium", consists of sections 1–9 and the appendix of this article (cf. "Intertemporal Price Equilibrium", pp. 186–209 and 225–27), and chapter 7, "The Disturbances to the Intertemporal Price System due to Changes in the Volume of Money", consists of sections 10–12 (cf. "Intertemporal Price Equilibrium", pp. 210–25). These two chapters are not reprinted here.—Ed.]

[2] [Attached to the typescript there is a handwritten note with the headings and the respective pagination of the sections: "§1 Influence of prices in successive stages of production on the structure of production: the problem. 1–4. §2 Plan of the investigation; vertical division of labour, prices guide the assignment of goods to the stages of production, synchronisation requires double correspondence, price system of higher order. 5–11. §3 Effects of changes in data in multi-stage production without money. 11–23. §4 Effects of the use of money. 24–26. §5 The idea of the circuit of money. 27–33. §6 Obstacles to adjustments to changes in data in the money economy. 33–39. §7 Demand for consumers' goods and demand for producers' goods. 40–46. §8 The money flow and original changes in real capital (technical-physical changes). 47–51. §9 Say's theorem and the multi-stage money economy (and the possibility of general gluts). 52–60. §10 The general significance of indirect exchange (. . .)". At the bottom of the page Hayek added, "pp. 9–24, abbreviate radically!"—Ed.]

only determine the prices of consumable goods—as has been assumed up to now—but also the prices of means of production and of semi-finished goods. Besides the prices obtained *alternatively* for one and the same good at distinct points in time, we will now turn to the *successive* prices obtained for a good passing through the distinct stages of its production. From this new point of view the linkage between present and future becomes even tighter than already evident under the previous assumptions. This is so because all the prices resulting from exchange among producers, on the one hand, can only be explained as based on the expectation of certain future prices of the final product and, on the other hand, determine those future prices through their influence on the structure of production and on the future provision of goods. Thus this investigation led to the question of to what extent the influences of money will determine *the structure of production*. As a first step towards answering this question we will have to investigate the multiple formation of prices, which characterises every good on its way through the process of production, in its significance for maintaining the process of production. Thereby we will remain faithful to the guiding principle of this investigation, that is, to ascertain the influences of money on the course of the economy by means of a comparison with those exchange ratios that would be brought about without the existence of money. Thus we have to investigate the 'original determinants' and the 'function' of the relative height of the prices of products and of means of production for the case of a fictitious barter economy, and for this purpose we will reconsider the transition from a barter to a money economy as already analysed before. The influences of money on this new group of price relations and thereby on the structure of production can only be analysed based on this reconsideration.

[Subsequent to this extension of our assumptions a further approximation to reality will become necessary, namely abandoning the assumption that the circumstances that determine the temporal structure of prices can be *foreseen*. The assumption of foresight has indeed provided the prerequisite for the static theory of the price relations between means of production and products, yet beyond what is offered by general theory hardly more can be said on this topic than results by mere implication from the analysis of chapter 6 to this special case. In contrast, the problems characteristic of the extension of our analysis become apparent only when turning to *disturbances* of the state of equilibrium and asking whether and how a new equilibrium is attained. It is this question which marks the transition from a static to a dynamic approach. In addition, this question makes it possible (as has been the case with regard to the effects of monetary exchange in a single-stage economy[3]) to emphasise

---

[3] [This refers to chapters 6 and 7 above, that is, to the approach of Hayek's "Intertemporal Price Equilibrium".—Ed.]

the differences which must exist in an actual economy experiencing the passage of time compared to an economy characterised by the hypothetical ideal of self-contained, interdependent equilibrium relationships.][4]

Theoretical investigations of the type undertaken in the preceding chapters are of significance only insofar as they provide the starting point for a process of decreasing abstraction. The inclusion of the circumstances just noted within the sphere of our considerations marks a crucial step in this process. Only thereby can we justify the far-reaching hypothetical simplification, to which we have adhered up to now and which represents the most important tool of all theory. Existing theory should not be reproached for the extensive use it makes of this tool, but for its insufficient honouring of the obligation implied by this use: that is, the obligation to abandon these consciously introduced simplifications and to investigate how the results will thereby be affected. It is to this second part of the tasks of theoretical research that this study attempts to contribute. Apparently it is just these new elements now to be included in our considerations that will lead us to problems, which hitherto lack any systematic investigation, yet are of crucial importance for the applicability of the results already derived.

2.

In the preceding chapters this investigation has assumed, of course, that the consumers' goods coming to the market are not readily available in certain quantities, but must be *produced*. Accordingly, it was supposed that the quantity supplied of each of these goods depends on the price to be realised and that production is time-consuming so that after a change in data a new state of equilibrium cannot be attained instantaneously but only after the necessary change of the quantities produced affected the market for consumers' goods. However, we neglected the fact that as a rule many economic subjects participate in the production of a consumers' good, each of them only contributing a part of the work necessary for its completion, exchanging among them (by purchase and sale, respectively) the respective results of all these contributions. Until now we tried to evade the problems created by this circumstance by assuming that the production of every good, from the production of required raw materials to the manufacturing of tools and machines up to its final stage, is concentrated in an economic unit directed by a single will, so that only the produced consumers' goods will be exchanged among these units.

Now we will take account of the fact that there is not only a horizontal division of labour among the economic units, referring to the variety of con-

[4] [The passages in brackets are crossed out in the typescript.—Ed.]

sumers' goods, but also a *vertical division of labour* with regard to the production of goods in *several stages*, which are distinct both from a technical and an economic point of view. Accordingly, we face a category of prices which differ from those hitherto considered in their dependence as well as their influence on the other prices. The most obvious peculiarity of these prices is that they do not govern the distribution of consumers' goods, but the extent to which the intermediary products (tools and raw materials) required for the production of consumers' goods will be provided; and to some degree this task is performed independently from the prices realised for consumers' goods and often before these goods even exist and are able to yield prices. Thus, prices *determine the assignment* of intermediary products *among the individual stages of production*, yet these are *not* the same prices that guide the distribution of consumers' goods and thereby indirectly influence the provision of the means of production, rather this function is fulfilled by particular prices. Notably the prices of consumers' goods can influence the provision of the means of production only by their impact on *the prices of goods produced in the different stages*. Although these prices must exhibit a certain equilibrium relation to the prices of consumers' goods, this relation can be disturbed by those special determinants that affect these prices only; and as long as the equilibrium relation between prices is not restored, the provision of the means of production will not correspond to that required for the sale of the final product.

In order to recognise the significance attributed to these prices in their effect on the structure of production we must first ascertain the conditions for a steady course of the economic process to be fulfilled by the system of all prices and the structure of production. In addition, to judge the disturbances of this process caused by deviations of these prices due to the use of money, we have to examine how an economy without money would react to a disturbance of the state of equilibrium and how a new equilibrium would be re-established. For this purpose we will, for the last time and only briefly, base our considerations on the working of the imagined barter economy.

The most general conditions, which the structure of production must fulfil at any moment, for the *steady* maintenance of production can be best captured by the notion of *synchronisation*.[5] "Every economy of permanent existence in

---

[5] Cf. on this John Bates Clark, *The Distribution of Wealth: A Theory of Wages, Interest and Profits* (New York: Macmillan, 1899 [reprinted, Kelley, 1965]) [cf. chapter 20, "Production and Consumption Synchronized by Rightly Apportioned Capital"—Ed.]; and later Wilhelm Lexis, *Allgemeine Volkswirtschaftslehre*, 2nd ed. (Leipzig and Berlin: Teubner, 1913), pp. 187ff. [pp. 187–92], and Hans Mayer, "Produktion", in *Handwörterbuch der Staatswissenschaften*, 4th revised edition, ed. Ludwig Elster, Adolf Weber, and Friedrich Wieser, vol. 6 (Jena: Fischer, 1925), of which the section "Die zeitliche Gestaltung der Produktion" [that is, "the temporal structure of production"—Ed.] (pp. 1115–16) is here referred for all of the following discussion. [Hayek added a handwritten note: "Some other demonstrations may be found in the system of the mathematical school. Cf. for example . . .", followed by an illegible reference.—Ed.]

order to satisfy the steadily revolving needs requires a temporal structure of production so that all the various consumers' goods are supplied in an even and steady flow. This can only be accomplished by arranging the production process in such a way that in each period of the economic process—that is, to put a sort of cross section through the temporal course of production—*all the numerous states of conversion*, which the various goods must pass on their way from the production of raw materials to the final product, *coexist side by side* and that to all these stages the various means of production required for further conversions, like raw and auxiliary materials, tools, appliances, machines and so on, are assigned in ever constant quantities."[6] In an exchange economy the assignments to the individual stages of production depend on the prices of the products of these stages, and thus the accomplishment of such a synchronised structure of production presupposes a certain relation between the prices of the products of these stages. In effect, the sum of the prices paid for all the goods used at a certain stage of a branch of production must correspond to the total price of the products of the subsequent stage.[7] Suppose this were not the case, that is, the price sum of the quantity of the means of production prepared at a certain stage did not correspond to the total price to be realised from the quantity of products that can be manufactured from these means. Then as a consequence the quantity of the means of production provided in the earlier stage of production would be changed and thus the quantitative correspondence among the goods available in the various stages disturbed; yet, this correspondence is a prerequisite for the steady maintenance of production. Thus the temporal equilibrium of production requires a *double correspondence* among the goods always available in the individual stages of production: the quantity of these goods available in each stage must correspond to the quantity available in the subsequent stage *in the technical sense* that this latter quantity, no less and no more, can be produced, yet, in addition, these two quantities of goods must also correspond *in value terms*, that is, realise the same prices and thus be exchanged against each other without any leftovers.

The fact that equilibrium requires that *technical factors determine a certain price relation* between certain quantities of various goods establishes an especially close connection between these prices and makes them distinct from the general price system as a particular type of relationship. The primary prices of consumers' goods determine *which* of the many *needs* begging for satisfaction shall be satisfied. Besides there is a group of derived prices, depending on the former, which determine *the kind and the quantity of the goods to be pro-*

---

[6] Mayer, ibid., p. 1115 (emphasis added).

[7] [Consistently interpreted, the condition should be that "the sum of the prices paid for all the goods used at a certain stage" should "correspond to the total price of the product as realised from sales to the subsequent stage". Note also that Hayek uses the term 'total price' (in contrast to 'unit price') as synonymous to proceeds or revenue.—Ed.]

duced and later on to be distributed at the market for consumers' goods; yet *these prices* will not determine the distribution among the consumers. These prices of a new type do not constitute an autonomous element within the existing price system, as in the case of the price of a newly introduced consumers' good. Neither do the respective goods compete with consumers' goods for sale, and therefore cannot directly influence the system of consumers' goods' prices. With regard to this system these prices are no more than an irrelevant repetition of the price of the consumers' good, a repetition, unable to interfere with the self-contained system of prices of consumers' goods—self-contained because only the prices realised for consumers' goods provide the basis for the demand for consumers' goods, so that therefore demand and supply of *consumers' goods* of necessity coincide.

Thus, in equilibrium the prices of means of production and of the products manufactured from them must coincide and will be identical in relation to the remainder of the price system; therefore after a disturbance to equilibrium in order to fulfil their function they *must* change jointly at one stroke. However, as a matter of fact the physical consequences of a change in data can affect the individual stages only successively, thus after a change in data the determinants of the individual prices can also change only successively so that the *correspondence between prices* as a necessary prerequisite for maintaining equilibrium cannot always be fulfilled. As long as there is only exchange of consumers' goods, all prices belong so to say to just one level and thus any change in data affects them simultaneously. Yet by including the means of production among the objects of exchange the price system acquires a *new dimension*, a *superstructure* built above the linear system of consumers' goods prices, so that now different degrees of mutual dependency may be distinguished. Changes in data will now first only affect submarkets, into which the whole system of exchange relations has been partitioned; prices which by the nature of the equilibrium system should only move jointly and uniformly now become capable of autonomous changes.

In the course of this investigation we will pursue the effects of changes in data with regard to such a *'price system of higher order'*, thus turning attention from the mere description of the conditions of *equilibrium* to the analysis of the *reaction mechanism* set in motion by a change in data. This will elucidate the significance of the structure of the price system, reflecting the differentiated relations among prices, for the undisturbed maintenance of the economic process. Yet, prior to this, it appears suitable to represent this mutual dependency of prices in a different way schematically.

As we still proceed under the assumption of pure barter, the means providing for the purchase of the producers' goods required for the production of the consumers' good consist only in the price realised for the consumers' good. Therefore the suppliers of producers' goods can sell them only to producers of the consumers' goods, so that the remuneration they can realise for their efforts as a whole is limited by the price of the consumers' good, which is just manufactured from such producers' goods. In this way the whole of exchange relations is subject to a definite order. While *the persons which bring consumers' goods to the market exchange them only to the smallest part against other consumers' goods, the producers of producer's goods*[8] *exchange them to the greater part or exclusively* (this will be the case for those who contribute the original means, labour and land) *against consumers' goods*. In a market for consumers' goods naturally any person intends to acquire goods other than those supplied by oneself, consequently the exchange is between goods of which *either* the one *or* the other may realise *permanently* a more favourable price and thus induce the producer to increase production. In contrast, considering the exchange between goods of different stages of production, in this case the change in price and quantity produced of one good must necessarily bring about a change in price and quantity produced of the other good *in the same direction*. As a consequence any change in an exchange relation will be propagated through a definite chain of further exchanges, yet without the possibility that this change will give rise to a change in the participants of exchange,[9] as would happen as a rule at a market purely for consumers' goods.

Under conditions of barter, demand can only react to a change in the supply of a producers' good by drawing on goods, hitherto used otherwise, for the purpose of purchasing the producers' good in increased supply (or by devoting goods, hitherto used for these purchases, to other more advantageous purposes) once the change in the quantity supplied has been propagated to the stage of consumers' goods. The converse will happen if the demand for consumable products changes. The prices to be permanently realised by the consumers' goods (and also by the means of production used in manufacturing them) can only be ascertained once sufficient time has passed for the new starts or the closings of production in the preceding stages, initiated by the change in demand for the final product, to fully exert their effect on the supply of consumers' goods. In the meantime, however, in both cases the products of the individual stages of the branches of production, although produced in changed quantities, will realise a total price which has not yet been influenced by this change in quantity but is equal to that realised before this change. Evidently, these prices stand outside the relationships of the general price system and therefore the volume of production thus determined need not correspond to the sales ultimately possible. These prices do not result from the demand

---

[8] [Although "producers of producers' goods" is the literal translation of the German text, possibly the intended meaning would be rendered better by "suppliers of the means of production", as this would explicitly comprise the supply of original means of production.—Ed.]

[9] [The phrase "participants of exchange" is possibly a typing error; a reasonable conjecture instead might be "relations of exchange".—Ed.]

for the final product manufactured from the respective producers' goods and therefore they cannot signal if the market will absorb the *final product*. Rather, it is the demand for the final product *in the quantity already at the market*, which determines these prices. The changed quantity of the producers' good realises a total price as if the quantity of the consumers' good manufactured from it would be the same as the quantity of the consumers' good currently exchanged at the market. Yet, if this is not case, then *production will still be guided by prices which under prevailing conditions cannot be realised*.[10] Possibly due to this circumstance the unit price for the producers' good may change in the opposite direction compared to what will happen if the changed supply meets the ultimately relevant demand for consumers' goods. As a consequence a change in the quantity produced may be induced opposite to that necessary for attaining the state of equilibrium.

[. . .][11]

For the following arguments it is not necessary to go beyond these hints about the conditions of intertemporal equilibrium with regard to the prices of consumers' and producers' goods. Therefore we will now turn to the so-called disturbances of the equilibrium relationships, that is, the unexpected changes in data and their effects, to which up to now we have referred only in occasional digressions.

3.

As long as we still abstract from the existence of money, the following *types of changes in data* come into question as causes of disturbances of equilibrium: *First*, the supply of original means of production may change (the supply of produced means of production is economically determined, thus at best an incidental destruction of such goods by natural disasters, etc., could be considered as a change in data); such a change may consist in a change in the absolute quantity available of every good as well as in a change in their distribution among the individual economic subjects. *Second*, the technical relation between means of production and products may change, e.g., due to inventions, so that now from the same quantity of means of production a higher quantity of products can be manufactured. And *third*, among consumers the relative appraisal of the individual consumers' goods may change. In a multi-stage exchange economy each of these changes in data will affect the various elements of the price system only successively, that is, as the respective changes in the

---

[10] [That is, the conditions prevailing when the new production is coming to the market.—Ed.]

[11] [Here is a gap in the typescript, possibly due to a deletion by Hayek. The text continues with the following paragraph, which is crossed out in the typescript.—Ed.]

quantities of the various goods move through the different stages of production. Thus this movement gives rise to a *sequence of a series of different price systems*, each of which is only maintained for a moment, because each carries in itself the cause for the next change and thus in this sense does not constitute an 'equilibrium system'. For our purpose we are only interested if this chain of changes will be nothing more than a stepwise approach towards a new state of equilibrium so that accordingly each single change would be in the very direction leading to the new state of equilibrium. Or may the changes in individual prices, and the changes in the quantities produced thereby induced, tend in the opposite direction of what would be ultimately required for attaining equilibrium? In the latter case the initiating disturbance of the state of equilibrium would even be aggravated, because in the first instance the price mechanism brought about not adjustment but on the contrary a change in the opposite direction as would be compatible with the new conditions. This is the question to be examined for all three cases.

We start with the relatively trivial *first case*, the *change in the disposable quantity of the original means of production*. For concreteness (and so as not to refer all the time to all possible eventualities) we assume that—e.g., by the discovery of a new deposit of ore—the supply of some raw material *increases* considerably. How would the price system under a commodity clearing as described above react to such a change and what would be the shifts in the structure of production necessary before a new state of rest could be attained?

The potential demand for the increased supply of the raw material will come primarily from those firms that already have processed it in the past. At the moment when the increased supply comes for the first time to the market, these firms will have brought their product to the market in the same quantity still as before. Thus their means for purchasing the increased quantity of the raw material are limited by the price realised for the quantity of their product just produced, less manufacturing costs (that is, the prices of complementary producers' goods). The increased quantity of the raw material can therefore realise a total price not higher than that realised by the quantity necessary for the manufacturing of the product as *currently* available at the market. The implied fall in the unit price of the raw material may have the effect that other industries which up to now did not use it will turn to it, or that industries which already used it will use it in greater quantities as a substitute for other raw materials. However, it is equally probable that in these industries the manufacturing of the increased quantity of the raw material requires also the use of a greater quantity of complementary producers' goods; in this case the share of the price available for the purchase of our raw material will be thereby diminished and the additional demand coming from these industries possibly compensated.

Taking all these circumstances into account, it may well be possible that the demand for the producers' good now available in a greater quantity[12] can change instantaneously. Yet, it remains a fact that for all those industries which due to the increased supply of the raw material are able to increase the quantities produced the sum available for the purchase of all the required means of production cannot be greater than the sum realised for the current product. However, as long as they *expect* that the total price of the final product now producible in a greater quantity will *not exceed or be even smaller than* that of the quantity currently produced, that is, as long as they assume an elasticity of demand not greater than unity, the above fact will not change their dispositions. For if they expect to realise *less* for the increased product than for the current one, there will be no incentive to spend the same amount as before for raw materials, etc. In this case they will devote only that part of the proceeds from past production to the purchase of raw materials which they expect to recover from the sale of the increased product, any difference being used for personal consumption or for the opening up of a new branch of production.

As long as we assume that the change in the price of the final product induced by the change in its quantity will be correctly foreseen, the only interesting case is when the expected total price of the increased final product exceeds that realised for the unchanged quantity. This would result in a difference between the price of the raw material and the price of the product manufactured from it. For some time this difference could not be capitalised on because those producers equipped for manufacturing the raw material did not yet have at their disposal the proceeds from the greater quantity of the final product to be produced, while other producers lacked the fixed capital and the knowledge necessary for manufacturing it. In a money economy in such a case credit would fill the gap by providing a loan to the manufacturer, which would enable the exploitation of the profit opportunity offered by this price difference. However, in the barter economy the possibility of the granting of such a credit does not exist, because the owners of raw materials would only be ready to exchange them against quantities of consumers' goods,[13] which in turn due to their variety can never be traded, in contrast to money, as a kind of homogeneous working capital. Banning the alternative that the owners of raw materials are ready to 'wait' (an assumption that cannot be justified), the price realised for a unit of their increased product will not only be less than the current price, but also less than the price to be realised once the increase in production has reached the stage of final products. Therefore it would be unprofitable to exploit the new sources of the raw material now to the same

---

[12] [That is, the raw material in question.—Ed.]
[13] See above, p. [93—Ed.].

degree as will be the case when the increased final product eventually has come to the market. Moreover, even in those firms where the raw material had been produced before the discovery of new deposits, due to the competition from the new sources the employment of labour would become unprofitable to a greater extent than in the final position. Thus while the new firms will merely not be able to extend their production to the quantity ultimately possible, the old firms will have to restrict temporarily the quantities produced more sharply than required after the final adjustment of the market to the new situation. [Therefore in the meantime these firms require less of other goods and labour than will be the case permanently, so that temporarily these goods and labour will move into other branches of production where production will increase, albeit only temporarily, too. The same must result in all the stages which are part of this branch of production. This is so because only when the increased volume of the final product has come to the market for consumers' goods, will it be possible that due to the fall in price new groups of buyers shift their 'purchasing power' from other purposes to the product in question.][14]

In the meantime *prices will be formed in all stages of production which can only be explained by the fact that the increased supply of producers' goods meets a demand based on the price for the still unchanged supply of products manufactured from these producers' goods.* Accordingly, the quantities produced will not be those corresponding to the new equilibrium price of the product. Therefore, the price realised by the final product when it eventually comes to the market in increased quantity will still not represent a permanent price. This will therefore induce a readjustment of its quantity, which will then again pass through all the stages of production. Depending on whether the price to be realised by the new final product is greater or smaller than the price for the quantity produced before, the individual stages of production will experience movements of the complementary means of production—either leaving for other branches of production or conversely entering from other such branches, yet with the effect that the use in the branch of production in question will turn out as unprofitable.

In any case, a new state of equilibrium would eventually be attained by such a stepwise adjustment, if it were possible to assume that in the meantime the demand for the final product remained constant. However, this cannot be the case, because all the temporary shifts, which are part of any adjustment process, affect the supply of other goods and in turn the effective demand for the final product of the branch of production in question. This means nothing less than that the price for the final product, too, at no time will signal whether an unchanged quantity can be sold permanently at the given price. This is so because among the determinants of this price there are some which necessar-

---

[14] [The sentences in brackets are crossed out in the typescript.—Ed.]

ily will cease to exist the moment this price has been realised. Even taking the realised price for the final product as a guide has the consequence that the volume of production will be determined by prices, for the recurrence of which *the preconditions on the side of demand are not fulfilled.* The prices on which the demand for the final product is based belong in some sense to a previous system of equilibrium, which has just been destroyed by the increased final product coming to the market. Yet, we are already aware, from our investigation of indirect exchange, of the consequences when the formation of prices is not exclusively determined by the current demand and supply of goods.[15]

Here it is the case that results of previous exchanges play a part in the determination of subsequent acts of exchange, be it in the form of money proceeds or in the form of goods purchased for subsequent processing or resale. This, however, will destroy the self-contained character of the system, which is a prerequisite for the instantaneous attainment of equilibrium. Accordingly, any change will induce *in principle* an infinite chain of further shifts without a state of rest ever being reached. The essential *similarity* of the *effects* of *indirect exchange* and of *multi-stage production* in this regard becomes evident when recognising that basically each purchase for resale, even when the resale is subsequent to the processing of the purchased good, represents a kind of indirect exchange. *Even when no medium of exchange is used,* multi-stage production will give rise to all the effects earlier described for the case of indirect exchange, and in fact to a still greater degree. For the use of a medium of exchange splits up direct exchange into just two separate acts, so that a change in the supply of a consumers' good will make itself felt as a change in demand in the same market by the time the realised price will be spent again. Yet, in a barter economy a change in the supply of a means of production will as a rule affect the demand for other goods, exerted by the owners of this means of production, only when the change in the quantity of the means of production has been *passed right through the whole series of exchanges to the market for consumers' goods.* Here the whole process of production will be inserted between the change of supply and the change of demand based on it, and the circle of exchanges will not be closed before the increased final product has been sold and the price realised for it has been returned to the owners of the means of production.

In the case discussed the consequences derived from this fact are relatively minor. Due to the assumption that the effect of the change in the quantity of the final product on its price can be foreseen, the case could be eliminated where the total price of the increased final product lies below that of the current unchanged product. In the converse case, we found out that the new state of equilibrium would be approached no longer instantaneously but only asymptotically; yet although in the course of this process numerous tempo-

[15] See chapter 5.

rary misdirections of production would occur, on the whole the tendency to a new, if unattainable,[16] state of rest would not be crucially disturbed. However, as soon as we assume, closer to the actual facts, that the producer of the raw material and its subsequent purchaser are not able to correctly foresee the price ultimately realised by the increased final product, the adjustment process will become much more complicated and induce much graver misdirections than those hitherto described.

Finally, let us [stay with the case already examined but][17] assume again that the total price of the increased final product will be smaller than that of the quantity produced before. Then as a rule this drop in the total price will make itself felt only when the increased final product arrives at the market, or possibly when the products of the last but one stage of production are offered to the final producer. Until this moment, in every stage of production, which the increased intermediary products pass successively, demand will be based on the yet higher total price realised for the current product (less the higher costs for the increased semi-finished goods and raw materials). Prices will therefore induce an expansion of production not justified by the demand for consumers' goods. This means, that 1. in all stages of production new complementary producers' goods are attracted from other branches, which however will become unusable, once the increased final product arrives at the market; 2. durable means of production will be manufactured, which would be profitable only at the current price, which however *cannot* be sustained; 3. as part of the final product becomes unsaleable, stocks pile up, which subsequently by restricting production push the price below the equilibrium price; and finally, 4. due to the temporary shifts of the producers' goods resulting from the excessive increase in production, even the final product will always be confronted with a demand derived from the current, yet transient structure of production, and which thus does not provide a reliable indicator for the sales possible in the state of equilibrium.

Thus, under the circumstances considered, the prices formed as a direct consequence of the change in data will lead to changes in production which are not required by the new constellation of data and are not conducive to the approach towards a new state of equilibrium; in contrast, these prices *lead away from equilibrium* and will turn out as generating losses.

The *second* case of changes in data mentioned above, changes in the technical relations between means of production and product, is equivalent to the first one. This is so because from an economic point of view the increase in the efficiency of a means of production resulting from an invention has just the same effect as an increase in its quantity proportional to the increase in

---

[16] [The word is crossed out in the typescript.—Ed.]

[17] [The passage in brackets is crossed out in the typescript.—Ed.]

efficiency. Therefore it is only *the third case*, the change in data in the form of an original change in consumption, that is, of the consumers' needs, which requires further investigation.

We will again put the case more concretely and assume that some day, due to a change in tastes, a product is demanded more strongly in place of another one, and that this product is manufactured in numerous stages from a specific raw material, of which it is the most important use. Then, for a time the increased demand just meets an unchanged supply, and the increased demand will only bring about a rise in the price of the *product*. In the first of the cases already discussed the crucial reaction of demand to an original change in the supply of a raw material could only take place when the increased final product had reached the market for consumers' goods. Similarly, now in the case of an original change in demand the immediate reaction would only concern the production of the raw material. Until the increased quantity of the raw material has passed all the stages of production, the quantity of the final product can only increase to the extent made possible by a more intensive processing of the raw materials and semi-finished products available at the individual stages. For this purpose, it will be necessary in all the stages to attract new complementary producers' goods from other branches of production; however, the increased use of these producers' goods is due to the high unit price of the final product which can be realised only temporarily. Yet, as soon as the increase in the manufacturing of raw materials induced by the rising prices has brought about increased production in all consecutive stages and the increased final product has arrived at the market for consumers' goods, at least part of the attracted complementary producers' goods becomes unusable. At this moment the price of the final product must change and this would once more change the profit opportunities of the production of raw materials. Here again the two cases must be distinguished of the elasticity of demand being greater or less than unity, and correspondingly of the total price of the increased production of consumers' goods being smaller or greater than that of the smaller quantity produced before. Again we are primarily interested in the case of an elasticity greater than unity, so that the total proceeds must fall due to the increase in supply.[18] Under this precondition the production of raw materials must be reduced again. However, as long as in the intermediate stages there are still greater quantities of products available than necessary for the reduced production of raw materials, even this cur-

---

[18] [Apparently, there is an error in this passage: The case of the elasticity of demand being *greater* than unity (that is, of elastic demand) implies the total price (proceeds) of the increased production being *greater* (and not smaller) than that of the smaller quantity produced before. Consequently, in this case of elasticity greater than unity the total proceeds must *rise* (and not fall) due to the increase in supply. Thus, the case analysed in the following is that of *inelastic* demand.—Ed.]

tailed quantity will only realise the smaller total price that corresponds to the excessive increase in the final product. This will then give rise to an excessive decline in the production of raw materials. Even if these fluctuations do not feed back on demand, the state of equilibrium will thereby be approached only slowly. Yet, naturally each of these changes in the structure of production does affect demand and thus each adjustment to demand results in a change in demand, so that in principle the state of equilibrium will never be actually attained, even if in the course of time the deviations from equilibrium will become so small as to be practically irrelevant.

The outcome of this somewhat lengthy discussion of the conditions of barter within a production process based on the division of labour is its essential similarity with the case of indirect exchange: Once there has been a change in the original data, a complete state of rest will *never* be attained. The reason is that the original data constitute only one part of the determinants of prices, while the other part consists of the results of the preceding period of exchange; the latter, however, cannot be considered as given because of the induced changes in the consecutive period. *The maintenance of equilibrium requires that all the remaining products which have not been consumed at the end of the period and therefore enter the next period as 'historical' data (and also the media of exchange left* over as proceeds from exchanges in the hands of the economic subjects) *must precisely correspond to those having been available at the beginning of the period.* Yet this means nothing more than that the state of equilibrium must already have been attained in the preceding period, and consequently if equilibrium is not attained in this period, it cannot come about in the next period. As already seen in the discussion of indirect exchange, the idea of equilibrium is strictly confined to closed economic periods, where none of the determinants of the economic process is itself the result of economic activity. This very condition can no longer be fulfilled if the same goods recurrently constitute the object of exchange (whether as goods to be processed or as media of exchange).

[For our investigation of the essential effects of the use of a medium of exchange, that is, the deviations of prices from their 'natural' formation, the insight is crucial that even in the barter economy phenomena of the same type may arise as already discussed for the use of money. Under the simple conditions assumed before all deviations from the theoretically derived direct tendency towards equilibrium were only made possible by the introduction of money. Now, in contrast, we have become familiar with disturbances to this adjustment process, which must come about—without accounting for the existence of a medium of exchange—as a consequence of any change in data and which must be taken into consideration when ascertaining the deviations brought about by money in comparison to the course of the barter economy.][19]

---

[19] [The paragraph is crossed out in the typescript.—Ed.]

4.

After the investigation of the manifold resistances to the prompt adjustment to a change in data in the case of a barter economy with a vertical division of labour our subject will be the effects of the use of money in such an economy. Then a first conjecture might be that the similar resistances already discussed as a consequence of the use of money will add to the former ones, and that the money economy with a vertical division of labour will be confronted with even greater obstacles to the attainment of equilibrium. However, this will not be the case, on the contrary, a simple consideration demonstrates that the existence of money will facilitate and shorten the adjustment of the process of production to a change in data.

In the money economy where only consumers' goods are exchanged every shift of purchasing power among the economic subjects gives rise to a change in the direction of demand because of the distinct individual preferences, consequently full equilibrium will never be attained. In the barter economy with a vertical division of labour the difficulties of adjusting the structure of production to the demand for consumers' goods derive from a different problem: Here the demand for the various means of production is not determined by the respective price of the consumers' good, but by the price realised in the immediately subsequent stage. Thus the possibility to exploit potential price differences between means of production and product is ruled out because of the incommensurability of the prices paid in terms of various goods for the products of the individual stages of production and because of the lack of capital tradable in a homogenous unit of account. In this respect matters crucially change with the introduction of money.

With the introduction of a medium of exchange, which offers the possibility of calculation by comparing the different prices, the fact will lose its significance that in the sphere of producers' goods the persons disposing of certain incomes vary. In contrast to consumers, the producers in their role as entrepreneurs direct their demand with a common goal in mind. Whoever of the producers is in the position to dispose of greater sums of money, will direct demand to one and the same location, namely where the differences in prices between products and producers' goods offer the greatest opportunities for profit. It is thus the calculation in terms of money, that is, the identity of the goal of all firms[20] created by the homogeneity of the price good in all acts of exchange, which eliminates the deviations from equilibrium; in a barter economy these deviations arise because the demand for the required means

---

[20] Cf. on this Mayer, "Untersuchung", part 1, p. 21: "The entrepreneur qua entrepreneur has only *a single homogeneous goal*: To acquire with the means at his disposal (his 'capital') the *greatest money income possible*."

of production by any producer directly depends on the prices currently realised for the respective product. In these cases in the money economy the adjustment to a change in data will thus occur even more swiftly than in a barter economy with an equally developed division of labour. This circumstance demonstrates once more the absurdity of neglecting the 'veil of money' in any explanation of the processes of the mature exchange economy, as the process described thereby would be virtually impossible without money.

There is thus a quintessential difference in the price formation of producers' goods between a barter and a money economy. In the former the means for the purchase of the product of any stage of production is given by the price currently realised for the product of the next stage, even if the product of the next stage has been manufactured from different quantities than those currently purchased. In the latter every means of production is sold in a general market where the purchasing power—which from the point of view of producers is considered as capital instead of income—is directed at those demands that offer the greatest prospects of profit, that is, where the difference between the expected price of the product and its costs is greatest. Therefore in a money economy any change in the prices of consumers' goods immediately will give rise to adjustments of demand in all stages of production to the changed prices of the final product. Similarly, any change in the profit margin of a specific branch of production, due to a change in the supply of original means of production or in the technique of production, will be exploited immediately; it is no longer necessary to wait until the expected price for the changed quantity of the consumers' good in question has ultimately been realised.

In a money economy the adjustment of the apparatus of production to a change in data encounters considerably fewer frictions than *could* be the case in a barter economy. In the money economy the prices of consumers' goods can directly affect the demand for the products of all stages of production, and even the change in the prices of consumers' goods expected consequent upon a change in the conditions of production can be anticipated in the demand for the means of production. Thereby, the exclusive dependence of the prices to be realised in any stage of production on those currently realised in the consecutive stage vanishes, and instead is replaced by the direct connection between the price of a means of production and the *expected* price of the product to be manufactured from it.

Thus the distribution of the funds of purchasing power available for the purchase of the required producers' goods automatically adjusts to any given demand for consumers' goods. Here it can only be pointed out as a brief remark that this distribution will be controlled by the rate of interest. We will turn to this issue more deeply when considering the effects of a shift in demand between consumers' and producers' goods. Before we must discuss in some detail the so-called circuit of money, from consumers' goods through all the stages of production back to consumers' goods, as most curious ideas prevail about the alleged disturbances due to changes in this circuit.

5.

From ancient times the idea of the circuit of money has played a significant role in economic theory.[21] According to this idea, in a mature exchange economy money moves in a closed circuit, leading it from consumers' goods through the various stages of production back into the hands of consumers; moreover a certain steadiness within this circuit should be preserved. Although, like all over-simplified schemes, it has perhaps caused more harm than good for the understanding of the structure of the exchange economy, it is today deeply rooted in economic thought. Therefore despite the indisputable danger of all such pictures, it might be preferable to replace it by elaborating another more suitable schematic presentation of the external order of the exchange relationships. This will be the subject of the following section before we proceed in the analysis of the crucial connections.

The main shortcoming of the common idea of the closed circuit of money[22] consists in its total neglect of the facts of the sequence of time and of the simultaneous existence of a multiplicity of circuits, which are autonomous in a certain sense. Yet, both these facts cannot be ignored once we turn to an economy where a medium of exchange is used and where production is multistage. If we look at the circuit of money of an exchange economy composed of successive acts of exchange, we must be aware that the different elements of a circuit refer to different points in time and conversely that the acts of exchange carried out simultaneously make up the parts of different circuits. Based on a graphical representation used by Lexis for the presentation of synchronised production,[23] the following diagram attempts to clarify these facts.

---

[21] In Germany this idea owes its popularity in particular to Adolph Wagner; cf. *Sozialökonomische Theorie des Geldes und Geldwesens* (Leipzig: Winter 1909), and J. J. O. Lahn, *Der Kreislauf des Geldes und Mechanismus des Sozial-Lebens* (Berlin: Puttkammer and Muehlbrecht, 1903), published pseudonymously by Wagner's disciple Nicholas A. Johannsen, who in America became well-known as a crisis theorist, as well as Ernst Wagemann, *Allgemeine Geldlehre*, vol. 1: *Theorie des Geldwertes und der Währung* (Berlin [Jena: Fischer], 1923). In the American literature the same idea plays an important role in the familiar works of Foster and Catchings; cf. in particular their *Money* and *Profits*, Publications of the Pollak Foundation, no. 8 (Boston and New York: Houghton Mifflin, 1925). On these authors' theory cf. my "Widersinn des Sparens" [translated as "The 'Paradox' of Saving"—Ed.].

[22] Cf. the interesting comments in Josef F. Feilen, *Die Umlaufsgeschwindigkeit des Geldes* (Berlin and Leipzig: de Gruyter, 1923), pp. 56ff. [pp. 56–65].

[23] Cf. Lexis, *Allgemeine Volkswirtschaftslehre*, p. 188.

We start from the fact that the process of production in every stage is not a singular event but is continuously recurring, and that each complete process of production consists of processes occurring at different points in time in the individual stages. The vertical columns depict the periodically maturing products of the individual stages of production, with the ordinate representing the time dimension and the numbers running from bottom to the top standing for the consecutive points in time. The stages of production are depicted horizontally, in the sequence from left to right. Of the five stages of production visualised, following Lexis, the first can be identified as the production of raw materials, the second as semi-finished products, the third as final products, the fourth as wholesale trade, and finally the fifth as retail trade. This example is, of course, arbitrary and neglects the fact, to be noticed immediately, that every stage of production uses not just one, but several complementary products. In the course of the production process every single good moves along the lines pointing diagonally upwards to the right from one stage of production to the next. For example, the raw material $_1P_1$ manufactured in the first period moves to the production of semi-finished goods, which it leaves at the end of the second period as $_2P_2$, in order to enter one period later as the final product $_3P_3$ the stage of wholesale trade and so on. Simultaneously with the transfer of the product of one stage of production to the next, the receiving stage must transfer the proceeds realised for the product just finished as the price paid for the new purchases of raw materials or products for the sake of processing them. The diagram depicts the path of these money payments as the dashed lines ascending from the right to the left, contrary to the movement of the goods, and thus reaching ever earlier stages with the progress of time.[24]

In observing these movements we will provisionally abstract from the prices paid for complementary goods, including labour, and concentrate on the path representing that part of the price paid for the consumable product which falls upon the raw material that is the starting point of the whole series of production processes. Then the price paid for the raw material also represents the next demand for the consumers' good. In the diagram the price paid for the raw material $_5P_1$ thus constitutes the basis of the demand for consumers' goods in the next period, and the path seemingly terminating to the left and above $_5P_1$ continues in fact with the consumers' good $_6P_5$. To take account of this fact, we would have to imagine the whole area depicted in the diagram as the rolled-up surface of a cylinder, with the money flows moving around the cylinder in an *ascending spiral*. The same is also true of the circuit of goods, as we have assumed the producer of raw materials to be the sole consumer of final products so that, for example, the flow of goods seemingly terminating

---

[24] [In the separate folder (box 105, folder 1) containing Hayek's notes there is a three-dimensional representation of this diagram, here included as fig. 1.3.—Ed.]

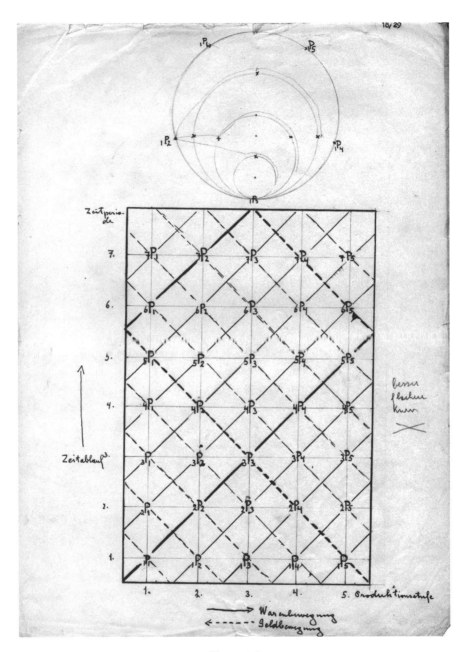

Figure 1.2

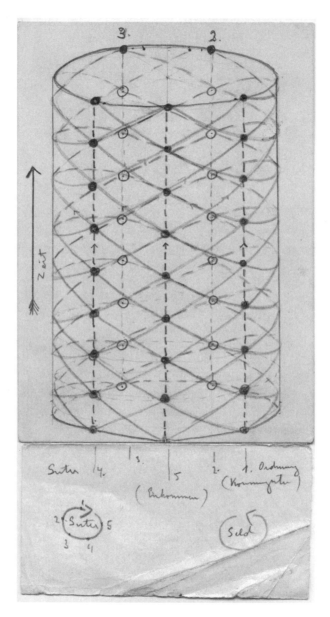

Figure 1.3

above $_5P_5$ continues to the left to $_6P_1$ and provides the starting point for a new chain of production ($_6P_1-_7P_2$ and so on).

The idea of likening the depicted circuit scheme to the rolled-up surface of a cylinder provides the opportunity to take account in our scheme of the hitherto neglected *difference in the length of the individual processes of production* (that is, the unequal number of stages of production contained in each of it) and thereby of the unequal length of the various circuits of money. Inside the cylinder representing the five-stage process of production we may imagine the surfaces of correspondingly smaller cylinders, representing processes of production with four or three or still fewer stages, and outside of it an arbitrary number of further cylindrical surfaces, representing processes with more than five stages. Furthermore, the different duration of the production process within the individual stages may be depicted by corresponding differences in the distances between the points representing the various stages, or similarly by the different steepness of the lines representing the path of goods.

The scheme will become still more complicated if we do not pursue just the path stretching from a raw material to the final product, but the manufacturing of the product from all its various constituent factors of production. The complementary goods used in every stage of production for the processing of intermediate products are as a rule themselves the result of a multi-stage process. Moreover, the complementary goods have absorbed in each of these stages of their production several other complementary goods, too. Thus, instead of the simple spiral depicted in our diagram, *every final product would constitute the end point of a whole bundle of spirals, of different length and branching out again and again,* which might thus be best compared with a river system made up of a main river and many tributaries and branches of different length.[25] [For the purpose of illustration such a bundle of spirals representing the production of *one* good is depicted in the diagram. Of course, in a similar way the circuit of the money paid for the product passing through all the stages and branches of production must be depicted.][26]

However, strictly speaking, such a depiction would still not suffice. A more or less complete diagrammatic representation of all these relations would have to take into account that original as well as produced *means of production* of almost any type will be used in the manufacturing of not just one, but of

[25] [Notably, Friedrich Wieser used an analogous simile for describing the passage of goods through succeeding stages of production: "The productive movement terminates in the household. Toward this goal the materials are carried in the current of production from one stage of development to the next, like the waters of a river flowing from one level to another towards the estuary." (*Social Economics*, p. 66)—Ed.]

[26] [The two sentences in brackets are crossed out in the typescript. Apparently this diagram is fig. 1.4, which in the typescript is on a separate page following fig. 1.2.—Ed.]

Figure 1.4

even *very many different products*. To include this in our scheme, a number of different circles of production would have to meet in every stage of production, and every stage in turn would be the starting point of spirals of different lengths and with multiple branches. The paths through which the products of a certain stage of production must pass before they have become consumable should thus be represented by such a bundle of spirals, with the spirals starting from below at a common point and branching out upwards. Both with regard to the origin and to the destination of its product every stage of production would thus constitute a point of intersection of entire bundles of spirals, which can be imagined but hardly drawn in a diagram.

Another fact to be integrated into a full account of the relationships of the circuit of production is that a great part of the means of production employed at a stage will not be immediately used up, but may serve for numerous periods, as will be typically the case for machines, tools and buildings. These *durable means of production*, or "work goods" (Wieser),[27] thus will continue to render their service even if they are not replaced to the extent of their wear and tear. Provisionally restricting our attention to the circuit of the stationary economy, the use of such durable means of production can be introduced into our scheme by assuming that the existing stock of these machines, etc., just consists of so many pieces as is the number of periods for which every machine can be used. Thus the wear and tear of the existing stock of machines can be compensated by the annual increment of just one machine.

The merit of this scheme lies in demonstrating how at every point in time price formation at current markets depends on the prices and the quantities produced in the past and how it itself influences price formation in future periods. The flows of money incomes and goods meeting each other at the market at a specific point in time are represented by the lines that a cross section will cut out from our scheme. As shown in the simplified depiction of such a cross section in fig. 1.2, it comprises all the elements of a complete process of production. Thus it conforms precisely to the picture of the simultaneous operation of all the single processes as sketched by elementary theory. However, in our view it is essential to notice that this scheme shows that the products and the money proceeds of all the different stages of production simultaneously coming to the market belong to quite different circuits. Thus at a given point in time goods of the different stages, each belonging to a different production chain, confront at the market a sum of money expenditure, composed in turn of money flows of the same number and in different phases of their circuit. In a perfectly stationary economy each of these money flows will be composed of elements, which strictly correspond to the elements of the money flows currently in a different phase; and similarly, each of the goods at the market belongs to a chain of production such that its preceding and subsequent elements are identical to the products coming currently to the market from the different stages of the same process of production. Accordingly, the course of such a stationary economy will not differ from that of the hypothetical barter economy considered earlier. For the purely static part of the analysis there are no new insights to be gained from this scheme, except that it points to the immense intricacy of the relations that must be taken into account in examining the reactions to disturbances of equilibrium.

[27] [Wieser introduced the term "work goods" (*Werkgüter*) for denoting capital goods that are part of fixed capital in his *Theorie der gesellschaftlichen Wirtschaft*, pp. 50–51; cf. *Social Economics*, pp. 66–67.—Ed.]

6.

This depiction of the external course of the circuits of money and production does not contribute much to their explanation. Rather, it necessarily just stops short where the very theoretical task begins, namely the explanation of the circumstances which determine the course of the specific circuit. Nevertheless it appears to me that the improved depiction of this external course is an essential means for avoiding the various fallacies and misconceptions, which are facilitated by the usual, overly simplified idea of the 'circuit'. For the scheme as developed above highlights the fact that into every market enter the flows of a very great number of various 'circuits' in their different phases and that equilibrium tends to be established among all the acts of exchange, which constitute the elements of these 'circuits'. This insight will to a large extent safeguard against the common error of regarding the orbits of this circuit as more or less constants, that is, as independent of current price formation. For the flow of money is not bound to follow a fixed circuit through the stages of production, although this idea is much furthered by considering a *closed* circuit; rather at any time the circuit may branch off, because its movement is guided by prices and any price change will change its course. Indeed, this crucial insight just constitutes the onset of all economic problems.

Thus, the relations depicted in this scheme become interesting only when we start asking about the causes which determine the orbits of the flows of money and goods and consider the consequences to which a change in these determinants will give rise.

At first, these examinations of the determinants of the circuit of money will serve to refute an erroneous, yet common view. According to this view, at some point the money flow might become deficient for ensuring the sale of all the products coming to market, or spontaneous shifts of demand among the various stages of production might even give rise to increases or decreases in production not based on the relation between the supply of means of production and the demand for consumers' goods. The falsity of this view becomes evident when we turn to the market where at every point in time the prices are formed that determine the future course of the flows of money and goods. This market is to be regarded as a cross section of our cylinder, and it comprehends in a synchronised mode the complete process of production, that is, the products of all stages of production. Therefore, in these markets the products of all these stages compete for every sum of money that is part of any circuit, and conversely the proceeds from the products of all the stages of production may be used for purchasing products of any stage. Although presumed all too easily by the overly simplified notions of the circuit, there is no such thing as a money flow that must pass—on a fixed route—the various stages of production one after another, so that if the flow increases at a specific place the corresponding increase in demand could reach the higher stages only successively. Rather, every swelling of some of the many circuits running in parallel will, at any stage that it encounters, branch off into other circuits. According to current market conditions and price expectations the money flow will leap quite freely into other circuits. Hence, the fact that today the demand for consumers' goods has increased by additional amounts of money does not mean that tomorrow only the demand for goods of the second order, the following day only that for goods of the third order, and so on back to the original means of production, will increase temporarily.[28]

Rather, the increase in the proceeds from certain consumers' goods will cause, already in the next period of production, the demand for all the means of production from which it is manufactured to rise in due proportion. This comes about not only because the higher proceeds from the sale of these consumers' goods will be evenly spread to all earlier stages of production, but also because the improved profit opportunities in this branch of production will attract sums used before in other circuits. Taking for the moment the proportion between the demand for consumers' goods and for means of production as fixed, then demand will distribute itself among the different stages of every branch of production so that it corresponds in each stage to the expected price of the very share of the final product imputed to the contribution of the means of production of this stage. Thus, if presently the *quantity* of means of production assigned to this stage is less than that corresponding to the saleable quantity of the final product, the unit price of this means of production will rise above the equilibrium price and induce its disposal at a greater quantity; conversely, if too great a quantity of the means of production in question is assigned to a stage, then its price will decline and induce a decrease in its production. In the same way every change in the expected price of the final product will redistribute demand among the various branches of production.

Hence, that part of the whole money flow coming to the market that is devoted not for purposes of consumption but for continuing production will be distributed automatically to the various stages of production in such a way as to guarantee that at the expected product prices the whole product can be sold at prices covering costs. [On another occasion[29] I have demonstrated with regard to the well-known theories of Foster and Catchings that the above result is possible for any arbitrary relation between the demand for consumers' and producers' goods provided this relation is determined by the proportion between real demand and real supply, and not by amounts of money entering or disappearing from the circuit. There cannot be any doubt that within the sphere of production the circuit cannot be considered as a given fact indepen-

---

[28] [The marginal note attached here is illegible.—Ed.]
[29] Cf. Hayek, "Widersinn des Sparens".

dent of prices, but on the contrary the course of the circuit will be fully determined by them. Whether the money flows follow their previous orbits or not, will thus depend on whether they are confronted with precisely the same structure of production as before, that is, with the same quantities of goods assigned to the various stages and branches of production, or not.][30] Here the movements of the money flow are thus never the cause of price changes, but always the effect of preceding changes in the relation between the supply of means of production (including changes in their technical usability) and changes in the direction of the demand for consumers' goods.[31] A glut in some stages of production can therefore only originate from disturbances in the structure of production so that the necessary price relations (conforming to the technical relations[32]) among the goods of the various stages of production cannot be established; yet, the origin will never lie in a deficiency of the money flow available for the purchases of the products of this stage of production.[33]

However, there is a more serious problem than this naïve idea of the harm due to 'rambling money flows', namely that of the effects of real changes in data on the monetary price system of higher order. Indeed, it has been demonstrated above that due to the existence of money certain difficulties discussed earlier on disappear, in particular now the demand for goods of every stage of production *directly* depends on the demand for final products. Yet, the fact remains that the physical effects of a change in some stage of production will reach the subsequent stages only successively, and as long as this is the case, the economy cannot exhibit a stable equilibrium and therefore the auxiliary construction of the synchronisation of all processes cannot be utilised. As our earlier scheme had shown the meaning and significance of this auxiliary construction, its inapplicability makes the crucial difference for the dynamic problem to which we will turn now from the relationship on which the static approach was based. In contrast, under dynamic conditions the products and money proceeds of all the phases of a production process simultaneously coming to the market will not always correspond to the respective earlier phases of the chains of production, and thus the fiction of synchronisation will lose its meaning. Moreover, production guided by the current prices of all

[30] [The passage in brackets is crossed out in the typescript.—Ed.]

[31] [This passage, which is difficult to comprehend, might be due to a slip of the pen. Possibly the words "the relation between" should be deleted.—Ed.]

[32] See above, p. [94—Ed.].

[33] As the cause of a glut can never be found in the deficiency of the money flow but only in the real structure of production (which, however, in turn may be determined by money in a way to be analysed below), this cause of a glut cannot be eliminated by an addition to the volume of money or any other increase in the money flow. Cf. on this my paper "Widersinn des Sparens", already cited above. [With regard to terminology, in the following '(general) glut' stands for the slightly old-fashioned *(allgemeine) Absatzstockung*, while the simpler *Überproduktion* has been translated as 'overproduction'.—Ed.]

the other stages of production cannot guarantee that the quantities of goods presently sold will continue to find a purchaser at unchanged prices without new changes in data. When after a change in demand or supply the prices in the various stages of production change, these price changes do not yet ultimately determine whether in the future it is possible to sell the same quantities of the means of production. Rather, this decision must again be postponed until the changed volume of production has affected the supply of consumers' goods. Consequently, when deciding upon the quantities to be produced, producers must look for guidance not only at currently prevailing prices, but primarily at expected price changes, the extent of which they cannot assess with certainty. Their search for such guidance becomes still more difficult as they can form expectations about future prices only on the basis of current prices. Yet, during the transition to a new equilibrium the relative height of current prices may prove deceptive as during this transition phase the relation among the various prices must necessarily be in disequilibrium;[34] in particular, the relation between the prices of means of production and of the products manufactured from them will diverge from the relation of their technical transformation, and thus cannot be maintained. Of course, the producers are aware that such differences between the prices of products and means of production cannot be maintained, yet their decisions about the volume of future production will differ according to whether they expect the eventual adjustment to be brought about by a change in product prices[35] or by a change in the prices of means of production. For example, the cheapening of production and respective increase in the supply of some means of production will in the first instance lead to a strong decline in its price; yet after the due increase in the final product it will turn out that either its price falls to such an extent that production must be curtailed again or conversely its price remains at a value sufficient even to make a further increase possible.

Even with a monetary organisation of exchange the principal difficulties for an instantaneous adjustment to changes in data persist; these are due to the vertical division of labour and consequently to the non-uniform dependence of the various prices one on another. Here the prices are not formed uniformly, as in a single row; rather the prices of products of consecutive stages of production are differently, and more closely, related to each other than the prices of the products of the same order belonging to different branches of production. Therefore a state of equilibrium will not be attained automatically and instantaneously, as the prices formed in the various stages of production may affect the volume of production in these stages in a way ultimately not justified by possible sales. The view that the automatic and instantaneous

[34] [Hayek uses the English term 'disequilibrium' in the German text.—Ed.]
[35] [In the typescript the phrase reads, "change in product", an apparent typing error.—Ed.]

attainment of a state of equilibrium among all prices would guarantee the sale of all goods coming to the market is of utmost importance because it also forms the basis of Say's famous law of markets.[36] It is well-known that this theorem, which may be regarded the first formulation of the modern idea of equilibrium, denies the possibility of a general glut and up to now has not been refuted in this regard. Nevertheless it would be premature to conclude from the above arguments, as has often been done,[37] that Say's theorem is only valid for the barter economy, but loses its applicability as soon as the goods coming to the market, instead of being exchanged directly one against another, are exchanged against money. We will postpone the discussion of the significance of Say's theorem and the actual limits of its validity until we have examined more closely the effects of shifts between the demand for consumers' goods and for means of production. However, as long as we disregard temporary disturbances of this proportion and thus take the relative magnitude of the demand for means of production as given, it is easy to show that the difficulties of adjustment to a change in data mentioned above may well lead to partial gluts, but will never be the cause of a general glut comprehending almost all branches of production.

Let us then assume that the relative magnitude of the volume of money available for the purchase of means of production is permanently fixed and given, or at least that it does not change suddenly but only continuously and steadily in one direction. Then, in this case, the changes in the relative assignments of goods to the various stages of production and thus the adjustment to changes in price expectations are limited in a way that general overproduction caused by erroneous price expectations will be impossible. For the scarcity of the 'fund of capital' available to be invested in the various stages of production will make itself felt by restricting investment to those productions that promise the highest return, and thus this scarcity will be enforced by the level of the rate of interest and the corresponding relation between the prices of consumers' goods and of means of production. [Thus suppose the case of an erroneous expectation of a general rise in prices (that is, not just a rise in the prices of all the products of a single branch of production, which in any

---

[36] [Jean-Baptiste Say (1776–1832) defended, against contemporary theories of underconsumption, the thesis of the impossibility of general overproduction with the argument that goods will only be exchanged against goods and thus the total supply of goods must equal the total demand for goods. This is the main idea of Say's famous *Théorie des débouchés* (or 'Law of Markets'). Cf. Jean-Baptiste Say, *Traité d'économie politique*, 1803, translated from the fourth edition (1819) as *A Treatise on Political Economy* (Philadelphia: Claxton, Remsen, and Haggelfinger, 1880; reprinted, New York: Kelley, 1971, and New Brunswick: Transactions, 2001).—Ed.]

[37] Cf. most recently in particular Rudolf Stucken, *Theorie der Konjunkturschwankungen* (Jena: Fischer, 1926), pp. 4ff. [pp. 4–6], and Leonard Miksch, *Gibt es eine allgemeine Überproduktion?* (Jena: Fischer, 1929).

case could only give rise to a *partial* overproduction) or an erroneous expectation that despite an increase in all or most final products their prices will not change, although in view of the income stream available for the purchase of these final products their prices must remain stable or fall, respectively. Even in these cases misguided expectations will not cause an excessive expansion of production in the higher stages of all branches of production, because the competition for the limited supply of money capital will drive up the rate of interest to the level where only production that promises the highest yield relative to the amount of capital needed will appear profitable.][38] Under the conditions assumed the consequence of these erroneous price expectations can only be that in *some* branches of production too many means of production will be assigned to the higher stages so that sales at prices covering costs will become impossible. Yet, there can never result an excessive expansion of the production of producers' goods in general or as a consequence a general discrepancy between the prices of products and of means of production.

7.

It is worthwhile to pursue more closely the connection between the relative magnitude of the demand for consumers' and producers' goods and the structure of production, although the ultimate solution of this question would only be possible within the framework of a fully developed theory of interest, which is out of the question here. It is best to start by turning to the effect of the investment of new savings, that is, the case that the demand for producers' goods increases at the expense of the demand for consumers' goods.[39] The proposition that new saving can only bring about an increase in the volume of production by enabling a greater and more productive 'roundaboutness' in the methods of production has been demonstrated so fully by the classical analysis of Böhm-Bawerk that it does not require further examination. It is only necessary here to go further into certain monetary aspects of the phenomenon.[40]

[38] [The passage in brackets is crossed out in the typescript.—Ed.]

[39] [The next two sentences are taken from "Widersinn des Sparens", p. 405 (cf. "The 'Paradox' of Saving", reprinted, p. 94).—Ed.]

[40] The following up to the end of the paragraph [that is, of section 7—Ed.] is taken almost literally from my article "Widersinn des Sparens", where I go into more details with regard to various special types of capital formation. On the question whether the value of the raw materials, semi-finished goods and other means of production, coming to the market in every period, can exceed the value of the consumers' goods, coming to the market at the same time, I should add that its erroneous denial dates back at least to Adam Smith. Cf. "The value of the goods circulated between the different dealers never can exceed the value of those circulated between the dealers and [the] consumers; whatever is bought [by the dealers] being ultimately destined to be sold to the consumers . . . Though the annual purchases of all the consumers, therefore, are

The questions which interest us are as follows: how does the increase in the money flow *available for productive purposes* following the investment of new savings distribute the additional demand for means of production through the economic circuit, and under what conditions is this distribution effected in such a way as to achieve the purpose of saving with the smallest possible disturbance? For the sake of simplicity, we may assume that the path from the original means of production to the final product is of equal length for all factors of production, although, in fact, this differs for the particular original means of production according to the stages of production where they are employed; so that the assumed uniform length of the roundabout ways of production only corresponds to the average length of the various processes which lead to the production of a consumers' good. We assume, therefore, that, for example, the value of all means of production coming to the market during one period is eight times as great as the value of the consumers' good produced during the same period, and the latter is sold for 1,000 units of money. We disregard the differences in value conditioned by interest, that is to say, we make the assumption that interest on capital employed, together with the remuneration of the original means of production, is paid out only in the highest stage of production. The whole process of production and the circuit of money connected with it can then be represented schematically in the following way:[41]

[. . .]

The way in which the movement of prices will effect this adjustment on the shortest possible path given that the volume of money remains unchanged has been investigated in my essay "Gibt es einen 'Widersinn des Sparens'?", already mentioned several times. Here we are mainly interested in the question how the same process would evolve, if the volume of money did not

---

at least equal in value to those of all [the] dealers, they can generally be transacted with a much smaller quantity of money; the same pieces of money, by a more rapid circulation, serving as the instrument of many more purchases of the one kind than of the other" (*An Inquiry into the Nature and Causes of the Wealth of Nations* [1776] (London: Routledge, 1903), book 2, chapter 2, paragraph 88, p. 247. [For a slightly different version of this passage cf. *The Glasgow Edition of the Works and Correspondence of Adam Smith*, vol. 1, ed. R. H. Campbell and A. S. Skinner (Oxford: Oxford University Press, 1976; reprinted, Indianapolis: Liberty Press, 1981), p. 322. See *Prices and Production*, reprinted, pp. 226–27, for a discussion of the same passage.—Ed.]

[41] [This paragraph has been cut out from "Widersinn des Sparens", p. 406, and pasted into the typescript. (The translation follows "The 'Paradox' of Saving", reprinted, pp. 94–95, with some slight modifications, which are due to the fact that the translation was based on a revised version of the German article.) The schematic representation, which is missing from the typescript, refers to "Scheme A" ("Widersinn des Sparens", p. 406; cf. "The 'Paradox' of Saving", reprinted, p. 96). Apparently, the remainder of the section was planned to follow this article closely, yet with the exception of the next two paragraphs has not been preserved in the typescript. According to the pagination at this point five pages are missing.—Ed.]

remain constant, but, as actually happens as a rule, the increase in production initiated an increase in money. For this end we assume that, just like in Scheme B,[42] the relation of the demand for consumers' goods to the demand for means of production changed from 1,000:8,000 to 900:8,100, or from 1:8 to 1:9, so that the number of stages increased correspondingly from 9 to 10. Now let us assume that at the moment when the enlarged product comes on to the market, the volume of money is increased, for example, by 100 units. For the time being we assume that this additional sum is spent exclusively on consumers' goods and we will later on compare this with the case when they are spent on producers' goods.

Because of this, the demand for consumers' goods again increases from 900 to 1,000, while the sums available for means of production remain unchanged, so that the relation between the demand for the two groups of goods changes from 900:8,100 to 1,000:8,100, that is the relative size of the demand for means of production in comparison with the demand for consumers' goods falls from 9 times to 8.1 times the latter. The transformation of production conditioned by this, in the form of a shortening of the roundabout methods of production, comes about in the manner presented in Scheme C, as the number of stages of production, under our assumption of an equal distribution among stages, must then be 8.1 [   ][43]

8.

The process of readjustment of the structure of production generated by every shift between the demand for consumers' and producers' goods is directly induced by a shift in the price relations between these goods so that alternative methods of production become profitable. Such shifts of demand, as far as indeed *shifts* of demand are concerned, and not the appearance of additional, unfounded demand, will not disturb the general equilibrium[44] between demand and supply. Yet, it must not be ignored that such shifts of demand, and as a consequence of prices, among *stages* of production are principally

[42] ["Scheme B" refers to the corresponding table in "Widersinn des Sparens", p. 408 (cf. "The 'Paradox' of Saving", reprinted, p. 97), which depicts the case of an increase in saving. From here on the text follows again "Widersinn des Sparens", p. 423 (cf. "The 'Paradox' of Saving", reprinted, p. 114).—Ed.]

[43] [The last two paragraphs are from a single page of the typescript, the only surviving one of the remainder of this section. The second of these two paragraphs again has been cut out from "Widersinn des Sparens", p. 423 (cf. "The 'Paradox' of Saving", reprinted, p. 114) and pasted into the typescript. The text breaks off with a page break.—Ed.]

[44] ['General equilibrium' is the literal translation of the German text; yet from the context it seems plausible that what Hayek had in mind was 'aggregate equilibrium', that is, equilibrium between the aggregates of demand and supply.—Ed.]

of a different significance than the same shifts among *branches* of production. While shifts of prices of the latter type already account for the ultimate decision about the possibility of selling the products of the respective branch of production, shifts of prices of the former type will succeed in their effect on the methods of production only if the ultimately realised price of the final product coincides with the expected price. As a rule this can and will be the case if the cause of the shift of demand is 'real', but not if it is generated by an increase in the volume of money, because then, as has been shown, sooner or later a tendency to re-establish the earlier state[45] will prevail. Indeed, in the latter case a shift of demand may change the relative weight of the various stages in all branches of production in such a way that the available means of production cannot be employed in their entirety, that is, give rise to a general glut. Below we will discuss the relationship between this insight and Say's famous theorem, to which it stands in a certain opposition. Before that, however, we will investigate how far such price shifts among stages of production may also result from *original* changes in the supply of the means of production, that is, without a change in the demand for consumers' goods in its relation to the demand for means of production, brought about by consumers themselves or 'externally' by the appearance of new purchasing power.

Apart from these two cases[46] a change in the relation between demand and supply, and thereby in the relative height of the prices, in the various stages of production can result only from two causes: either changes in the physical quantity or quality of the existing means of production, which also includes the case of inventions or discoveries making such new quantities or qualities accessible, or changes in the valuation of the existing means of production, and thereby also in the demand directed at their replacement. Indeed, the latter case can never be regarded an original change, but rather the consequence of one of the already mentioned types of initiating changes. Nevertheless, it must be treated here separately, because it covers a series of essentially similar phenomena[47] which although happening in the sphere of production are characterised by shifts in demand as well as supply. To see this more clearly, it is advisable to analyse more precisely the demand for producers' goods, which up to now has been just confronted with the demand for consumers' goods. There are three main components to be distinguished, first, proceeds from circulating capital turned over, second, earned amortisation quotas of fixed capital, where in both cases the amounts available for new investments depend on the realisation of certain prices for goods already produced, and finally, new savings to be invested for the first time, possibly augmented by a

---

[45] [That is, the earlier state of equilibrium.—Ed.]

[46] [That is, the changes in the demand for consumers' goods referred to in the last sentence of the preceding paragraph.—Ed.]

[47] [In the typescript a word is missing after "similar"; "phenomena" is a conjecture.—Ed.]

fourth item, the additional producer credits already mentioned. This demand for means of production is confronted, on the one hand, by the steady flow of services of the original means of production (the services of labour and land) and, on the other hand, by the existing stock of produced means of production to be used up in the shorter or longer term.[48]

Starting with the changes originating from the supply side and neglecting in this regard the practically less important cases of the accidental destructions of already existing produced means of production by natural disasters etc., then the following two types of supply changes will be considered: either the physical quantity of the supply of one or several original means of production changes or due to technical progress the usability and thereby the economically relevant quality of original or produced means of production improves. If, for the sake of simplicity of the presentation, we restrict our attention to increases of supply, then as an immediate effect the price of the product of the stage of production in question will fall. The extent of this price fall, and in particular whether the price fall is so strong that the whole proceeds realised for the increased quantity will decrease—that is, whether demand will turn out as elastic or inelastic—depends at first on the expected and ultimately on the realised changes in the price of the final product. However, the quantity of this final product can only increase at a later point in time. As long as the increase in production has not affected all stages of production, neither will there be equilibrium between the prices of the means of production and the final product, nor will the auxiliary construction of synchronisation be applicable to the structure of production. Consequently, the existing price relations will provide no proper guide, neither for the producers of the branch of production in question—who perhaps are able to predict the effect on the price of the final product—nor also for all other economic subjects.

Apart from its influence on the demand for the products of the various stages of production concerned, such an original change in the supply of the means of production will also shift, as a whole, the relative value[49] of the supply of means of production and of the supply of consumers' goods. This

---

[48] This distinction, here undertaken for a different purpose, may perhaps help in clarifying both the term 'supply of capital', so important for the explanation of the rate of interest, and the meaning of capital as a value and capital as a quantity, dealt with as opposing notions in the literature. Accordingly, applying the above idea, the supply of capital relevant for the determination of the rate of interest would be identified as the amount available at a time for new investment, composed as described in the text; it would thus be ascertained only in value terms and in relation to the magnitude of the demand for consumers' goods. The supply is confronted by the existing stock of produced means of production, which determines the possibilities for use and therefore the *demand* for capital; the magnitude and composition of this stock, jointly with the magnitude of the demand for consumers' goods determines the yields to be achieved. (Cf. also my book, *Geldtheorie und Konjunkturtheorie*, pp. 123ff. [pp. 123–24; cf. *Monetary Theory and the Trade Cycle*, reprinted, pp. 150–51.—Ed.])

[49] [The German typescript reads, unintelligibly, "in the relative value".—Ed.]

can generate a discrepancy between, on the one hand, the relation of the demand for consumers' goods to that for means of production and, on the other hand, the relation of the supply of consumers' goods to that of means of production, thus giving rise to further shifts in the structure of production.

Certainly the 'replacement capital' available for reinvestment is incomparably more important in volume than the savings destined for new investment, and therefore the demand for means of production depends very strongly on changes in the valuation (and respectively the yield) of the existing capital goods. Nevertheless, even without any changes in the volume of saving, it is possible or even probable that in value terms the relation between the supply of means of production and of consumers' goods will shift differently from the relation between the demand for means of production and for consumers' goods. This is related to the fact that the value of the existing means of production can change due to technical-physical changes of the type already mentioned. Consequently, the actually earned amortisation quotas available for reinvestment will change, too, yet as the owners of the means of production—encouraged by the methods of bookkeeping—strive for the maintenance of the *originally* invested capital, they will react not by changes in their expenses for the maintenance of capital, but rather with increases or decreases in their consumption. (For this reason we will in general expect that the reaction of the demand for means of production to changes in the income stream as a whole differs in its extent depending on whether this demand is mainly based on replacement capital or on new savings. In the first case the quest for maintaining capital values might take precedence over consumption, while in the second case the endeavour for a steady provision of consumers' goods might be stronger, so that savings represent that part of the surplus more prone to strong fluctuations.)

To correctly acknowledge the significance that inventions and discoveries possibly may give rise to different changes in the value of the supply of means of production, on the one hand, and in the value of the demand for means of production, on the other hand, we have to consider the resulting increase of the productive forces available. For this increase in productive forces may not always bring about an increase, but a decrease as well, in the relative value of the supply of means of production (compared with the supply of consumers' goods). One reason is that inventions—as has been emphasised by Sidgwick[50] and Cannan[51]—will not always induce a lengthening, but possibly also

---

[50] Henry Sidgwick, *The Principles of Political Economy*, 1st ed. (London: Macmillan, 1883), p. 158, 3rd ed. (1901) [reprinted, Bristol: Thoemmes Press, 1996], p. 176 [pp. 159–60]. [Henry Sidgwick (1838–1900), Cambridge economist and philosopher, in his synthesis of classical and utilitarian thought foreshadowed to some extent the accomplishments of Alfred Marshall.—Ed.]

[51] Edwin Cannan, *Wealth: A Brief Explanation of the Causes of Economic Welfare*, 1st ed. (London: King, 1914), pp. 135ff. [pp. 135–36], 3rd ed. (1928) [reprinted as vol. 5 of *The Collected Works of Edwin Cannan* (London: Routledge and Thoemmes Press, 1997)—Ed.], pp. 138ff. [pp. 138–39],

a shortening, of the roundaboutness of the efficient methods of production, so that in the latter case the relative value of the quantity of means of production necessary to produce a certain quantity of consumers' goods may decrease.[52] Yet, this outcome may also be brought about just[53] because, for example, an increase in the usable forces of nature relative to the quantity of the existing produced means of production will as a rule (that is, if the demand for these forces of nature is elastic) lead to an increase in the incomes thereby realised and thus in the demand for consumers' goods.

If as a consequence of such a change the relative magnitude of the demand for producers' goods exceeds the relative magnitude of the supply of the means of production,[54] this must, of course, result first in an increase in real capital and then, due to this increase, in a rise in the production of consumers' goods. If saving had brought about such an increase in real capital, then (due to this saving) a temporary contraction, combined with a fall in prices, would have preceded the rise in the supply of consumers' goods. In contrast, here neither such a temporary contraction nor a fall in prices of consumers' goods will happen, so that the increase in production will be guided by the still unchanged prices of consumers' goods. As a possible consequence the expansion of production may first proceed without the required lengthening in the roundaboutness of production, and only the fall in prices due to the increase in the supply of consumers' goods will necessitate the choice of more roundabout methods of production.

9.

The preceding sections have described the specific structure of the 'price system of higher order', that is, the complete price system of a structure of production based on a vertical division of labour. This will turn out of crucial significance for one of the most contested problems of economics, the correctness or not of the famous 'law of markets' of J. B. Say and James Mill.[55] The

---

and recently more detailed in *A Review of Economic Theory* (London: King and Son, 1929) [reprinted as vol. 8 of *The Collected Works of Edwin Cannan*—Ed.], pp. 262ff. [pp. 262–65].

[52] [This corresponds to the notion of 'capital-saving' technical progress, which for a given structure of production decreases the marginal product of capital relative to that of labour. For this classification cf. John Richard Hicks, *The Theory of Wages* (London: Macmillan, 1932; 2nd ed., 1963], pp. 121–25.—Ed.]

[53] [That is, without any reference to the structure of production.—Ed.]

[54] [Hayek's somewhat unfortunate formulation ought to be read as, "If . . . the relation of the demand for producers' goods to that for consumers' goods exceeds the relation of the supply of producers' goods to that of consumers' goods . . ."—Ed.]

[55] On the question of the origin of this theory cf. now in particular Jacob H. Hollander's "Editor's Introduction" to David Ricardo's *Notes on Malthus' "Principles of Political Economy"*, ed. Jacob H. Hollander and Theodore E. Gregory (Baltimore: Johns Hopkins Press; London: Ox-

correctness of this doctrine of the impossibility of general overproduction is directly evident for a linear price system, that is, in the case that only consumers' goods are exchanged and the mutual dependency of all prices is principally of the same type. Yet, on the contrary, its validity appears to me very restricted, once closer relationships within the price system are exhibited of a type, such that the *possibility to sell* a certain (producers') good is conditioned on the product manufactured from it realising a *certain* price. Now there are certain goods (and services of these goods) that can only be sold at all, that is, at any arbitrary price, if the goods which can be manufactured from them realise a certain minimum price; therefore, unlike the pure consumers' goods market, there is a necessity that certain price relations are realised.

As this problem is of fundamental importance for the theory of the trade cycle, although most adherents to the—in my view principally correct—monetary approaches have taken an all too easy way out,[56] it must be treated here in some detail. For inasmuch as the various authors attempted to identify money as the cause of general gluts, they have done so almost exclusively in the extremely simplified form of trying to show that for one or other reason the volume of money will become deficient for purchasing the goods supplied at given prices, and thus will cause a slump in prices. Even if correct, such an explanation of a price fall would not solve the crucial problem of the theory of the trade cycle. For this main problem does not consist in the fact of a one-time fall in prices, but rather in the question owing to what circumstances the evolution of the economy will, in the absence of external disturbances, recurrently lead to a situation where for some time a great part of the existing producers' goods and the services of labour cannot be sold. These general gluts, not solely crises or industrial fluctuations as such, constitute the central theoretical problem, which cannot be solved by assuming a discrepancy between the supply of goods and the volume of money, that is, general overproduction in relation to the existing volume of money. The crucial problem is how it can happen that it becomes unprofitable to maintain production, and thus that producers' goods become unusable, which cannot be explained by too low an absolute level of all prices, but rather always only by a shift in the relative height of the various prices. In this regard, for the time being we neglect the role of payments to be effected periodically in amounts fixed in terms of money, the significance of which must be examined separately. Then we have to look for the crucial cause not in the general movement of all prices, but in

---

ford University Press, 1928); on the German literature cf. the fine work by Miksch, *Gibt es eine allgemeine Überproduktion?*

[56] Cf. besides Miksch, *Gibt es eine allgemeine Überproduktion?*, already cited, my review of this book in *Zeitschrift für Nationalökonomie*, vol. 1, January 1930, pp. 625–26, as well as Stucken, *Theorie der Konjunkturschwankungen*, and finally the theory of Foster and Catchings, repeatedly cited, and my critique of it in "Widersinn des Sparens".

the well-known fact that such a 'general' movement never concerns all prices uniformly, but always results in specific relative shifts of prices, which are the reason why some branches of production become unprofitable.

Of course, for a theoretical explanation it would not suffice to ascertain empirically that indeed the prices of the means of production fall later and more slowly than the prices of consumers' goods (supposing that this would be the case at all), and thus to explain the lack of profitability of the branches of production in question by pointing to this fact of experience. Rather, it is necessary to explain *why* certain shifts within the price system will occur regularly. The indispensability of such a procedure in this case becomes obvious by acknowledging the deficiency of the usual distinction between the prices of consumers' goods and of the means of production, which in most observations of facts is the only one taken into account. Yet, it neither suffices for explaining those shifts in the price system which bring about general gluts, nor is the initiating cause always a decrease in the volume of money available for the purchase of consumers' goods, as presumed by naïve monetary explanations.

Obviously, a general glut can only come about when the prices realised for the products are not sufficient to cover the costs of production and beyond that to ensure a profit. Yet it remains undecided, whether this shift in relation to the earlier state, where production had been profitable, comes about by a fall in product prices or a rise of all (or certain) prices of the means of production. The observations at the upper turning point militate against the first assumption, while the experience that the fall in the prices of the means of production usually precedes the fall in product prices cannot be easily accommodated with the second assumption, as apparently this should quickly re-establish the profitability of production. Yet, a more detailed analysis of the changes in the apparatus of production associated with an expansion in the equipment of the means of production generated by an increase in the volume of money,[57] makes it possible to overcome these difficulties and at once points out the limits of Say's theorem.

Now the changes in the structure of production, analysed in its most general outline in the section mentioned above, shall be examined by focusing in more detail on the changes in the use and in the prices of the goods of various types. For the understanding of the relationships in question it is of fundamental importance that the means of production available for making up the apparatus of production can be distinguished in the following respect: One part of these means of production can only be used in certain stages of production, and thus will become usable at all only when the structure of production has reached a degree of capital intensity which encompasses these stages (to this type belong in particular certain machines, semi-finished goods etc.). Yet an-

[57] See section 7 above.

other part (in particular raw materials and labour) are usable in many or even in all stages of production and according to the degree of capital intensity will be used in greater quantities in the lower or in the higher stages of production. Perhaps these two main types of means of production can most effectively be classified by following Wieser,[58] who in this regard denoted capital goods as specific or versatile (with respect to their use in various stages of production). (Our use of the word "capital goods" instead of Wieser's "means of production"[59] shall signify that here the distinction refers to the different importance of these goods in the capitalistic structure of production, that is, their usability in only few or in many stages within this structure.)[60]

If the demand for means of production rises relative to the demand for consumers' goods, then the restructuring of production necessitated by this rise can only be accomplished by transferring some of the means of production usable in different stages from lower to higher stages; in the higher stages they will be employed in the manufacturing of intermediate products which mostly cannot be used in lower stages. Prerequisite for such a shift is a *decrease* in the price margin between products and means of production, which is equivalent to a fall in the rate of interest. These decreases in the price margin will always result from a relative increase in the demand for means of production, either—in the case, here discussed, of an increase in the demand for means of production due to an increase of money—by an absolute rise in the prices of the means of production, or—in the case of a rise in the demand for means of production due to saving—by an absolute fall in product prices.[61]

---

[58] Wieser, *Theorie der gesellschaftlichen Wirtschaft*, pp. 61ff. [pp. 61–64; cf. *Social Economics*, pp. 81–85—Ed.].

[59] [Or "productive means", as translated in *Social Economics*, p. 81.—Ed.]

[60] Here we can only touch the extremely important problem of the shifts within the price system as a whole that are brought about by every transition to more capital-intensive methods of production. Yet, it should be noted as strange indeed that this question, of utmost significance for any detailed explanation of the trade cycle, has not been investigated hitherto at all. Such an investigation might offer a theoretical foundation for a classification of prices according to their behaviour during the course of the cycle. This would afford the possibility to business cycle research to replace the notion, by no ways clear or unequivocal, of goods of different price sensitivity or the quite superficial distinction between raw materials and manufactured goods by a more relevant one.

[61] At first glance, it might not be evident why a decrease in that price difference and the associated fall in the rate of interest should induce *not only* the adoption of longer processes of production *beside* the presently existing ones, which are more productive per unit of time, but shall result in means of production being pulled out of the shorter, per unit of time more profitable processes and transferred into the seemingly less profitable ones or, for short, that the longer *replace* the shorter processes. Thus, in the course of such an expansion of capitalistic production the longer, yet per unit of time less profitable methods of roundabout production will be adopted not beside, but instead of the shorter, yet per unit of time more profitable methods. This is so because the absolute yield (coupled with a lower yield per unit of time) of the longer

This price movement, resulting from every shift between the demand for consumers' goods and for means of production, can best be clarified by the picture of an opening and closing fan, the sticks of which correspond to the different stages of production and the respective distance between them to the price differences between the goods of these stages. A relative increase in the demand for means of production (that is, the transition to more capital-intensive production) and the consequent rise in the prices of the means of production would then correspond to the closing of the fan, a relative increase in the demand for consumers' goods to the opening of the fan, the width of which would also represent the respective level of the rate of interest. Moreover, every such movement of prices must be associated with a change in the quantitative distribution of the means of production among the different stages. Thus when the price fan closes, a greater part of the means of production usable in numerous stages of production will be redirected towards the higher stages (the lower sticks of the fan); thereby the process of production will be expanded to a greater number of stages, that is, relocated towards the outside edge of the fan. The opening of the fan (an increase in the price differences) must in contrast mean a redirection of the versatile means of production towards the lower stages of production (the upper sticks of the fan) and simultaneously a shortening of the process of production.[62]

The transition from shorter to longer processes of production can be effected without encountering special obstacles by integrating step by step those means of production to be devoted for more distant periods of consumption. In contrast, the regress of the process of production to a less capital-intensive structure due to a relative increase in the demand for consumers' goods will be associated with particular phenomena. Such a regress may become necessary if the regular addition of new saving to which production had become adjusted stops at once, or if other circumstances of a temporary nature have led for a while to an excessive expansion of the demand for means of production. For example, this would be conceivable if at a given rate of interest technical improvements made longer processes than the existing ones profitable, yet without *at the beginning* requiring more means of production than the existing shorter ones for their implementation. Only in the course of the restructuring towards a more capital-intensive process of production—when not only its first stages have been started, but at the same time each of the increased number of stages of production also requires original means of production—the entire capital requirement for this process of production will be

---

processes of production can only be realised, if more capital than available up to now will be employed by them, so that also capital until now used in shorter processes must be supplied to the longer ones.

[62] [The simile of the price fan reappears in *Prices and Production*, reprinted, p. 248.—Ed.]

recognised, the rate of interest will rise, and the process must be abandoned.[63] Yet, the typical case of an inevitable fall in the relative demand for means of production might be the one already mentioned; here the rise in the relative demand in the past has been caused by an increase in the volume of money, yet once the increase in the volume of money ceases, approximately the old[64] relation between the demand for consumers' goods and for means of production must re-establish itself. In this case the return of the demand for consumers' goods to its prior level and the opening of the price fan thereby brought about at first will make it more advantageous to use the versatile means of production in the stages closer to consumption, and consequently they will become too expensive to be used anymore in the still existing long processes of production. At the same time the specific means of production attached to the higher stages—'fixed capital', like machines, buildings, etc., attached to them, as well as the semi-finished goods manufactured in these stages, which can only be transformed into consumable goods by passing through numerous lower stages of production—will fall in their price, or for the moment will become absolutely unsaleable.

Thus, while within the longer processes, which cannot be maintained due to the change in the relation between the demand for consumers' goods and producers' goods, there is an excess of specific and a shortage of versatile means of production, at the beginning the relation will be just the reverse within the shorter processes of production. Here the existing supply of means of production usable in many or all stages of production would suffice for enabling the start of this shorter process at full strength, yet there will be a lack of the required specific means of production, necessary for each stage of this production process. The lower stages of production (closer to consumption) will be able to employ the available versatile means of production, in particular available labour, only when the restructuring of this new process of production has come so far that the lower stages have been filled with the required semi-finished goods etc., too. However, this process takes time, and during this time a part of those means of production, no more sufficient for the longer processes, yet still not required for the shorter ones, will remain unemployed. In this way the situation is brought about, so often described in times of cri-

---

[63] This case of a non-monetary cause of an excessive expansion of the production of producers' goods thus should be added to the case of violent fluctuations of saving, already mentioned in my book, *Geldtheorie und Konjunkturtheorie*, p. 121 [cf. *Monetary Theory and the Trade Cycle*, reprinted, p. 149—Ed.].

[64] We cannot investigate the interesting problem whether the increase in the volume of the means of production brought about by an increase in the demand for means of production (even if merely temporary) may not also change the proportion in which the individual economic subjects will divide the gross yield of their activities (apart from additional sums of money) between consumption and production. Thus this problem is tantamount to whether the relation between the demand for consumers' and producers' goods can be permanently shifted in favour of the latter.

ses, that both, on the one hand, machines, factories and products, and, on the other hand, raw materials and labour are unemployed, and apparently cannot cooperate with one another due to the intervention of some higher power or even because the money needed to keep things going is lacking. It is indeed paradoxical that the goods which cause the crisis because of their scarcity are those same goods which during the crisis come to the market in excessive amounts and therefore become unsaleable. The explanation is to be found in that the presently existing labour force, in particular, owes its capability of earning a wage sufficient for the sustenance of life only to the special capitalistic structure of production; if this capitalistic apparatus turns out temporarily as too big to be maintained, this labour force cannot be fully employed as long as the necessary restructuring of production has not been completed.

It is therefore not the means of production or capital per se that will become scarce in the crisis and of which the price will rise, but those producers' goods that can also be used for the manufacturing of consumers' goods by means of shorter processes and that are thus not irrevocably attached to the longer process; they correspond therefore to the free capital disposable for new investment (in contrast to capital already invested). As has been demonstrated on another occasion,[65] it is this free capital that alone determines the volume of the supply of capital, and thereby from the supply side influences the rate of interest. And it is the shortage of free capital that brings about the rise in the interest rate in boom and crisis, fully compatible with the simultaneous decrease in the yield of current equipment, of ultimately fixed capital. The relationship between the movement of the interest rate in a proper sense and the yield of long-term equipment is thus indeed analogous to that between the movement of interest and rent, being based as it is on the same opposition, from which Wieser derived the differences in the movements of interest and rent, namely the price movement of versatile means of production (or "cost productive means") and those "specific" to certain uses.[66]

To conclude this section I want to refer to a passage, in which more than twenty years ago Arthur Spiethoff[67] dealt with these crucial questions in a manner very similar to this approach. In his article "Der Kapitalmangel in seinem Verhältnis zur Güterwelt"[68] he wrote: "What is the very meaning of overproduction (and capital shortage) for the nature of the relation of the

---

[65] Cf. *Geldtheorie und Konjunkturtheorie*, pp. 123f. [pp. 123–24; cf. *Monetary Theory and the Trade Cycle*, reprinted, pp. 150–51.—Ed.]; see also above, p. 123.

[66] [Cf. again Wieser, *Social Economics*, p. 81.—Ed.]

[67] [Arthur Spiethoff (1873–1957), German economist, as professor at the University of Bonn (1918–38) a colleague of Schumpeter, in his eclectic contributions to business cycle research attempted to fuse theoretical and historical approaches.—Ed.]

[68] In Schmoller's *Jahrbuch für Gesetzgebung, Verwaltung und Volkswirtschaft im Deutschen Reiche*, vol. 33, no. 4, 1909, p. 44. [Precisely, the title is, "Der Kapitalmangel in seinem Verhältnisse zur Güterwelt".—Ed.]

goods to each other? It represents (both in the capitalist and in the socialist order) abundance and shortage at the same time. It is the same as with all supplementary (complementary) goods and the famous pair of gloves, of which one glove has been lost. The missing glove is shortage, and the only remaining one is unusable in its solitariness and therefore abundance. Precisely the same is the case with the goods affected by overproduction. They are abundant, because they cannot be used without the goods necessary to complement them; and of the latter there is shortage, because they are needed to use the former. Thus, here one and the same situation represents abundance as seen from one side and shortage as seen from the other side."

10.

The inevitably lengthy investigations of this section should have clarified that the influences emanating from money on the direction and volume of production are much more complicated and far-reaching than the effects usually and exclusively attributed to changes in the general price level. Even though the *permanent* determinant of the type and direction of all productive activity is the relation of the real supply to the demand of real origin, monetary influences can for some time bring about such imbalances in the structure of production that temporarily a great part of the productive forces becomes unusable. The connections in this regard are by no means always so simple that rising prices must cause a rise in production or falling prices a fall in production. There would indeed be no influence at all of price changes on the volume of production if the goods of higher and lower order were affected uniformly and simultaneously. However, if this is not the case, then the effect of the same price change on production will be of opposite direction whether it first acts on the goods of higher order or first on the goods of lower order.[69] In particular, for all changes of production, especially for increases in the volume of production, what is crucial for the undisturbed maintenance of production is not that the product prices realised be constant, but that prices are realised which cover costs. This implies, however, that among the prices of means of production a certain proportion, corresponding to the respective structure of production, must be secured. This presupposes in turn that the quantities of the means of production assigned to every stage of production are just, and no more than, sufficient to maintain the current process of production. It is crucial for the maintenance or obstruction of production as a whole if and how far a monetarily induced shift of demand between these stages of production may temporarily change this relative assignment of goods to the different stages.

[69] Cf. on this Eulenburg, "Die Preisbildung in der modernen Wirtschaft", pp. 270ff. [pp. 270–73].

Taking the above arguments for granted, it becomes clear how little the confrontation of movements of the *general* price level to the changes of the average volume of production *as a whole*, prevalent in the usual investigations on the influence of money on production, may contribute to the solution of the problem. Neither do changes of the general price level depict the crucial causal factor, the shifts within prices, nor do the various statistical numbers on the change in the so-called volume of production indicate anything of the processes essential for the future development, that is, of the relative development of the different stages of production. Rather, it is plausible to assume that whenever monetary effects have an impact on the volume of production this will change production in the various stages in more or less different directions. Now as the technique of statistical inquiries implies that in the measurement of the volume of production greater weight is attached to the higher compared to the lower stages, all these so-called index numbers of production must even be considered as providing highly misleading foundations for examining the actual effects of price movements on the volume of production. As theoretical concepts the price level and the volume of production are equally useless, both representing just averages, change in which cannot tell us anything about those processes by which the monetary influences actually affect production, that is, shifts in the structure of prices and production.

From the foregoing it must be concluded that stabilising the general price level will by no means eliminate the monetary disturbances to production. Moreover, a regulation of the volume of money directed at the stabilisation of the price level may even bring about such disturbances that eventually the ultimate aim, the stabilisation of the price level, could prove impossible. For there can be no doubt that once the structure of production has been subjected to a far reaching disproportionality, no regulation of money whatsoever, except by initiating a vigorous increase in prices, can prevent that temporarily a great part of goods will become unsaleable and thereby the average price level will fall. Apart from that there would be utterly no justification for a policy that attempted to compensate the inevitable relative fall in the prices of a great number of goods by raising the prices of other goods just sufficiently for stabilising the price level. Yet, here these changes in the general value of money, on which the analyses of such phenomena often focus exclusively, are by no means the causes, but rather (as has been often erroneously objected to all monetary explanations of these processes) they are themselves the effect of prior ('real') shifts in the structure of production; however, these shifts are in turn conditioned by monetary influences, which have happened below the surface of a stable price level, which misleadingly indicated indifference.

Thereby it should also have become evident that by confining, as usual, the theory of money to a theory of the value of money, that is, to an explanation of the general value of money in contrast to an explanation of the influence of money on the relative height of prices, phenomena of the greatest importance fall outside the limits of this approach; it thus becomes incapable of a satisfactory solution even of the problem on which it itself focuses. Rather, as already discussed in the introductory chapters, the reconsideration of the whole system of economic theory necessitated by the introduction of indirect exchange and money remained undone, resulting in the unfortunate separation of the theory of money from general economic theory on which it was grafted in a completely inorganic way. Thus, introducing the assumption of indirect exchange and money did not initiate a progressive development of general economic theory; instead the mechanism inherent in general economic theory was tacitly assumed as given and monetary phenomena considered as merely superficial processes unable to modify the crucial determinants.

The conclusions to be drawn for the method of monetary research, or, better, for the method of theoretical research of the money economy, are therefore that we should not confine ourselves to investigating just the newly introduced phenomenon of money and the determination of its value. Rather, what is needed is a reworking—taking proper account of the newly introduced determinant[70]—of the whole field of economic theory, which up to now has been treated under the preliminary assumption of a barter economy.[71] We are already in a position to point out how the new theoretical picture of the economy, based on these extended foundations, will differ from that which takes only the economy's natural data into account: The rigid system of mutual dependencies within closed time periods typical for statics must be replaced by an exposition of principally open-ended processes, for the explanation of which comprehensive equilibrium systems will not suffice. The periodically recurring movements of the static system will be superseded by phenomena of movements of a different kind. These movements will be made up of a sequence of partial equilibria,[72] each derived, by using the tools of static theory, as causally emanating from the preceding state, yet never to be deter-

---

[70] [That is, of money.—Ed.]

[71] This view formulated as a postulate is already to be found in Schumpeter, *Wesen und Hauptinhalt*, pp. 280 and 281: "It is simply impossible to treat monetary theory as such. Yet, on the other hand, it [monetary theory] is *indispensable* for understanding the processes of an exchange economy. This is a very significant difference between the exchange economy and an isolated economy. We cannot understand it fully without the phenomenon of indirect exchange, because without it the processes become essentially different", and: "Above all, monetary theory as usually presented constitutes nothing less than an integral part of price theory. Rather it has become common practice to treat monetary theory as a separate subject and in discussions of pure theory to remove the 'veil of money', which covers the economic processes." Cf. also Mitchell, "The Role of Money in Economic Theory".

[72] [In the German text Hayek uses the uncommon term *Teilgleichgewichte*, here translated as "partial equilibria". In any case, this is not meant to denote the opposite of 'general equilibrium', but possibly a sequence of equilibria over time, none of which is a 'full' (or intertemporal) equilibrium.—Ed.]

mined by inserting the extra-economic data into the system of simultaneous equations which characterises static theory. A case, already closely discussed,[73] will serve as the typical example of a process to be explained by the theory of a money economy. This is the case in which the double correspondence, required by equilibrium, between value and quantity of the goods existing in consecutive stages of production cannot be taken for granted so that there will be for some time a sequence of unstable positions. If in economics we shall speak of dynamic theory at all, then it will be problems of this type where this term is most suitable.

After all this we must not forget that the phenomena discussed are not only the consequence of the use of money, but will already be brought about by every instance of indirect exchange, as represented by every trade, every purchase for the sake of repurchase, and therefore almost every activity of production. In any case, these consequences become apparent with particular clarity if a medium of exchange of variable quantity is used; and it has been the effects of changes in this quantity by which we demonstrated the peculiar problems resulting from indirect exchange. It would, however, be premature to conclude that *only* changes in the *volume* of money may bring about such serious disturbances to the economic process. There are at least three other aspects, hitherto neglected here, which may suggest influences of the use of money on the economic process. These are: 1. the fact that the existence of long-term contracts of fixed payments in terms of money introduces a rigid element into the price system, which up to now has been here ignored; 2. the fact, also hitherto not taken into account, that the demand for goods as expressed in money terms can change, at every point in time, not only due to changes in the volume of money, but also due to the speed by which amounts received will again be spent (changes in the so-called velocity of money); and finally 3. the related phenomenon, similar in its effect to a change in the velocity of money, that in some transactions the generally accepted medium of exchange may be replaced by a mere claim to the medium of exchange, not in itself to be considered as money—a phenomenon that renders the assumption, used up to now, of an unchanged volume of money as practically irrelevant. A comprehensive evaluation of the effects of money on price formation, and thereby on the whole economic process, must therefore be postponed until these phenomena have been clarified sufficiently.

[73] [For example, in chapter 5 above.—Ed.]

135

Appendix
The Exchange Value of Money: A Review[1]

The work under review sets out to "extract the essential contribution of money from the tightly-knit relationships of prices and income characterising the capitalist market economy and to develop the contents of a purely economic theory of money in an exact fashion".[2] In line with prevailing views, the author believes that he can achieve this objective by a systematic investigation of the factors that determine the value of money, that is, the general exchange value of money. The theoretical justification and conceptual demarcation of the 'general exchange value of money' as a tool of economic theory appear hardly problematic to him. However, as an investigation into the determinants of the price level—conceding theoretical relevance to this concept—this work has distinct merit. Even for those who are less convinced of the importance of its subject of investigation, like every careful piece of research it has much of value to offer.

The study takes the 'equation of exchange' in I. Fisher's formulation[3] as its starting point, although Neisser quite properly emphasises that this equation does not in the least constitute a theory of the value of money.[4] All that it does is to highlight the basic factors schematically and to delineate clearly what an explanation of the value of money must accomplish. The book in the main relies on a conventional framework—surely an advantage rather than a draw-back in the face of the widespread cult of originality in our field. It undoubtedly represents a valuable contribution to the current literature on money by its lucid and thorough clarification of an often muddled terminology and by its solid grounding in the marginal productivity theory of distribution, which is by now quite generally accepted.

Although partially superseded by more recent studies,[5] the introductory

---

[1] [Review of Hans Neisser, *Der Tauschwert des Geldes* (Jena: Fischer, 1928). First published in *Weltwirtschaftliches Archiv*, vol. 29, January 1929, pp. 103–6. Translated by Grete Heinz with minor amendments by the editor. Hans Philipp Neisser (1895–1975), German economist, worked at the Kiel Institute for the World Economy, 1928–33, until he was forced to emigrate. In the United States he taught at the University of Pennsylvania and eventually, from 1943 to 1965, at the New School for Social Research in New York.—Ed.]

[2] Neisser, *Tauschwert des Geldes*, p. v.

[3] [Cf. Irving Fisher, *The Purchasing Power of Money* (New York: Macmillan, 1911), 2nd ed. rev. (1913) reprinted as vol. 4 of *The Works of Irving Fisher*, ed. Barber. Neisser refers in *Tauschwert des Geldes*, p. 2n., to the German translation, *Die Kaufkraft des Geldes* (Berlin: Reimer, 1916; reprinted, 1922), of the first edition.—Ed.]

[4] [Cf. *Tauschwert des Geldes*, p. 11.—Ed.]

[5] [See, e.g., Gottfried Haberler, *Der Sinn der Indexzahlen: Eine Untersuchung über den Begriff des Preisniveaus und die Methoden seiner Messung* (Tübingen: Mohr, 1927), to which Neisser refers in the preface (*Tauschwert des Geldes*, p. v).—Ed.]

remarks about the theoretical possibility of ascertaining the prevailing price level are well worth reading, whether or not one fully agrees with them. The author's subsequent arguments about the relationship between the quantity theory of money and the so-called income theory are on the whole well taken.[6] It must be noted that his general criticism of the income theory hardly does justice to some of its variants, such as Wieser's, which takes as its starting point the relatively independent variability of real and nominal income confronting one another, a point also made by Neisser.[7] On the other hand, the author should be highly commended for insisting that money represents 'pure demand', which does not, as is the case in a barter economy, require that goods be offered simultaneously, so that thereby money "acquires a life of its own".[8]

Next, Neisser gives a detailed and thorough explanation of the concept or rather the several concepts of velocity of circulation and establishes the connection between velocity and the amount of individual cash balances in a clear way. At the outset of the discussion we do find the inaccurate statement that there is always an *inverse proportional* relationship between the velocity of circulation and average cash balances, whereas in reality these two magnitudes must always move *in opposite directions, but not necessarily* in inverse *proportion*. (The objection applies not only when one talks of the absolute size of cash balances, but also when one considers cash balances as a proportion of income, an approach wisely introduced by Neisser.)[9] But this inaccuracy does not adversely affect the subsequent exposition, in which the author does an excellent job of analysing the factors that determine the velocity of circulation by tracking down all the theoretically conceivable processes. Despite the special merits distinguishing this part of the study from most other works on this sub-

[6] [Income theories relate the circulation of money (the stock of money times its velocity of circulation, or $M \times V$) not to the nominal value of transactions $(P \times T)$, as in Fisher's equation of exchange $(M \times V = P \times T)$, but to nominal income $(P_r \times \Upsilon)$. Accordingly, in the corresponding equation of income theory, $M \times V_r = P_r \times \Upsilon$, velocity must be reinterpreted as 'income velocity', $V_r = V(P_r \times \Upsilon) / (P \times T)$, where the fraction used for conversion is occasionally referred to as the 'velocity of circulation of commodities'. A well-known contemporary exposition of income theory was Joseph A. Schumpeter, "Das Sozialprodukt und die Rechenpfennige: Glossen und Beiträge zur Geldtheorie von heute", *Archiv für Sozialwissenschaft und Sozialpolitik*, vol. 44, no. 3, 1917–18, pp. 627–715, reprinted in *Aufsätze zur ökonomischen Theorie*, ed. Erich Schneider and Arthur Spiethoff (Tübingen: Mohr, 1952), pp. 29–117, and translated as "Money and the Social Product", *International Economic Papers*, vol. 6, 1956, pp. 148–211. For Wieser cf., e.g., *Theorie der gesellschaftlichen Wirtschaft*, pp. 187–89, translated, *Social Economics*, pp. 262–65.—Ed.]

[7] [Cf. *Tauschwert des Geldes*, pp. 11–12.—Ed.]

[8] [Ibid., p. 13.—Ed.]

[9] [Cf. ibid., pp. 16–17. The point of Hayek's criticism is not crystal clear, as the proportion of cash balances relative to nominal income must by definition be reciprocal to the income velocity of money (see note 6 above). Possibly, Hayek's argument relates to the distinction between income velocity and simple velocity.—Ed.]

ject, we will not delve any further into this topic. For this neglect the reviewer's prejudice, which leads him to mistrust the whole concept of velocity of circulation, may be to blame. Even Neisser's study is unable to dispel his scepticism as to the relevance to theoretical economics of average magnitudes like—by the author's own definition—the velocity of circulation. The reviewer feels that these average values can contribute nothing to the understanding of phenomena of any kind and can only explain changes in other equally irrelevant average magnitudes such as the so-called 'general' value of money.

After a brief section "simply restating the findings of monetary theory"[10] about notes and coins, there follows a comprehensive discussion of credit money, which I consider the most valuable part of the whole book. It treats a whole series of questions, notably the origin and the limitations of bank credit, with praiseworthy clarity and thereby eliminates many misunderstandings. What Neisser has to say in the subsection about book money and the origins of cheque money, and especially his demonstration[11] that bank deposits originating from cash payments and from the granting of credit are basically indistinguishable should once and for all dispel presently still widespread misconceptions. His critical dissection in the following part of A. Hahn's widely discussed views is among the most perceptive treatments of Hahn's controversial theories.[12] In the same subsection Neisser also makes some excellent observations about the effect of even relatively small changes in the interest rate on the profitability of individual industries as well as on the price level.

The subsequent subsections about the money market and note-issuing banks are equally stimulating. In the subsection on the money market the author shows the critical importance of the demand for cash not only for the theory of the money market but for the theory of credit as well. His approach is equally fruitful in the next subsection on note-issuing banks. We must limit ourselves here to two of the points he raises. One concerns the appropriateness of the cover provisions for deposits in note-issuing banks. He proposes that a certain minimum of cash balances that fall due on a daily basis could be left uncovered, but that for amounts above that minimum the cover provisions should be the same as for bank notes.[13] Another point deals with the opposition between the 'verification theory' and the 'dominance theory'[14] of discount policy, where Neisser rightly judges the former theory as definitively wrong.

[10] Ibid., p. 40.

[11] Ibid., pp. 52–56. [Hayek referred to this passage again in his *Monetary Theory and the Trade Cycle*, reprinted, pp. 131–32.—Ed.]

[12] [Cf. L. Albert Hahn's *Volkswirtschaftliche Theorie des Bankkredits* (Tübingen: Mohr, 1920). On Hahn, see below, pp. 173–74.—Ed.]

[13] [Cf. *Tauschwert des Geldes*, pp. 86–87.—Ed.]

[14] [The 'verification theory' maintained that the role of discount policy was just to follow the market rate, whereas according to the 'dominance theory' discount policy was capable of regulating the market rate. See ibid., pp. 91–92.—Ed.]

To be able to do at least partial justice to the major ideas presented at the end of the book, we must completely pass over the following chapter on the "determination of the national quantities of money and goods",[15] which in the main deals critically, if not originally, with the theory of international trade. The last chapter concerns the mutual influences of money and the quantity of goods. The author first raises the question to what extent an expansion in the quantity of money might trigger an increase in production. After an unnecessarily involved discussion, the author upholds the prevailing view that at most a very modest effect can be expected from the expansion of money. He subsequently offers a valuable discussion on the alleged adjustment of the quantity of money and credit to the 'demand for money', that is, the amount of turnover in commodities. He thereupon turns to the question whether commercial bills can serve as a basis for note issue, that is, to the problem of the so-called 'classical creation of money'.[16] Neisser makes it clear that this doctrine completely misinterprets the function of the rate of interest and states that "only the interest rate policy of the note-issuing bank, rather than any mechanism in the creation of bank credit", can "bring about a parallel movement [in the quantity of goods and the volume of credit]".[17] However, the sole argument Neisser can offer for justifying the desirability of such a parallel movement is an uncritical reference to the dogma of the necessity of a stable price level. In this regard he fails to follow up on the critical remarks that he introduces in discussing the definition of the concept of inflation.

The systematic analysis is supplemented by three appendices covering war loans and price rises, the theory of transfers,[18] and bimetallic and parallel currencies,[19] which somewhat disrupt the structure of the book. It might have

---

[15] [Ibid., chapter 5.—Ed.]

[16] [The idea of the 'classical creation of money' (*klassische Geldschöpfung*) had been introduced into German monetary debate by the banker Friedrich Bendixen (1864–1920). In his *Das Wesen des Geldes*, 4th ed. (Munich and Leipzig: Duncker and Humblot, 1926 [1st ed., 1906]) he advocated the 'classical' principle of issuing notes in exchange for sound commercial bills as a safeguard against inflation.—Ed.]

[17] *Tauschwert des Geldes*, p. 148.

[18] [The so-called transfer problem deals with the economic forces determining the consequences of transfer payments for the donor and recipient countries. After World War I the debate of the transfer problem focused on the issue of German reparation payments.—Ed.]

[19] [A bimetallic system is characterised by money consisting of, or being convertible into, two precious metals, e.g., gold and silver, with a fixed relative price. In contrast, in a system of parallel currencies there exist two (or more) distinct monies, the unit of each one defined as a fixed amount of a precious metal, respectively, yet with a flexible relative price between the two monies (see *Tauschwert des Geldes*, pp. 199–200). Note that Neisser's discussion of parallel currencies bears a family resemblance to the idea of 'competing currencies' to which Hayek turned in his later monetary writings (see, e.g., F. A. Hayek, "Choice in Currency", in *New Studies in Philosophy, Politics, Economics, and the History of Ideas* (Chicago: University of Chicago Press; London: Routledge, 1978), pp. 218–31, reprinted as chapter 3 of *Good Money, Part II: The Standard*, ed. Stephen Kresge, vol. 6 (1999) of *The Collected Works of F. A. Hayek*).—Ed.]

been more appropriate and more effective to publish them separately. The application of research results presented earlier in the book to more or less current problems demonstrates at any rate the solid foundation that the theoretical analysis provides for solving specific questions.

While the book offers nothing essentially new, its critical summary and sifting of all the intellectual currents that dominate serious discussions about monetary problems today move us a step forward. The book's conservative character makes it all the more apparent how far we have come in clarifying the major problems and in what areas the expansion of firm knowledge about the way things work is still needed. The very fact that such a book merely summarises familiar material proves that the German literature on money has reached a respectable level within just the last six to eight years and that, in contrast to previous decades, it can now hold its own in comparison with English or American literature on the subject.

TWO

THE PURCHASING POWER OF THE
CONSUMER AND THE DEPRESSION[1]

The lot of the economist to-day is a hard one. Everybody else may feel justi-fied in taking a rather optimistic view at least of the somewhat more remote future. Even if the immediate outlook is as gloomy as at present the rapid progress of knowledge in the technical sciences seems to secure a brilliant future to mankind and a speedy overcoming of our present economic troubles. To the economist the situation of his own branch of knowledge gives no rea-son for such confidence. Not that progress has here been slower than in other sciences. But it lacks that application to the problems of actual life which is essential if our knowledge is to be useful; and while in other lines of knowl-edge the practitioners in the field which a science treats are trained at least in its fundamentals, I think it is no exaggeration to say that the men who should apply economics to practical problems make no use of the progress it has made during the last century. It rather seems as if economics loses in influence on practical affairs as it increases in technicality. So it comes that the econo-mist not only sees the causes of the present difficulties in a disregard of the teaching of his science which has not decreased but rather increased, but most look with the greatest misgivings to the future.[2]

Indeed, when we look back a century and compare, e.g., the debates which took then place in the House of Commons on any economic problems with the discussions of similar problems in any of the present parliaments there remains

---

[1] [On the title page of the typescript there is a handwritten note by Hayek, dated October 2, 1964: "This, if I remember correctly, was a lecture I gave at Cambridge in January 1931 before going to London to give the lectures on *Prices and Production*." Hayek did remember correctly; he presented this lecture to the Marshall Society at the University of Cambridge at the end of Janu-ary 1931. The text follows the typescript as revised in Hayek's handwriting; obvious errors have been silently corrected.—Ed.]

[2] [Hayek expressed very similar ideas on the economist's "unfortunate situation today" in the introductory paragraph of "Capital Consumption", in F. A. Hayek, *Money, Capital and Fluctua-tions: Early Essays by F. A. Hayek*, ed. Roy McCloughry (London: Routledge and Kegan Paul; Chi-cago: University of Chicago Press, 1984), p. 136, which is a translation of "Kapitalaufzehrung", *Weltwirtschaftliches Archiv*, vol. 36, July 1932; a new translation is to appear in *Capital and Interest*, ed. Lawrence White, vol. 11 (forthcoming) of *The Collected Works of F. A. Hayek* (Chicago: Univer-sity of Chicago Press; London: Routledge).—Ed.]

little doubt that the standard of general education on economic matters and the respect for expert knowledge has, if anything, decreased. A comparison of the situation to-day and a century ago is particularly interesting because it appears that the economic problems which seemed then of main importance and the ones we have to face now are of striking similarity. The effects of machinery—to-day we say rationalisation—of falling prices, the causes of a glut of the markets, the problem of protection to agriculture and the wide problem of population which promises to come to great importance during the next decades have been main problems of the 'twenties and 'thirties of the nineteenth as well as the twentieth century. It was mainly in the discussion of these problems that the main body of the classical doctrines in economics was evolved and one should expect, therefore, that these doctrines should be as interesting to the present public as they were then. Nor did our ancestors fare ill when they followed the advice of the economists. It was by the introduction of the principle of free trade with all its implications as demanded by the leading school of economists that the civilised world emerged from the period of depression which followed the Napoleonic wars and entered upon that singular epoch of brilliant progress in the second half of the nineteenth and the first years of the twentieth century. But in that happy period the teachings of the 'dismal science'[3] seem to have been entirely lost from the consciousness of the public; and when the new calamity arose they were ready to make it ten times worse by sinning again and again against the most elementary economic principles.

I do not think that I need to explain to you what I mean when I say that we have got in a vicious circle; that all over the world we are constantly making matters worse by some kind or other of state interference, and then feel ourselves compelled by the worse situation to interfere anew. It is not necessary to be a liberal of the old fashion to recognise that we would be better off if in the last decade the governments had made fewer well-intentioned attempts to help on all sides. But if we have done badly in this regard in the past, I think there is danger that we will do much worse in the future. While politicians are disregarding the teaching of orthodox economics they seem to be the more ready to swallow the new theories discovered by practical men. It seems as if, as the influence of scientific economics diminishes, the influence of a kind of pseudo-economics is constantly gaining ground as the general situation becomes worse. At present the easiest way to become a famous economist is probably to make oneself the advocate of some popular prejudice and to give

[3] [The pejorative characterisation of classical political economy as a 'dismal science' is due to Thomas Carlyle; cf. his "Occasional Discourse on the Negro Question", *Fraser's Magazine*, vol. 40, December 1849, pp. 670–79, reprinted in *Critical and Miscellaneous Essays: Collected and Republished*, vol. 6 (London: Chapman and Hall, 1869), pp. 171–210.—Ed.]

it, by clothing it in the language of economics, the outward appearance of a scientific theory.

For this lecture I shall single out one of these new theories which seems to me the clearest expression of an idea which is at the root of nearly all of them and which is at the same time the most dangerous delusion to which men could give themselves at the present moment. It is the new gospel which is now broadcasted in and from the United States: that what we need in order to get rid of our troubles is only an increase of the purchasing power of the consumers. It is not a lack of capital, so the doctrine goes, but an insufficiency of the purchasing power of the consumers which prevents us from producing more. Of capital there is plenty, unused machinery everywhere, and with the existing equipment we could easily make the output of consumers' goods twice and even three times as large if we could only find buyers for it. The obvious consequence is that we have simply to increase wages, to spend as much as we can, to 'buy now' instead of to-morrow and, if necessary, even to strengthen the purchasing power of consumers by additional money in order to make full use of the existing resources. Mr. Hoover, Mr. Ford, and Messrs. Foster and Catchings[4] have for so long a time hammered these doctrines into the minds of the American public that they seem recently to have become there the received creed. But it is not because it has just now become the general fashion that this doctrine seems so particularly dangerous; it is because it only openly states what for many years has already been the tacit foundation of practical politics that it seems to me of tremendous importance whether economists will succeed in correcting public opinion on that point or whether we are going to continue to act on that erroneous assumption. It is probably not too much to say that the fate of our civilisation will depend upon whether this fallacy is in time recognised.

[4] [These are, of course, the thirty-first American president, Herbert Hoover (1874–1964); the car maker Henry Ford (1863–1947); and the economist-pamphleteers William Truffant Foster (1879–1950) and Wadill Catchings (1879–1969). Hoover, whose presidency (1929–33) was overshadowed by the outbreak of the Great Depression, in 1930 initiated a 'buy now campaign' as a means for combating the depression; it turned out largely ineffective, similar to the better-known campaign orchestrated by the National Recovery Administration in 1933 under Hoover's successor, Franklin D. Roosevelt. Ford was the founder of the Ford Motor Company, famous for paying high wages with the intention both to reduce labour turnover and to boost workers' purchasing power. Foster and Catchings were among the best-known contemporary advocates of underconsumptionist doctrines; many of their writings were published by the Pollak Foundation, founded and financed by Catchings and directed by Foster. See, e.g., their *Profits*, Publications of the Pollak Foundation, no. 8 (Boston and New York: Houghton Mifflin, 1925). Hayek had critically examined their approach in "Gibt es einen 'Widersinn des Sparens'?" *Zeitschrift für Nationalökonomie*, vol. 1, November 1929, pp. 387–429, translated as "The 'Paradox' of Saving", *Economica*, no. 32, May 1931, pp. 125–69, reprinted as chapter 2 of *Contra Keynes and Cambridge: Essays, Correspondence*, ed. Bruce Caldwell, vol. 9 (1995) of *The Collected Works of F. A. Hayek.—*Ed.]

The task for the economists, however, is particularly difficult. While the popular explanation is so easy to understand and seems so obvious, the real problem is exceedingly complicated. It is probably a particularly good instance of the reasons why economics is so unpopular. But I cannot say that the economists themselves are quite free from blame for their ill success in educating the general public on this problem. They have scarcely themselves come to an agreement on this problem; and still less have they succeeded in making their opinions clear and intelligible to the intelligent laymen.

The main difficulty, for the economist and for the general public, rests probably with the term capital which has too many different and too little concrete meanings. I have, therefore, found it useful to avoid that term as long as possible and to try to base the explanation of the essential connections on a little more concrete descriptions of the changes in the methods of production which take place when the amount of capital available changes. The fundamental concept which in one of the different meanings of the term capital shall serve in its place is the relative magnitude of the demand for producers' goods made during a period of time to the demand for consumers' goods exercised during the same period of time. This concept is as it stands, however, not as definite as may seem at first glance and requires some further explanation. While the demand for consumers' goods is something quite definite as it refers only to one, namely the last stage of the way which every good has to pass before it becomes ripe for consumption,[5] and because we have only to think of the goods which are actually bought by the consumers during a period of time, it would of course be entirely arbitrary if we let the magnitude of what I have called demand for producers' goods depend on the entirely accidental fact whether any good or its components has to change hands more or less often during its process of production, i.e., whether the successive process necessary to complete it is carried on by one firm or divided between a greater or smaller number of different firms. On the other hand it is no less clear that we cannot count every piece of goods just once in its process of production, for the very thing I want to bring out by this concept is the fact that the total quantity of producers' goods needed during a period of time is, under the existing methods of production, several times larger than the output of consumers' goods of the same period. Any cursory glance on the economic organisation of society shows that far more work is devoted to the produc-

---

[5] [The underlying idea is Böhm-Bawerk's, that the various industries making up the economy can be arranged linearly into successive stages, from the first stage of raw materials to the final stage of the production of consumers' goods. Here, as in the first edition of *Prices and Production*, 'lower stages' are those nearer to, and 'higher stages' those more distant from, consumption. Cf. *Prices and Production*, 1st ed. (London: Routledge, 1931; 2nd ed rev., 1935), reprinted in *Business Cycles, Part I*, ed. Hansjoerg Klausinger, vol. 7 (2012) of *The Collected Works of F. A. Hayek*, p. 231n.25.—Ed.]

tion of producers' goods (including all kind of intermediate products) which will help to produce consumers' goods in some more or less distant future, than is devoted to the production of consumers' goods for the use in the current period. And we get a general idea about the proportion of the demand for consumers' goods to the demand for producers' goods when we learn that, e.g., in the United States the money payments for consumers' goods form only about one twelfth of the total of all payments made.[6] But these figures are distorted by the accidental fact noticed before, namely the degree of integration or specialisation in the particular line of production.

What we have to do to get a useful concept of the relative demand for producers' goods is to count each good and all the component elements of each good as many times as it takes periods of time for them to pass through the process of production. If we take, e.g., the month as the period and assume that the production of the consumers' goods takes on the average three months if we count all work on the machinery and implements required and used up in the process of production, then the demand for producers' goods was three times as large as the demand for consumers' goods. You will probably understand what I mean better from this diagram, which I have prepared for another purpose, than from any verbal explanation.[7]

That our division of the process of production into separate stages the products of which are counted as separate producers' goods is made quite irrespective whether these intermediate products actually change hands at this stage and, therefore, whether any demand for the producers' goods in the ordinary sense of the word is exercised on the markets, does not make our concept as artificial as may seem. Whether any producer invests new money in producers' goods by actually buying more or whether he does so by prolonging his process of production and therefore for some time selling less—we might say he buys his own products from himself in order to subject them to a further process of production—amounts to the same thing. In a state of equilibrium[8] this total demand for producers' goods will be identical with the total amount of producers' goods of all kinds (original means of production and intermediate products) which are necessary to secure the continuous out-

---

[6] [In "The 'Paradox' of Saving", reprinted, p. 93n., and later on in *Prices and Production*, reprinted, p. 226, Hayek attributed this observation to Marius W. Holtrop, *De Omloopssnelheid van het Geld* (Amsterdam: Paris, 1928), p. 181; cf. the abridged version translated into German by Erich Schiff as "Die Umlaufsgeschwindigkeit des Geldes" and reprinted in *Beiträge zur Geldtheorie*, ed. F. A. Hayek (Vienna: Springer 1933; reprinted, Berlin, Heidelberg, and New York: Springer, 2007), p. 186.—Ed.]

[7] [The diagram has not been preserved. It is a plausible conjecture that this diagram exhibited the triangular structure of stages of production which Hayek was to use in the LSE lectures; cf. for example *Prices and Production*, lecture 2, figure 2, reprinted, p. 225.—Ed.]

[8] [That is, in a state of *stationary* equilibrium.—Ed.]

put of the same quantity of consumers' goods which is currently produced. It is probably clear that under the prevailing system of production this demand for producers' goods will always be several times greater than the demand for consumers' goods. The only thing which probably requires some further explanation is the way in which durable goods, in particular instrumental goods as machinery which lasts for more than one period, is taken account of. The answer is that only that part of these durable goods is included in the aggregate demand for producers' goods which is used up and renewed during a period of time.

In a state of equilibrium, as I said before, the demand for producers' goods of a period will be identical to the amount of the producers' goods actually used in that period. But the magnitude of this demand may increase or decrease irrespective of whether the supply of consumers' goods has changed before or not. It will, therefore, be necessary to investigate the circumstances determining the magnitude of that demand somewhat closer.

The main part of the demand for producers' goods made during any period of time will always consist of the returns obtained from the sale of the output of the preceding period, which are reinvested in production and not consumed. Whether the demand for producers' goods will remain the same will therefore in the first place depend upon whether not more than actual profits and the remuneration of the original means of production, land and labour, are used for consumption. But we must not forget that in the ordinary course of business a great many firms will always not only make no profits at all but suffer losses and, therefore, be unable to reinvest an amount equivalent to the costs of their output. This will, e.g., regularly be the case in trades which decline because of a change of fashion, etc. In this case it would be necessary in order to keep the demand for producers' goods at the same level that these losses be made up by new savings, e.g., savings made out of the extraordinary profits made in the trades favoured by the change of fashion. Only the amount of savings which exceeds this amount necessary to compensate for losses, or net savings may be considered an addition to the demand for producers' goods.[9] It is perhaps not unnecessary to insist upon this rather obvious fact because there seems to exist very generally the impression that the amount of capital once existing is a magnitude which will continue to exist in-

---

[9] [In the typescript this reads, "consumers' goods", which is obviously a typing error. This passage on 'net savings' was taken over into *Preise und Produktion* (Vienna: Springer, 1931; reprinted, 1976), pp. 48–49, and reproduced in "A Rejoinder to Mr. Keynes", *Economica*, no. 34, November 1931, p. 402n.5, reprinted as chapter 5 of F. A. Hayek, *Contra Keynes and Cambridge*, p. 163n.12. Note that, with appropriate concepts of profits and losses, net saving thus defined is equivalent to the excess of gross saving over depreciation allowances.—Ed.]

dependently of human decisions.[10] This is partly explained by the fact that if one speaks of capital or capital goods one is inclined to think of durable goods only, which, however, form only a part of the total of producers' goods existing at any moment. It is one of the main objects of this form of exposition to show that entrepreneurs are constantly called upon to decide whether they find it possible and attractive to reinvest as much in their line of production as they did before.

Net savings (and net losses) are however not the only means by which the total demand for producers' goods may be changed. The same effect is obtained if additional money (in the form of bank loans) is given to entrepreneurs and used by them in production or if, on the contrary, money is paid back to the banks by the entrepreneurs and their total funds in this way diminished. And the same effect as by an increase of money in the hands of the entrepreneurs is brought about by a decrease of money in the hands of the consumers, and the same effect as by a decrease of money in the hands of the entrepreneurs by an addition of new money given to consumers. This leads us to the next point, the importance of the relative magnitude of the demand for producers' goods.

It is only this relative magnitude of the demand for producers' goods compared with the demand for consumers' goods which is of importance. But what is the meaning and effect of a proportional[11] increase or decrease of the demand—and in consequence, of course, production of producers' goods?

The fact that the demand for producers' goods made during a period of time is several times greater than the demand for consumers' goods means in the first instance that a proportionally larger share of the available total resources is devoted to the satisfaction of future wants than is used to satisfy the

[10] [This remark refers to the controversy about the permanency of capital between Eugen von Böhm-Bawerk and John Bates Clark, which foreshadowed Hayek's own capital debate with Frank Knight. On this issue cf. Avi J. Cohen, "The Mythology of Capital or of Static Equilibrium? The Böhm-Bawerk/Clark Controversy", *Journal of the History of Economic Thought*, vol. 30, June 2008, pp. 151–71. Eugen von Böhm-Bawerk (1851–1914), professor of economics at the University of Vienna and for some time minister of finance, as a member of the second generation contributed, jointly with Friedrich Wieser, to the transformation of Carl Menger's foundational ideas into a distinctive Austrian school. His own work focused on the theory of capital and interest. John Bates Clark (1847–1938), professor of economics at Columbia University, 1895–1923, was pivotal in propagating the marginal productivity theory of distribution; cf. his *The Distribution of Wealth: A Theory of Wages, Interest and Profits* (New York: Macmillan, 1899; reprinted, Kelley, 1965). Frank H. Knight (1885–1972), a classical liberal, taught at the University of Chicago, 1928–52; in the 1930s his *Risk, Uncertainty and Profit* (Boston: Houghton Mifflin, 1921; reprinted, Chicago: University of Chicago Press, 1985) was used as a textbook at LSE. Both Clark and Knight entertained the notion of capital as a fund and were critical of the Austrian emphasis on the time dimension of capital.—Ed.]

[11] [Apparently, what Hayek means by 'proportional' is 'relative'.—Ed.]

current demand for consumers' goods. This, in turn, implies that the process of production lasts on the average as many periods as the demand for producers' goods is greater than the demand for consumers' goods. This becomes immediately clear if you think that the fact that the process of production takes on the average three periods implies that during any period of time the goods needed in this and in the next two periods must be in process.

The reason why men chose such long-lasting or, as has become customary to say, round-about methods of production[12] is, of course, that by the use of such methods the product of the available original means of production may be increased, within practical limits almost indefinitely. And how far the round-about processes of production may be extended depends, as we have seen, on the proportion between the current demand for producers' goods and the current demand for consumers' goods.

We are now ready to attack the two main questions of our problem. These two questions are: first, can the demand for consumers' goods ever be too small to make the employment of all available producers' goods impossible? And secondly: what happens if the demand for consumers' goods increases relatively to the demand for producers' goods? I hope to show you that the answer to the first question is no and that the effect of an increase of the relative demand for consumers' goods is an economic crisis and unemployment, and the effect of a continued tendency to an increase of the relative demand for consumers' goods lasting stagnation combined with a progressive using up of the existing capital.

The assertion that there is too little demand for consumers' goods to buy the current output at remunerative prices[13] is only another way of saying that too much is invested in production relatively to the existing demand for consumers' goods. But how is this to be understood? We have seen that the demand for producers' goods may be any number of times greater than the demand for consumers' goods and that this would only mean that production would be carried on by longer round-about processes, i.e., that the output of consumers' goods in terms of physical units would be increased and the cost per unit decreased.

You see in the second diagram[14] what would happen if, e.g., the demand for producers' goods had become four times instead of three times as large as the demand for consumers' goods. Still it will be possible to sell the output

---

[12] [The notion of 'roundabout methods of production' refers to Böhm-Bawerk's idea of the productivity of time, that is, the superiority of processes with a longer average period of production. Cf. also the editor's introduction to F. A. Hayek, *Business Cycles, Part I*, pp. 25–26.—Ed.]

[13] [This is the assertion of the underconsumption theory as put forward, e.g., by Foster and Catchings.—Ed.]

[14] [This diagram must have been in all likelihood the counterpart to that in *Prices and Production*, lecture 2, figure 3, reprinted, p. 231.—Ed.]

of consumers' goods at a remunerative price because total costs, or the payment for all original factors of production will still be not greater than the demand for consumers' goods. Only the amount of intermediate products produced in a period of time will have increased. And even during the period of transition to longer round-about methods of production which are started because of an increase of the relative demand for producers' goods there will arise no real difficulties and only a temporary and necessary accumulation of unsold consumers' goods will take place; the amount of consumers' goods which have not been sold because of the saving will be needed to meet the demand in the interval of time between the moment when the last goods manufactured by the shorter old process are finished and the moment when the first goods produced in the longer new process are ready. So long as the demand for producers' goods increases relatively to the demand for consumers' goods or remains at least in the same proportion to it there is therefore no reason why there should be any unused resources. And in fact it is only in periods when we may be sure that the demand for producers' goods is increasing relatively to the demand for consumers' goods, in periods of a boom, that we find no unused resources except what are temporarily unemployed because of a shift from one employment to another.

But what will happen if the demand for consumers' goods increases relatively to the demand for producers' goods? There are several reasons why this may happen. A wave of prodigality may take hold of the people; gross income may be transferred by the interference of authority from people who would invest or reinvest it to people who will spend it on consumers' goods; or—probably the most important case for the explanation of cyclical fluctuations—the demand for producers' goods may for a time have been artificially increased by additional credits granted to producers and will, therefore, of necessity decrease again as soon as the banks stop to add to the circulation, enforced saving[15] ceases, and consumption tends to come into its own rights. For my next purpose I need not to distinguish between these different causes of a relative increase of the demand for consumers' goods; the effects will be essentially the same in whatever way it is brought about.

To understand these effects we must follow the successive steps by which the changes in the method of production are brought about somewhat more in detail than we did for the opposite case. That a relative increase of the demand for consumers' goods will cause a shortening of production[16] is rather obvious. It is also rather natural that such a shortening of the process of production will imply a loss in the value of the durable instruments of produc-

---

[15] [On the idea of 'forced saving', cf. the next chapter of this volume and the editor's introduction to F. A. Hayek, *Business Cycles, Part I*, pp. 21–25.—Ed.]

[16] [More precisely, this should read, "a shortening of the process of production".—Ed.]

tion which are adapted to the longer processes of production. The interesting thing, however, is that the transition to shorter round-about methods of production will temporarily make the employment of part of the available resources impossible and may even be considered as the regular cause of cyclical unemployment so that, far from bringing unemployed resources into employment, additional demand for consumers' goods which is not based on a preceding expansion of production will tend to increase unemployment.

Now what is it what really happens when the process of production is shortened? It means that the amount of intermediate products produced in any period of time must decrease relatively to the production of consumers' goods. This again implies that a larger proportion of the available resources must be used in the lower stages and a smaller proportion in the higher stages. But not all producers' goods can be used in different stages of production and, therefore, be shifted from the higher to lower stages and *vice versa* as the need arises. The original means of production, land and labour, will in general be applicable in all stages. The same will be true with a great many raw materials and with certain implements of not very specialised character. But all kinds of highly specialised machinery and almost all semi-manufactured goods will be applicable only in the particular stage for which they have been made and will not allow of being shifted to another stage. I shall call producers' goods of this type which are applicable to only one or a very few stages of production 'specific' producers' goods, while the goods which can be used in many stages of production I shall call, for lack of a better term, 'non-specific' producers' goods.[17]

Such a shifting of producers' goods to lower stages of production can only be effected by a rise of the prices offered there relatively to the prices offered in the higher stages of production. This will be the very effect of an increase of the demand for consumers' goods relatively to the demand for producers' goods. The increase of the demand for consumers' goods will first cause a rise of the prices of consumers' goods. This rise will increase the price margins between consumers' goods and the product of the immediately preceding stage of production which again will make investment in the last stage of production relatively more profitable than in the higher stages. Funds will be shifted to it until the price margins between all stages of production have generally risen. This tendency will be strengthened by the decrease of the demand for producers' goods in general which will make for a cumulative fall of the prices of producers' goods in the higher stages of production. The increase of the price margins between the stages of production means that money there invested will bring greater profits, or that the natural rate of interest has risen.

[17] [The same distinction had already been introduced in "Investigations into Monetary Theory", this volume, pp. 127–28; cf. also *Prices and Production*, reprinted, pp. 243–44.—Ed.]

But, as I said before, only a part of all producers' goods can be transferred from one stage of production to another and, therefore, be used in the shorter as well as in the longer process. The specific goods which have been adapted to the longer process only will become useless while it will be necessary to produce new specific goods adapted to the shorter process. And the main thing is that the old, longer process will immediately become unprofitable and, therefore, be stopped, while it will last some time until the new shorter process will be completed and, therefore, absorb all the available non-specific goods.

I begin with the effect on the old, longer process: the increase of the demand for consumers' goods without a preceding increase of production has made it necessary, because it would take too much time to produce the additional goods by the long process, to withdraw part of the producers' goods employed in it in order to produce the additional goods demanded by quicker, though less effective, methods. This transfer of producers' goods from higher to lower stages of production, which this means, can only be effected by paying higher prices, i.e., by using what is saved in the shorter process on interest in paying more for the producers' goods needed. But the rise of the prices of these goods will make it unprofitable to continue production by the longer process. The diminished quantity of non-specific goods remaining available for the longer process will in particular also decrease the productivity of the specific goods used in conjunction with them in any stage of production, these will fall in price, their production will become unprofitable and be discontinued. Production may go on in that part of the longer processes of production where the loss is borne by the already existing specific goods which cannot be shifted to other employments and where this loss in value is sufficient to make up for the increased price of the non-specific goods required, and so long as there are such intermediate specific products which were produced when their production was still profitable. But the general effect of the new and more pressing demand for consumers' goods will be an almost sudden stoppage of work in at least all the higher stages of production of the longer processes of production.

It may seem hard to believe that a comparatively small withdrawal of producers' goods for the satisfaction of more immediate needs should have so far-reaching effects on production in general. But when one has seen what our present, the capitalistic method of production really means it will not be so difficult to understand why nothing short of a certain proportional magnitude of the demand for producers' goods will be sufficient to keep the process of production going on at its present degree of round-aboutness. Any decrease below that proportion will stop it almost immediately.

But while the non-specific producers' goods, particularly the supplies of workmen employed in those higher stages, have thus been thrown out of use because their number has proved insufficient and, therefore, their price too high for the demands made by the long processes of production, it is by no means necessary that the total quantity of them which can no longer be used in the long processes will immediately be absorbed in the short processes which are being started anew. Quite the contrary: the shorter processes will have to be started at the very beginning and will only gradually absorb all the available producers' goods as the product progresses towards consumption and as the successive stages are supplied with the necessary intermediate products. While in the longer processes production ceases almost immediately as the change in relative prices of specific and non-specific goods in favour of the latter and the rise of the rate of interest make them unprofitable, these goods will find employment only as the shorter processes are approaching completion. The final adaptation will be still more retarded by the initial uncertainty in regard to the methods of production which will ultimately prove profitable, after the temporary scarcity of consumers' goods has disappeared. Entrepreneurs will justly hesitate to make investments suited to the overshortened process, i.e., investments which would enable them to produce with relatively little capital and a relatively great quantity of original means of production.[18]

It seems something of a paradox that the very same goods[19] the scarcity of which has been the cause of the crisis should become unsaleable as a consequence of the same crisis. But the fact is that while, after the growing demand for ready consumers' goods has taken away part of the non-specific producers' goods required, the remaining are no longer sufficient for the long processes and the particular kinds of specific goods required for the processes which would be just long enough to employ the total quantity of those non-specific goods are not yet available. The situation would be like that of the people of an isolated island, if after having constructed from savings and by using up all existing capital an enormous machine which was to provide them with all necessities, they found out that they had exhausted all their savings before the new machine could turn out its product. They would then have no choice but to give up temporarily the work on the new process of production and to devote their labour to producing their daily food without any capital. Only after they had succeeded in saving a new stock of food might they try to get the new machine into operation. In the actual world, however, where the accumulation of capital has permitted a growth of population far beyond the number which could find food without that capital, the single workman will in general not be able to produce without the help of capital enough for a living and he will, therefore, become unemployable. And the same will apply to all goods and services whose use requiring the cooperation of others which,

---

[18] [Apart from some stylistic modifications, this paragraph and the next were taken over into the text of *Prices and Production*, reprinted, pp. 256–58.—Ed.]

[19] [That is, the non-specific producers' goods in question.—Ed.]

after a change in the structure of production of the kind described, may not be available in the necessary quantity.

Theoretically the situation may be described thus: while in the usual demand schedule it is supposed that any supply of any producers' goods may immediately be sold at some price, the fact that under the capitalistic system of production a different total of producers' goods available required a different equipment of specific and mostly durable goods which it takes considerable time to produce makes it impossible to find buyers for the current supply of non-specific and non-durable goods and services (particularly labour) before that new equipment is ready. And because of the constant use of such equipment the total supply of labour has increased to such an amount that without capital it might not obtain a price at all. No price of labour might, therefore, be low enough to give employment to all workmen in such a situation.[20]

The capitalistic machinery will do its service only so long as we are satisfied to consume not more than the immediate output of that part of our total resources which under the existing organisation is devoted to the current output of consumers' goods. *Every* increase of consumption, if it is not to disturb the existing machinery, must be preceded by new savings, even if the existing durable equipment is sufficient for that increase of production, because the continuous production on that enlarged scale requires an increase of the intermediate products of all stages which must exist in any moment and which are no less capital than the durable instruments. The appearance that we could at will immediately increase the output by the use of the existing machinery is deceitful. Whatever technical experts may tell us about what they consider the enormous existing unused capacity, there is in fact no possibility to increase output to that extent.[21] They—and all the economists who believe that 'capital' is superabundant—are deceived by the fact that a great deal of the durable instrumental goods, machinery, houses and the like, are adapted to a far greater production. But they overlook that 'capital' consists not only of durable goods but that to use the existing machinery a great many non-durable goods and services which are now used to provide for immediate wants would have to be invested in long lasting processes to bear fruit only in a relatively distant future. The existence of unused resources is therefore no proof that capital is abundant and consumption insufficient. Quite the contrary, it is a sign that we cannot use the existing equipment because the immediate de-

---

[20] [This paragraph has found its way only into the German version, *Preise und Produktion*, p. 91n.1; cf. the translation of this passage added in *Prices and Production*, reprinted, editor's note, p. 258.—Ed.]

[21] [Hayek elaborated this theme later on in his "Technischer Fortschritt und Überkapazität", *Österreichische Zeitschrft für Bankwesen*, vol. 1, June 1936, sections 9 and 10, translated as "Technical Progress and Excess Capacity" and reprinted as chapter 8 of F. A. Hayek, *Money, Capital and Fluctuations*, cf. pp. 174–78; also to be included in F. A. Hayek, *Capital and Interest*.—Ed.]

mand for consumers' goods is too pressing to allow of the available liquid resources being invested in the long processes for which we have the necessary equipment.[22]

It is, therefore, also out of the question that the unused resources could be brought into employment by an additional demand for consumers' goods; or rather, that the total amount of unused resources could be diminished in this way. It would only have the effect that the tendency towards a temporary excessive shortening of the process of production is intensified and the crisis made more acute. This situation makes it rather seem desirable that during the crisis and in the early stages of depression the demand for consumers' goods be curtailed and that it should only rise again as the output of the new shorter process comes on the market. This is exactly what is caused by cyclical unemployment which reduces the demand for consumers' goods for so long as a greater demand could only be satisfied by a transition to very short and ineffective methods of production. For this reason one could almost call unemployment nature's own remedy against the disturbances caused by the preceding excessive use of the available resources for capital purposes.

But we must not let ourselves be deceived by the fact that in the past cyclical fluctuations have been the regular cause of unemployment. Exactly the same effects as from a return of consumption to its old proportion[23] relatively to the demand for producers' goods will flow from any relative increase of the demand for consumers' goods from whatever source it comes. The effects are even worse if consumers' demand is artificially and continuously increased by authoritative interference. The effect will then be a permanent depression, accompanied by a continuous using up of the existing capital. This may be the result from the increase of government expenditure in general and of attempts of intentioned transfers of gross income from people who would invest it to people who will spend it on consumers' goods, and probably also from all attempts to redistribute property. When we learn from a recent publication[24] that the proportion of public expenditure to the total national income has risen in Germany from 11.5% in 1913 to 28.6% in 1929 and in most other European countries from between 10–14% to between 20–25%, while in the United States the same proportion has risen in this period only from 6.5% to 8%, it becomes rather very probably that this form of an authoritative inter-

---

[22] [Again this paragraph reappears with some stylistic modifications in *Preise und Produktion*, pp. 92–94.—Ed.]

[23] [The typescript reads, "own proportion", which is presumably a typing error.—Ed.]

[24] Fritz Karl Mann, *Die Staatswirtschaft unserer Zeit: Eine Einführung* (Jena: Fischer, 1930). [Cf. pp. 50 and 55 for the numbers on Germany, and the other European countries and the United States, respectively. Note that present-day statistics, although their estimates of the absolute levels of the share of public expenditure in income are lower, confirm Hayek's assertion of a change in these ratios, that is, the approximate doubling for most European countries.—Ed.]

ference in favour of consumption has been a very effective influence making for the chronic unemployment which we observe in most European States.

If we look at this problem from this point of view the much abused phrase of a 'crisis of capitalism' becomes a new meaning. It may very well be that we are in a crisis of capitalism, but not because the capitalistic system has proved a failure but because for more than a decade we have been systematically destroying capital. We have done so hesitatingly and planlessly in the past, and the effects have yet been compensated by new inventions which made even the smaller capital more effective. But if the new fashion to belittle the importance of saving and to stimulate consumption in every possible way should become general we will very soon do so systematically and quickly. But we cannot afford to use up our capital because the population of the civilised countries, numerous as it has become, can live on the present standard and perhaps at all only because of this capital: But if we should go on to use it up the increasing difficulties will make it more and more difficult ever to stop this process and in the end sheer necessity would probably compel men to fight and kill one another until their number has been sufficiently reduced to live without capital.

THREE

A NOTE ON THE DEVELOPMENT OF THE DOCTRINE OF 'FORCED SAVING'[1]

The enhanced interest in the problem of 'Forced Saving', due to recent developments in the theory of industrial fluctuations, has led to the discovery of so many more or less distinct allusions to that subject in the works of earlier writers that the sketch of the development of that doctrine, which I attempted in the first chapter of my *Prices and Production*[2] has rapidly become out of date. Since, in addition to the several early references to this problem which have recently been noticed by other writers, I have now discovered what is, perhaps, their common source, it may be worth while to redraw my previous sketch of the development of this doctrine.

Although it is impossible at the present time to show conclusively whether or in what way Jeremy Bentham's teaching on this point was disseminated at the time when he formulated his opinions, it now appears to me to be practically certain that the earliest—and also the clearest and most elaborate— statement of this theory is to be found in the writings of that author. In a passage which received its final form in 1804—though it was probably sketched much earlier, and not published until 1843 in his *Manual of Political Economy*[3]—

---

[1] [First published in *Quarterly Journal of Economics*, vol. 47, November 1932, pp. 123–33, and reprinted as chapter 7 of *Profits, Interest and Investment. And Other Essays on the Theory of Industrial Fluctuations* (London: Routledge, 1939). The text is that of the reprint.—Ed.]

[2] *Prices and Production* (London: Routledge, 1931), pp. 17–19. Part of the material used in the following note has already been mentioned in the German edition of the same work, published shortly after the English edition under the title of *Preise und Produktion* (Vienna: Springer, 1931 [reprinted, 1976]), pp. 18–20. [Hayek used the findings of this article for extending the corresponding passages in the second edition of *Prices and Production* (1935), pp. 18–20; cf. the variorum edition reprinted in *Business Cycles, Part I*, ed. Hansjoerg Klausinger, vol. 7 (2012) of *The Collected Works of F. A. Hayek* (Chicago: University of Chicago Press), pp. 206–10.—Ed.]

[3] *The Works of Jeremy Bentham*, published under the superintendence of his executor, John Bowring, vol. 3 (Edinburgh: William Tait, 1843 [reprinted, Bristol: Thoemmes Press, 1995]), pp. 31–84. The *Manual*, as there reprinted, though the only edition which is reasonably complete, obviously does not represent a complete manuscript which Bentham intended to be published in that form, but rather a compilation by the editor from different manuscripts and some fragments published by Dumont. Nor is it true, as is frequently asserted, that all parts of the *Manual*, as printed there, date back to 1793. A cursory inspection of the Bentham manuscripts in University College, London, shows that the material in the published *Manual* belongs to quite different

he deals in some detail with the phenomenon which he calls 'Forced Frugality'. He seems to have hit upon this idea in exactly the connection in which one would expect it to occur first; and his influence on almost all economists of the early nineteenth century probably accounts for the fact that the idea is mentioned again and again in this period in very similar terms, even though his own statement did not appear in print until a much later date.

It might be expected that the author of the *Defence of Usury*,[4] who was an acute observer of the effects of the Fixation of Prices[5] and who had adopted as his *leitmotiv* for the study of the art of Political Economy the statement that "industry is limited by capital",[6] would turn his attention to the problem of whether government measures might not lead to an increase of that capital. Indeed, the first example of the "broad measures" of governments (i.e., such measures as "have for their object the augmentation of wealth in all its shapes without distinction") which Bentham discusses among what he calls Non-agenda of the state, is headed "Forced Frugality".[7]

---

periods and that there is, in addition to it, a good deal of apparently very interesting unpublished material. A critical edition of all the economic writings of Bentham is urgently needed. [Jeremy Bentham (1748–1832), philosopher and legal reformer, was a major propagator of the idea of utilitarianism. A critical edition meeting Hayek's desiderata is *Jeremy Bentham's Economic Writings. Critical Edition Based on His Printed Works and Unprinted Manuscripts*, ed. Werner Stark, 3 vols. (London: Allen and Unwin, 1952, 1954; reprinted, London: Routledge, 2004). As Stark points out, the *Manual* as published in the Bowring edition mixed up two distinct sources, the main part of it consisting of a manuscript written after 1800 and designed to be published under the title *Institute of Political Economy*, into which a few pages from the original *Manual* of 1795 had been inserted, namely pp. 57–65 in vol. 3 of the Bowring edition (cf. Werner Stark, introduction to *Economic Writings*, vol. 1, pp. 49–50). Hayek's references are almost exclusively to the *Institute* (now reprinted in *Economic Writings*, ed. Stark, vol. 3, pp. 303–80; the original manuscript of the *Manual* is reprinted in vol. 1, pp. 219–73).—Ed.]

[4] [*Defence of Usury, showing the impolicy of the present legal restraints on the terms of pecuniary bargains* [1816], reprinted in *Works*, ed. Bowring, vol. 3, pp. 1–29, and in *Economic Writings*, ed. Stark, vol. 1, pp. 121–207.—Ed.]

[5] Cf. Bentham, *Manual*, ed. Bowring, chapter 3, section 22, p. 66.

[6] [Cf. *Economic Writings*, ed. Stark, vol. 1, p. 225: "the limitation of industry by the limitation of capital" as "the groundwork of the whole", a passage missing from the Bowring edition of the *Manual*; cf. also Bentham's unpublished postscript to the *Defence of Usury*, where he referred to "the principle 'No more trade than capital', or 'Capital limits trade'" (cf. *Economic Writings*, ed. Stark, vol. 1, pp. 201–4). Later on John Stuart Mill restated the principle that "industry is limited by capital", cf. his *Principles of Political Economy*, ed. William James Ashley (London: Longmans, Green, 1909; new edition, 1921), book 1, chapter 5, paragraph 1, p. 63; cf. *Principles of Political Economy, Part 1*, ed. John M. Robson, vol. 2 (1965) of the *Collected Works of John Stuart Mill* (Toronto: University of Toronto Press; London: Routledge and Kegan Paul; reprinted, Indianapolis: Liberty Fund, 2006), p. 63.—Ed.]

[7] Bentham, *Manual*, ed. Bowring, chapter 3, section 4, p. 44. [Cf. also *Economic Writings*, ed. Stark, vol. 3, p. 342. Hayek's quotation is inaccurate: it should read, "measures having for their effect, or their object . . ." Cf.: "*Agenda* and *non-agenda* are the economic activities of the govern-

"By raising money," he writes, "as other money is raised, by taxes (the amount of which is taken by individuals out of their expenditure on the score of maintenance), government has it in its power to accelerate, to an unexampled degree, the augmentation of the mass of real wealth. By a proportionable sacrifice of present comfort, it may make any addition that it pleases to the mass of future wealth; that is, to the increase of comfort and security. But though it has it in its power to do this, it follows not that it ought to exercise this power to compel the community to make this sacrifice."[8]

And after a lengthy discussion of this form of Forced Frugality, which does not concern us here, Bentham continues:—

The effect of forced frugality is also produced by the creating of paper money by government, or the suffering of the creation of paper money by individuals. In this case, the effect is produced by a species of indirect taxation, which has hitherto passed almost unnoticed.[9]

Bentham then proceeds to study, as example 2 of his "broad measures" among the *non-agenda*, the effects of increasing money in some detail. "Labour," he begins, "and not money, is the real source of wealth."

All hands being employed, and employed in the most advantageous manner, wealth—real wealth—could admit of no further increase; but money would be increasable *ad infinitum*. The effect of every increase of money (understand, of the ratio of the quantity of money employed in the purchase of things vendible, to the quantity of things vendible for money) is to impose an unprofitable *income tax* on the incomes of all fixed incomists.[10]

---

ment: in so far as they promote happiness, they are desirable and hence *agenda*; in so far as they do not, they are undesirable and hence *non-agenda*" (Stark, introduction to vol. 3, p. 40.—Ed.]

[8] [*Manual*, ed. Bowring, chapter 3, section 4, p. 44; cf. also *Economic Writings*, ed. Stark, vol. 3, p. 342. Here and in the following, slight inaccuracies in Hayek's quotations with regard to punctuation will not be explicitly noted.—Ed.]

[9] [*Manual*, ed. Bowring, pp. 44–45. Hayek's quotation of the first sentence is inaccurate and should read, ". . . or the suffering the creation of paper money on the part of individuals", followed by a paragraph break. This passage is not in the Stark edition.—Ed.]

[10] Here Bentham appends the following very interesting footnote, which is curious as an early attempt to estimate the quantitative importance of this phenomenon: "The following is an indication of the indirect income tax resulting from the increase [from increase] of money: In Britain (anno 1801) money is about £72,000,000; income about £216,000,000 (72:216::1:3). Each [*Each*] million added to *money* adds therefore *three* millions for ever to *pecuniary income*; and this (setting aside the 15 per cent for ever—£150,000—for profit on the million if employed in the shape of capital) without addition to real income. If, in every year, £2,000,000 be added to money (*plus* £300,000 for an equivalent to the addition made as above to real wealth) then in 36 years (anno 1837) the nominal or pecuniary amount of a mass of real income equal to the amount of 1801, will be doubled, i.e., become £432,000,000; to which will be added £10,800,000 for an equiva-

If, on the introduction of the additional money into circulation, it pass in the first instance into hands which employ it in the way of unproductive expenditure, the suffering from this tax remains altogether uncompensated; if before it come into any hands of that description, it have come into hands by which it has been employed in the shape of capital, the suffering by the income tax is partly reduced and partly compensated. It is reduced by the mass of things vendible produced by means of it: a mass by the amount of which, were it not for the corresponding increase in the mass of money, the value of the mass of money would *pro tanto* have been increased, and the prices of things vendible decreased. It is in a certain degree, though in a very inadequate degree, compensated for by the same means; viz., by the amount of the addition made to the quantity of sensible wealth—of wealth possessing a value in the way of use. Here, as in the above case of forced frugality, national wealth is increased at the expense of national comfort and national justice.[11]

After some further remarks on the same subject, which there is no need to quote here, Bentham continues:

No sooner, however, does such additional sum of money pass on from the hands by which it is employed in the shape of capital, into those hands by which it is employed in adding to unproductive expenditure, than its operation in the way of making an addition to real wealth is at an end. No sooner does it go in addition to money employed in the purchase of articles for consumption, than its power of producing an addition to the mass of the matter of real wealth is at an end: thenceforward and for ever it keeps on contributing by its whole amount to the increase in prices, in the same manner as if from the mines it had come in the first instance into an unproductive hand, without passing through any productive one.[12]

---

lent to the intermediate addition to real wealth (£300,000 × 36). But the £432,000,000 of 1837, being worth not more than the £216,000,000 of 1801, each £100 of the £432,000,000 will be worth but £50 of the £216,000,000; that is, the income of each *fixed incomist* will, by that time, have been subjected to an indirect income tax of £50 per cent. He whose pecuniary income of 1837 is double what it is in 1801, will in point of *wealth* be neither a *gainer* nor a *loser* by the change. Not [*Not*] so in point of *comfort*. For by so much as he is a gainer in wealth the *one* way, by so much is he the loser in the *other*; and by the nature and constitution of the human frame, sum for sum, enjoyment from *gain* is never equal to the suffering from loss." [*Manual*, ed. Bowring, p. 45n.; cf. also *Economic Writings*, ed. Stark, vol. 3, p. 348.—Ed.]

[The quotation in the text is from *Manual*, ed. Bowring, p. 45; cf. also *Economic Writings*, ed. Stark, vol. 3, p. 344. Hayek's quotation is inaccurate. It should read, "the incomes of fixed incomists".—Ed.]

[11] [*Manual*, ed. Bowring, p. 45; cf. also *Economic Writings*, ed. Stark, vol. 3, pp. 348–49.—Ed.]

[12] [*Manual*, ed. Bowring, p. 46; cf. also for a slightly different version *Economic Writings*, ed. Stark, vol. 3, p. 349. Hayek's quotation is inaccurate. In the final sentence, "increase in prices" should read, "increase of prices".—Ed.]

As an historical fact, however, Bentham thinks that

> It is a matter of uncertainty what part, and even whether any part (of the increase of wealth) has been produced by the addition to money, since without any such addition it might have been produced as well as by it.[13]

Shortly after Bentham had given definite shape to his thoughts in 1804 (from his manuscripts it seems clear that he had been working on them at least as early as 1801—perhaps much earlier) he noticed that he had already been anticipated. On March 22nd, 1804, he wrote to his French editor, Dumont:

> I had been working at, and thought to have finished a concise view of the influence of money in the increase of wealth as a specimen of the 'Præcognita', preparatory to the practical part—the Agenda and Non-agenda. But, just now, I got returned from Trail my Thornton and your Wheatley; and I see few ideas in my papers that are not to be found somewhere or other in their books. What I could hope to do would be little more than substituting method to chaos, and keeping clear of contradictions, which are to be found in both, but more particularly in Wheatley. The moral is that I should go quietly back to Evidence. . . .[14]

---

[13] [*Manual*, ed. Bowring, p. 46; cf. also *Economic Writings*, ed. Stark, vol. 3, p. 350. The exact quotation is, "and as to the addition of wealth, it is a matter of uncertainty what part, and even whether any part, has been produced by the addition to money, since without any such addition it might have been produced as well as by it."—Ed.]

[14] See *Works*, ed. Bowring, vol. 10: *Memoirs and Correspondence*, p. 413. [Cf. also *The Correspondence of Jeremy Bentham*, ed. J. R. Dinwiddy, vol. 7: *January 1802 to December 1808* (Oxford: Clarendon Press, 1988), letter 1841, pp. 262–63. Hayek's quotation is slightly inaccurate: the spelling should be "Non-Agenda"; in the following sentence it should read, "I have got returned"; and an ellipsis should be inserted before the final sentence. 'Præcognita' means, "which should be known in order to understand something else" (*Webster's Revised Unabridged Dictionary*, ed. Noah Porter [Springfield, MA: G & C. Merriam Co., 1913]). James Trail (1745–1808) was an old friend of Bentham and member of Parliament for Oxford, 1802–6. On Thornton and Wheatley see below. The reference to "Evidence" is to Bentham's efforts between 1803 and 1812, from which three published works emanated: *A Treatise on Judicial Evidence*, extracted from the manuscripts and translated into English by Etienne Dumont (London: Baldwin, Craddock, and Joy, 1825); *The Rationale of Judicial Evidence*, in 5 vols., ed. John Stuart Mill (London: Hunt and Clarke, 1827; reprinted, New York and London: Garland, 1978), and finally the posthumous compilation "An Introductory View of the Rationale of Evidence", in *Works*, ed. Bowring, vol. 6.—Ed.] Bentham had already read Thornton two years before and had praised him highly in a letter to Dumont dated June 28th, 1802. He wrote, "This is a book of real merit—a controversy with him would be really instructive. I have tumbled it over but very imperfectly, that not being the order of the day, and for fear of calling off my attention, and absorbing my capacity of exertion. But, one of these days, I may not improbably grapple with him. Admitting all his facts with thanks—agreeing with him in almost all his conclusions—but disputing with him what seems (as far as I have yet seen) to be his most material conclusion, viz., that paper money does more

While Wheatley's *Remarks*[15] seem, however, to contain nothing upon the problem which interests us here, Thornton had indeed expressed similar thoughts in the following paragraph of his *Paper Credit*[16]:

> It must also be admitted that, provided we assume an excessive issue of paper to lift up, as it may for a time, the costs of goods though not the price of labour, some augmentation of stock will be the consequence; for the labourer according to this supposition, may be forced by his necessity to con-

---

good than harm. Here is a book of real instruction, if the French are wise enough to translate it; the style clear, plain, without ornament or pretension; the reasoning close." (*Memoirs and Correspondence*, ed. Bowring, p. 389.) [Cf. also *Correspondence*, ed. Dinwiddy, vol. 7, letter 1705, p. 63.—Ed.] Dumont seems to have taken the hint. At least, the *Bibliothèque Britannique* of Geneva, where, in earlier years, Dumont had published part of the *Manual* and other manuscripts of Bentham, published in its volumes XXI–XXIII (1802 et seq.) six long extracts from Thornton's book, announcing at the same time a forthcoming French translation. [The *Bibliothèque Britannique* was a monthly journal of literature, sciences and the arts published in Geneva, from 1796 to 1816, when it transformed into the *Bibliothèque Universelle*. The translation by Dumont of Thornton's *Paper Credit* (see below), indicated in the text, was published as *Recherche sur la nature et les effets du credit du papier* (Geneva: Bibliothèque Britannique, 1803). Pierre Etienne Louis Dumont (1759–1829) was a French writer and the editor of numerous works of Bentham in French.—Ed.]

[15] John Wheatley, *Remarks on Currency and Commerce* (London: Cadell and Davies, 1803 [reprinted, Bristol: Thoemmes Press, 1991]). [John Wheatley (1722–1830) was a lawyer and economist; his monetary writings mostly concurred with the Bullionist position.—Ed.]

[16] Henry Thornton, *An Enquiry into the Nature and Effects of the Paper Credit of Great Britain* (London: J. Hatchard, F. and C. Rivington, 1802), p. 263 [pp. 263–64; cf. the American edition (Philadelphia: Humphreys, 1807), p. 170; reprinted in *A Select Collection of Scarce and Valuable Tracts and Other Publications on Paper Currency and Banking*, ed. James Ramsey McCulloch (London: Murray, 1857), which is reprinted as vol. 3 of *Classical Writings on Economics* (London: Pickering and Chatto, 1995), p. 306. Cf. also the reprint *An Enquiry into the Nature and Effects of the Paper Credit of Great Britain together with his Evidence given before the Committee of Secrecy of the Two Houses of Parliament in the Bank of England, March and April 1797, some Manuscript Notes, and his Speeches on the Bullion Report, May 1811*, ed. F. A. Hayek (London: Allen and Unwin, 1939; reprinted, New York: Kelley, 1991), p. 239. Hayek's quotation is inaccurate. It should read, "It must be also admitted that, provided we assume an excessive issue of paper to lift up, as it may for a time, the cost of goods though not the price of labour, some augmentation of stock will be the consequence; for the labourer, according to this supposition, may be forced by his necessity to consume fewer articles, though he may exercise the same industry. But this saving, as well as any additional one which may arise from a similar defalcation of the revenue of the unproductive members of the society, will be attended with a proportionate hardship and injustice." Henry Thornton (1760–1815) was an outstanding monetary theorist of the nineteenth century, famous for his contribution to the debates during the restriction period and, jointly with Francis Horner (1778–1817) and William Huskisson (1770–1830), for the authorship of the *Bullion Report*.—Ed.] Attention has already been drawn to this remark of Thornton by Prof. C. Bresciani-Turroni, *Le vicende del marco tedesco* (Milan: Univ. Bocconi ed., 1931), p. 240. [For a translation see Costatino Bresciani-Turroni, *The Economics of Inflation: A Study of Currency Depreciation in Post-War Germany*. With a foreword by Lionel Robbins, trans. Millicent E. Sayers (London: Allen and Unwin, 1937; reprinted, London: Routledge, 2003), p. 186.—Ed.]

sume fewer articles, though he may exercise the same industry. But this saving, as well as any additional one which may arise from a similar defalcation of the revenue of the unproductive members of the society will be attended with a proportional injustice and hardship.

The next and much more detailed exposition of this phenomenon which I have noticed—that of Malthus in his review of Ricardo's *High Price of Bullion*[17]—I have already quoted at some length in *Prices and Production*. Here I only want to draw the attention of the reader to the striking similarity between the phrasing of Malthus and that of Bentham. Since my mention of Malthus in this connection, my attention has been drawn to an almost simultaneous discussion of the same problem by Dugald Stewart which, however—like Bentham's contribution—did not appear in print until many years afterwards.[18] In a series of memoranda, which he wrote in 1811 for Lord Lauderdale,[19] on

[17] *Edinburgh Review*, vol. 17, February 1811, pp. 363 et seq. [pp. 363–64; reprinted in *The Works of Thomas Robert Malthus*, ed. E. A. Wrigley and David Souden, vol. 7: *Essays on Political Economy* (London: Pickering, 1986), pp. 46–48—Ed.]. Cf. also Ricardo's reply in the appendix to the fourth edition of his pamphlet on *The High Price of Bullion: A Proof of the Depreciation of Banknotes* (London: Murray, 1811) [reprinted in *The Works and Correspondence of David Ricardo*, ed. Piero Sraffa, vol. 3: *Pamphlets and Papers, 1809–1811* (Cambridge: Cambridge University Press, 1951; reprinted, Indianapolis: Liberty Press, 2004), pp. 99–127—Ed.]. "If such a distribution of the circulating medium were to take place, as to throw the command of the produce of the country chiefly into the hands of the productive classes—that is, if considerable portions of the currency were taken from the idle and those who live upon fixed incomes, and transferred to farmers, manufacturers and merchants, the proportion between capital and revenue would be greatly altered to the advantage of capital; and, in a short time, the produce of the country would be greatly augmented.

"Whenever, in the actual state of things, a fresh issue of notes comes into the hands of those who mean to employ it [them] in the prosecution and extension of [a] profitable business, a difference in the distribution of the circulating medium takes place, similar in kind to that which has been last supposed; and produces similar, though, of course, comparatively inconsiderable effects, in altering the proportion between capital and revenue in favour of the former." [Malthus, "Review of Ricardo", p. 364; reprinted, *Works*, ed. Wrigley and Souden, vol. 7, p. 47—Ed.] The continuation of the passage is quoted in *Prices and Production*, 1st ed., p. 18 [reprinted, p. 206—Ed.]. [Thomas Robert Malthus (1766–1834), important classical economist, is best known for his views on population and his debate with Ricardo on the possibility of general gluts. David Ricardo (1772–1823) was the prime theorist (in the modern sense of abstract model-building) among the classical economists.—Ed.]

[18] Cf. *The Collected Works of Dugald Stewart*, ed. Sir William Hamilton, vol. 8 [that is, *Lectures on Political Economy*, vol. 1—Ed.] (London: Hamilton, Adams; Edinburgh: Constable, 1855 [reprinted, London: Thoemmes Press, 1994]), pp. 440–49. The reference to Dugald Stewart in this connection I owe to Prof. Jacob Viner. [Dugald Stewart (1753–1828), Scottish philosopher, had succeeded Adam Ferguson at the University of Edinburgh in the chair of moral philosophy and became the first biographer of Adam Smith.—Ed.]

[19] Lord Lauderdale had discussed the danger of a "forcible conversion of revenue into capital" or a "forced increase of capital", although in a slightly different context, already in 1804 in his

the *Bullion Report* and which were reprinted as an appendix to his *Lectures on Political Economy*, he objects to the over-simplified formulation of the quantity theory, employed in the reasoning of the *Bullion Report*,[20] and stresses the more "indirect connection between the high prices and an increased circulating medium".[21] He quotes first a statement from a letter by Lord Lauderdale that

> "*By the same act* with which a bank increases the circulating medium of a country, it issues into the community a mass of fictitious capital, which serves not only as circulating medium but creates an additional quantity of capital to be employed in every mode in which capital can be employed", and then adds: "The explanation you have given of the process by which this affects the price of commodities, coincides so exactly with my own ideas that it would be quite superfluous for me to follow out the speculation any farther. The radical evil, in short, seems to be, not the mere over-issue of notes, considered as an addition to our currency, but the anomalous and unchecked

---

Inquiry into the Nature and Origin of Public Wealth (Edinburgh: Constable, 1804), pp. 262, 267–68. [Cf. the second edition, 1819, reprinted, New York: Kelley, 1962, pp. 258, 264, and 265. Lauderdale refers to the accumulating fund destined for extinguishing the public debt whereby the annual contribution (of £6 million) would be "withdrawn from the acquisition of commodities . . . and *forcibly converted into capital*" (first edition, p. 262); yet he doubts whether a nation could "with impunity, either forcibly abstract a sum so large . . . from expenditure in consumable goods of its produce and manufacture; or *forcibly accumulate its capital* with such rapidity" (p. 267); and he objects to the plan "of abstracting from expenditure, and *forcibly converting into capital*" (p. 268) such a sum (emphasis added). James Maitland, 8th Earl of Lauderdale (1759–1839), was an English politician and a strong defender of the *Bullion Report.—*Ed.]

[20] [*Report, together with Minutes of Evidence, and Accounts, from the Select Committee on the High Price of Gold Bullion* (London, 1810), the octavo edition reprinted as *The Paper Pound of 1797–1821: A Reprint of the Bullion Report*, ed. Edwin Cannan, 2nd ed. (London: King, 1925; reprinted, New York: Kelley 1969); cf. also the reprint in *Scarce Tracts on Paper Currency*, ed. McCulloch. The *Bullion Report* addressed the question of the causes of the high price of bullion (that is, of unminted gold in terms of Bank of England notes, which were at a par with minted gold). This divergence in price had been made possible by the 1797 Restriction Act, by which, during the Napoleonic wars and in the face of a severe external drain, the Bank of England had been prohibited to redeem its notes into gold. Under these circumstances the 'bullionists' identified the over-issue of notes as the cause of the price rise, and recommended the resumption of cash payments by the Bank. In contrast, the 'anti-bullionists' sided with the Bank of England in maintaining that over-issue was impossible as long as only solid 'real bills' were accepted for discounting. The report, authored by Francis Horner, Henry Thornton, and William Huskisson and vehemently supported in the House by David Ricardo, argued along the lines of the bullionists, yet failed to win the approval of Parliament in 1811. For a more detailed account cf. F. A. Hayek, "The Period of Restrictions, 1797–1821, and the Bullion Debate in England", chapter 11 of *The Trend of Economic Thinking: Essays on Political Economists and Economic History*, ed. W. W. Bartley III and Stephen Kresge, vol. 3 (1999) of *The Collected Works of F. A. Hayek.—*Ed.]

[21] *The Collected Works of Dugald Stewart*, ed. Hamilton, vol. 8, p. 440. [Indeed, this is Lauderdale quoted by Stewart. The quotation is slightly inaccurate. It should read, "indirect connexion between high prices and an increased circulating medium".—Ed.]

extension of *credit* and its inevitable effect in producing a sudden augmentation of prices by a sudden augmentation of demand. The enlarged issue deserves attention, chiefly as affording a scale for measuring how far this extension has been carried. The same degree of credit, if it could have been given without the intervention of paper currency, would have operated in exactly the same way upon prices, and upon everything else."[22]

Stewart then discusses some different opinions stated by Thornton, in the *Bullion Report*, and by Huskisson,[23] and proceeds to draw a conclusion which, in a curious way, anticipates the subject, and even the formulation, of a well-known recent controversy:[24]

I have dwelt the longer on this particular view of the subject, considered in contrast with that adopted by Mr. Thornton (and apparently sanctioned in the last passage quoted from the *Bullion Report*) because the two opinions lead obviously to two very different conclusions concerning the nature of the remedy suited to the disorder. The one opinion suggests the propriety of limiting credit through the medium of a restricted currency; the other of limiting the currency through the medium of a well regulated and discriminating credit. If the radical evil were merely an excess of the circulating medium, operating as such without the combination of any other cause, it would follow that a reduction of this quantity, by whatsoever means it were to be brought about, and however violent the effects which it might threaten, would be the only measure competent to the attainment of the end. But if, on the other hand, this excess be only symptomatic of another malady, with which, from particular circumstances, it happens to be co-existent (of an extension of credit, to wit, calculated to derange the pre-existing relations of demand

---

[22] Ibid., p. 440 [pp. 440–41]. [The second part of the quotation is inaccurate. It should start with, "The explanation you have given of the process by which this affects the prices of commodities, coincides so exactly with all my own ideas . . .", and the beginning of the penultimate sentence should read, "The enlarged issues deserve attention . . ."—Ed.]

[23] [Cf. William Huskisson, *The Question Concerning the Depreciation of our Currency Stated and Examined*, 3rd ed. (London: Murray, 1810), reprinted in *Scarce Tracts on Paper Currency*, ed. McCulloch.—Ed.]

[24] Cf. John Maynard Keynes, *A Tract on Monetary Reform* (London: Macmillan, 1923), p. 184 [reprinted as vol. 4 (1972) of *The Collected Writings of John Maynard Keynes*, ed. Austin Robinson and Donald Moggridge (London: Macmillan; Cambridge: Cambridge University Press), p. 146—Ed.], and Prof. Edwin Cannan's article "Limitation of Currency or Limitation of Credit?", *Economic Journal*, vol. 34, March 1924, pp. 52–64, reprinted in the author's *An Economist's Protest* (London: King, 1927), pp. 370–84 [which is reprinted as vol. 6 of *The Collected Works of Edwin Cannan* (London: Routledge and Thoemmes Press, 1997). In his controversy with Keynes, Cannan argued for the limitation of currency, yet also denied the possibility of banks to create circulating media; cf. Hayek's criticism in his otherwise very favourable review of *An Economist's Protest* in *Zeitschrift für Nationalökonomie*, vol. 1, November 1929, pp. 467–70.—Ed.]

and supply) then in that case the restriction and *regulation* of this credit, ought to be regarded as the primary object, and the reduction of our circulating medium attended to solely as an indication that the cure is progressive.[25]

Stewart adds that, in his opinion, a repeal or relaxation of the anti-usurious laws "would go to the root of the mischief by a process more effectual, and at the same time more gentle and manageable in its operation, than any other that I can imagine",[26] and quotes in corroboration of that view the passage from Thornton in which this author anticipated Wicksell's theory as to the effect of a money rate of interest which is below the 'natural' rate.[27] A little later, Stewart comes back to this point, insisting that "the *primary* cause of the depreciation is the artificial cheapness in the rate at which, in consequence of the laws against usury, the use of money may be obtained".[28] And before he concludes this letter (which was written in March, 1811) he mentions that he has just seen the article (by Malthus) in the *Edinburgh Review* of February and that he was agreeably surprised to find the passage to which I have already alluded, which he quotes in full.[29]

After all this, there can be little doubt that the theory of 'forced saving' was fairly widely known among monetary writers in the early nineteenth century; and I should not be surprised if a closer study of the literature of the time revealed still more discussions of the problem.[30] Indeed, Prof. A. M. Marget

[25] *The Collected Works of Dugald Stewart*, ed. Hamilton, vol. 8, p. 443. [Apart from punctuation, the only inaccuracy in Hayek's quotation is at the beginning of the third sentence, which should start, "If the radical evil were merely an excess of circulating medium . . ."—Ed.]

[26] Ibid. [Until the Bank Charter Act of 1833 existing usury laws prohibited the Bank from raising the discount rate above five percent. Cf. on this F. A. Hayek, "The Dispute between the Currency School and the Banking School, 1821–1848", chapter 12 of F. A. Hayek, *The Trend of Economic Thinking*.—Ed.]

[27] Thornton, *Paper Credit*, p. 287 [cf. the American edition (1807), p. 183; *Scarce Tracts on Paper Currency*, ed. McCulloch, p. 319; *Paper Credit*, ed. Hayek, pp. 253–54—Ed.]. The passage is quoted and discussed in my *Prices and Production* [1st ed.], pp. 12, 13 [reprinted, pp. 201–2—Ed.].

[28] *The Collected Works of Dugald Stewart*, ed. Hamilton, vol. 8, p. 447.

[29] Ibid., pp. 448–49.

[30] Since these lines were first published [in 1932—Ed.], Professor Jacob Viner, *Studies in the Theory of International Trade* (London: Allen and Unwin, 1937), pp. 189–96, has given an even more extensive list of such further early discussions of the problem than I should have expected. His main additional references are: Robert Torrens, *An Essay on Money and Paper Currency* (London: Johnson and Co., 1812) [reprinted in the *Collected Works of Robert Torrens*, ed. Giancarlo de Vivo, vol. 1 (Bristol: Thoemmes Press, 2000)—Ed.], pp. 34ff. [pp. 34–41]; Thomas Robert Malthus, "Review of Tooke" [titled "Thoughts and Details on the High and Low Prices of the Last Thirty Years"—Ed.], *Quarterly Review*, vol. 29, April 1823, p. 239 [reprinted, *The Works of Thomas Robert Malthus*, ed. Wrigley and Souden, vol. 7, p. 253—Ed.]; Lord Lauderdale, *Further Considerations on the State of the Currency* (Edinburgh: Constable, 1813), pp. 96–97; John Rooke, *A Supplement to the Remarks on the Nature and Operations of Money* (London: Baldwin, Cradock, and Joy, 1819), pp. 68–69; Thomas Tooke, *Considerations on the State of the Currency*, 2nd ed. (London: Murray,

has noted a rather general allusion to it in R. Torrens' *Essay on the Production of Wealth*.[31] But it would be surprising if an idea, which was discussed as widely as this one was, should in the course of time be entirely forgotten; and this was by no means the case here. John Stuart Mill in the fourth of his *Essays on Some Unsettled Questions of Political Economy*—"On Profits and Interest"—written in 1829 or 1830, goes at least so far as to mention that, as a result of the activity of bankers, "revenue" may be "converted into capital; and thus, strange as it may appear, the depreciation of the currency, when effected in this way, operates to a certain extent as a forced accumulation".[32] But he believed then that this phenomenon belonged to the "further anomalies of the rate of interest which have not, so far as we are aware, been hitherto brought within the pale of exact science".[33] The early editions of his *Principles* seem to contain nothing on this point. But in 1865, in the sixth edition, he added to his chapter on "Credit as a Substitute for Money" a footnote which so closely resembles the statement by Malthus that it seems very probable that something—perhaps the publication of D. Stewart's *Collected Works*, in 1855, containing the discussion to which we have already referred (including the quotation from Malthus)—had directed his attention to the earlier discussion of the point.

1826), pp. 23–24; Thomas Joplin, *An Illustration of Mr. Joplin's Views on Currency* (London: Baldwin, Cradock and Joy, 1825), pp. 28ff. [pp. 28–29], and *Views on the Currency* (London: Ridgway, 1828), p. 146. [Robert Torrens (1780–1864), a retired army officer and journalist, was the author of a classic defense of the currency principle. Thomas Tooke (1774–1858), an English merchant, is considered the preeminent member of the banking school; incidentally, at LSE Hayek occupied the chair for economics and statistics named after Tooke. John Rooke (1780–1856), British political economist and geologist, was an advocate of free trade. Thomas Joplin (circa 1790–1847), banker, was best known for his advocacy of joint-stock banks and criticism of the monopoly of the Bank of England; his contributions to contemporary monetary debate, although original, were largely neglected.—Ed.]

[31] Robert Torrens, *An Essay on the Production of Wealth* (London: Longman, Hurst, Rees, Orme, and Brown, 1821), pp. 326 et seq. [pp. 326–327; reprinted, *Collected Works*, ed. de Vivo, vol. 3—Ed.]. The reference is given by Prof. Arthur W. Marget in his excellent article on "Léon Walras and the 'Cash Balance Approach' to the Problem of the Value of Money", *Journal of Political Economy*, vol. 39, October 1931, p. 598.

[32] John Stuart Mill, *Essays on Some Unsettled Questions of Political Economy*, 2nd ed. (London: Longmans, Green, Reader, and Dyer, 1874), p. 118 [as reprinted in *Essays on Economics and Society, Part 1*, vol. 4 (1967) of the *Collected Works of John Stuart Mill*, ed. Robson, p. 307. John Stuart Mill (1806–73) was a British classical economist and moral philosopher, whose *Principles of Political Economy* was the leading textbook before the advent of Marshall's *Principles* and of neoclassical economics.—Ed.]. I owe this reference to Mr. Victor Edelberg. [Victor Edelberg was at the time a graduate student at LSE and soon to publish a paper on "The Ricardian Theory of Profits", *Economica*, no. 39, February 1933, pp. 51–74.—Ed.]

[33] Mill, *Essays on Some Unsettled Questions of Political Economy*, p. 114. [Cf. reprinted, ed. Robson, p. 305. Hayek's quotation is inaccurate. It should read, "further anomalies in the rate of interest".—Ed.]

The footnote, which qualifies a statement made in the text that credit serves only to transfer capital from one person to another, is as follows:—

> To make the proposition in the text strictly true, a corrective—though a very slight one—requires to be made. The circulating medium existing in a country at a given time is partly employed in purchases for productive, partly for unproductive, consumption. According as a larger proportion of it is employed in the one way or in the other, the real capital of the country is greater or less. If, then, an addition were made to the circulating medium in the hands of unproductive consumers exclusively, a larger portion of the existing stock of commodities would be bought for unproductive consumption, and a smaller for a productive, which state of things, while it lasted, would be equivalent to a diminution of capital; and, on the contrary, if the addition made be to the portion of the circulating medium which is in the hands of producers, and destined for their business, a greater portion of the commodities of the country will be, for the present, employed as capital, and a less portion unproductively. Now an effect of this latter character naturally attends some extensions of credit, especially when taking place in the form of bank notes or other instruments of exchange. The additional bank notes are, in ordinary course, first issued to producers or dealers, to be employed as capital; and though the stock of commodities in the country is no greater than before, yet as a greater share of that stock now comes by purchase into the hands of producers and dealers, to that extent what would have been unproductively consumed is applied to production, and there is a real increase of capital. The effect ceases, and a counter-process takes place, when the additional credit is stopped, and the notes called in.[34]

Only fourteen years after this remarkably clear statement by John Stuart Mill, we find that exposition of the theory of 'forced saving' to which the modern developments can be pretty definitely traced. Whether Léon Wal-

---

[34] Mill, *Principles of Political Economy*, ed. Ashley, p. 512 [cf. *Principles of Political Economy, Part 2*, ed. John M. Robson, vol. 3 (1965) of the *Collected Works of John Stuart Mill*, p. 528n.65. There are two inaccuracies in Hayek's quotation. In the second sentence the final passage should read, "purchases for productive, and partly for unproductive consumption", and the final passage of the fourth sentence, "a greater portion of the commodities in the country will for the present be employed as capital, and a less portion unproductively".—Ed.] This passage in the *Principles* has been pointed out by Prof. Marco Fanno in his article "Cicli di produzione, cicli di [del] credito e fluttuazioni industriali", *Giornali* [*Giornale*] *degli Economisti*, vol. 46 (4th series), May 1931, p. 31 of the reprint [p. 360 of the *Giornale*; translated as "Production Cycles, Credit Cycles and Industrial Fluctuations", in *Structural Change and Economic Dynamics*, vol. 4, December 1993, p. 428, reprinted in *Business Cycle Theory: Selected Texts 1860–1939*, vol. 2: *Structural Theories of the Business Cycle*, ed. Harald Hagemann (London: Pickering and Chatto, 2002), p. 252.—Ed.]

ras, who in 1879 devoted a long section of his *Théorie Mathématique du Billet de Banque* to a discussion of it, had been directly influenced by Mill is not known; but it seems quite probable. That Walras inspired K. Wicksell and, through Wicksell, all the later German authors who dealt with the problem, there can be little doubt. But Walras' very interesting discussion was practically forgotten, until attention was recently drawn to it by Professor Marget in the article quoted above. Indeed, Walras there gives more than his disciple Wicksell—or any other author up to quite recent times. In a section headed "Accroissement du Capital par l'émission des Billets de Banque",[35] he analyses, in great detail, what he calls the undeniable fact that "L'émission des billets de banque pour une certaine somme permet une augmentation dans la quantité du capital pour une somme égale".[36] He sees clearly that the expansion of bank credit "crée non pas un capital nouveau, mais une demande nouvelle de capital, et le capital lui-même reste à créer"; in consequence, "la proportion de la production des revenues consommables et des capitaux neufs est changée, il y a diminution dans la quantité des uns et augmentation dans la quantité des autres".[37] The situation is not quite the same as in the case of a sudden and considerable increase in saving, because

dans le cas de l'émission des billets de banque, comme cela aurait aussi lieu dans le cas de la découverte de monnaie métallique, il y a augmentation de demande d'un côté sans diminution de demande de l'autre, et, par suite, augmentation dans la valeur totale de la production. Ainsi: *L'émission de billets de banque pour une certaine somme amère, pendant toute la période d'émission, une hausse du prix des produits consistant en revenus consommables et capitaux neufs qui se mesure approximativement par le rapport du montant de l'émission au montant du revenu*

---

[35] Cf. Léon Walras, "Théorie mathématique du billet de banque" [1879], reprinted in *Études d'économie politique appliquée* (Lausanne: Rouge; Paris: Pichon, 1898 [2nd ed., 1936]), pp. 348–56. [Reprinted as vol. 10 of Auguste et Léon Walras, *Oeuvres économiques complètes* (Paris: Economica, 1992), pp. 318–26; translated by Jan van Daal as "Mathematical Theory of Banknotes", in *Studies in Applied Economics*, vol. 2 (London: Routledge, 2005), pp. 280–85. The translation of the section heading reads, "Capital increase because of the issue of banknotes", ibid., p. 280.—Léon Walras (1834–1910) has become famous as the founder of the Lausanne school, which fused the Marginal Revolution with a distinctly mathematical approach. Beyond developing the notion of general equilibrium as an important instrument for dealing with economic statics, he struggled to introduce money into general equilibrium analysis.—Ed.]

[36] [Ibid., p. 349 (*Oeuvres*, p. 319; *Studies*, p. 280: "the issue of a certain amount of banknotes allows an increase in the quantity of capital to an equal amount"); the passage is emphasised in the original.—Ed.]

[37] [Ibid., p. 350 (*Oeuvres*, p. 320; *Studies*, p. 281: "does not create new capital, but creates an additional demand for capital. The capital itself remains to be created"; in consequence "the proportions of the production of consumer and capital goods are changed in the sense that the former decreases and the latter increases"). Hayek's quotation is inaccurate; it should read "*revenus*" instead of "*revenues*".—Ed.]

social antérieur. Ce phénomène est transitoire: une fois l'émission terminée, la hausse en question disparaît, et il ne subsiste plus que celle provenant de la dépréciation du métal précieux.[38]

Finally, Walras elaborates this theory in algebraic form and gives an arithmetical example in order to show what the practical importance of the phenomenon may be.

In Wicksell's exposition,[39] this idea, although only briefly mentioned, becomes an integral part of his theory as to the effect of a money rate of interest which is different from the equilibrium rate. From Wicksell, the idea was taken over by Mises,[40] who elaborated it still further, and from Mises by Schumpeter.[41] Through their influence, it has recently become quite a familiar feature of German writings on the subject,[42] even before the interest in these problems was further stimulated by the new, and apparently independent, de-

[38] [Ibid., p. 351 (*Oeuvres*, p. 321; *Studies*, pp. 281–82: "In the case of an issue of banknotes, just as in the case of the unearthing of metallic money, there is an increase in demand on one side, without a decrease in demand on the other, and, consequently, the production's total value would increase. Hence: *during the period of issue of a certain amount of banknotes the price rise of the products, both consumer goods and new capital goods, can be measured approximately by the ratio of the amount of the issue to the amount of social revenue beforehand.* This phenomenon is transitory: once the issue is finished, the price increase in question will disappear and only the price increase arising from the depreciation of the precious metals will remain.") Hayek's quotation is inaccurate; it should read "*amène*" instead of "*amère*".—Ed.]

[39] Knut Wicksell, *Geldzins und Güterpreise: Eine Studie über die den Tauschwert des Geldes bestimmenden Ursachen* (Jena: Fischer, 1898 [reprinted, Aalen: Scientia, 1968]), pp. 103, 142 [that is, correctly, pp. 102 and 143; translated as *Interest and Prices: A Study of the Causes Regulating the Value of Money*, trans. Richard F. Kahn (London: Macmillan, 1936; reprinted, New York: Kelley, 1965, and Auburn, AL: Ludwig von Mises Institute, 2007), pp. 111 and 155. Knut Wicksell (1851–1926), Swedish economist, professor at the University of Lund from 1903 to 1917, attempted a synthesis of Austrian capital theory and the theory of marginal productivity within Walras's general equilibrium framework. His most original contribution was to monetary theory, where he emphasised the indirect mechanism of money on prices by way of its impact on the money rate of interest.—Ed.].

[40] Ludwig von Mises, *Theorie des Geldes und der Umlaufsmittel* (Munich and Leipzig: Duncker and Humblot, 1912) [the second revised edition (1924) translated as *The Theory of Money and Credit*, trans. Harold E. Batson (London: Cape, 1934; reprinted, Indianapolis: Liberty Press, 1981).—Ed.].

[41] Joseph A. Schumpeter, *Theorie der wirtschaftlichen Entwicklung* (Munich and Leipzig: Duncker and Humblot, 1912) [the second revised edition (1926) translated as *The Theory of Economic Development*, trans. Redvers Opie (Cambridge, MA: Harvard University Press, 1934). Joseph Alois Schumpeter (1883–1950) studied at the University of Vienna and, after a short spell as Austrian minister of finance in 1919, taught at Graz, Bonn, and ultimately, from 1932 to 1950, at Harvard. In his theory, credit creation and forced saving are vital for the furthering of innovation and progress.—Ed.].

[42] These more recent German developments have been discussed, in some detail, in an article by Dr. Erich Egner, "Zur Lehre vom Zwangssparen", *Zeitschrift für die gesamte Staatswissenschaft*, vol. 84, no. 3, 1928, pp. 529–60.

velopment of similar ideas among the Cambridge School of Economists. Mr. D. H. Robertson's 'Imposed Lacking' and Professor Pigou's 'Forced Levies'[43] are, of course, just the same thing as Bentham's 'Forced Frugality', J. S. Mill's 'Forced Accumulation' and the 'Erzwungene Sparen' or 'Zwangssparen' of Wicksell and the German authors. Mr. J. M. Keynes, however, who discusses the same problem in his *Treatise on Money*,[44] rejects this terminology and prefers to speak simply of investment being in excess of saving; and there is much to be said in favour of this. Unfortunately, however, Mr. Keynes uses the terms 'saving' and 'investing' in a sense quite different from the usual one, so that, for some time, the danger of confusion may make difficult the acceptance of what is perhaps the better terminology.

[43] [Cf. Dennis H. Robertson, *Banking Policy and the Price Level: An Essay in the Theory of the Trade Cycle* (London: King, 1926), reprinted as vol. 3 of *The Development of Monetary Theory, 1920s and 1930s*, ed. Forrest Capie and Geoffrey E. Wood (London: Routledge, 2000), p. 49; and Arthur Cecil Pigou, "Correctives of the Trade Cycle", in *Is Unemployment Inevitable? An Analysis and a Forecast. A Continuation of the Investigations Embodied in "The Third Winter of Unemployment"*, ed. Walter Layton (London: Macmillan, 1925), p. 100, reprinted in *Business Cycle Theory: Selected Texts 1860–1939*, vol. 3: *Monetary Theories of the Business Cycle*, ed. Hagemann, p. 128; cf. also Pigou, *Industrial Fluctuations*, 2nd ed. (London: Macmillan, 1929), reprinted as vol. 6 of *Collected Economic Writings* (London: Macmillan, 1999), pp. 251 and 253. Dennis Holme Robertson (1890–1963), Cambridge economist, incorporated monetary factors and the mechanism of forced saving, in the guise of idiosyncratic terminology, into his theory of the business cycle. Arthur Cecil Pigou (1877–1959), Cambridge economist and the successor of Alfred Marshall as professor of political economy, 1908–43, combined in his theory of the business cycle monetary and psychological factors.—Ed.]

[44] John Maynard Keynes, *A Treatise on Money*, 2 vols. (London: Macmillan, 1930), vol. 1, p. 171 [reprinted as vols. 5 and 6 (1971) of *The Collected Writings of John Maynard Keynes*; cf. vol. 5, p. 154—Ed.].

FOUR

THE PRESENT STATE AND IMMEDIATE PROSPECTS OF THE STUDY OF INDUSTRIAL FLUCTUATIONS[1]

However one defines *Konjunkturforschung*[2] there can be little question that its present state, as well as its prospects and tasks in the immediate future, is determined more by the extent of our present understanding of the causes operating in this field than by the amount of descriptive material at our disposal—the latter representing the constantly changing object to which we have to apply our theoretical knowledge. In the following attempt to discuss the "present state and the immediate prospects of *Konjunkturforschung*" this term will therefore be interpreted in the sense of the general theory of industrial fluctuations and not as referring to the technique and method of current observation practised by the various economic services

It can hardly be denied that this branch of economic theory has made considerable progress during the last ten years and that the state of our knowledge is considerably more satisfactory than a generation or even a few years ago; and it is probably also true that there is comparatively more agreement among theoretical economists interested in this field than among the contemporaries who are largely interested in factual description. At least in so far as the factors determining the boom and the immediate causes of the crisis are concerned there is to-day no fundamental difference between the views of say Spiethoff, Cassel, Wicksell, and Mises[3] and a large group of writers who in other respects hold very different views—J. Åkerman, B. M. Anderson, Bresciani-Turroni, Budge, Eucken, Fanno, Fasiani, Haberler, Halm, Landauer, Machlup, Morgenstern, Robertson, Robbins, Röpke, Strigl, and Adolf Weber.[4] The achieve-

---

[1] [First published as chapter 6 of F. A. Hayek, *Profits, Interest and Investment. And Other Essays on the Theory of Industrial Fluctuations* (London: Routledge, 1939); translated from "Der Stand und die nächste Zukunft der Konjunkturforschung", in *Festschrift für Arthur Spiethoff*, ed. Gustav Clausing (Munich: Duncker and Humblot, 1933), pp. 110–17.—Ed.]

[2] [That is, 'business cycle research' or the 'study of industrial fluctuations'.—Ed.]

[3] [For biographical information on these authors see above, pp. 131, 63, 169, and 58.—Ed.]

[4] [Johan Henryk Åkerman (1896–1982), a Swedish economist, professor at the University of Lund, in the 1930s contributed to business cycle research and reviewed Hayek's *Preise und Produktion* in the *Zeitschrift für Nationalökonomie*, vol. 5, no. 3, 1934, pp. 372–79. Benjamin McAlester Anderson Jr. (1886–1949) was an American banker and economist in the Austrian tradition; for his monetary theory see *The Value of Money* (New York: Macmillan, 1917; reprinted, Grove City, PA:

ment of the last few years which must not be underestimated is the clearer insight we have at last gained into a process often vaguely seen but never before adequately described or explained: the process by which misdirections of capital caused by credit expansion will in the end, when consumers' demand grows too rapidly, lead to a scarcity of capital which makes it impossible to use a large part of the equipment which has been adapted to a state where capital was more abundant. The most important advance in this field is undoubtedly the more careful analysis of this state of "simultaneous scarcity and

---

Libertarian Press, 2005). Costatino Bresciani-Turroni (1882–1963), Italian economist, is best known for his succinct analysis of the German hyperinflation, *The Economics of Inflation: A Study of Currency Depreciation in Post-War Germany*, trans. Millicent E. Sayers (London: Allen and Unwin, 1937; reprinted, London: Routledge, 2003). Siegfried Budge (1869–1941) taught monetary theory at the University of Frankfurt until his dismissal in 1933. Walter Eucken (1891–1950) was professor at the University of Freiburg, 1927–50, where he became one of the founders of the Freiburg school of economics and law, and of ordoliberalism. Marco Fanno (1878–1965) was an important Italian economist of the interwar period; Hayek highly esteemed Fanno's contributions to the theory of money and the cycle and chose one of his essays for translation in *Beiträge zur Geldtheorie*, ed. F. A. Hayek (Vienna: Springer, 1933; reprinted, Berlin, Heidelberg, and New York: Springer, 2007). Mauro Fasiani (1900–1950) taught public finance in Turin, Sassari, Trieste, and, from 1934, Genoa. Gottfried Haberler (1900–1995), Austrian economist and a friend of Hayek from their days in Vienna, became professor at Harvard, 1936–71; in the 1930s he worked on a systematic analysis of the business cycle eventually to appear as *Prosperity and Depression* (Geneva: League of Nations, 1937). Georg Nikolaus Halm (1901–84) was a German economist; Hayek thoroughly discussed Halm's doctoral thesis, "Das Zinsproblem am Geld- und Kapitalmarkt", *Jahrbücher für Nationalökonomie und Statistik*, vol. 125 (3rd series, vol. 70), nos. 1 and 2, 1926, pp. 1–34 and 97–121, in *Monetary Theory and the Trade Cycle* (London: Cape, 1933), reprinted in *Business Cycles, Part I*, ed. Hansjoerg Klausinger, vol. 7 (2012) of *The Collected Works of F. A. Hayek* (Chicago: University of Chicago Press), p. 160. Carl Landauer (1891–1983), German socialist economist and journalist, taught at the Handelshochschule Berlin, 1926–33, and after his forced emigration at the University of California, Berkeley, 1934–59. Fritz Machlup (1902–83), Austrian economist and another friend of Hayek from their student days, immigrated to the United States in the 1930s and taught at the University of Buffalo, Johns Hopkins University, and Princeton University. In 1933 Machlup had just published *Börsenkredit, Industriekredit und Kapitalbildung* (Vienna: Springer, 1931; reprinted, Frankfurt: Frankfurter Allgemeine, 2002); a revised version was translated by Vera C. Smith as *The Stock Market, Credit and Capital Formation* (London: Hodge, 1940). Oskar Morgenstern (1902–77) accomplished his habilitation at the University of Vienna with his monograph *Wirtschaftsprognose: Eine Untersuchung ihrer Voraussetzungen und Möglichkeiten* (Vienna: Springer, 1928); in 1931 he succeeded Hayek as the director of the Austrian Institute for Business Cycle Research. Presently, he is best known for his collaboration with John von Neumann (1903–57) in the foundation of game theory. Dennis Holme Robertson's most important contribution in this respect was *Banking Policy and the Price Level: An Essay in the Theory of the Trade Cycle* (London: King, 1926), reprinted as vol. 3 of *The Development of Monetary Theory, 1920s and 1930s*, ed. Forrest Capie and Geoffrey E. Wood (London: Routledge, 2000); for biographical information see above, p. 170. Lionel Robbins (1898–1984), head of the Economics Department at LSE, 1928–60, closely cooperated with Hayek during the 1930s; in 1933 he was just writing *The Great Depression* (London: Macmillan, 1934; reprinted, Auburn, AL: Ludwig von Mises Institute, 2007), very much along Austrian lines. Wilhelm Röpke

abundance" (Spiethoff),[5] which is somewhat inadequately described by the terms 'scarcity of capital' or 'scarcity of circulating capital', an analysis which has led to the conclusion that this scarcity of capital is simply relative over-consumption. In addition to the demonstration, which this implies, that the under-consumption theories are logically indefensible,[6] the most important step in this direction was the regained understanding of the function of the rate of interest—and particularly of its necessity even in a stationary state—which had been badly obscured by the temporary fashion of interest theories based on purely 'dynamic' considerations or merely on considerations of banking liquidity.[7] Perhaps not much less important for the increasing agree-

---

(1892–1966), German economist, before 1933 professor of economics in Jena, Graz, and Marburg, combined Austrian ideas on the origins of the crisis with the recommendation of expansionist policies to combat deep depressions; cf. for a summary of his views *Krise und Konjunktur* (Leipzig: Quelle and Meyer, 1932), translated as *Crises and Cycles* (London: Hodge, 1936; reprinted, Auburn, AL: Ludwig von Mises Institute, 2007). After his forced emigration Röpke taught in Istanbul and Geneva, and in post-war Germany became an advocate of the model of the Social Market Economy. Richard Strigl (1891–1942), a student of Böhm-Bawerk, contributed to the Austrian theory of capital and the cycle; in the 1930s he taught at the University of Vienna and the Hochschule für Welthandel. Adolf Weber (1876–1950), German economist, was professor of economics and public finance at the University of Munich, 1921–48. His main contribution to monetary business cycle theory had been his *Depositenbanken und Spekulationsbanken: Ein Vergleich deutschen und englischen Bankwesens*, 3rd ed. (Leipzig: Duncker and Humblot, 1922).—Ed.]

[5] [Cf. Arthur Spiethoff, "Krisen", in *Handwörterbuch der Staatswissenschaften*, 4th ed. rev., ed. Ludwig Elster, Adolf Weber, and Friedrich Wieser, vol. 6 (Jena: Fischer, 1925), p. 78; translated in an abridged version as "Business Cycles", in *International Economic Papers*, vol. 3, 1953, reprinted in *Business Cycle Theory: Selected Texts 1860–1939*, vol. 2: *Structural Theories of the Business Cycle*, ed. Harald Hagemann (London: Pickering and Chatto, 2002), p. 193, where the passage is translated as "at the same time shortage and superfluity".—Ed.]

[6] [On Hayek's critique of underconsumption theories, in particular those of Foster and Catchings, see p. 143n.4 above.—Ed.]

[7] This was, of course, written [in 1933—Ed.] before Mr. Keynes with his *General Theory* started in this country a fashion very similar to that which had prevailed in Germany in the nineteen-twenties [cf. John Maynard Keynes, *The General Theory of Employment, Interest and Money* (London: Macmillan 1936), reprinted as vol. 7 (1971) of *The Collected Writings of John Maynard Keynes*, ed. Austin Robinson and Donald Moggridge (London: Macmillan; Cambridge: Cambridge University Press)—Ed.]. The statement in the text refers to Schumpeter's 'dynamic' theory of interest and particularly to L. Albert Hahn's *Volkswirtschaftliche Theorie des Bankkredits* (Tübingen: Mohr, 1920), which contains a discussion of "the rate of interest as a price for the loss of liquidity" [ibid., p. 102—Ed.] which at the time attracted much attention and gave rise to extensive discussions. [This footnote was added to the 1939 translation. On the famous debate of Schumpeter's 'dynamic' theory of interest expounded in his *Theorie der wirtschaftlichen Entwicklung* (Munich and Leipzig: Duncker and Humblot, 1912), see Eugen von Böhm-Bawerk's review, "Eine 'dynamische' Theorie des Kapitalzinses", Schumpeter's reply, "Eine 'dynamische' Theorie des Kapitalzinses: Eine Entgegnung", and Böhm-Bawerk's rejoinder, "Schlußbemerkungen", all in *Zeitschrift für Volkswirtschaft, Sozialpolitik und Verwaltung*, vol. 22, no. 1, 1913, pp. 1–62, and no. 3, 1913, pp. 599–639 and pp. 640–56, respectively. For a reprint of Böhm-

ment on fundamentals was the abandonment of the idea, based on the more naive monetary theories of the trade cycle, that all that was required to abolish industrial fluctuations was the stabilisation of the price level; this last advance, however, was probably due less to the theoretical argument of a few economists than to the bad disappointment caused by the crisis of 1929 following a period of fairly stable prices.[8]

This important agreement on fundamentals must, however, neither deceive us into disregarding the important differences between the formulations by the various authors, which indeed are such that in many instances it is difficult to recognise the fundamental similarity of their views, nor make us forget that even the common general outline of these explanations still contains problems the solution of which has hardly yet been attempted. We have as yet very little of that developed theory of the formation, maintenance, transformation and consumption of capital which takes account of the different degrees of mobility and adaptability of the different kinds of capital goods[9] and their distribution between the various stages of production which we need if we are to be able to translate the abstract scheme of our explanation into more concrete terms. To give only one example of how little we really know about the dynamics of capitalistic production, it may be mentioned that even such a fundamental concept as that of 'maintaining capital intact' is still exceedingly vague and obscure in its meaning—although, of course, problems like that of the correspondence between (new) savings and (new) investments, which play such a great role in all the theories belonging to this group, can hardly be intelligently discussed without a clear conception of what is meant by maintaining capital intact.

But even if we can hope that these conceptual difficulties still inherent in the present formulation of our theory will be gradually cleared up in the course of further discussion,[10] there are undeniably other chapters of the ex-

Bawerk's review see Böhm-Bawerk, *Kleinere Abhandlungen über Kapital und Zins*, ed. Franz X. Weiss (Vienna: Hölder-Pichler-Tempsky, 1926; reprinted, Frankfurt: Sauer and Auvermann, 1968), pp. 520–85, and for Schumpeter's reply see Schumpeter, *Aufsätze zur ökonomischen Theorie*, ed. Erich Schneider and Arthur Spiethoff (Tübingen: Mohr, 1952), pp. 411–51. In the 1920s the German banker and economist Lucien Albert Hahn (1889–1968) had propagated the idea of inflationary credit created by the banks.—Ed.]

[8] [For Hayek's case on the 1929 crisis cf. his "Das Schicksal der Goldwährung", *Der Deutsche Volkswirt*, vol. 6, February 12 and 19, 1932, pp. 642–45 and 677–81, translated as "The Fate of the Gold Standard" and reprinted as chapter 3 of *Good Money, Part I: The New World*, ed. Stephen Kresge, vol. 5 (1999) of *The Collected Works of F. A. Hayek.*—Ed.]

[9] [Here 'mobility' and 'adaptability' denote the opposites of what Hayek in other places had termed the 'specificity' and 'complementarity' of capital goods. Note that in the German version Hayek does not speak of "different kinds of capital goods", but of "durable and non-durable capital goods" (cf. "Der Stand und die nächste Zukunft", p. 111).—Ed.]

[10] [Cf. Hayek's own contributions to this discussion, "The Maintenance of Capital", *Economica*, n.s., vol. 2, August 1935, pp. 241–76, reprinted as chapter 3 of F. A. Hayek, *Profits, Interest and Investment*, and "Maintaining Capital Intact: A Reply to Professor Pigou", *Economica*, n.s., vol. 8,

planations of industrial fluctuations which are in a much less satisfactory state. As soon as we proceed from the causes of the crisis proper to the explanation of the more advanced stages of the depression and of the process of liquidation which restores some sort of equilibrium, that is as soon as we turn to the problems which at the present moment are most intensively discussed, we find hardly any agreement between the various writers and I doubt whether anyone can pride himself on having a clear picture of these complicated processes. Yet it seems to me as if the better insight we have gained into the crucial problems of the crisis proper had also improved prospects of progress in this field. If this process of liquidation and adjustment which follows the crisis is still largely unexplored, this is probably due to the fact that it can be understood only on the basis of a correct explanation of the crisis; and if there is reason to be optimistic about recent progress on the latter point, we are probably also justified in now expecting more rapid progress in the former field. But the attempts (of which Mr. Keynes' *Treatise on Money* is probably the most interesting[11]) made so far to clear up these (in a methodological sense) secondary complications which arise during the depression, all suffer from the defect that they proceed from an assumed position of disequilibrium without a sufficient explanation how this has arisen.

How confused ideas still are with respect to the problems of the liquidation and readjustment of the economic system after a crisis is well illustrated by the vague and indefinite way in which in recent years financial journalists and others have discussed the problem of liquidation of the present depression. The analysis of the crisis shows that, once an excessive increase of the capital structure has proved insupportable and has led to a crisis, profitability of production can be restored only by considerable changes in relative prices, reductions of certain stocks, and transfers of means of production to other uses. In connection with these changes, liquidations of firms in a purely financial sense of the word may be inevitable, and their postponement may possibly delay the process of liquidation in the first, more general sense; but this is a separate and special phenomenon which in recent discussions has been stressed rather excessively at the expense of the more fundamental changes in prices,

---

August 1941, pp. 276–80, both to be included in *Capital and Interest*, ed. Lawrence White, vol. 11 (forthcoming) of *The Collected Works of F. A. Hayek.*—Ed.]

[11] For a discussion of Mr. Keynes' views and the way in which confusions inherent in his fundamental concepts have vitiated his comprehensive attempt to clear up those complications cf. my "Reflections on the Pure Theory of Money of Mr. J. M. Keynes", *Economica*, no. 33, August 1931, pp. 270–95; "A Rejoinder to Mr. Keynes", *Economica*, no. 34, November 1931, pp. 398–403; and "Reflections on the Pure Theory of Money of Mr. J. M. Keynes (continued)", *Economica*, no. 35, February 1932, pp. 22–44. [Reprinted as chapters 3, 5, and 6 of *Contra Keynes and Cambridge: Essays, Correspondence*, ed. Bruce Caldwell, vol. 9 (1995) of *The Collected Works of F. A. Hayek*. Hayek's "Reflections" are a two-part review of Keynes's *A Treatise on Money*, 2 vols. (London: Macmillan, 1930), reprinted as vols. 5 and 6 (1971) of *The Collected Writings of John Maynard Keynes.*—Ed.]

stocks, etc. A theoretical problem of great importance which needs to be elucidated in this connection is the significance, for this process of liquidation, of the rigidity of prices and wages, which since the great war has undoubtedly become very considerable. There can be little question that these rigidities tend to delay the process of adaptation and that this will cause a 'secondary' deflation[12] which at first will intensify the depression but ultimately will help to overcome these rigidities. The main problems in this connection, on which opinions are still diametrically opposed, are, firstly, whether this process of deflation is merely an evil which has to be combated, or whether it does not serve a necessary function in breaking these rigidities, and, secondly, whether the persistence of these deflationary tendencies proves that the fundamental maladjustment of prices still exists, or whether, once that process of deflation has gathered momentum, it may not continue[13] long after it has served its initial function.

Such an induced[14] process of deflation (i.e., a process not deliberately brought about by the central banks and which might occur equally under a purely metallic currency) raises problems of the most interesting kind. Quite apart from the fact which has always been emphasised, probably rightly, by men of practical experience, that it is very questionable whether such a deflation can be successfully combated by the ordinary means of central banking policy, it is quite possible that a general expectation of a continued fall of prices may have very peculiar effects and may invert certain rules which apply under normal conditions: it is for instance at least conceivable that a fall of the prices of consumers' goods, which creates the expectation of still lower prices in the future, may make the current production of consumers' goods appear more profitable than investments which will help the production of consumers' goods in the future, and thus will lead to a reduction of the proportion of capital used in the production of consumers' goods. This influence of price expectations on the structure of production and the closely connected questions of changes in the velocity of circulation of money or the cash balances held are problems which urgently require study within the general framework of a theory of intertemporal price relationships. What is needed is a fusion of

---

[12] [On the notion of 'secondary deflation' cf. the editor's introduction to this volume, pp. 5–15.—Ed.]

[13] [The German version, "Der Stand und die nächste Zukunft", p. 113, reads, "it may continue"; the word "not" was added in the translation.—Ed.]

[14] Since this was written I have learnt that the term 'induced' deflation has been used by American economists, probably more logically, in the exactly opposite sense, to describe a deflation induced by the banking system. 'Spontaneous' deflation would probably have been a better term for what is meant in the text. [For the concept of induced deflation as used by American economists see, e.g., Jacob Viner, *Balanced Deflation, Inflation, or More Depression* (Minneapolis: University of Minnesota Press, 1933), pp. 13–19, reprinted in *The Development of Monetary Theory, 1920s and 1930s*, ed. Capie and Wood, vol. 4.—Ed.]

the results of the study of three groups of problems, up till now discussed in separate sections of economic theory: the capital problem which results from the fact that cash balances are capital from the point of view of the individual but not for society as a whole; the monetary problem of changes in the velocity of circulation; and in price theory the problem of intertemporal exchange relationships. It is only from such a development that we can expect that advance in the theory of interest, making it more realistic and concrete, which I have discussed in another place.[15]

Finally, as the last and most important of the problems which urgently require solution, we might mention the mechanism of the re-absorption of the unemployed productive forces—men as well as equipment—at the end of a depression and particularly the role of credit expansion in this process. Although the general principles raise here no great difficulties, and although in particular it is probably generally recognised to-day that the need for additional credit in this connection is a genuine need for additional capital, it must be admitted that the traditional analysis of the effects of credit expansion cannot be applied to this case without considerable modifications. The reason for this is that in this situation the expansion of credit for investment purposes will not lead to a diversion of productive resources into more 'round-about' processes of production with a consequent decrease of the current output of consumers' goods, but merely to a redistribution of the available supply of consumers' goods among a greater amount of factors of production. The re-employment of equipment and men, to employ whom it has not been profitable before, is made possible in this case by a reduction of real wages.[16] This reduction of real wages through a rise in the prices of consumers' goods compared with such a reduction brought about by a lowering of money wages has, however, the disadvantage that this rise of prices of consumers' goods, caused by the increase of demand before supply has increased, will lead to a rise in the rate of interest. As, however, in this situation money wages are not likely to rise in consequence of a rise in the prices of consumers' goods, the effects of credit expansion will be less harmful than under conditions of full employment. It is at least conceivable that in this case, in analogy to the case of an ex-

[15] *Monetary Theory and the Trade Cycle*, chapter 5. Perhaps I might also mention here that it was essentially the considerations indicated in the text which have led me to collect a number of important contributions to these problems, which had not been available in one of the generally understood languages, in a volume called *Beiträge zur Geldtheorie* (by M. Fanno, M. W. Holtrop, J. G. Koopmans, G. Myrdal, and K. Wicksell).

[16] As will be apparent from the first essay in this collection I believe now that this statement is incorrect as far as the beginning of the recovery is concerned; it applies only to the more advanced stages of the boom, when the supply of consumers' goods begins to fall short of demand. In the following sentence of the text 'profits' should be substituted for 'interest'. [This footnote was added to the 1939 translation. The essay referred to is "Profits, Interest and Investment", chapter 1 of Hayek, *Profits, Interest and Investment*, reprinted as chapter 8 of this volume.—Ed.]

pected continued fall of the prices of consumers' goods considered before, the rise of prices accompanying the increasing employment will create the expectation of still higher prices in the future and thus stimulate investment.

All this is, of course, no real attempt at a solution of these problems, but merely an indication of the lines on which such a solution must be sought. And among the problems which now urgently require a solution, the effects of a credit expansion under dynamic conditions certainly takes first place, just because we are now fairly clear as to what these effects are in an otherwise stationary system. It is not to be expected that further research in this direction will force us to change our views on the general principles involved. But as a further example of the unexpected conclusions to which we may be led if we apply these general principles to more complicated conditions, some further remarks may be added here on the effects of credit expansion in a progressive society. This case is particularly interesting because in a society where population and capital are growing credit expansion could only be avoided at the price of a continuous fall not only of the prices of consumers' goods but also of the factors of production, i.e., incomes, which would undoubtedly create very serious frictions. In an economic system with a high rate of voluntary saving it is, however, by no means impossible that at the critical moment, when credit expansion has to be slowed down and the further increase of incomes and the demand for consumers' goods relatively to investment threatens to lead to a crisis, the continued saving at a high rate may more than offset the tendency towards an increase of consumption and thus prevent the crisis. The conditions under which this might be the case would be not only that credit expansion has not proceeded at too fast a rate, and that it is slowed down very gradually, but also that the part of the supply of free capital[17] which is due to voluntary savings is large compared with the part due to an expansion of credit. If these conditions are satisfied the result might be that for a time the current voluntary savings will be used to take over, as it were, the capital created by means of forced saving; and current savings would then have to serve, not to make further new investment possible, but merely to maintain capital which has been formed in anticipation of these savings. And although even in this case the forced saving will not have increased the total amount of capital that can be accumulated in the long run, it will at least not lead to the crisis which would be the inevitable consequence if it were not for the con-

[17] [According to Hayek's definition the supply of free capital consists of "earned amortization quotas (or proceeds from circulating capital which has been turned over), new savings and perhaps additional credits" (cf. "Capital Consumption", in *Money, Capital and Fluctuations: Early Essays by F. A. Hayek*, ed. Roy McCloughry (London: Routledge and Kegan Paul; Chicago: University of Chicago Press, 1984), pp. 157–58n.9; cf. the German original, "Kapitalaufzehrung", *Weltwirtschaftliches Archiv*, vol. 36, July 1932, pp. 96–97n.2; a new translation is to appear in F. A. Hayek, *Capital and Interest*).—Ed.]

tinued voluntary saving. It is possible that this fact explains why at the present moment (1932)[18] certain countries with a high rate of saving (in particular, France) are in a less depressed condition than most others.

The list of such problems yet waiting for a solution could, of course, be continued almost indefinitely. But this fact does not detract from the value of the progress of our knowledge in recent years, of which we have spoken at the beginning of this article, nor does it give support to the views of those who object to the simplified constructions and abstract deductions from which we start and usually impute to those who use them an unwarranted neglect of the further complications. If we are now in a position to attack these further problems with a chance of success, this is mainly due to the fact that we are at last in a position to state the skeleton of our explanation in a logically consistent manner. Nobody can hope that we shall soon be in a position to give a final answer to all the important questions in this field. The concrete forms in which these phenomena manifest themselves in the real world are far too complex and variable, and the process by which theoretical and descriptive work mutually supply each other with questions and their answers is far too slow to justify much optimism in this respect. Our success in recasting an important part of traditional theory into a logically consistent system and in refuting at the same time some of the most widely held fallacies is no small achievement and should prove a great help in further developments. This confidence need not be shaken by certain deplorable tendencies in the economic literature of the most recent times. It cannot be denied that the present crisis, as is true of almost all earlier crises, has enormously swollen the literature of our subject, and that not only errors of the most primitive kind have been revived by outsiders, but that even competent scholars appear to have lost their heads and in their anxiety to help quickly have proposed remedies which are hardly compatible with their theoretical views. But once the problems of the present crisis have ceased to be as pressing as they are now, further research will not only have new important material at its disposal, but will also be able to base itself on a stream of secured knowledge which may be temporarily submerged but certainly not stopped by the present flood of dilettante literature.

[18] [The date was added in the 1939 translation. —Ed.]

FIVE

RESTORING THE PRICE-LEVEL?[1]

The belief that we could restore prosperity by raising prices to the level at which they stood in the last of the prosperous years has secured a strong hold on the imagination of the public. That something is wrong with the system of prices ruling at the present time, and that considerable changes in this price-structure will be necessary before industry in general is once more prosperous, cannot, of course, be denied. The existence of such mal-adjustments has always been recognised as the dominant feature of any depression. The peculiarity about the doctrine which is so popular today, however, is that it does not direct attention to the relationship between the existing prices of different commodities, but concentrates upon the relationship between a fictitious average of all these prices and a similar fictitious average at some date in the past.

This attitude, which is comparatively recent, results from the discussion of a special and quite distinct set of problems. When, in the years immediately after the War,[2] economists had the task of convincing statesmen and the general public that the policy of covering budget deficits by means of the printing presses would be disastrous, they had to use an over-simplified explanation of the effects of changes in the quantity of money and to illustrate their arguments by a few simple figures. The public learned that lesson only

---

[1] [The original typescript is preserved in the Friedrich A. von Hayek Papers, Incremental Material, box 105, folder 11, Hoover Institution Archives, Stanford University; the cover bears the pencilled remark "for London General Press, Dec. 1933". In the 1920s and 1930s the London General Press appears to have been a publisher of pamphlets, speeches, and the like on banking and financial matters. Occasional authors included Sir Henry Strakosch (*A Financial Plan for the Prevention of War*, 1929), Sir Josiah Stamp (*The Present Position of Rationalisation*, 1930), and Sir Walter Layton (*The Economic Situation of Great Britain*, 1931). As Hayek's typescript was not put into print by the Press, it is published here for the first time. However, an Italian translation appeared as "Una politica errata: il rialzo artificiale dei prezzi" (in the biweekly *La Borsa – Quindicinale dei mercati finanziari*, no. 25, March 3, 1934, pp. 3–4). This source has been pointed out to me by Antonio Magliulo; cf. his paper presented to the Annual Conference of the European Society for the History of Economic Thought (ESHET), 2011 (Istanbul), titled, "Hayek and the Great Depression of 1929: Did He Really Change His Mind?"—Ed.]

[2] [That is, World War I.—Ed.]

too well, and developed an almost superstitious faith in index numbers, but, in economics, "a little knowledge is a dangerous thing"[3] and often tends to displace important considerations which sound common sense would dictate. In this particular case, the simple rules of thumb, which served well enough in one situation, became definitely misleading in another.

It is undeniably true that any rapid changes in the price-level will be harmful and will in particular tend to disorganise production, if they are expected to continue. It is, however, quite a different proposition to argue that it is not the *changing*, but the *changed*, price-level which is harmful; and that it is therefore desirable, if a change has occurred in one direction, to bring about another change in the reverse direction in order to return to what is considered to be the normal price-level. The evil effects of this delusion were experienced in this country after the war-time inflation, when an attempt was made to use deflation in order to restore prices to the pre-war level, which was then considered normal.[4]

Certainly there were people to whom such a policy brought relief and partial compensation for the losses suffered during the preceding period of inflation. And there were others, upon whom new losses were inflicted by the process of deflation. But the essential point to remember is that, while the lasting effects of a change in the price-level concern only the distribution of income (some benefiting and others suffering to the same extent), every new monetary change will, by paralysing production immediately or ultimately, reduce the social income as a whole. As in so many other cases, the correction of the change in the distribution of income between classes may be accomplished only at the cost of reducing incomes in the aggregate.

It is important to distinguish clearly between these two entirely different aspects of monetary changes. The first kind, which is due to the existence of long-term contracts for fixed money payments, would also occur if all prices changed at the same time, in the same direction and to the same degree. Any increase in the price-level would harm the creditor and assist the debtor; and the reverse would be true of any reduction in the price-level. But, in this case, there need not be any considerable or lasting effect on the volume of production or employment. Interest and the repayment of debts are not costs of production in the sense that they will change as output increases or decreases; and a change in the burden of debt will not therefore make production in general either more or less profitable. It may ruin or enrich individuals; it may drive

---

[3] [Proverbial phrase, first used by Alexander Pope (1688–1744) in his poem *An Essay on Criticism*, 1709: "A little learning is a dangerous thing; / drink deep, or taste not the Pierian spring: / there shallow draughts intoxicate the brain, / and drinking largely sobers us again."—Ed.]

[4] [This refers to Great Britain's price deflation after World War I and possibly to the deflationary consequences of its return to the pre-war (and overvalued) parity of the pound in 1925.—Ed.]

numerous producers into bankruptcy and make their plant, land, or other instruments of production pass into other hands, and thus temporarily derange the markets; but, if this process is not interfered with, it will not prevent a speedy resumption of production on the former scale.

The really important effect on the volume of production, on the other hand, has nothing to do with the absolute level of prices. It is connected with changes in the relative prices of individual commodities and services—changes which will always be caused by the same forces which bring about violent changes in the price-level. In general terms, that group of prices which represents the cost of production of other commodities will change relatively to the prices of these commodities. It is such disparities between prices which exist at any one moment which may clog the wheels of production and cause tremendous losses to society as a whole. And, although it is desirable to preserve, or to restore, justice between debtors and creditors, it is even more important to get production going again. But there is no reason to assume that the same measures will serve both ends. On the contrary, it is quite probable, from all we know, that the policy which would now help debtors by restoring the price-level to some former figure, would also bring about a further disorganisation of production.

The reason is that the process by which a change in the price-level is brought about necessarily involves considerable changes in the relation between individual prices. It is, of course, impossible by any conceivable measure to change all prices at the same time or to the same degree. Nor would this, if possible, have the desired effect. But still less is there any reason to suppose that the shifts between different prices, which will occur during such a process of 'reflation' would be in the right direction. There is only one thing certain about them: that they will lack in one quality which is essential for a return to lasting prosperity—that of creating expectations which are likely to be realised.

The change in relative prices brought about by changes in the quantity of money will necessarily be of a temporary nature. They will tend to be reversed as soon as the quantity of money ceases to change further, and they will in the meantime have misdirected production into channels which will ultimately prove unprofitable. From all we know, it is highly probable that such misdirections of production by a price structure which is temporarily distorted by monetary changes, is the fundamental cause of crises and depressions. Surely, to create new mal-adjustments of production, with the inevitable consequence of a new depression later, is too high a price to pay for the speeding up of a process of recovery already under way.

About a year or so ago, it is true, it might have been argued with some appearance of justification that this was not merely a question of speeding up recovery, but the only way out of a vicious spiral of deflation which, month by month, was carrying us into deeper depression. But whatever may have been the merits of the argument for the deliberate expansion of credit while prices continued to fall, it must be borne in mind that we have recently entered upon a new phase of the depression. The deflationary process came to an end as soon as a period of relatively stable prices had created hopes of further stability; more definite signs of recovery then became noticeable and can now no longer be mistaken. The problem now is, not what we must do to prevent the depression from getting worse, but whether anything can be done to speed up the process of recovery.

As we have already suggested, it cannot be denied that a deliberate attempt to raise the price-level would probably have this immediate effect; but it would be very dangerous in the long run. Even apart from the objection that the prosperity so created would probably be of a very transitory nature, such a policy would be faced by other very serious difficulties. There is no scientific criterion whatever, on which to fix a particular price-level as the goal of such a policy. The price-levels of 1931, 1929, 1926, or perhaps even 1921 or 1914 might be proposed with very much the same degree of justification. And for reasons already stated, the restoration of any one of these price-levels would certainly not have the effect that the position of any individual would be made the same as it was in the year chosen as the standard. In many lines of industry, where costs have already been adjusted but would follow a new upward movement only tardily, the effect of raising prices to the 1929 level would be similar to that of a major inflation. In others—and particularly in those where the clamour is loudest—the result would probably be very disappointing. It is not surprising that the industries in which the burden of old debts is heaviest, and therefore the demand for a reduction in the value of money most pressing, are, at the same time, the industries whose difficulties are much older than the present depression, and have certainly not been brought about by monetary changes. In particular, the hope of the farmers, in America and elsewhere, that their difficulties can be overcome by any kind of monetary manipulation are certainly illusory. But to hold out hopes which are certain to be disappointed is highly dangerous. If the restoration of the 1929 price-level does not do the trick, equally strong forces will press for the restoration of the 1921, or even some higher, level. And as the arguments against the restoration of the 1929 price-level are hardly less strong than those against a larger dose of inflation, it would be difficult to resist such a demand when once the former had been accepted.

But the decisive argument against any such experiments at the present stage seems to me to be one which has not yet been mentioned. Any process of recovery which leads to fairly stable conditions must involve the adapting of relative prices and methods of production to existing circumstances. And the most important condition which must be satisfied if this process is to continue at a fairly rapid rate is that these circumstances are expected to remain stable.

The confidence of the entrepreneurs that their calculations based on existing prices will not again be upset by unforeseen changes is of greater importance for reviving the demand for the industries now most depressed than any other single factor. If anything can be done to help recovery it is by reducing uncertainty as regards future policy, and by facilitating the adaptation to the given conditions of production. There is ample scope for action in this direction in other fields, but little in that of monetary policy, where the essential requisite is stability.

That no deliberate action should be taken to raise prices in general, does not, of course, mean that all individual prices will, or should, remain where they are. There can be little doubt that, with the gradual return of confidence and the resumption of investment activity, some prices will rise considerably without any deliberate action to secure that end. In fact, it is rather probable that the next real problem which will arise for the monetary authorities will be just the reverse from what is commonly supposed: namely to prevent this upward revision of some prices from degenerating into a general price movement with all the disturbing effects which such a movement always has upon industrial stability. But although the time when this problem will have to receive serious attention is perhaps not quite so far distant as is commonly supposed, it has, unfortunately, not yet arrived.

Appendix: Excerpt from a Letter, F. A. Hayek to Gottfried Haberler, December 20, 1931[1]

The problem of deflation gives me much headache. Machlup in his letter[2] to you of 5th is certainly wrong, 1. because after the crisis the 'formal or spurious capital disposal'[3] does no longer exist, on the contrary the crisis is the consequence of the fact that the additional sums of money have become income, that is, its proportions have shifted back again towards consumption. The required shortening of the roundaboutness of production would also result without deflation. 2. Because it is by no means sure that a mobilisation of surplus cash balances would bring about a relative increase in the demand for producers' goods.[4] But I cannot agree with your criticisms, too, although the differences between us are small. 1. If the deflation is induced, then it will stop only after costs of production have decreased stronger than prices, and as long as this is not the case any attempt to combat deflation will only delay the attainment of a new equilibrium. 2. A *general* fall in prices, although not to the extent experienced in the recent years, is conceivable very well without any deflation, if after a breakdown of production for some time more goods (due to a shortening of the roundaboutness of production, the liquidation of stocks, etc.) come to the market than planned. 3. The fact that prior to 1929 prices should have been allowed to fall is just an indicator for the extent of the inflation that indeed happened. Yet, just as without any tendency of a falling price trend the cyclical reaction to inflation would undershoot the equilibrium level of prices, it appears plausible to me, even if not strictly deducible theoretically, that similarly in a case of relative inflation[5] the cyclical fall in prices will be stronger, too.—On these problems I am having correspondence with you and with Machlup and Röpke, and I am discussing them here a lot, and I will try to put down my opinions on paper and eventually send it to you.

---

[1] [As pointed out in the editor's introduction, this is the only letter preserved from correspondence between Hayek, Haberler, Machlup, and Röpke on the topic of deflation (see the Gottfried Haberler Papers, box 65, Hoover Institution Archives, Stanford University). The excerpt reprinted here gives a snapshot of Hayek's opinion on this topic as it had evolved at the end of 1931, shortly after he had arrived in London. The translation is by the editor.—Ed.]

[2] [The letter from Machlup to Haberler, December 5, 1931, has been lost.—Ed.]

[3] [In his *Börsenkredit, Industriekredit und Kapitalbildung* (Vienna: Springer, 1931; reprinted, Frankfurt: Frankfurter Allgemeine, 2002), p. 16, Machlup speaks of the 'formal' or additional purchasing power created by bank credit; cf. the slightly revised passage in the translation, *The Stock Market, Credit and Capital Formation*, trans. Vera C. Smith (London: Hodge, 1940), pp. 14–15.—Ed.]

[4] [The identification of the disbursements of surplus cash balances as a monetary cause of the boom was a major novel argument in Machlup's contribution; cf., e.g., *The Stock Market*, p. 15.—Ed.]

[5] [Haberler had coined the term 'relative inflation' for denoting the case of credit creation accompanied (due to growth in output) by a stable price level.—Ed.]

SIX

CAPITAL AND INDUSTRIAL FLUCTUATIONS: A REPLY TO A CRITICISM[1]

A sympathetic criticism of the kind to which the views of the present author have been subjected by Messrs. Hansen and Tout in a recent issue of *Econometrica*,[2] offers a welcome opportunity of clearing up some points upon which I have obviously not yet been sufficiently explicit. The critical comments of the two authors are mostly directed against points where real difficulties present themselves; and while I think I can answer their main objections, it is probable that I can do so more profitably by means of a further systematic development of my thesis than by wasting time on the comparatively unimportant discussion of whether these developments were already implied in my earlier statements, or whether the interpretation put upon these by Messrs. Hansen and Tout can, or cannot, be justified from the admittedly sketchy and incomplete exposition in *Prices and Production*.[3]

Messrs. Hansen and Tout have stated my theory in the following series of propositions:[4]

---

[1] [First published in *Econometrica*, vol. 2, April 1934, pp 152–67, and reprinted in a revised version as an appendix to F. A. Hayek, *Prices and Production*, 2nd ed. (London: Routledge, 1935), pp. 132–62; in the reprint Hayek added the subtitle "A Reply to a Criticism". The text is that of the reprint.—Ed.]

[2] Alvin H. Hansen and Herbert Tout, "Annual Survey of Business Cycle Theory: Investment and Saving in Business Cycle Theory", *Econometrica*, vol. 1, April 1933, pp. 119–47. [In their survey Hansen and Tout concentrated on a comparative critique of F. A. Hayek's *Prices and Production*, 1st ed. (London: Routledge, 1931), reprinted in *Business Cycles, Part I*, ed. Hansjoerg Klausinger, vol. 7 (2012) of *The Collected Works of F. A. Hayek* (Chicago: University of Chicago Press), and John Maynard Keynes's *A Treatise on Money*, 2 vols. (London: Macmillan, 1930), reprinted as vols. 5 and 6 (1971) of *The Collected Writings of John Maynard Keynes*, ed. Austin Robinson and Donald Moggridge (London: Macmillan; Cambridge: Cambridge University Press). Alvin Harvey Hansen (1887–1975), American economist, was professor at the University of Minnesota and, from 1937 to 1957, at Harvard University. In the 1930s his main field of research was business cycle theory; later he became pivotal for introducing Keynesian thought to the United States.—Ed.]

[3] [When here and in the following Hayek refers in the reprinted version to "the preceding lectures", this has been substituted by the original reference to *Prices and Production*.—Ed.]

[4] [The remainder of this section is a quotation from Hansen and Tout, "Annual Survey", pp. 133–35, inserted into the text as reprinted in Hayek, *Prices and Production*, 2nd ed.—Ed.]

Thesis Number 1. That depression is brought about by a shrinkage in the structure of production (i.e., a shortening of the capitalistic process). In Hayek's view, the phenomenon of depression *is* a shrinkage in the structure of production. Dynamic forces may bring about various effects on economic life, but unless they have the specific effect of shortening the process of production, depression will not follow therefrom. Nor does depression ever assume any other form than that of a shrinkage in the structure of production. In short, depression may be defined as a shortening of the capitalistic process of production.

Thesis Number 2. The leading cause (there are, however, others) which brings about, either directly or indirectly, a shortening in the process of production, is the phenomenon of *forced* saving.

Thesis Number 3. An elongation of the process of production caused by *voluntary* saving tends to remain intact; or at least, there is no inherent reason why such an elongation *must* necessarily be followed by a shrinkage in the structure of production.

An increase in voluntary saving would cause an enlarged demand for producers' goods in relation to consumers' goods, and this would raise the prices of goods in the higher stages of production in relation to those of the lower stages.[5] The consequent narrowing of the price margins or, in other words, the lower rate of interest, would thus make possible a permanent elongation of the process of production.

Thesis Number 4. A lengthening of the process of production caused by forced saving (the money supply not having been held neutral) cannot possibly be permanently maintained, but must necessarily be followed by a shortening in the process of production.

An increase in money supply (bank credit) made available to entrepreneurs would cause an increase in the demand for producers' goods in relation to consumers' goods, and this would raise the prices of goods of the higher order in relation to those of the lower order. The consequent elongation of the process of production could not, however, be maintained, because a reversal in the price relationship of higher and lower order goods would appear as soon as the money supply ceased to increase owing to the fact that spending and saving habits had not changed. Thus, a shrinkage in the artificially elongated process of production would inevitably occur.

[5] [Here Hansen and Tout adhere to Hayek's terminology of the first edition of *Prices and Production*, where 'lower stages' denoted those nearer to consumption, and the converse for the 'higher stages'. In the second edition (p. 53n.1, reprinted, p. 231n.25) Hayek substituted 'later' and 'earlier' for 'lower' and 'higher' stages, which is also how he uses these terms below.—Ed.]

Thesis Number 5. An increase in consumer demand occasioned by an increase in the supply of money (over and above what may be necessary to hold money neutral) inevitably brings about a shortening in the process of production, and so causes depression.

An increased supply of money made available directly to consumers would cause an increase in the demand for consumers' goods in relation to producers' goods, and would thus raise the prices of goods of the lower order in relation to those of the higher order, and this would inevitably bring about a shortening in the process of production.

Thesis Number 6. That excessive public expenditures and taxation, by increasing the ratio of spending to saving, will force a shortening in the process of production and so cause prolonged depression or business stagnation.

An increase in spending would cause an increased demand for consumers' goods in relation to producers' goods, and this would raise the prices of goods of the lower order in relation to those of the higher order. The consequent widening of the price margins between the lower and higher order goods, or, in other words, a higher rate of interest, would, therefore, bring about a shortening of the process of production.

Thesis Number 7. That the supply of money should be kept constant, except for such increases and decreases as may be necessary (1) to offset changes in the velocity of circulation, (2) to counteract such changes in the co-efficient of money transactions as are occasioned by the amalgamation of firms, and the like, and (3) to provide for any changes in non-monetary means of payment, such as book credit, that may be taking place. (A distinction is thus made between a 'constant' money supply and a 'neutral' money supply.)

Thesis Number 8. That any change in money supply (other than that necessary to hold money neutral) is harmful because it necessarily brings about, eventually, a shortening in the process of production. (a) If the increased money supply goes to entrepreneurs, the process of production is first elongated, but, subsequently, necessarily shortened, returning to its previous status, or to a still shorter process. (b) If the increased money goes first to consumers, the shortening of the process of production takes place at once, and the process remains permanently shortened.

Thesis Number 9. That an increase in production and trade forms no justification for an increase in bank credit.

Thesis Number 10. That a period of depression should not be counteracted by any inflation of the money supply, though, in theory, there is the possibility that during the acute stages[6] of the crisis, while the capitalistic structure is tending to shrink more than will ultimately prove necessary, a nicely regulated increase might prove beneficial. The impossibility of such skilful management makes this an unimportant exception.

1.

With one exception, I fully agree that this formulation of my views is a fair and accurate summary of my position. Even the unimportant exception is probably only a slip of the pen, and is satisfactorily cleared up in the later discussion. But, as it may have confused some readers, I should like to emphasise at the outset that I should never say, as stated in thesis number 2 that forced saving can ever *directly* bring about a shortening of the process of production. Forced saving means essentially a lengthening of the process of production and the crucial point is that, in my view, it is these elongations which are likely to be partly or wholly *reversed* as soon as the cause of the forced saving *disappears*.

The first major difficulty which Messrs. Hansen and Tout discuss is connected with what they call my thesis number 1, namely, that the phenomenon of depression is equivalent to a shrinkage of the structure of production. Their difficulty here seems to me to turn on the distinction between a completed and an uncompleted structure, which I have probably failed to make sufficiently clear, and which is closely connected with the distinction between the effects of mere fluctuations in the rate of saving (or, more correctly, in the rate of investment) and the peculiar instability of capital created by means of forced saving. The best way of making these distinctions clear is probably to start with a general discussion of the effects of fluctuations in the means available for investment on the structure of production in general, and on the profitableness of the early stages in particular. From this discussion it will, I think, appear that, contrary to the opinion of Messrs. Hansen and Tout, it is not the mere fluctuations in the rate of investment which tend to make the earlier stages unprofitable but only, on the one hand, particularly violent fluctuations of this sort, and, on the other, fluctuations which make the net investment negative. Finally, concluding this part of the discussion, it will appear that, in the case of 'forced savings', it is not only impossible to keep the rate of investment constant, but that there will exist, as a necessary consequence of the 'forced saving', strong forces which tend to make the rate of investment negative.

---

[6] [In the original (Hansen and Tout, "Annual Survey", p. 135) this reads, "stage".—Ed.]

2.

Any lengthening of the process of production can only be completed over a period of time corresponding to the interval between the moment when the factors which are being shifted to an earlier stage are being invested, and the moment when their product matures. If the new, longer process is to be completed and maintained, this requires not only that the investment in the earlier stage must be constantly maintained, but also (except in a few rare cases, like the ageing of wine and the growing of trees) that further complementary investments must be made in the later stages.

From this it follows that, in any progressive society,[7] the particular forms in which investments are being made are determined by the expectation that, for some time to come, a similar stream of funds for investment will be forthcoming; and that, at any moment of time, only a fraction of the funds available for new investment will be used to start new processes, while the rest will be required to complete the processes already under way. On the simplifying assumption that the *total* length of the marginal processes which are made possible by an increase in the supply of investible funds, is always greater than the total length of any process already used, this situation can be represented by the following diagram. The curvilinear[8] triangle *ABC* represents, in the same way as the triangle I have used in *Prices and Production*, the stock of capital belonging to processes already completed. (The area of the curvilinear triangle *AB'C'* shows the stock of capital before the additions were begun.) The fully drawn stripes, beginning between *C* and *D*, represent incomplete processes, started at different moments in the past—and now in different stages of completion. The part of these stripes which is dotted represents the additional investment which is required to complete the processes. During every successive period of investment, part of the fund available will be used to start new processes, part to advance processes which are already under way, and part to complete the most advanced processes.

If at any moment savings fall by no more than had previously been used to

---

[7] [In the contemporary literature the term 'progressive society' denotes an economy where output is—for whatever reasons—growing over time; cf., e.g., Gustav Cassel, *The Theory of Social Economy*, new revised edition (London: Benn; New York: Harcourt, Brace and Co., 1932; reprinted, New York: Kelley, 1967), pp. 32–41. Here Hayek deals primarily with the transition to equilibrium (a stationary state) after an increase in saving.—Ed.]

[8] The reasons which make a curvilinear triangle of the kind shown in the text a more appropriate representation than the simplified form used in lecture 2 of *Prices and Production* are probably obvious. See *Prices and Production*, 2nd ed., p. 39 [reprinted, p. 222. The reference is to fig. 1, where the ordinate measures the number of stages (or the length of time of the process of production) and the abscissa both the original means of production used up and the output of consumers' goods produced in the process.—Ed.]

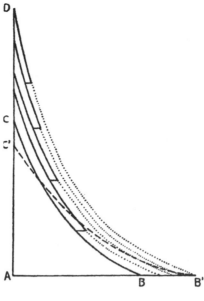

Figure 6.1

start new processes, the completion of the processes already under way will not be endangered. And since, at any moment, some of the unfinished processes will be completed, the amount of saving may continually fall off at a certain rate, and may reach zero at the moment when all the processes under way are completed.[9] There is, therefore, at any moment, a maximum rate at which the rate of saving may fall off, without interfering with the new processes already started. It is only when the decrease in saving is faster than this rate, at which the need for capital for the purpose of completing processes under way decreases, that the incomplete structure cannot be completed and some of the investments made in the earlier stages have to be abandoned.

Such an abandonment of early stages will, of course, mean that the average period for which the current supply of original factors is being invested is shortened even if, at the same time, a good deal of investment in new forms in later stages is taking place. In this case, however, investment in new forms need *not* mean *net* investment, since the losses on the abandoned earlier stages have to be offset against it.

---

[9] [From the requirement that savings become zero when all the processes under way are completed, it is clear that here Hayek speaks of 'net savings', that is, the excess of (gross) savings over depreciation.—Ed.]

3.

It is only another way of stating the same conclusions if one says that the total demand for producers' goods will fall off in consequence of a decrease in the demand for new producers' goods only if the latter declines faster than the replacement demand increases, in consequence of the preceding growth of the stock of producers' goods. And this brings me to a discussion of the famous argument[10] according to which any increase in the demand for productive equipment must lead to surplus capacity of plant producing that equipment, as soon as the demand for it[11] ceases to increase. Although this is rarely recognised, this is a typical instance where an expansion of an earlier stage of production can be maintained only if the further increase of capital makes it possible to complete the structure by adequate increases of capital in the later stages.[12]

From the very outset, it is important in this connection carefully to avoid a confusion which arises from the failure to distinguish between fluctuations in the demand for productive equipment of a particular industry, which arise from fluctuations in the demand for the product of that industry, and fluctuations in the demand for new producers' goods in general, which are connected with fluctuations in the supply of funds available for new investment. Here I am mainly concerned with the latter type of fluctuation. How far what is to be said about this particular case is also applicable to the former, depends upon the degree to which the concrete capital equipment in earlier stages is specialised to the production of equipment for a particular industry, or whether it can be more generally used. On this question of fact, I can only refer to an interesting article which was recently published by Mr. Seltzer,[13] who seems to show that the mobility of capital in this sense is far greater than is commonly supposed. Some other considerations on this point can be more appropriately discussed after I have dealt with the first type of fluctuation.

At first, therefore, I shall assume that the increase in investment is due to an increase in the supply of capital, and that the plant required to provide the

---

[10] [That is, the 'principle of acceleration of derived demand' or 'accelerator principle', cf. for a contemporary account Gottfried Haberler, *Prosperity and Depression: A Theoretical Analysis of Cyclical Movements* (Geneva: League of Nations, 1937), pp. 80–98.

[11] [That is, for productive equipment.—Ed.]

[12] A top-heavy structure of this kind is, therefore, an uncompleted structure in the sense that its earlier stages will be permanently employed only after they have helped to increase the equipment in later stages to such a magnitude that its replacement demand will fully use the capacity of the earlier stages. (The essential thing here, however, is not capacity in a technical sense, but sufficient employment to make amortisation of plant at current prices possible.)

[13] Lawrence H. Seltzer, "The Mobility of Capital", *Quarterly Journal of Economics*, vol. 46, May 1932, pp. 496–508. [Note that 'mobility of capital' corresponds to Hayek's notion of 'nonspecific producers' goods' introduced in *Prices and Production*, reprinted, p. 244.—Ed.]

new equipment is not adapted to the requirements of one industry only, but can be used fairly widely. The question then is whether, on the expectation of a continued growth of capital at about the same rate, it will appear profitable to expand the plant in the industries producing that equipment to a point where *any* decline in the current supply of new capital will make full use of that plant unprofitable.

The answer to this question is simply this: as long as the supply of capital does not decrease by more than the amount which has so far been used to construct the new plant[14] making that equipment, there is no reason why the demand for new equipment should fall off. In other words, the effect of a decrease in saving will simply be that the beginning of new roundabout processes will be stopped but, if the decrease does not exceed a certain rate, there is no reason why the already existing plant should not be continuously used to add to the equipment in later stages. And as the replacement demand due to earlier additions to this equipment will continue to rise, the supply of new savings may even continue to fall at a certain rate without affecting the employment of the plant producing this equipment. The situation is, therefore, completely analogous to the case of fluctuations in the rate of saving already discussed: it need not have any harmful effects, so long as the decline in the rate of saving does not exceed the amount which will permit the processes already begun to be completed.[15]

[14] It is assumed here that the construction of this additional plant for making the equipment in question can be carried out either with the help of similar plant already in existence, or of some other plant which can *also* be used to produce equipment for later stages. This, of course, will always be the case since no capital is created without the help of some capital already in existence, which if it is a question of adding an earlier stage of production to those already existing, must, ex definitione, mean that these capital goods have hitherto been used in later stages. It may be mentioned here, since this has occasionally been a cause of confusion, that any given capital good need not, and usually will not, belong to any one given 'stage' of production only. If it is used to produce other capital goods employed in different stages, and still more if it helps to produce durable goods, or is itself durable, it belongs to as many different 'stages' as different periods of time elapse from the moment in which we consider it, to the moments when the different final products which it has helped to produce are consumed. This, however, so far from making the concept of stages useless, is only a necessary distinction in order to explain the different ways in which the value of individual capital goods will be affected by changes in the supply of capital, the rate of interest, or other factors affecting the structure of production.

[15] [Here, Hayek's discussion may be interpreted to address two distinct aspects of the transition following an increase in the supply of saving: On the one hand, during a successful transition towards a more roundabout structure of production within the even flow of gross saving (or gross investment) the steady increase in replacement investment will be compensated by decreases in net investment until, when the new equilibrium or stationary state has been attained, all gross investment will be devoted for replacement and net investment will have vanished. On the other hand, even if the transition towards a more roundabout structure of production fails, e.g., because the higher level of voluntary saving will not be maintained, this need not generate a crisis, if the return to the prior equilibrium is effected merely by stopping the start of new

4.

The confusion on this point seems to result from a very common mistake—that of applying what is true of a single industry to industry as a whole. While, of course, the relative magnitude of the demand for equipment for a particular industry will depend upon the demand for the product of that industry, it is certainly not true to say that the demand for capital goods in general is directly determined by the magnitude of the demand for consumers' goods.[16] While it is true that some contemporary economists have come so much under the influence of the under-consumptionist fallacy that they are prepared to say that the savings will never lead to a corresponding increase in investment, because they involve a decline in the demand for consumers' goods, and are therefore only a harmful and undesirable phenomenon, I certainly need not discuss this with economists who accept as much of my fundamental position as do Messrs. Hansen and Tout. But, if one accepts the proposition that the magnitude of the total demand for producers' goods is not a simple derivative of the demand for consumers' goods, but that any given demand for consumers' goods can lead to methods of production involving very different demands for producers' goods, and that the particular method of production chosen will depend upon the proportion of the total wealth *not* required for immediate consumption, then we must certainly take the fluctuations in the supply of free capital,[17] and not the fluctuations in the demand for consumers' goods, as the starting point for this kind of analysis.

There is, therefore, no reason to suppose that a general increase in the demand for new capital goods, which is due to an increase in the supply of saving, must lead to a decrease in the demand for capital goods, as soon as the rate of saving begins to decline. And since I am still abstracting from the case where investment is financed by the creation of credit ('forced saving') or any other purely monetary changes, it is difficult to see what factors can affect the *total* demand for new capital goods, other than the supply of savings. Only if

---

processes and simultaneously completing the processes which have already been started before. Thus, in both instances, there is a limit up to which the rate of (net) saving may decrease without causing harmful effects.—Ed.]

[16] [This widely held proposition has been called the 'English view'; cf. Evan F. M. Durbin, *Purchasing Power and Trade Depression: A Critique of Under-Consumption Theories* (London: Cape, 1933), p. 147, see also the editor's introduction, this volume, pp. 15–17. It should be noted that this proposition links the level of the demand for capital goods to the *level* of the demand for consumers' goods; it is thus different from the accelerator principle, which links the level of the demand for capital goods to the *change* in the demand for consumers' goods. For another instance of Hayek's criticism cf. "Profits, Interest and Investment", chapter 1 of *Profits, Interest and Investment. And Other Essays on the Theory of Industrial Fluctuations* (London: Routledge, 1939), reprinted in this volume, especially pp. 222–23.—Ed.]

[17] [On Hayek's definition of "the supply of free capital" see p. 178n.17, above.—Ed.]

we assume that changes in the rate of interest which can be earned on new capital lead to hoarding or dishoarding, would a new cause of change be introduced. But this is one of the cases of monetary changes in the demand for consumers' goods which I shall have to discuss later on.

On this point, my argument so far amounts to this: that in so far as we abstract from monetary changes, the demand for consumers' goods can only change inversely with the demand for producers' goods, and in consequence, so far from having a cumulative effect in the same direction as the latter, will tend to offset it in the opposite direction.

There is, however, still the case of mere shifts of demand between different kinds of consumers' goods which, of course, will have some effect on the demand for particular kinds of capital goods. An unexpected shift of this kind will undoubtedly have the effect that provision made for the supply of new equipment in the industry from which demand has turned away will now prove excessive or, in other words, it will now become unprofitable to complete the longer processes in the expected way. But the total demand for new equipment will not be changed, and whether the equipment-producing plant already in existence will continue to be used or whether new plant will have to be built, will depend upon the technical considerations already mentioned.

5.

So much for the pure, or barter, theory of the subject (in the sense of the usual assumption of theory that money exists to facilitate exchange but exercises no determining influence on the course of things, or, in other words, remains neutral—an assumption which is almost always made though not expressed in these terms). The discussion of the active influence which may be exercised by money in this connection is best begun with the peculiar effect of forced savings, which will lead us to another of the points of discussion, namely, the effect of monetary changes on the demand for consumers' goods. For the peculiar characteristic of forced saving, which distinguishes its effects from those of voluntary saving, is simply that it leads necessarily to an increase in the means available for the purchase of consumers' goods. For this reason, my thesis number 4 about the impermanence of capital accumulated by forced saving is directly bound up with my thesis number 5 as to the effects of a direct increase in the monetary demand for consumers' goods, which Messrs. Hansen and Tout, quite consistently, also reject.[18]

The reason why forced saving will always lead to a subsequent increase in the money available for the purchase of consumers' goods, is fairly obvious

[18] [Cf. Hansen and Tout, "Annual Survey", pp. 140–43.—Ed.]

and will probably not be contested. Entrepreneurs are in this case enabled to attract factors of production from later to earlier stages, not by a corresponding transfer of funds from consumers' to producers' goods, but by additional money handed to them. This means that they will bid up the prices of these factors without there being a corresponding fall in the prices of other factors. Total money income will therefore increase, and this increase will in turn lead to an increase in the amount of money expended on consumers' goods. This increase in the expenditure on consumers' goods will necessarily follow in time upon the increase in the demand for factors. This lag will mean that, for some time after the demand for factors (or producers' goods) has ceased to increase (or when its rate of increase begins to slow down), the demand for consumers' goods will continue to increase at a faster rate; and so long as the increase in the demand for producers' goods is slowing down—and for some time afterwards—the monetary proportion between the demand for producers' goods and the demand for consumers' goods will change in favour of the latter.

The question turns, therefore, upon the effect of such a relative increase in the monetary demand for consumers' goods. The reply, in the particular case in question, however, is simplified, in comparison with the general problem, because, on our assumptions, two relevant points are given. We have in this particular case to assume that: (a) since it is the situation at the end of a boom, there are no unemployed resources, and (b) since the rate of credit expansion for productive purposes tends to be slowed down in spite of a continued rise in the monetary demand for consumers' goods, we cannot assume that the continued rise in this demand will lead to a renewed credit expansion. The much more difficult case of an increase in the monetary demand for consumers' goods, where these assumptions do not necessarily hold, as well as the problem why the rate of credit expansion cannot be sufficiently high to avoid this type of reaction, will be considered later on.

The relative rise in the price of consumers' goods will not only improve the competitive position of their producers on the market for original factors, but will also make it profitable for these to increase their output by the more rapid, even if more expensive, method of employing relatively more labour (original factors) in proportion to capital. And while their demand for all the non-specific factors of production (which can also be used in the latest stages of production) will continue to drive up the prices of these factors, the prices of the intermediate products specific to earlier stages of production will tend to fall relatively to their costs. And since the effect of this will not only tend to increase cumulatively towards the earlier stages but will also cause a shift of free capital towards the more profitable earlier stages,[19] it is easy to see how more and more of the earlier stages will tend to become unprofitable, until unem-

[19] [Apparently, this should read, "later stages".—Ed.]

ployment finally arises and leads to a fall in the prices of the original factors of production as well as in the prices of consumers' goods.

6.

Before I turn to the aspects of the situation where unemployed factors and unused lending capacity of all banks exist, and where, perhaps, delay in making the necessary adjustments has led to prolonged unprofitability causing deflation and a rapid general fall of prices, a little more must be said about the rate of credit expansion which would have to continue uninterruptedly if a reaction of the kind just discussed is to be avoided.

Messrs. Hansen and Tout merely speak of a *steady* rate of credit expansion[20] as a sufficient condition for a continuous and undisturbed rate of capital growth. I am not quite sure what 'steady' means in this context. But if it refers, as is probably the case, to a constant rate of increase in the total media of circulation, I think it can be shown that this is not sufficient to maintain a constant rate of forced saving; while it seems that any attempt to make the rate of credit expansion great enough to secure a constant rate of forced saving will inevitably be frustrated by counteracting forces which come into operation as soon as the process of inflation exceeds a certain speed.

A constant rate of forced saving (i.e., investment in excess of voluntary saving) requires a rate of credit expansion which will enable the producers of intermediate products, during each successive unit of time, to compete successfully with the producers of consumers' goods[21] for constant additional quantities of the original factors of production. But as the competing demand from the producers of consumers' goods rises (in terms of money) in consequence of, and in proportion to, the preceding increase of expenditure on the factors of production (income), an increase of credit which is to enable the producers of intermediate products to attract additional original factors, will have to be, not only absolutely but even relatively, greater than the last in-

---

[20] [Cf. Hansen and Tout, "Annual Survey", p. 139.—Ed.]

[21] I am compelled here—as I was in *Prices and Production*—to speak, for the sake of brevity, in terms of competition between the producers of intermediate products and the producers of consumers' goods (the present and future goods of Böhm-Bawerk's exposition) instead of speaking more correctly of competition between a continuous range of entrepreneurs in all 'stages' of production, which leads to all original factors being invested for a shorter or longer average period. [Böhm-Bawerk's exposition points to the fact that production takes time so that *present* intermediate goods can only be transformed into *future* consumers' goods; cf. Eugen von Böhm-Bawerk, *Kapital und Kapitalzins*, vol. 1: *Geschichte der Kapitalzinstheorien*, and vol. 2: *Positive Theorie des Kapitales*, 4th ed. in 3 vols. (Jena: Fischer, 1921), for a translation cf. *Capital and Interest*, 3 vols., trans. George D. Huncke and Hans F. Sennholz (South Holland, IL: Libertarian Press, 1959).—Ed.]

crease which is now reflected in the increased demand for consumers' goods. Even in order to attract only as great a proportion of the original factors, i.e., in order merely to maintain the already existing capital, every new increase would have to be proportional to the last increase, i.e., credit would have to expand progressively at a constant *rate*. But in order to bring about constant additions to capital, it would have to do more: it would have to increase at a *constantly increasing rate*. The rate at which this rate of increase must increase would be dependent upon the time lag between the first expenditure of the additional money on the factors of production and the re-expenditure of the income so created on consumers' goods.

It is true that in *Prices and Production* I have not only not discussed in detail[22] what rate of credit expansion is required to maintain a given rate of forced saving, but have simply assumed that that rate—whatever it was— could not be permanently maintained for institutional reasons, such as traditional banking policies or the operation of the gold standard.[23] But I think it can be shown without great difficulty that even if these obstacles to credit expansion were absent, such a policy would, sooner or later, inevitably lead to a rapid and progressive rise in prices which, in addition to its other undesirable effects, would set up movements which would soon counteract, and finally more than offset, the 'forced saving'.

That it is impossible, either for a simple progressive increase of credit which only helps to maintain, and does not add to, the already existing 'forced saving', or for an increase in credit at an increasing rate, to continue for a considerable time without causing a rise in prices, results from the fact that in neither case have we reason to assume that the increase in the supply of consumers' goods will keep pace with the increase in the flow of money coming on to the market for consumers' goods. In so far as, in the second case, the credit expansion leads to an ultimate increase in the output of consumers' goods, this increase will lag considerably and increasingly (as the period of production increases) behind the increase in the demand for them. But whether the prices of consumers' goods will rise faster or slower, all other prices, and particularly the prices of the original factors of production, will rise even faster. It is only a question of time when this general and progressive rise of prices becomes very rapid. My argument is not that such a development is *inevitable* once a policy of credit expansion is embarked upon, but that it *has to be* carried to that point if a certain result—a constant rate of forced saving, or maintenance without the help of voluntary saving of capital accumulated by forced saving—is to be achieved.

[22] [This is the text as in the 1934 original; the reprinted version erroneously deleted the second "not" and thus reads, "I have not only discussed in detail".—Ed.]

[23] [Cf. *Prices and Production*, reprinted, pp. 254–55.—Ed.]

Once this stage is reached, such a policy will soon begin to defeat its own ends. While the mechanism of forced saving continues to operate, the general rise in prices will make it increasingly more difficult, and finally practically impossible, for entrepreneurs to maintain their existing capital intact. Paper profits will be computed and consumed, the failure to reproduce the existing capital will become quantitatively more and more important, and will finally exceed the additions made by forced saving.

It is important in this connection to remember that the entrepreneur necessarily and inevitably thinks of his capital in terms of money, and that, under changing conditions, he has no other way of thinking of its quantity than in value terms, which practically means in terms of money. But even if, for a time, he resists the temptation of paper profits (and experience teaches us that this is extremely unlikely) and computes his costs in terms of some index number, the rate of depreciation has only to become fast enough, and such an expedient will be ineffective. And since the gist of my argument is that, for the purpose under discussion, the rate of credit expansion and depreciation has to increase at an increasing rate, it will in time reach any desired magnitude.

7.

For these reasons, it seems to me that the hope of Messrs. Hansen and Tout based on a steady rate of forced saving is illusory. Whether there may not exist conditions under which temporary forced saving may take place without the evil consequences of a crisis, is quite another matter. That this will be possible only if the rate of forced saving is comparatively small, is probably obvious. Another condition which we already know is that the fluctuations in investment to which it gives rise keep well within the limits we have described. In another place,[24] I have tried to show that, if these conditions are combined with a third, namely, the presence of a relatively high rate of voluntary saving, which provides the means of taking over, as it were, the real capital which has been created but cannot be maintained by means of forced saving, the loss of this capital may be avoided. But in this case, the only one I know where such a loss will be avoided, the forced saving will only mean an anticipation but no net increase of the circulation of capital, because it can only be maintained if an equivalent amount of saving is to be forthcoming later. For this reason, I am even more doubtful than before whether forced saving can ever be a bless-

[24] "Stand und Zukunftsaufgaben der Konjunkturforschung", in *Festschrift für Arthur Spiethoff*, ed. Gustav Clausing (Munich: Duncker and Humblot, 1933), p. 110. [The correct title is "Der Stand und die nächste Zukunft der Konjunkturforschung", and the reference should be to pp. 115–16; cf. "The Present State and Immediate Prospects of the Study of Industrial Fluctuations", reprinted in this volume, pp. 178–79—Ed.]

ing as Messrs. Hansen and Tout think. This is quite irrespective of the question whether there is any sense in which the economist can legitimately say (as I have occasionally said myself)[25] that such decisions made against the will of those concerned may be 'beneficial'. But that touches the much wider problem of whether we possess any gauge by which to measure the satisfaction derived by those concerned, except their own preferences, shown in their decisions—a question which I cannot even begin to discuss here.

8.

It will be impossible within the compass of this article to discuss the further points made by Messrs. Hansen and Tout in the same orbit as those more fundamental problems already taken up. Particularly, the next and very important point as to the effect of an expansion of consumers' demand at a time when the productive forces are not fully employed, and banks are in a position to expand credits to producers, could be answered completely only in connection with a fully developed theory of the process going on during a depression. But, if it be assumed that these two conditions exist as a consequence of a preceding crisis (and a definite assumption as regards the reason *why* these conditions exist is essential for any answer), and if the explanation of the crisis which I have just discussed is accepted, it is difficult to see how the same phenomenon, which has brought about the crisis, i.e., the rise in the relative demand for consumers' goods, should also be the cure for it. The scarcity of capital, which, of course, is nothing else but the relatively high price of consumers' goods, could only be enhanced by giving the consumers more money to spend on final products. At least so long as there are no further monetary complications, particularly so long as it is not assumed that the expectation of a further fall in prices has led to hoarding, I see no way of getting over this difficulty. But before I proceed to the relation between these secondary monetary complications, and the underlying real maladjustments which have caused it, I must try to clear away what seems to me to be a confusion which has led Messrs. Hansen and Tout to apply their denial of the

---

[25] [Cf., e.g., F. A. Hayek, "Die Währungspolitik der Vereinigten Staaten seit der Überwindung der Krise von 1920, II", *Zeitschrift für Volkswirtschaft und Sozialpolitik*, n.s., vol. 5, no. 2, 1925, pp. 276–77; and "Das intertemporale Gleichgewichtssystem der Preise und die Bewegungen des 'Geldwertes'", *Weltwirtschaftliches Archiv*, vol. 28, July 1928, p. 66; translated, respectively, as "Monetary Policy in the United States After the Recovery from the Crisis of 1920" and "Intertemporal Price Equilibrium and Movements in the Value of Money", reprinted in *Good Money, Part I: The New World*, ed. Stephen Kresge, vol. 5 (1999) of *The Collected Works of F. A. Hayek*, pp. 118–19 and 217–18; as well as *Monetary Theory and the Trade Cycle* (London: Cape, 1933), reprinted in F. A. Hayek, *Business Cycles, Part I*, pp. 143–44.—Ed.]

capital-destroying effect of additions to consumers' credits, not only to the peculiar situation of an advanced depression, but also generally.

The essence of the confusion on this point seems to me to lie in the contrast which my critics try to establish in several places between what they call "nominal" changes in the relative monetary demand for consumers' goods and producers' goods, and the "real changes in the demand for consumers' goods occasioned by a fundamental modification in time preference for present and future goods".[26] It seems to me that, to assume that this rate of time preference can have any effect other than through the relative demand for these two classes of goods, or can have any immediate effects different from those of any other cause affecting that relative demand, is an attempt to establish a purely mystical connection. The mere fact that, even without a monetary change, any change in the distribution of the command over existing resources will, under a given set of individual time preferences, lead to quite different proportions between capital and income, should suffice to make this quite clear.[27]

Nor can I see how the two authors can combine their acceptance of the idea that forced saving can be brought about by monetary causes, without a change in the rate of time preference, with a general denial that monetary causes may also lead to 'forced dis-saving'. In principle, any change in the relative demand for the two categories of goods, whether brought about by actual shifts of monetary demand from one to the other, or merely by unilateral increases or decreases without corresponding changes on the other side, will *tend* to lead to corresponding changes in the relative amounts produced. The differences between these two cases (a shift and a unilateral change) are, *first* that the shift of an amount of money from the demand for consumers' goods to the demand for producers' goods changes the proportion between the two much more effectively than a mere unilateral increase or decrease by the same amount; and, *second*, that the changes in the quantity of money, which are implied in the second type of change, will lead to further changes which may counteract or offset the tendency created by the change in relative demand. This will be particularly true if a change in relative demand is accompanied

---

[26] [Hansen and Tout, "Annual Survey", p. 141.—Ed.]

[27] This fact is partly realised by the authors who, however, seem to underestimate its importance, mainly because they think only of the effects of a change in the distribution of *income*; and while this is obviously the only factor which will affect *new savings*, the total supply of free capital depends even more on turnover or amortisation of existing capital. Any change in that stock of existing capital, brought about by monetary causes, will, by means of the consequent redistribution of the command over resources, tend to affect the relative demand for producers' and consumers' goods. If the monetary causes have led to a destruction of capital, this change will necessarily be permanent. If they have led to the creation of additional capital goods, the effect on relative demand *may* be, at least to some extent, permanently to increase the relative demand for capital goods.

by an absolute reduction in demand and if, at the same time, costs (i.e., the prices of the original factors of production) are rigid. In this case, deflationary tendencies are likely to set in, which may more than counter-balance the effect of the changed relative demand. But, in spite of these further complications which seem likely to arise, the principle seems to me to be true, and to comprise even what seems to Messrs. Hansen and Tout a *reductio ad absurdum* of the argument,[28] namely that a unilateral decrease in the demand for consumers' goods may lead to a lengthening of the structure of production. Although I fully admit that, because of the probable complications, this case is very unlikely to materialise, I do not think that it is entirely impractical. Would Messrs. Hansen and Tout deny that, e.g., increased hoarding on the part of a class of very small rentiers who reduced their consumption of agricultural products might not lead, via the reduction of wages, first in agriculture and then generally, to an increase in the real quantity of labour corresponding to a constant amount of money invested in industry, and therefore of capital?

9.

The analysis of this and similar cases would help to bring out an important distinction which Messrs. Hansen and Tout tend to overlook: the distinction between the tendencies set up directly by a given monetary change, and the effects of the further monetary changes which may, and perhaps even probably will, but need not, be induced by this first change. A sharp dividing line is the more necessary here since the tendency in current discussions is either to take these secondary monetary changes for granted, without ever mentioning them, or to fail to demonstrate why, and under what conditions, they should follow the first change.

These considerations bring me back to the problem of the relation between the demand for consumers' goods and the prices of capital goods. I should not deny that there may be conditions where, e.g., the expectation of a general price fall has led to extensive hoarding, and where any change in this expectation may lead to such dishoarding of funds available for investment as to outbalance the initial effect of the increase in the demand for consumers' goods.[29] Nor is it inconceivable that a similar situation may prevail as regards bank lending. There can also be no doubt that, in connection with these secondary monetary complications, *general* price movements, apart from the changes in relative prices, will be of the greatest importance, and that any-

[28] [Cf. Hansen and Tout, "Annual Survey", p. 143n.20.—Ed.]

[29] Cf. my contribution to the *Festschrift für Arthur Spiethoff* [cf. "The Present State and Immediate Prospects"—Ed.], quoted above.

thing which stops or reverses the general price movement may lead to induced monetary changes, the effect of which on the demand for consumers' goods, and producers' goods, may be stronger than the initial change in the quantity of money.

But one has to be careful not to fall into the error apparently made by Messrs. Hansen and Tout—that of assuming that, in all cases, where the prices of consumers' goods and producers' goods move in the same direction (e.g., upwards), this may not be accompanied by changes in their relative height, which would produce exactly the same effect as if there were no general price movement. Their general proposition that changes in the relative prices of consumers' goods and producers' goods will not have the same effect when they are accompanied by a universal movement in the same direction as when they find expression in an absolute movement in different direction, is only true under the following assumptions: (1) that the expected general price movement is relatively great compared with the relative price changes; (2) that, at the same time, the general movement does not exceed the limits beyond which—as experience has shown at least in cases of considerable inflation—costs begin to move more rapidly than prices; (3) that money rates of interest do not adapt themselves to the expected rate of general price change.[30]

Further, it is necessary to be careful to make clear the special assumptions under which these further complications are likely to arise. The deflationary tendencies, which are assumed to exist in most of the reasoning of the kind discussed, are not a necessary consequence of any crisis and depression, but are probably due to resistances to the necessary readjustments, caused by rigidity of prices, the existence of long term contracts, etc. I am far from underrating the importance of these phenomena. What I am pleading for is only that, for analytical purposes, these tendencies should carefully be kept sepa-

---

[30] It is a curious fact that the discussion of the supposedly different effect of changes in the relative demand which are due to changes in the supply of money leads the two authors to argue—in effect, if not explicitly, and on what seems to me to be wrong grounds—what they had previously denied, namely that capital accumulated by means of 'forced saving' will not be permanent. If it were true that when, after a change in the supply of money, "equilibrium is finally established, the [their] relation (between the prices of consumers' goods and the prices of producers' goods) [the words within the brackets are Hayek's emendation—Ed.] will be found [to be] unaltered unless the effects of the transition period have been such as to change permanently the time preference of the income receivers [of income receivers]" (Hansen and Tout, "Annual Survey", p. 143), then, no doubt, the greater part of the real capital created by means of forced saving would be lost. But I think it will be clear by now why I should be very reluctant to use this argument in defence of my position.

Messrs. Hansen and Tout think that such a permanent change in the time preference of the income receivers "is not unlikely, since an increase or decrease in money supply is likely to increase [or decrease] the real income of the community" [ibid.—Ed.]. This seems to show conclusively that what they have in mind is not the effect on the quantity and distribution of resources, but on individual time preferences.

rate and not confused with one another. Only in this way can we hope ultimately to unravel the tangle of different forces at work during a depression,
and to arrive at that detailed explanation of the depression which I cannot
even attempt here. But to deny the existence of certain tendencies merely because they are likely to be counteracted by others, does not seem to me to be
a promising procedure.

10.

The objections raised by Messrs. Hansen and Tout to what they call my theses
7, 8, 9, and 10, are partly based on arguments which I have already discussed
and partly introduce further complications which any programme of practical
policy has to face and which I admit I have not investigated sufficiently. But it
is obviously impossible to develop my ideas further, in this connection, or to
try to make good these deficiencies here.

There are only two more points upon which I wish to touch. The first is that
the concept of neutral money was meant in the first place to be an instrument
of theoretical analysis and not necessarily a tool of practical policy.[31] Its purpose was to bring out clearly the conditions under which we could expect the
economic process in a money economy to correspond perfectly to the picture
drawn by the theory of equilibrium and, incidentally, to show what we should
have to consider as the peculiar active effects caused by monetary changes.
In a sense, of course, this would also set up an ideal of policy. But it is by no
means inconceivable that considerations other than the direct monetary influences on prices, such as the existence of long term contracts in fixed sums
of money, the rigidity of prices, and such like institutional factors, may make
such an attempt entirely impracticable, because it would set up frictions of a
new kind. In that case, the task of monetary policy would be to find a work-
able compromise between the different incompatible aims. But, in this case,
one would have to be clear that certain important determining and disturbing
influences arising from monetary causes would remain in existence, and that
we should always have to remain conscious of this fact. Or, in other words,
that even under the best practicable monetary system, the self-equilibrating
mechanism of prices might be seriously disturbed by monetary causes.

The second point is that up to 1927 I should, indeed, have expected that
because, during the preceding boom period, prices did not rise—but rather
tended to fall—the subsequent depression would be very mild. But, as is

---

[31] [Cf. also similarly F. A. Hayek, "Über 'neutrales Geld'", *Zeitschrift für Nationalökonomie*, vol. 4,
October 1933, pp. 659–61, translated as "On 'Neutral' Money" and reprinted as chapter 6 of
F. A. Hayek, *Good Money, Part I: The New World.*—Ed.]

well known, in that year an entirely unprecedented action was taken by the American monetary authorities, which makes it impossible to compare the effects of the boom on the subsequent depression with any previous experience. The authorities succeeded, by means of an easy-money policy, inaugurated as soon as the symptoms of an impending reaction were noticed, in prolonging the boom for two years beyond what would otherwise have been its natural end. And when the crisis finally occurred, for almost two more years, deliberate attempts were made to prevent, by all conceivable means, the normal process of liquidation. It seems to me that these facts have had a far greater influence on the character of the depression than the developments up to 1927, which from all we know, might instead have led to a comparatively mild depression in and after 1927.[32]

[32] [On these issues cf. Hayek's elaboration in "Das Schicksal der Goldwährung", *Der Deutsche Volkswirt*, vol. 6, February 12 and 19, 1932, pp. 642–45 and 677–81, translated as "The Fate of the Gold Standard" and reprinted as chapter 3 of F. A. Hayek, *Good Money, Part I: The New World*.—Ed.]

SEVEN

INVESTMENT THAT RAISES THE DEMAND FOR CAPITAL[1]

The purpose of this essay is to state a proposition which underlies the modern 'monetary over-investment theories' of the trade cycle in a form in which, as far as I know, it has never before been expressed, but which seems to make this particular proposition so obvious as to put its logical correctness beyond dispute. This, of course, does not necessarily mean that the theories which rely largely on this proposition provide an adequate account of all or any trade cycles. But it should do something to show the inadequacies of those current theories which completely disregard the effect in question. It should, moreover, clear up some of the confusion and misunderstandings which have made it so difficult to come to an agreement on the purely analytical points involved.

It will surprise nobody to find the source of this confusion in the ambiguity of the term capital. In static analysis, the term capital refers equally to the aggregate value of all capital goods and to their 'quantity', measured in terms of cost (or in some other way). But this is of little significance because in equilibrium these two magnitudes must necessarily coincide. In the analysis of dynamic phenomena, however, this ambiguity becomes exceedingly dangerous. In particular, the static proposition that an increase in the quantity of capital will bring about a fall in its marginal productivity (which for the purposes of this article I shall call the rate of interest), when taken over into economic dynamics and applied to the quantity of capital goods, may become quite definitely erroneous.

1. The Relative Significance of the Amount of Investment and of the Form that it Takes

The assumption that an increase in the quantity of capital goods will necessarily decrease the return to be expected on further investment is gener-

---

[1] [First published in *Review of Economic Statistics*, vol. 19, November 1937, pp. 174–77, and reprinted as chapter 2 of F. A. Hayek, *Profits, Interest and Investment. And Other Essays on the Theory of Industrial Fluctuations* (London: Routledge, 1939). The text follows the reprint.—Ed.]

ally treated as obvious. It is, therefore, desirable to state the actual relations between the two magnitudes in a form which may, perhaps, sound somewhat paradoxical. The main thesis of this article will be that the effect which the current production of capital goods will have on the future demand for investible funds will depend not so much on the quantity of capital goods produced, as on the kind of capital goods which are produced or on the particular forms which current investment takes, and that an increase in the current output of capital goods will frequently have the effect not of lowering but of raising the future demand for investible funds, and thereby the rate of interest.

Each separate step of the argument which leads to this conclusion is a familiar and obvious proposition. The first main point is that most investment is undertaken in the expectation that further investment, for which the equipment that formed the object of the first investment will be needed, will take place at a later date. This may be expressed by saying that current investment will be guided by the expectation that investment will continue at a certain rate for some time to come, or that the rate of interest will stay at a certain figure. The success of current investment will depend upon this expectation being fulfilled. Most individual acts of investment must be regarded, therefore, as mere links in a chain which has to be completed if its parts are to serve the function for which they were intended, even though the chain consists of separate and successive acts of different entrepreneurs. The manufacturer of any kind of machines who increases his plant can do so only in the expectation that the users of these machines will at some later time be willing to install additional machines, and that these machines may be wanted only if somebody else will later be willing to invest in their products, etc.

The first investment of such a chain, therefore, will be undertaken only if it is expected that in each link of this chain a certain rate of interest can be earned. But this does not mean that, *once this investment has been made*, the process of further investments will not be continued if conditions change in an unfavourable direction—if, for example, the rate of interest at which money can be borrowed rises. If the investments already made are irrevocably committed to the particular purpose, this provides a margin within which the total profits to be expected on the whole chain of successive investments may fall without affecting the profitability of the further investments still needed to complete the process. For if the fixed capital already created is specific to the particular purpose, it will, of course, be used even if the return covers little more than the cost of using it (but not interest and amortisation); and since the owners of this fixed capital will find it in their interest to use it so long as they get only a little more than mere operating cost, nearly the whole amount which it was originally expected would be earned as interest and amortisation becomes available, as it were, as a premium on investment in the later stages of the process. The amount by which entrepreneurs in these later stages need to pay less for the products of the earlier stages, because the equipment there is already in existence, thus becomes available for expenditure on the completion of the process. And the greater the amount of investment which has already been made compared with that which is still required to utilise the equipment already in existence, the greater will be the rate of interest which can advantageously be borne in raising capital for these investments completing the chain.

2. 'Completing Investments' and the Rate of Interest

Obviously then, the demand for capital at any particular moment depends not so much on the productivity that the existing structure of real capital would have if completed—the long term schedule of the productivity of investment—as on the proportion between that part of it which has already been completed and that part which has yet to be added to complete it. Only for a very small fraction of the total investments—the marginal investments which represent the beginning of new chains of investment—will the demand for funds promptly react to a change in the rate at which capital can be borrowed. For the rest, the demand for capital will be highly inelastic with respect to changes in the rate of interest.

The consequences of this can readily be shown by a schematic example. Assume that past investments have been guided by the expectation that a rate of interest of 4 per cent would continue to rule for some time, but that in order to complete the investments which have been undertaken in this expectation a greater supply of loanable funds would be required than is actually forthcoming. Assume further that, if investments in the recent past had been guided by the expectation of a 5 per cent rate of interest, the amount of further loans required to continue these investment processes would just exhaust the current supply. This does not mean that once investments have been undertaken in the expectation of a rate of 4 per cent, a rise of the interest rate to 5 per cent—that is, to the figure which, if correctly foreseen, would have represented an equilibrium rate—will now be sufficient to reduce demand for loans to the level of the supply. If a considerable part of the equipment to be used has already been produced, many investments, which it would never have been profitable to start if a rate of interest of 5 per cent had been foreseen, will be well worth while continuing, even at a rate much higher than 5 per cent. The loss will fall entirely on those entrepreneurs who in the past, in the expectation of the lower rate of interest, have already erected new plant, etc. But the concessions in price, below their actual cost of production, which they will be compelled to make, will enable the other entrepreneurs, whom they supply with equipment, to go on with the installation of new machinery, which would not have been possible if developments had been foreseen correctly from the outset. The construction of a large hydro-electric plant that would have been profitable if the rate of interest had remained at 4 per cent will prove unprofitable if the rate of interest rises. But, once it has been constructed and charges for electric power adjusted to get maximum profit over current expenditure, it will give rise to a further demand for capital for the installation of electric motors, etc., which will not be sensibly reduced even by a rate of interest much higher than 5 per cent.[2]

How far the rate of interest will have to rise to bring the demand for loans down to the available supplies will depend, as we have seen, on the proportion between that part of the complete investment processes which had been carried out before the unexpected rise in the rate of interest occurred, and that part of this total expenditure which has yet to be incurred. If, in a particular instance, interest at 4 per cent on the capital already invested and amortisation of that capital would have represented 30 per cent of the expected price of the final commodity in the production of which it was to be used, then interest charges involved in utilising the existing plant and its products would have to rise so as to absorb the whole of this 30 per cent of the final price, before the demand for capital for this purpose would be effectively curtailed. If, of the remaining 70 per cent of the expected total cost of the final product, 15 per cent was allowed for further interest at 4 per cent, interest rates would have to rise to approximately 12 per cent before the profitability of the investments completing the process already begun would be reduced to zero.

Against this whole argumentation it might be objected that it completely ignores the effect of the rise in interest rates on current replacement of the capital in the 'earlier stages' which has partly or entirely lost its value. It is certainly true that these items of equipment will not be replaced. But the implication that this will in any way relieve the demand for funds for investment is certainly erroneous. In so far as those items in the normal course of affairs would already need replacement, these replacements would have been financed out of amortisation currently earned. They would not have constituted a demand on the funds available for investments. But if—and this is more likely—they have not yet become ripe for replacement, the amortisation earned would temporarily be available for investment elsewhere. The fact that no amortisation or only a reduced quota will be earned will then mean a reduction of the supply of investible funds, that is, it will represent a factor which tends to raise rather than lower the rate of interest.

---

[2] Cf. my *Monetary Theory and the Trade Cycle* (London: Cape, 1933), pp. 224f. [pp. 224–25, reprinted in *Business Cycles, Part I*, ed. Hansjoerg Klausinger, vol. 7 (2012) of *The Collected Works of F. A. Hayek* (Chicago: University of Chicago Press), p. 158—Ed.].

3. Causes of an Urgent Demand for Funds for Completing Investments

The causes which are likely to bring about such a situation remain to be considered. Under what conditions will the demand for the additional capital required to complete a given capital structure drive up the rate of interest to a figure very much higher than the rate which is compatible with the permanent maintenance of that structure?

In principle the answer is surely clear. Anything which will lead people to expect a lower rate of interest, or a larger supply of investible funds, than will actually exist when the time comes for their utilisation, will in the way we have suggested force interest rates to rise much higher than would have been the case if people had not expected such a low rate. But, while it is true that an unexpected decrease in the rate of saving, or an unforeseen appearance of a new demand for capital—a new invention for instance—may bring about such a situation, the most important cause practically of such false expectations probably is a temporary increase in the supply of such funds through credit expansion at a rate which cannot be maintained. In this case, the increased quantity of current investment will induce people to expect investment to continue at a similar rate for some time, and in consequence to invest now in a form which requires for its successful completion further investment at a similar rate.[3] It is not so much the quantity of current investment but the direction it takes—the *type* of capital goods being produced—which determines the amount of future investment required if the current investments are to be successfully incorporated in the structure of production. But it is the amount of investment made possible by the current supply of funds which determines expectations about the future rate of investment and thereby the form that the current investment will be given. We can now see the justification for the somewhat paradoxical form in which the main thesis of this article was originally stated. An increase in the rate of investment, or the quantity of capital goods, may have the effect of raising rather than lowering the rate of interest, if this increase has given rise to the expectation of a greater future supply of investible funds than is actually forthcoming.

---

[3] For a somewhat fuller statement of these connections see my articles "Preiserwartungen, monetäre Störungen und Fehlinvestitionen", *Nationalökonomisk Tidsskrift*, vol. 73, no. 1, 1935, pp. 176–91 (also a French version [titled, "Previsions de prix, perturbations monétaires et faux investissements"—Ed.] in the *Revue des Sciences Economiques*, vol. 9, October 1935, pp. 165–81) [cf. the translation as "Price Expectations, Monetary Disturbances, and Malinvestments", chapter 4 of *Profits, Interest and Investment*, reprinted as chapter 7 of *Good Money, Part I: The New World*, ed. Stephen Kresge, vol. 5 (1999) of *The Collected Works of F. A. Hayek*—Ed.], and "The Maintenance of Capital", *Economica*, n.s., vol. 2, August 1935, particularly pp. 268 et seq. [pp. 268–73; cf. reprinted in F. A. Hayek, *Profits, Interest and Investment*, pp. 122–29; to be included in *Capital and Interest*, ed. Lawrence White, vol. 11 (forthcoming) of *The Collected Works of F. A. Hayek*—Ed.].

If this proposition is correct, and if its assumptions are empirically justified, this means that much of the purely monetary analysis of the trade cycle now current is built on very insufficient foundations. If it is correct, the common assumption that the expected return on investment, or the 'marginal efficiency of capital', can be treated as a simple decreasing function of the quantity of capital goods in existence, or of the current rate of investment, will have to be abandoned, and with it much of the argument based on the supposed tendency of the 'marginal efficiency of capital' to fall more rapidly than the money rate of interest.[4] If past investment is often found to make further investment more rather than less profitable, this would also mean that the rise of the rate of interest towards the end of a boom—which so many authors believe can be explained only by *monetary* factors affecting the *supply* of loanable funds[5]—can be adequately explained by *real* factors affecting the *demand*. It shows, moreover, that a purely monetary analysis, which runs in terms of mere rates of investment without analysing the concrete structure of these investments and the influence which monetary factors can have on this real structure of production, is bound to neglect some of the most significant elements in the picture. And, perhaps, it also explains why a careful analysis of the time structure of production (*not* in terms of an 'average' period of production)[6] is a necessary basis for a satisfactory analysis of the trade cycle.

[4] [The target of this attack is of course Keynes's *General Theory*, where a marginal efficiency of capital falling more rapidly than the rate of interest is identified as an obstacle to full employment; cf., e.g., John Maynard Keynes, *The General Theory of Employment, Interest and Money* (London: Macmillan, 1936), reprinted as vol. 7 (1971) of *The Collected Writings of John Maynard Keynes*, ed. Austin Robinson and Donald Moggridge (London: Macmillan; Cambridge: Cambridge University Press), pp. 173 and 219.—Ed.]

[5] [In Hayek's terminology the supply of 'loanable funds' is a concept analogous to the supply of 'free capital'.—Ed.]

[6] [This is one of the many instances, after 1934, where Hayek rejected the idea of an 'average period of production', which he himself had used as a simplification in *Prices and Production*. See also the editor's introduction, this volume, pp. 34–36.—Ed.]

EIGHT

PROFITS, INTEREST AND INVESTMENT[1]

1. Introduction. In this essay an attempt will be made to restate two crucial points of the explanation of crises and depressions which the author has tried to develop on earlier occasions. In the first part I hope to show why under certain conditions, contrary to a widely held opinion, an increase in the demand for consumers' goods will tend to decrease rather than to increase the demand for investment goods. In the second part it will be shown why these conditions will regularly arise as a consequence of the conditions prevailing at the beginning of a recovery from a depression.

The main point on which this revised version differs from my earlier treatments of the same problem is that I believe now that it is, properly speaking, a rate of profit rather than a rate of interest in the strict sense which is the dominating factor in this connection. In particular it seems that the mechanism through which an increase in the demand for consumers' goods may lower the investment demand-schedule (and consequently employment) involves an increase in a rate of profit which is distinct from, and may move independently of, the money rate of interest, although it is often confused with the latter and indeed performs many of the functions commonly attributed to it. It will be argued here that it is this rate of profit which 'orthodox' economists, consciously or unconsciously, often had in mind when they spoke of the rate of interest equalising saving and investment, or of the rate of interest depending on the scarcity of real capital. It will be argued further that this rate of profit is in many respects much more effective and fundamental than the rate of interest. And while it is easy to understand why economists who were brought up to think mainly in 'real' terms should refer to this rate of profit as

---

[1] [First published as chapter 1 of *Profits, Interest and Investment. And Other Essays on the Theory of Industrial Fluctuations* (London: Routledge, 1939). As pointed out in the editor's introduction, this volume, p. 15, this essay had originally been destined for the final chapter of Hayek's capital book—which ultimately became *The Pure Theory of Capital* (London: Macmillan, 1941), reprinted, ed. Lawrence White, as vol. 12 (2007) of *The Collected Works of F. A. Hayek* (Chicago: University of Chicago Press; London: Routledge)—but then grew into a separate study of its own.—Ed.]

the rate of interest, there can be no doubt that this practice has caused a great deal of confusion and that a more careful separation of the two concepts is necessary.[2]

A second correction of a similar nature concerns the inadequate distinction I had formerly drawn between the movements of money wages and the movement of real wages. Although the argument of *Prices and Production*[3] clearly implied a *fall* of real wages during the later stages of the boom (as is shown particularly by the discussion of the increasing 'price margins' between the various stages of production[4]), this was obscured by the emphasis on the rise of money wages—which is only a symptom that the fall in real wages is having its effect on the demand for labour. There may, however, also have been some confusion between the different ways in which changes in the prices of raw materials and changes in the rate of wages operate. This point will be separately considered in section 9 below.

Apart from these two corrections the main difference between the present version and the older ones is that I am here trying to show the same tendencies at work under different and, I hope, more realistic assumptions. We shall start here from an initial situation where considerable unemployment of material resources and labour exists, and we shall take account of the existing

---

[2] The classical economists were by no means unaware of the fact that the relationship between the rate of profit and the rate of interest properly speaking presented a problem. One of the earliest questions proposed for discussion at the Political Economy Club (by G. W. Norman on February 4th, 1822) was "Is there any necessary connection between the rate of Profit and the rate of Interest?" (Political Economy Club, *Minutes of Proceedings, etc. [1899–1920, Roll of Members and Questions Discussed, 1821–1920, with documents bearing on the history of the Club*—Ed.], vol. 6 (London: Macmillan, 1921), p. 11). [George Warde Norman (1793–1882) was director of the Bank of England for more than fifty years and contributed to classical monetary thought. The Political Economy Club, founded in 1821, with its regular meetings and discussions constituted a major institutional link for the community of the classical economists.—Ed.] The confusion only began when economists, probably because of the special associations attached to the word profit since Marx, began to shun this term and to use interest instead. Although in many connections, particularly when the term interest is used merely as a generic description of the income from capital in general, as in the theory of distribution, this use of the term may do no harm, it is definitely misleading in 'dynamic' analysis.

[3] [*Prices and Production* (London: Routledge, 1931; 2nd ed. rev., 1935), reprinted in *Business Cycles, Part I*, ed. Hansjoerg Klausinger, vol. 7 (2012) of *The Collected Works of F. A. Hayek.*—Ed.]

[4] [The 'price margin' is the relation between the price of a good produced in a stage of production and the unit costs expended (for wages and intermediate products) in its production; cf., e.g., *Prices and Production*, reprinted, p. 248. Note that with a linear structure of production where consumers' goods are produced in the last stage of production while in the first stage only original means of production (labour) are used, 'real wages', that is, wages in terms of consumers' goods, are determined by the whole sequence of price margins linking the costs (wages) of the first stage to the price of the good produced in the last stage.—Ed.]

rigidity of money wages and of the limited mobility of labour. More specifically, we shall assume throughout this essay that there is in the short run practically no mobility of labour between the main industrial groups, that money
wages cannot be reduced, that the existing equipment is fairly specific to the
purposes for which it was made, and finally, that the money rate of interest
is kept constant. Terms like income, profits, wages, yields, etc., will throughout, unless the contrary is expressly indicated, be used to refer to amounts of
money (as distinguished from the corresponding 'real' magnitudes).

The earlier presentation of essentially the same argument in *Prices and Production* has been frequently criticised for its failure to take account of the existence of unused resources. It still seems to me that to start first from a position of equilibrium was logically the right procedure, and that it is important
to be able to show how from such an initial position cyclical fluctuations may
be generated. But this ought to be supplemented by an account of how such
cyclical fluctuations, once started, tend to become self-generating, so that the
economic system may never reach a position which could be described as equilibrium. This I shall try to do here and I hope to show that to introduce these
more realistic assumptions strengthens rather than weakens my argument.

In a sense the assumptions made here, and particularly the assumption of
complete immobility of the rate of interest and of complete rigidity of money
wages maintained through the greater part of this paper, are as artificial as the
opposite assumption made on the earlier occasions. And I should like to emphasise at once that this paper does not attempt to give a comprehensive or
complete account of the causes of industrial fluctuations. It provides merely
another theoretical model which ought to help to elucidate certain essential
relationships. In particular I want to warn the reader that I do not mean to assert that the rate of profit actually does play quite the role which it is here assumed to play. What I am concerned with is to show how it would act if the
rate of interest failed to act at all. I believe that this throws important light
on the function of the rate of interest. But it is vain to ask for empirical confirmation of this particular mechanism. All that is relevant for my purpose is
whether under the assumed conditions it would act as I describe it.

To concentrate discussion on matters directly relevant to the main problem
I have here in general avoided the special terminology of the 'Austrian' theory
of capital. Although I still regard this theory essentially right and even as indispensable for a more detailed analysis, I can see that in the simplified form
in which I had to use it in my former book it may be more misleading than
helpful. And a systematic discussion of these problems must be reserved for
another occasion.[5]

---

[5] [Thereby Hayek refers to his ongoing work on the capital project which evolved into *The
Pure Theory of Capital.*—Ed.]

Part One

2. The Ricardo Effect. Since throughout this essay we shall frequently have to make use of a proposition of general character, we shall begin by explaining it in its general form quite apart from its special application to problems of industrial fluctuations. Its substance is contained in the familiar Ricardian proposition that a rise in wages will encourage capitalists to substitute machinery for labour and vice versa.[6] Adapted to our present purpose it can best be restated by means of a schematic example. Assume that the labour used directly or indirectly (in the form of machinery, tools, raw materials, etc.), in the manufacture of any commodity is applied at various dates so that Ricardo's "time which must elapse before the commodity can be brought to the market"[7] is two years, one year, six months, three months, and one month respectively for the various amounts of labour used.[8] Assume further that the rate of interest is 6 per cent and that in the initial position the per annum rate of profit on the capital invested in the various kinds of labour is equal to the rate of interest. Assume then that while wages remain constant the price of the product rises by 2 per cent (which means that real wages fall in proportion). The result of this on the rate of profit earned on the various kinds of labour is best shown by a table (see table 8.1).

The amount of profit earned on the turnover of any amount of labour will be equal to the difference between the wages and the price of the marginal product of that labour. If the price of the product rises this will increase the amount of profit on each turnover in a corresponding proportion irrespective of the length of the period of turnover; and the *time rate* of profit will be increased accordingly much more for labour invested for short periods than on labour invested for long periods. In the case shown by the table the per annum rate of profit is raised, by a rise in the price of the product of only 2 per cent, from 6 to 7 per cent on the two years' investment and from 6 to 30 per cent on the one month's investment. This will, of course, create a tendency to use proportionately more of the latter kind and less of the former kind of labour, i.e., more labour in the last stages of the process and less in the form of ma-

---

[6] David Ricardo, *On the Principles of Political Economy and Taxation* [1817, 3rd ed. 1821], as reprinted in *The Works of David Ricardo*, ed. John Ramsey McCulloch (London: Murray, 1846), pp. 26f. [pp. 26–27; cf. *The Works and Correspondence of David Ricardo*, ed. Piero Sraffa, vol. 1 (Cambridge: Cambridge University Press, 1951; reprinted, Indianapolis: Liberty Press, 2004), pp. 39–41—Ed.].

[7] [*The Works of David Ricardo*, ed. McCulloch, p. 25, *The Works and Correspondence of David Ricardo*, ed. Sraffa, vol. 1, p. 37.—Ed.]

[8] These various intervals refer to different amounts of labour used in *one and the same* technical process, not to different processes. A change to more or less 'capitalistic' processes would be brought about by changes in the proportions of the amounts of labour invested for the various intervals.

Table 8.1

	Labour invested for				
	2 years	1 year	6 months	3 months	1 month
Initial *amount* of profit on each turnover in per cent	12	6	3	1.5	0.5
	(*all corresponding to 6 per cent per annum*)				
Add 2 per cent additional profit on each turnover due to rise of price of product:	14	8	5	3.5	2.5
	which corresponds to a per annum rate of profit of:				
	7	8	10	14	30
	per cent				

chinery or for other work of preparatory character, till by a fall of the marginal product of the former and a rise of the marginal product of the latter kind of labour the time rates of profit earned on capital invested in each become once more the same. Or in other words: a rise in the price of the product (or a fall in real wages) will lead to the use of relatively less machinery and other capital and of relatively more direct labour in the production of any given quantity of output.[9] In what follows we shall refer to this tendency as the 'Ricardo Effect'.

[9] This proposition can be demonstrated by a slight adaptation of the useful diagram employed by Professor Lange to explain the determination of the rate of interest (Oskar Lange, "The Place of Interest in the Theory of Production", *Review of Economic Studies*, vol. 3, June 1936, p. 165). [See fig. 8.1 on following page.—Ed.]

Along the abscissa *OP* is measured the total quantity of labour used in a particular process of production which, it is assumed, can be distributed in various ways between investment for one year and investment for two years. The amount of labour invested for one year is measured from the right to the left so that the remaining portion of the abscissa measures the amount of labour invested for two years. Any point of the abscissa corresponds therefore to a given distribution of the fixed total of labour between the two kinds of investments. The marginal productivity of labour invested for two years (measured along the ordinate *OY* and on the assumption that the complementary amount of labour is invested for one year) is then shown by the curve sloping down from the left to the right, while the marginal productivity of the various amounts of labour invested for one year is similarly represented by the curve sloping down from the right to the left.

It can now be easily shown that the distribution of labour between the two kinds of investments will be determined by the rate of real wages. Assume wages at first to be equal to *OW*. Equilibrium requires that the amount of profits on two year investments (neglecting compound interest) be exactly twice the amount of profits on one year investments. These profits are represented by the distances *RT* and *RS* respectively and the condition of equilibrium is therefore that *RT* = 2*RS*. Assume now that real wages are lowered from *OW* to *OW*¹. The point at which profits

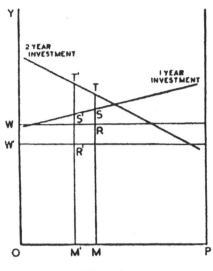

Figure 8.1

3. The Operation of the 'Ricardo Effect' in the Later Stages of the Boom. We can now apply these considerations to the special case of the rise in prices and fall in real wages which usually occurs in the later stages of the boom. We shall consider an economic system at a point somewhere half-way through a cyclical upswing, when excess stocks of consumers' goods have been absorbed, and employment in the consumers' goods industries is high so that any further rise in demand for consumers' goods will lead to a rise in their prices and a fall in real wages. For the present we shall just take it as a fact—and it is probably one of the best established empirical generalisations about industrial fluctuations—that at this stage prices of consumers' goods do as a rule rise and real wages fall.[10] With the reasons why this should regularly be the case, i.e., why the output of consumers' goods should fail to keep pace with the demand for consumers' goods, we shall be concerned in the second part of this essay. But

---

on two year investments $R^1 T^1$ will now be exactly twice the profits on one year investments $R^1 S^1$ will in consequence be shifted to the left, i.e., to M^1. In consequence of the fall in wages the proportional amount of labour used for one year investments will have increased from PM to PM^1, and the corresponding proportional amount of labour invested for two years reduced from OM to OM^1. And the same would apply, of course, to any other pair of investment periods of which the one is longer and the other shorter.

[10] [This alleged fact, of a counter-cyclical movement of real wages, underlying not only Hayek's but even more so Keynes's theory, had been already contested in the well-known article by John T. Dunlop, "The Movement of Real and Money Wage Rates", *Economic Journal*, vol. 48, September 1938, pp. 413–34.—Ed.]

while in this stage unemployment in the consumers' goods industries will have become insignificant, there may still exist a fairly substantial unemployment in some of the capital goods industries.

Our next problem is what effect the rise of prices and profits and the fall of real wages in the consumers' goods industries will have on the separate investment demand-schedules (the schedules of the 'marginal efficiency of capital'[11]) of the different kinds of capital goods. We shall at first be concerned with the effect of such a rise in prices relatively to cost on the demand for capital goods on the part of the various individual industries, particularly the consumers' goods industries. We shall see later how essential it is, not at once to aggregate the separate investment demand-schedules of the various industries, but carefully to distinguish between the effects which the causes we are considering will have on the demand for different kinds of capital goods. It will be seen then how misleading a premature combination of these separate demand-schedules into one general investment demand-schedule may become in a world where labour (and existing equipment) is not homogeneous, but often very specific to particular purposes, and where, therefore, an increase in the demand for one kind of labour of which there is no more available can in no way offset a decrease in the demand for other kinds of labour of which there is still an unemployed reserve.

Of the three main influences on which the profitability of producing the different kinds of capital goods will depend—their expected yield, their cost of production, and the rate of interest—it will be their yield[12] with which we shall here be mainly concerned. It is with respect to the effect of changes in final demand on the yield of various types of capital goods that our first divergence from prevalent views arises; for it is usually taken for granted that the yield of capital goods in general will move parallel with, or at least in the same direction as, expected final demand.[13] Now this is true enough of capital

---

[11] [This is Keynes's term (see above, editor's note, p. 211) for the expected 'internal rate of return' (or rate of profit) associated with a specific capital good. Implicitly, with a given rate of interest, it defines a demand schedule ('the demand price') for the capital good in question. See, e.g., John Maynard Keynes, *The General Theory of Employment, Interest and Money* (London: Macmillan, 1936), reprinted as vol. 7 (1971) of *The Collected Writings of John Maynard Keynes*, ed. Austin Robinson and Donald Moggridge (London: Macmillan; Cambridge: Cambridge University Press), chapter 4.—Ed.]

[12] It is probably justifiable to assume that expected yields will as a rule move, if not by the same amounts, at least in the same direction as current yields. Whether that is the case or not, however, till it becomes necessary explicitly to bring in expectations, we shall here simply speak of the yield, implying that current and expected yield do move in the same direction.

[13] This appears to be regarded as so obvious that it is rarely explicitly stated, except by some general reference to the fact that the demand for capital goods is 'derived' from the demand for consumers' goods. It is rather instructive that the most elaborate and influential work dealing with these problems in recent years, Mr. Keynes' *General Theory*, does not contain, as far as I can

goods (or rather durable consumers' goods) which without any further collaboration from labour will directly serve consumption. But it is much less obvious in the case of labour-saving equipment; that is, machinery in the ordinary sense of the word; and it is still less obvious in the case of machinery to make machinery and so forth.

It is here that the 'Ricardo Effect' comes into action and becomes of decisive importance. The rise in the prices of consumers' goods[14] and the consequent fall in real wages means a rise in the rate of profit in the consumers' goods industries, but, as we have seen, a very different rise in the time rates of profit that can now be earned on more direct labour and on the investment of additional capital in machinery. A much higher rate of profit will now be obtainable on money spent on labour than on money invested in machinery.

The effect of this rise in the rate of profit[15] in the consumers' goods industries will be twofold. On the one hand it will cause a tendency to use more labour with the existing machinery, by working over-time and double shifts, by using outworn and obsolete machinery, etc. On the other hand, in so far as new machinery is being installed, either by way of replacement or in order to increase capacity, this, so long as real wages remain low compared with the marginal productivity of labour, will be of a less expensive, less labour-saving or less durable type.

To illustrate this last point it is convenient to consider for the moment a society where machines are not bought but only hired from the producer. The demand for the services of machines required by the consumers' goods industries, and therefore the rent offered for their hire, will undoubtedly rise in consequence of the increased demand for consumers' goods. But it will not rise to the same extent for different kinds of machinery. A fall in real wages will raise the value of the less labour-saving machinery more than that of more labour-saving machinery, and stimulate the production of the former at the expense of the latter. And similarly with respect to more or less durable ma-

---

see, any discussion of how a change in final demand affects the yield of the various types of investment goods.

[14] It should be noted that the relevant rise in the prices of consumers' goods is not the absolute rise, but the rise relatively to costs of production. This means that an absolute rise in prices may not have the effects assumed here if it is not in excess of an independent rise in costs, and that constant prices may have the same effect as a rise in prices if costs fall (in consequence of improved technique, previous investments, etc.). The essential point is what happens to profits.

[15] Here and throughout the further exposition 'the rate of profit' stands for the profit schedule (or the rate of profit on any given output) and the expressions 'a rise in profits' and 'a fall in profits' must be understood to refer to a rise or fall of the whole profit schedule. On occasions it will also be necessary to speak for the sake of brevity of *the* rate of profit in groups of industries, although this is not intended to suggest that there will be a uniform rise of the profit schedules in these industries. All that is meant is that the rates of profit will tend to rise, to various extents, above the given rate of interest.

chinery. Whether it pays to make machinery more durable will depend on whether the last additional investment by which the life of the machine can be lengthened will bring the same per annum rate of return as the direct use of labour; and if real wages fall it will evidently be profitable to provide the same services from less durable machinery than before.

4. The Rate of Profit and the Rate of Interest. The rise of the rate of profit in the consumers' goods industries will then create a tendency for any given quantity of output to be produced with comparatively less capital and comparatively more labour. But, it might be objected, must not the rate of profit always become equal to the rate of interest, which we have assumed to remain constant? That is, will not production always be expanded to the point where the marginal rate of profit is equal to the rate of interest? Now this is probably[16] quite true of the *marginal* rate of profit; but this in no way constitutes an objection to our argument. What we are concerned with are not marginal rates of profit but the rates of profit on any given output and with any given method of production (or the profit schedules or profit curve for all possible outputs and all the various methods of production); and the main point is exactly that the only way to make the marginal rate of profit equal to any given rate of interest if real wages have fallen is to use a larger proportion of labour and a smaller proportion of capital. If real wages fall and the profit schedule of any given firm is thereby raised, and if the rate of interest remains constant,[17] this will in the first instance mean that more labour will be used with the given machinery till the rate of profit on the marginal unit of labour is once again equal to the given rate of interest. And when it comes to additions to, or replacements of, existing machinery, it will again be the level of the profit schedule and not marginal profits which will determine the kind of machinery that will be installed. Or, to put the same thing differently, a fall in real wages means that the proportion of capital and labour at which the marginal rate of profit on money spent on either will be the same, will be changed in favour of labour, whatever the marginal rate of profit. If, by keeping the rate of interest at the initial low figure, marginal profits are also kept low, this will only have the effect of a reduction in cost, that is, it will raise the figure at

[16] At any rate in so far as *expected* marginal profits are concerned. It is, however, by no means unlikely that in the course of such a process of expansion entrepreneurs will find again and again that the prices of their products have unexpectedly risen and that therefore retrospectively marginal profits were persistently higher than the rate of interest.

[17] [Note that prices of capital goods also remain constant so that the ratio between wages and the rental price of capital (that is, the rate of interest applied to the price of capital goods) does not change, too. It is this observation on which the critics of the 'Ricardo effect' will base their case. Cf. the editor's introduction, this volume, p. 19.—Ed.]

which the supply of and the demand for final output will be equal; but it will not affect the tendency to produce that output with comparatively less capital, a tendency which is caused, not by any change in the rate of interest, but by the shift in the position of the profit schedule.

5. The Role of Expectations. Another possible objection which must be briefly considered here is connected with the expectations of entrepreneurs about future price movements. So far we have considered the effects merely of a single rise in prices of consumers' goods and of the corresponding fall in real wages in the consumers' goods industries; and the argument implied that entrepreneurs expect that this higher rate of profit will continue. But a change in current prices may conceivably affect prices in more than one way and it therefore becomes necessary to consider more explicitly the role played by expectations of the entrepreneurs. That if entrepreneurs doubt the permanence of the increased demand they will not be inclined to increase the permanent capacity of their plant, and that therefore any idea about a normal price level which is being exceeded will operate in favour of short term rather than long term investment, will probably be granted. But it might at first appear that if entrepreneurs expected prices to continue to rise indefinitely this would have the contrary effect, that is, would favour investments for long periods. If entrepreneurs did expect a very considerable rise of prices to take place at a fairly distant date, say two years ahead, and if they assumed that prices would then remain high for a fairly long period afterwards, this might indeed stimulate long period investments. But the expected distant rise in prices would have to be very considerable indeed to counterbalance the tendency towards less capitalistic[18] investments caused by a rise in current prices and profits.[19] If prices,

---

[18] I am using 'capitalistic' and more and less 'capitalistic' here very much in the same sense in which Mr. Kaldor in a recent article "Capital Intensity and the Trade Cycle", *Economica*, n.s., vol. 6, February 1939, pp. 40–66 [reprinted as chapter 6 of his *Essays on Economic Stability and Growth*, vol. 2 of *Collected Economic Essays* (London: Duckworth, 1960; 2nd ed., 1980)—Ed.], uses the terms 'capital intensity' and 'capital intensive' as a somewhat too literal rendering of the German terms *Kapitalintensität* and *kapitalintensiv*. I have used these German terms myself in the original edition of "The 'Paradox' of Saving" [that is, in "Gibt es einen 'Widersinn des Sparens'?", *Zeitschrift für Nationalökonomie*, vol. 1, November 1929, p. 409n.—Ed.]. But the translators (was it Dr. Tugendhat or Mr. Kaldor himself?) wisely chose to translate them by 'roundaboutness' and more and less 'capitalistic'. Cf. "The 'Paradox' of Saving", as reprinted in *Profits, Interest and Investment*, p. 233n. [This reprint contains minor revisions; the passage in question is not in the translation that appeared in *Economica*, no. 32, May 1931, pp. 125–69, reprinted in *Contra Keynes and Cambridge: Essays, Correspondence*, ed. Bruce Caldwell, vol. 9 (1995) of *The Collected Works of F. A. Hayek*—Ed.]

[19] A reference to the numerical example used before in the text will easily show this. The point is that the expected rise in prices (as a rate per annum) will have to be greater than the rise in the (per annum) rate of profits on current transactions which depends, not simply on the rate

however, are merely expected to continue to rise at the rate at which they have already risen, this will as a rule create the expectation of a continued opportunity to make high profits on short term investments (i.e., it will operate as a rise of the 'prices of present goods' relatively to the 'prices of future goods' of pure theory[20]), and since the faster prices rise the greater the profit on current turnover is likely to be, the expectation of a continued rise of prices (unless it is an expectation of a rise at a continuously accelerating rate) will operate in favour of short term and against long term investments in the same way as a mere rise in present prices.

6. The Two Factors in the Operation of the Acceleration Principle. The significance of the results so far obtained can perhaps be made clearer if we relate them to a well-known doctrine, the so-called 'acceleration principle of derived demand'. This doctrine, into the long history and the detail of which we need not enter here, essentially asserts that, since the production of any given amount of final output usually requires an amount of capital several times larger than the output produced with it during any short period (say a year), any increase in final demand will give rise to an additional demand for capital goods several times larger than that new final demand. The demand for capital goods according to this theory is the result of final demand multiplied by a given coefficient.[21] We shall refer here to the two factors which determine this product as the 'multiplicand' and the 'multiplier' respectively, the former being final demand and the latter the ratio at which this final demand is transformed into demand for capital goods. (This 'multiplier' with which the acceleration principle operates must, of course, not be confused with *the* Multiplier which plays such

---

at which prices have already risen, but on the ratio of the difference between cost and prices caused by this rise to the period of turnover. If we take the figures used before, where the rise of current prices by 2 per cent (which may be due to a rise of prices extending over the course of some months) has increased the amount of profit on one month's investments from 1/2 to 2 1/2 per cent, it would require the expectation of a further rise of prices of no less than 46 per cent over the next two years in order to make a two years' investment and a one month's investment equally attractive as they were before. And a still greater expected rise in prices would be necessary in order that long period investments should actually be stimulated. [In the original, due to an obvious slip of the pen, the third sentence starts, "If we take the figures used before, where the rise of current profits [*sic*] by 2 per cent . . ."—Ed.]

[20] [Following Böhm-Bawerk, production means that present (capital) goods are to be turned into future (consumers') goods; in the case here considered it becomes profitable to shorten the time span needed for turning present into future goods. On Böhm-Bawerk's approach see above, editor's note, p. 197n.21.—Ed.]

[21] [Note that in this sentence Hayek explicitly refers to a relationship between levels of demand, in contrast to the common understanding of the accelerator principle as relating the demand for capital goods to the *change* in the demand for final goods. On the 'accelerator principle' and the so-called 'English view' of derived demand see the editor's note above, p. 194n.16.—Ed.]

an important role in Mr. Keynes' theories.[22] We shall later—in section 14 below—have occasion to reintroduce this 'multiplier' of the acceleration principle in its inverse form under the name of the 'Quotient'.)

The characteristic feature of the doctrine of the acceleration principle in its widely current form is that this 'multiplier' with which the acceleration effect operates is assumed to be constant—presumably because it is supposed to be determined solely by technological rather than by economic factors. In consequence any change in the 'multiplicand'—final demand—is assumed to lead to proportionally a much greater change in the same direction in the demand for capital goods. We have seen, however, that under certain conditions an increase in final demand may lead to a decrease of the 'multiplier'; the provision for supplying the increased demand may be made by using less capital than before per unit of expected demand. And this change will affect not only new investment but equally current replacement demand.

Even if the 'multiplier' decreases, however, this does not yet necessarily mean that total demand for machinery and other capital goods on the part of the consumers' goods industries will decrease. Whether this will be the case or not will evidently depend on whether the 'multiplicand', final demand, grows more or less rapidly than the 'multiplier' decreases. The effect on the demand for machinery of a tendency to increase capacity for final output may or may not be compensated by the tendency to use less expensive kinds of machinery. The net effect will depend on a number of circumstances: the magnitude of the rise in final demand, the durability of the machinery used in the past, the relative magnitude of the demand for additional machinery and of replacement demand (which depends on the two former factors) and finally, on the magnitude of the rise in the rate of profits. It is quite likely, at least as long as the rise of profits is confined to the consumers' goods industries, that aggregate demand for machinery will increase—although it will be demand for different kinds of machinery.

But this is not yet the end of the story. We have so far only considered the situation in the industries serving the consumers directly. We must now subject the situation in the other industries to a similar analysis.

7. The Structure of Capitalistic Production. If the idea of a fairly homogeneous aggregate demand for capital goods, more or less directly derived from the demand for consumers' goods, were an adequate description of reality, little more would have to be said about the subject. An increase in the demand for consumers' goods that would lead to a decrease in the demand for capital

---

[22] [In Keynes's *General Theory* (cf. pp. 113–15) the 'Multiplier' is the ratio of the overall change in income (or effective demand) to the primary (or exogenous) change in expenditure from which it results.—Ed.]

goods, because the increase in the 'multiplicand' would be counterbalanced by a decrease in the 'multiplier' of the acceleration principle, would be just a theoretical possibility, rather unlikely to occur in real life. Although an increase in final demand would cause changes in the kinds of capital goods demanded, the capital goods industry[23] regarded as a unit would almost certainly experience an increase of employment.

But the crude dichotomy of industry into consumers' goods industries and capital goods industries is certainly wholly insufficient to reproduce the essential features of the complicated interdependency between the various industries in actual life. There is every reason to believe that there are as great differences between the position of the different kinds of capital goods industries as there are between them and the consumers' goods industries. The capital goods industries are not all equally adapted to supply the consumers' goods industries with any kind of equipment they may need; they are further organised in a sort of vertical hierarchy. This fact is essential for our further argument.

Even the concept of the 'stages of production' which was intended to supply in the place of the crude dichotomy a somewhat finer distinction is not quite adequate for the purpose. While this schematic representation brings out one essential fact, the importance of the specificity of existing equipment to a particular method of production, it gives the impression of a simple linearity of the dependency of the various stages of production which does not apply in a world where durable goods are the most important form of capital.[24]

Although it is useful to retain the concept of stages, it is necessary to substitute for our present purpose a somewhat more elaborate pattern for the simple linear arrangement. If we designate the production of consumers' goods as stage I, we can then classify the various industries which directly supply the consumers' goods industries with capital goods of various kinds as stages II, III, IV, etc., according to the more or less 'capitalistic' character of the equipment which they supply. Stage II would supply the consumers' goods industries with the least capitalistic type of requirements, such as the raw materials and their simplest tools. Stage III would supply them with equipment of little durability and machinery of the least automatic type. Stage IV would supply a somewhat more capitalistic (more durable or more labour-saving) type of machinery, and so on to stage V, VI, etc., in ascending order.

Stage II in turn would obtain its requirements from the higher or earlier stages, i.e., III, IV, V, etc., and distribute its demand between them according

---

[23] [For the sake of consistency, here and throughout the following "capital goods industry" has been substituted for Hayek's occasional use of "capital good industry".—Ed.]

[24] In *Prices and Production*, where I used the simple linear stage pattern, the argument was based on the assumption that all capital used was of the nature of circulating capital.

to the rate of profit ruling in stage II, and similarly for stage III, IV, V, etc.[25] It is evident that even this scheme, like every schematic representation, does some violence to reality. In particular, it still gives an undue impression of linearity of these relationships while in fact they may in many respects be rather circular in character.[26] But I think that it does at least to some extent reproduce essential features of the real organisation of industry. It shows that while some industries will be more or less directly and predominantly dependent on the demand for capital goods by the consumers' goods industries, others will be designed mainly to serve other capital goods industries, and still others will be suited almost exclusively to assist all other industries in the transition to more capitalistic, more labour-saving methods of production.

The further argument turns largely, it will be seen, on the specificity of large parts of industry to comparatively 'early' stages of production. But while it is, of course, a question of fact whether this condition is fulfilled in real life or not, and while there may be no single industry whose equipment is so completely specific to the production of particular kinds of capital goods that it can be used only for that and for no other purpose, nevertheless there is no doubt that many industries are largely 'specific to the early stages' in the sense that a large part of the output which they are capable of producing can be used only in that very indirect manner. That railroads and shipbuilding and a large section of the engineering industries depend to a great extent on the demand from other industries making capital goods, and that the iron and steel industry in turn is still a stage further removed from consumption (though perhaps to a smaller extent now than before the rise of the motor-car industry) is probably beyond doubt. And there can also be little question that in a modern advancing society[27] there are many specialised plants whose labour and equipment are adapted to provide all the other industries with labour-saving devices of one sort or another which it will be profitable to introduce only if the rate of profit earned with the older methods has fallen to a certain level. In a modern community, particularly after it has gone through a period of low profits and interest rates, quite a considerable proportion of its labour and equipment will be dependent for its employment on a continued transition to (or at least a continued use of) highly capitalistic methods by other industries. The employment of those sections of industry will therefore depend at least

---

[25] [In the original text apparently by mistake stage "III" has been left out of this listing.—Ed.]

[26] Cf. Fritz Burchardt, "Die Schemata des stationären Kreislaufes bei Böhm-Bawerk und Marx", *Weltwirtschaftliches Archiv*, vol. 35, January 1932, pp. 116–76 [this is the second part; cf. also the first part, vol. 34, October 1931, pp. 525–64—Ed.], which, although I cannot agree with all of it, still appears to me not only as the first but also as the most fruitful of all the recent criticisms of the 'Austrian' theory of capital.

[27] [The term 'advancing society' is here used as synonymous with 'progressive society' for a growing economy. See also the editor's note above, p. 190n.7.—Ed.]

as much on *how* the current output of consumers' goods is produced as on *how much* is produced.

8. The Effect on the Demand for Different Kinds of Capital Goods. With the help of this schematic representation of the interrelation between the various groups of industries we are now in a position to resume the main argument and to follow somewhat further the effects of a rise in the prices of consumers' goods and of profits in the consumers' goods industries. The first effect, as we have seen, is that while the total demand for capital goods on the part of the consumers' goods industries may possibly decrease but more likely will increase, this demand will be redistributed so that a greater share of it goes to the 'later' stages II, III, IV, etc., and a smaller share to the 'earlier' stages VII, VIII, IX, etc. The immediate result would then be that the industries belonging to the stages II, III, IV, etc., would experience an increase in the demand for their products while the industries belonging to the 'earlier' stages would experience a decrease in demand. For some time this will probably lead to a further increase in employment, of incomes, and of the demand for consumers' goods; the prices of the latter will rise further and the whole process will be further stimulated.

But as this process continues those capital goods industries the demand for whose products increases will gradually get in a position similar to that of the consumers' goods industries; that is, the industries in the stages II, III, IV, etc., will successively reach full employment, the prices of their products will rise, wages will fall relatively to the immediate product of these industries, and profits will rise; and in consequence these industries, too, will change to less capitalistic methods of production and shift their demand for capital goods from the types produced by the early stages to the types produced by the later stages. The industries corresponding to the early stages will find that the demand for their products on the part of more and more of the other industries will fall off.

It is not difficult to see how, as this process continues, a division of the industries into two groups will gradually arise: as profits are raised successively in more and more industries of the first group, the position of the industries in the second group, which specialise in the production of very labour-saving or particularly durable equipment, etc., will be more and more adversely affected. And although for a time the decline of these industries may not be strong enough to cause a general decrease in the demand for labour, the point will come when such a decline will set in; because, even if aggregate demand for labour at the existing wage level (if to express it as an aggregate has any meaning under the circumstances) continues to increase, it will be an increase in the demand for kinds of labour of which no more is available, while at the same time the demand for other kinds of labour will fall and total employment will consequently decrease.

While, so long as the decrease of the 'multiplier' of the acceleration principle through the Ricardo Effect affects only the relation between the last and all the preceding stages of production, it is very unlikely that this decrease will outbalance the increase of the 'multiplicand', final demand, the former effect becomes more and more important as it cumulates its effects through successive stages. It is essentially because a large part of final demand has to be transmitted through many successive 'stages', in each of which the amount of capital wanted to produce any given output will depend on the rate of profit earned there, that the magnitude of this 'multiplier' with which demand is transmitted becomes of decisive importance. And while at first, when profits have risen only in the consumers' goods industries and the 'multiplier' continues to operate with unabated intensity in the earlier stages, the total demand for capital goods will be little affected, yet gradually, as in more and more of the links of the long chain of stages through which demand must pass the ratio of transmission to earlier stages is reduced, the quantitative effects of the reduction in this ratio or multiplier must become greater and greater.[28]

[28] Perhaps this point might usefully be illustrated by a simple diagram [see fig. 8.2 on following page—Ed.] similar to those which I have used in this connection on earlier occasions [e.g., in *Prices and Production*, lecture 2—Ed.]. If in the rectangular triangle *ABC* the base *AB* measures current output (or sale) of consumers' goods (as a time rate at a moment), *CA* the maximum investment period of any of the factors used in the production of this output, the various shorter vertical distances between the line *CB* and the base *AB* the corresponding investment periods for the factors used in the further course of the process of production, the area of the triangle will (if for the purpose we disregard interest or profits) represent the magnitude of the stock of capital used in the production of the output. On the assumption that these various investment periods are spread evenly over the total length of the process (represented in the diagram by *CB* being a straight line), the proportion between the stock of capital and the output of any given period (say the output produced during an interval of the length AA^1, represented by the rectangle AA^1B^1B) will be uniquely determined by the length of the maximum investment period *CA*. This proportion is the same thing as the "multiplier" of the acceleration principle.

Assume now that final demand increases from *AB* to *AD*. If the 'multiplier' remains constant and the additional output is produced with the same amount of capital per unit of output, additional capital goods of an amount corresponding to the area of *BDC* will have to be produced, where the proportion of this quantity to the additional output produced during the unit period AA^1 will, of course, be the same as that between *ABD* [this should read, correctly, "*ABC*"—Ed.] and AA^1B^1B. If, however, as a consequence of a rise in profits the 'multiplier' is reduced, the increased final demand will give rise to a demand for capital goods which can be represented by some new triangle of smaller height, such as *ADE*. It is evident that if as a consequence of a rise in profits the maximum investment period is sufficiently reduced, the total new demand for capital goods represented by the area of *ADE* may be smaller than the original demand for capital shown by *ABC* (which was associated with a smaller final demand). But whether this is or is not the case is not so important as the fact that the demand for resources which are specific to

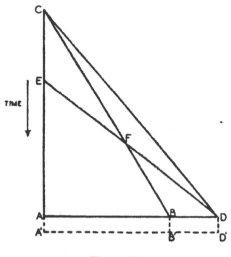

Figure 8.2

If the rate of interest had been allowed to rise with the rate of profit in the prosperous industries, the other industries would have been forced to curtail the scale of production to a level at which their profits correspond to the higher rate of interest. This would have brought the process of expansion to an end before the rate of profit in the prosperous industries would have risen too far, and the necessity of a later violent curtailment of production in the early stages would have been avoided. But if, as we assume here, the rate of interest is kept at its initial level and incomes and the demand for consumers' goods continue therefore to grow for some time after profits have begun to rise, the forces making for a rise of profits in one group of industries and for a fall in the demand for the products of another group of industries will become stronger and stronger. The only thing which can bring this process to an

the early stages (here those situated between *C* and *E*) will cease and unemployment will ensue here, while the increased demand in the later stages must exhaust itself in a rise in money wages in these stages without creating additional employment.

(Since the diagram shows only 'complete' structures in which there is no net investment and therefore total incomes equal to the receipts from the sale of consumers' goods, it does not show why in consequence of the cessation of investment in the early stages total money incomes should fall. But if it is remembered that so long as there is net investment total incomes will be larger than the receipts from the sale of consumers' goods, it will be clear why a reduction of employment in the investment goods industries will lead to a fall in total money incomes.)

The diagram can also be used to illustrate the case where the 'multiplier' is reduced in the later stages only but continues to operate with its original intensity in the earlier stages. Such a situation could be schematically represented if in the place of the straight lines *DE* or *DC* we use a broken line such as *DFC*.

end will be a fall in employment in the second group of industries, preventing a further rise or causing an actual decline of incomes. And if labour is not mobile between the two groups of industries a sort of equilibrium might ultimately be reached with a high rate of profit in the first group and no profits (or profits below the rate of interest) in the second group.

In fact, however, long before this position will be reached, in which there would be only on the one side a group of industries where the rate of profits had risen and on the other a group where yields had fallen, and when there will still be a large intermediate group where neither will have taken place, another adverse effect on profits in the investment goods industries will make itself felt, namely, a rise in costs.

9. *The Role of Raw Material Prices.* Up to this point nothing has yet been said on the complicated problem of the rise in costs and particularly of the rise in the prices of raw material on the profitability of the capital goods industries. The undoubted fact here is that during the upswing of the cycle raw material prices rise more than the prices of consumers' goods. If this must be regarded as an adverse influence on investment it leads to the apparent paradox that a rise in the 'real' value of raw materials (i.e., their value in terms of consumers' goods) has exactly the opposite effect on investment to that of a rise in real wages. The solution of this paradox lies in the fact that while labour, so far as provision for an expansion of output is concerned, is to a large extent a possible substitute for machinery, raw materials are required in practically fixed amounts per unit of output of any particular commodity. While, therefore, a rise in the price of either machinery or labour may increase the demand for the other of these two factors (and a fall in the price of one will decrease the demand for the other), a rise in the price of raw materials will not only decrease the demand for both labour and machinery, but will also discriminate against the latter because it will at the same time raise the cost of machinery. This means that as the demand for machinery falls in terms of consumers' goods and the prices of consumers' goods fall in terms of raw materials, the producers of machinery (even where the demand for their products has not yet been reduced by a fall in real wages) will be caught between falling prices of their products and rising costs,[29] and will have to curtail production. And this applies not only to raw materials proper. The same will be true of the hundred and one small cost items consisting of the prices of goods, some of them manufactured, such as fuels and lubricants, packing material and stationery, etc. The prices of these commodities which, unlike most labour, are not specific to a particular use but can be shifted between industries and stages

---

[29] [Note that consistently "falling prices" as well as "rising costs" are to be measured in terms of consumers' goods.—Ed.]

will for this reason often move differently from, and perhaps even in a direction contrary to, the prices of many of the products made from them.[30] It is these kinds of commodities, including the raw materials, which are capable of being turned rapidly and therefore at a fairly high rate of profits into consumers' goods, and the consumers' goods themselves, which are the 'circulating capital' which is getting scarce and therefore rises in price.[31]

10. The Decline of Investment. We have now concluded the demonstration of our first thesis, namely that an increase in the demand for consumers' goods may lead to a decrease in the demand for capital goods. It will be remembered that our argument referred throughout to a fairly advanced stage of the boom; and it is, of course, not argued that any rise in the rate of profit will decrease investment, but merely that, once the rate of profit rises in a sufficient number of industries beyond the rate to which the capitalistic structure of industry is adapted (or in the expectation of which much of the new investment has been started) it will have that effect. All that we were concerned to show is that once a certain point is passed, although the decline of investment may be postponed for a long time by keeping the rate of interest low, it is bound to come, and that the further the point is put off, the greater will be the rise in the rate of profit and consequently also the ultimate decline of investment. The rate of profit will in this case rise more and more, the tendency to increase output quickly will become stronger and stronger, and the range of capital goods that it will no longer be profitable to produce will become larger and larger. The 'critical point' where the process enters into the unstable phase has not yet been exactly defined; that will be one of the main tasks of the second part of this essay. But it must be clear already that this 'critical point' does not depend on 'full employment' in general being reached, but on the capacity to increase the output of consumers' goods as fast as demand increases.

Our main conclusion reached so far is perhaps that the turn of affairs will be brought about in the end by a 'scarcity of capital' independently of whether the money rate of interest rises or not. Up to this point the rate of interest has only been mentioned in passing. But while consideration of its

[30] The same may be true of certain kinds of wages in so far as some types of labour are mobile between industries and the rise of money wages in the consumers' goods industries raises wages of some labour also used in the capital goods industries. The case of mobility of labour is here, however, deliberately disregarded. The parallelism between the case of raw materials and some kinds of labour together with a certain confusion between the movement of real wages and the movement of money wages, has, however, to some extent misled me in the discussion of these problems in *Prices and Production*.

[31] It should perhaps be added here that owing to the great fluctuations in raw material prices the Ricardo Effect is likely to be particularly important through its effect on the demand for capital goods on the part of the raw material industries.

real significance will be deferred to the last sections of this essay, certain conclusions concerning the effects of its failure to rise with the rate of profit may conveniently be made explicit at this stage.

If the rate of interest were allowed to rise as profits rise (i.e., if the supply of credit were not elastic), the industries that could not earn profits at this higher rate would have to curtail or stop production, and incomes and the demand for consumers' goods and profits in the consumers' goods industries would cease to rise. In this way the investment for comparatively long periods, for the 'sustenance' of which the current supply of consumers' goods is insufficient, would be cut out. If, however, as we have assumed, the rate of interest is kept at the initial low figure (or if it constantly lags behind the movement of the rate of profits) and investments whose yield is not negatively affected continue in spite of the rise in final demand, the rise of profits in the late stages of production and the rise of costs will both come into play and will produce the result which the rate of interest has failed to bring about. The rise of the rate of profit on short as compared with that on long investments will induce entrepreneurs to divert whatever funds they have to invest towards less capitalistic machinery, etc.; and whatever part of the required reduction in total investment is not brought about by this diversion of investment demand towards less capitalistic type of machinery will in the end be brought about by a rise in the cost of production[32] of investment goods in the early stages.

Keeping the rate of interest low in spite of a rising demand for consumers' goods cannot prevent the rate of profit from rising; for just as long as the low rate of interest remains effective it will continue, by stimulating investment, further to increase incomes and the demand for consumers' goods; and so long as investment continues to increase, the discrepancy between prices and costs of consumers' goods must become progressively larger till the rise in the rate of profit becomes strong enough to make the tendency to change to less durable and expensive types of machinery dominant over the tendency to provide capacity for a larger output. Or, in other words, in the end the 'acceleration principle of derived demand' becomes inverted into a 'deceleration principle'—and the classical maxims that a scarcity of capital means a scarcity of consumers' goods, and that demand for commodities (= consumers' goods) is not demand for labour assert their fundamental truth.[33]

[32] Including probably a rise of money wages in these stages, which is, however, here excluded by our assumptions.

[33] [The 'classical maxims' to which Hayek alludes have been expressed, e.g., by John Stuart Mill, as the first fundamental proposition respecting capital, "that industry is limited by capital" (*Principles of Political Economy*, ed. William James Ashley (London: Longmans, Green, 1909; reprinted, New York: Kelley, 1976), book 1, chapter 5, paragraph 1, p. 63; cf. *Principles of Political Economy, Part 1*, ed. John M. Robson, vol. 2 (1965) of the *Collected Works of John Stuart Mill* (Toronto: University of Toronto Press; London: Routledge and Kegan Paul; reprinted, Indianapolis:

Some remarks should perhaps be added here on another subject which like the rate of interest will be considered more systematically later: the assumptions which are implied in our analysis with regard to the rate of saving or the 'propensity to consume'.[34] Prices of consumers' goods will rise and extra profits will be made on their production so long as a larger part of current money incomes than the replacement cost of current output of consumers' goods is spent on this output. This means that so long as an increase in the demand for consumers' goods proceeds from *net* investment,[35] or, in other words, so long as entrepreneurs invest more than *will* be saved out of the incomes thus increased, prices of consumers' goods must rise relatively to costs. We shall see later to what extent a low propensity to consume (or a great willingness to save out of given incomes) may extend the limits within which such an expansion can proceed without an ultimate breakdown. But even at this stage it must be clear that in order to prevent a rise in profits on consumers' goods nearly the whole additional income created by new net investment would have to be saved. And if in the later stages of the boom further increases in net investment lead first to an increase in the rate of profits and through it ultimately to a curtailment of investment activity, this will clearly be because the marginal propensity to consume is too high and not because it is too low. The apparent exhaustion of investment opportunities[36] at the end of the boom will then be due not to the fact that the investment opportunities which have existed before have all been taken up, but to the fact that because of the rise in the rate of profits in certain stages (that is the *increase* in demand) many kinds of investment which were profitable before have ceased to be so.

11. Depression and Revival. If in the short run labour is, as we have assumed, highly specific to its particular employment, the unemployment caused by the decline in investment activity will disappear only when investment of the kind in question becomes once again profitable—or in the long run when labour

Liberty Fund, 2006), p. 63), and that "demand for commodities is not demand for labour" (ibid., book 1, chapter 5, paragraph 9, ed. Ashley, p. 79; reprinted, ed. Robson, *Part 1*, p. 78).—Ed.]

[34] [This is another reference to Keynes's *General Theory*; cf., e.g., p. 90, which defines the 'propensity to consume' as the relationship between income and expenditure on consumption out of that income.—Ed.]

[35] On the somewhat complicated way in which net income and net investment must be defined in this context see my article on "The Maintenance of Capital", *Economica*, n.s., vol. 2, August 1935, now reprinted in *Profits, Interest and Investment*, pp. 83 et seq. [pp. 83–134].

[36] [This phrase refers to the then fashionable 'stagnation thesis'. For example, Nicholas Kaldor used it in his review (*Economic Journal*, vol. 49, March 1939, p. 91) of Alvin H. Hansen's *Full Recovery or Stagnation?* (New York: Norton, 1938). Joseph A. Schumpeter sketched the "theory of vanishing investment opportunity" in his *Business Cycles: A Theoretical, Historical, and Statistical Analysis of the Capitalist Process* (New York and London: McGraw Hill, 1939), pp. 1032–36, and referred to Hansen as "an admirable exposition of that theory" (p. 1032n.1).—Ed.]

has been gradually transferred to other industries. In order that investment of the former kind should be resumed it is necessary that profits in the late stages of production fall to the former level, or in other words, that the difference between real wages and the marginal product of labour in the late stages should be reduced. But it will inevitably take some time for the decrease in incomes earned in the investment goods industries to lead, *via* a fall of prices of consumers' goods, to a rise in real wages, a reduction of profits in the consumers' goods industries, and ultimately to a renewed stimulus to investment.

Prices of consumers' goods are notoriously sticky. At first, when the demand for such goods ceases to increase or even begins to fall, this will check the tendency to increase capacity and thus (by decreasing the 'multiplicand' of the acceleration effect without as yet changing the 'multiplier') will decrease employment also in those capital goods industries which till the end shared the prosperity of the consumers' goods industries. This will further intensify the decrease of incomes and of consumers' demand. When the prices of consumers' goods begin at last to fall, this will affect producers of consumers' goods the more the further they have gone in changing to methods with a high proportion of labour costs of production. But gradually, as employment falls in these industries, too, and as the producers with the highest proportion of labour costs are being eliminated, further falls in demand will lead to comparatively smaller reductions of production and employment. It is clear that this process will take longer according as the preceding boom has lasted longer and the tendency towards the adoption of more costly (less capitalistic) methods of currently producing consumers' goods has been carried further. Even if we disregard here completely any monetary complications which may be caused by the shock to confidence, this process of contraction may well last long enough for the volume of employment and of incomes to be considerably reduced. In the end, however, a new position of temporary quasi-equilibrium[37] would be reached in which, with a very low general level of employment, the demand for consumers' goods will once again have become equal to current output, and output and production will cease to shrink further.

At some stage of this process, however—either before this point is reached or soon afterwards—a contrary tendency brought about by the rise in real wages will make itself felt. We find now the obverse of what we have seen to happen during the later stages of the boom. While for a considerable time the factor dominating the demand for investment goods will be the decrease in the capacity needed in the consumers' goods industries (the 'multiplicand'

---

[37] [The term 'quasi-equilibrium' had already been used in this meaning by Dennis H. Robertson, "Industrial Fluctuation and the Natural Rate of Interest", *Economic Journal*, vol. 44, December 1934, pp. 652–53, reprinted in *Essays in Monetary Theory* (London: King, 1940), p. 86, and in *Essays in Money and Interest*, ed. John Hicks (London: Collins, 1966), p. 67.—Ed.]

of the acceleration effect), a point will come when this tendency will be overcome by the increase of the amount of investment that will be wanted for any given amount of output (i.e., of the 'multiplier'). The fall in the rate of profit and the rise in real wages will make a "substitution of machinery for labour"[38] profitable, and although at first the effect of this may be small, a point will be reached when the maintenance even of a small capacity of producing final output, corresponding to the reduced current demand for consumers' goods, by the more efficient, more capitalistic methods corresponding to the higher level of real wages, will lead to an increase of investment. Although with the given demand it will not be profitable to produce more consumers' goods (i.e., to produce a final output of greater total costs), it may well be profitable to increase investment beyond current amortisation in order to reduce costs of production. But this in turn will increase incomes and demand and the upward movement will start again.

It is not intended to give here a complete account of all the phases of the cycle and this rapid sketch of the forces operating during the downward swing of business activity must suffice to show that even during this phase it may be not so much the money rate of interest as the rate of profits and real wages which govern the decline and eventual revival of investment. We must, however, give more attention to the early stages of the process of revival. It is here that we shall have to face the crucial question which we have not yet answered, namely why it is that in the course of the recovery the supply of consumers' goods will become insufficient, or where the 'critical point' lies beyond which the expansion of investment will create an inherently unstable position. The second part of this essay will be devoted mainly to this problem.

Part II

12. Factors Governing the Revival of Investment. We shall assume that general activity has fallen to a very low level before investment and incomes begin to rise again. This means that unemployment will be very high, prices of consumers' goods and profits exceptionally low, and real wages comparatively high. The low rate of profits means here a low rate on working costs,[39] because if all costs were taken into account it may well be that in many cases prices do not even cover replacement costs and that there will be a general under-maintenance of capital.[40] In a sense the low rate of profit and the high

---

[38] [Cf. Ricardo, *Principles of Political Economy*, ed. McCulloch, p. 236; *Works and Correspondence*, ed. Sraffa, vol. 1, p. 388, for "the substitution of machinery for human labour".—Ed.]

[39] [Presumably, here working costs are to be interpreted as short-run variable costs.—Ed.]

[40] For some curious reason there appears to be less objection to the term under-maintenance of capital than to the term consumption of capital, although the two terms clearly mean the

real wages may even be regarded as a result of under-maintenance of capital, since the income generated by merely using (but not replacing) existing equipment will be lower than total replacement cost of current output, and the labour employed in producing current output will have to share this output with fewer people engaged in replacing equipment.

With high real wages and a low rate of profit[41] investment will take highly capitalistic forms: entrepreneurs will try to meet the high costs of labour by introducing very labour-saving machinery—the kind of machinery which it will be profitable to use only at a very low rate of profit and interest. The first increase of investment, induced by the high real wages, would not aim at producing a larger final output. It would entirely take the form of what Wicksell called a growth of capital in height and what Dr. Hawtrey has recently called a 'deepening' of capital.[42] Or, we might say, it is entirely due to an increase of

---

same thing. It is now probably generally admitted that some consumption of capital is a characteristic feature of every major depression (on this see now Solomon Fabricant, *Capital Consumption and Adjustment*, New York: National Bureau of Economic Research, 1938). But who has ever suggested, as is alleged by Mr. Keynes (*General Theory*, p. 329), that the boom is characterised by capital consumption? All that could be reasonably said is that towards the end of a boom an increasing tendency towards capital consumption develops which ultimately brings investment to a standstill. But long before there can be any question of net capital consumption the system will have gone far into depression. The opposite type of misunderstanding occurs in a recent article by Mr. N. Kaldor which in certain other respects resembles my present (and earlier) argument. (Cf. "Capital Intensity and the Trade Cycle".) In order to prove that the results of his analysis on the central point are different from those of the 'Austrian' theory (which in other respects they certainly are!) he asserts that "the proposition underlying the Austrian theory of the trade cycle—that the boom is characterised by the adoption of more capitalistic methods of production, and the depression by a return to less capitalistic methods—ought . . . to be reversed" [ibid., p. 56; reprinted, p. 137—Ed.]. I do not know whether any member of the 'Austrian School' has ever used this loose language, but it will be evident from the text that the terms boom and depression are far too vague to describe the real situation. (Is 'boom' equivalent to the whole upswing of the cycle and 'depression' to the downswing, or the former to the whole upper half and the latter to the whole lower half?) What I have argued before and is equally implied in all other versions of the Austrian theory of the trade cycle is that the transition to more capitalistic methods of production takes place during periods of low interest rates and *brings about* the boom, and that the transition to less capitalistic methods of production is caused by the high rates of interest and brings about the depression. This is of course very different from what Mr. Kaldor alleges to be the Austrian position and is practically identical with his own 'new' theory on this point. The only point on which I now want to modify this earlier statement is the substitution of high and low rates of profit for high and low rates of interest. [For another example of Hayek's willingness in 1939 to substitute 'profits' for 'interest' (as used in his pre-1939 writings) cf. his "The Present State and Immediate Prospects of the Study of Industrial Fluctuations", chapter 6 of *Profits, Interest and Investment*, reprinted in this volume, p. 177n.16.—Ed.]

[41] Wages, in terms of the immediate products of the industries concerned, will be even higher and the rate of profit even lower in the early stages than in the consumers' goods industries.

[42] Cf. Knut Wicksell, *Lectures on Political Economy*, vol. 1: *General Theory*, trans. Ernest Classen (London: Routledge, 1934 [reprinted, New York: Kelley, 1967, and Auburn, AL: Ludwig von

the 'multiplier' of the acceleration principle while the 'multiplicand' remains unchanged. The increase of investment outlay beyond current receipts from the sale of final output would therefore also be merely temporary, since once the equipment had been increased to the desired magnitude, replacement demand would again be no larger than receipts from the sale of final products. This at least would be so if the increase of investment did not in turn lead to an increase of incomes and thus to an increase in consumers' demand. But as consumers' demand will increase in consequence of the additional income generated by the new investment, the increase in investment will not only be maintained but will even be stimulated further.

This further increase of investment will mean that capital will now grow in 'height' and 'width' at the same time, that a process of deepening and a process of widening will proceed simultaneously. Or at any rate, so long as real wages and profits remain at the initial level, the tendency to produce any additional output with the use of a high proportion of capital will persist. And as in consequence of this investment final demand increases further, provision has to be made to produce a larger and larger output with these highly capitalistic methods. It is in this phase of the revival, before prices and profits begin to rise, that the acceleration principle operates with a constant (and very high) multiplier, that every (actual or expected) increase in the demand for consumers' goods will lead to a demand for a very great quantity of capital goods and that employment will grow rapidly in the investment goods industries.[43]

There can be little doubt that with much unused equipment in the consumers' goods industries and large surplus stocks in all the late stages of production it will be possible for recovery to proceed a long way before the prices of consumers' goods and profits will rise and real wages fall. And till the (present or expected) rate of profits begins to rise, investment will continue to take the highly capitalistic forms. But as every increase of net investment means that

---

Mises Institute, 2007]), pp. 163 and 266, and Ralph George Hawtrey, *Capital and Employment* (London: Longmans, 1937), p. 36. There is a slight difference in the distinctions drawn by the two authors, as Dr. Hawtrey applies his distinction to individual industries while Wicksell applied it to the economic system as a whole. The consequence is that an expansion of the very capitalistic industries at the expense of the less highly capitalistic ones would be treated as a case of mere widening by Dr. Hawtrey while Wicksell would have regarded it as a growth in height of the capital structure of the whole system. Much of what follows is implicit in the point made by Dr. Hawtrey that changes in the rate of interest are associated only with the deepening but not with the widening process—although we should have to substitute rate of profit for rate of interest.

[43] It should be remembered, however, that the acceleration principle will not begin to operate so long as there are unused resources of *all* kinds available. The relationship between the degree of employment and the operation of the acceleration principle is, however, exceedingly complex and cannot be discussed here. Detailed analysis would show that it can neither operate when there are unused resources of all kinds, nor when there are no unused resources, but only in the intermediate positions which will, of course, be the rule.

incomes grow more than the output of consumers' goods, it is clear that this process cannot go on indefinitely without causing a rise in prices and profits and thereby adversely affecting the profitability of the more capitalistic investment undertaken. What are the limits within which this process of expansion can proceed without causing a rise in prices and profits and thereby making the more capitalistic types of investment less profitable?

13. Inflationary and Non-Inflationary Increases of Money Incomes. In general terms the answer to our last question is obvious: the demand for consumers' goods arising out of the increased incomes must not increase faster than the supply of consumers' goods will be increased. And for a considerable time after the beginning of the recovery there will be no difficulty about increasing the output of consumers' goods rapidly. As has been mentioned already, the first impact of the increased demand will be met from the stocks accumulated during the depression—the only form in which some of the savings of the past could be stored up. In addition it will be possible, by taking idle equipment into use, to increase the current output of consumers' goods[44] not only quickly but also with an additional disbursement of working costs which will be considerably smaller than the value of the additional output (at current prices);[45] in consequence, even if all the new income created in the consumers' goods industries is immediately spent on consumers' goods, there will still be a surplus of output left to meet some part of the demand of those newly employed in the investment goods industries. Whatever is being saved by those engaged in currently turning out consumers' goods provides a further source from which the

---

[44] As it is sometimes alleged that the 'Austrians' were unaware of the fact that the effect of an expansion of credit will be different according as there are unemployed resources available or not, the following passage from Professor Mises' *Geldwertstabilisierung und Konjunkturpolitik* (Jena: Fischer, 1928), p. 49, perhaps deserves to be quoted: "Even on an unimpeded market there will be at times certain quantities of unsold commodities which exceed the stocks that would be held under static conditions, of unused productive plant, and of unused workmen. The increased activity will at first bring about a mobilisation of these reserves. Once they have been absorbed the increase of the means of circulation must, however, cause disturbances of a peculiar kind." [Cf. also the translation "Monetary Stabilization and Cyclical Policy", trans. Bettina Bien Greaves, in Ludwig von Mises, *On the Manipulation of Money and Credit*, ed. Percy L. Greaves (New York: Free Market Books, 1978), p. 125.—Ed.] In *Prices and Production*, where I started explicitly from an assumed equilibrium position, I had, of course, no occasion to deal with these problems.

[45] The reason why this unused equipment was not used although prices would have covered current outlay connected with it (factor cost) is, of course, that before the increase in demand prices obtainable for additional output would not have covered 'user cost' in addition to 'factor cost'. [Factor cost is the remuneration of the services of the factors of production; user cost is the loss in the value of capital equipment due to its being used for production compared with the alternative of its being not used but optimally maintained. For definitions of these terms along these lines cf. Keynes, *General Theory*, pp. 52–53; there the sum of factor and user cost is denoted as prime cost.—Ed.]

demand for consumers' goods on the part of those who produce investment goods can be supplied. And after a while the activities of the latter will begin to make a contribution to the current flow of investment goods.

But does not the mere fact that money incomes increase throughout this process prove that more is being invested than is being saved (i.e., that money that has not been earned in production becomes available for expenditure on products)? And does this not mean that the demand for consumers' goods must rise faster than supply? In the conditions which we are considering here the position is not as simple as this. If we started from a position of full employment the answer to those questions would indeed be 'yes'. New investment then would mean that resources are diverted from producing consumers' goods to producing capital goods; the larger money incomes would meet a decreasing output of consumers' goods; and the saving that is required to finance the new investment would in this case have to mean an actual decrease of consumption.

The situation is, however, different when the savings of one group of people are used to maintain formerly unemployed people while they are employed producing investment goods. In this case saving and investment on the part of the first group of people will not lead to a reduction of total consumption but only to a transfer of consuming power to a second group of people.[46] And

[46] It is in this case, and in this case only, that Adam Smith's famous dictum applies that "what is annually saved is as regularly consumed as what is annually spent, and nearly at [in] the same time too; but it is consumed by a different group [set] of people". (*An Inquiry into the Nature and Causes of the Wealth of Nations* [1776]), book 2, chapter 3, paragraph 18, 5th ed., ed. Edwin Cannan (London: Methuen, 1930), vol. 1, p. 320 [cf. *The Glasgow Edition of the Works and Correspondence of Adam Smith*, vol. 1, ed. R. H. Campbell and A. S. Skinner (Oxford: Oxford University Press, 1976; reprinted, Indianapolis: Liberty Press, 1981), pp. 337–38.—Ed.]). The main idea of this argument has been given wider currency through John Stuart Mill's "third fundamental theorem respecting capital", namely that "although saved, and the result of saving, it is nevertheless consumed"; or, as Mill puts it in another place, when income is saved, the savers "do not thereby annihilate their power of consumption; they do but transfer it from themselves to the labourers to whom they give employment" (*Principles of Political Economy*, chapter 1 [that is, correctly, book 1, chapter 5—Ed.], paragraphs 5 and 3, ed. Ashley, pp. 70 and 68 [cf. reprinted, ed. Robson, *Part 1*, pp. 70 and 67–68—Ed.]) In an economy with unemployed resources a fuller analysis would have to distinguish between three successive stages in the process of saving and investment: in the first stage it will be possible to invest more and at the same time to increase the output of consumers' goods so as to leave real wages of the increased number employed unchanged; in the second stage while it will still be possible to invest more without decreasing the output of consumers' goods, but the given (or only slightly enlarged) output of consumers' goods will have to be shared among the larger number of workmen now employed and real wages will fall; in the third stage a further increase of investment will be possible only at the price of an actual decrease in the output of consumers' goods, because it will involve a diversion of resources from the production of consumers' goods to the production of capital goods. While if we started from a position of equilibrium (as I did in *Prices and Production*), only the third case would be relevant, it is disregarded here because we assume that labour is completely immobile in the short run. It is, however, probably not without importance in some major booms.

since there is no reason why total consumption should be decreased in this case, there is also no reason why the part of the total money incomes which is available for expenditure on consumers' goods should fall. But this means that total money incomes must increase by exactly the amount by which saving and investment lead to the employment of formerly unemployed resources.

It can be easily shown that unless in this case money incomes were increased to the required extent, saving would have a definitely deflationary effect and, therefore, that an increase of money incomes within these limits would not be inflationary.[47] In the first instance it should be clear that when savings are used to redistribute consuming power so as to give people formerly unemployed a share in the current output of consumers' goods as remuneration for their producing investment goods, this means that the same income, or the titles to the same shares of the current output of consumers' goods, have to be paid out twice over: first to the people who save and invest that income, and then to the people who receive it for making capital goods and who spend it on consumers' goods. If the latter are, however, to step effectively into the gap in the flow of consumers' demand caused by the saving, they will have to be given, in addition to the money saved and invested by the others, and actually before that money reaches them, an amount of money sufficient to build up whatever cash balances they intend to hold when their income will be increased. Only if this is the case will they be able to start buying consumers' goods as soon as the others cease to do so: and only in this case will the money stream continue to reach the consumers' goods market at a constant rate.[48]

---

[47] The criterion for 'inflationary' or 'deflationary' seems to me to be as follows. There is neither inflation nor deflation if (1) there occurs no change in prices unless it is necessary for the restoration of equilibrium either that the production of the commodities affected should be increased or reduced, or that the recipient of the income affected should permanently (i.e., till the next real change) get a larger or smaller real income; and (2) if no price change necessary for this purpose is prevented. All monetary changes which do not fall in this category have the characteristic attribute that their effects are self-reversing, that is that they will cause further price changes which in the end will reverse the real change caused by the impact effect of the monetary change. (On the significance of these 'self-reversing changes' see my *Monetary Nationalism and International Stability*, Publications of the Graduate Institute of International Studies, no. 18 (London and New York: Longmans, Green and Co., 1937), passim [reprinted as chapter 1 of *Good Money, Part II: The Standard*, ed. Stephen Kresge, vol. 6 (1999) of *The Collected Works of F. A. Hayek*—Ed.].) Applied to the present case this means mainly that unless it is necessary that the output of consumers' goods should be reduced the prices of consumers' goods should not fall relatively to costs.

[48] Some considerations of this sort were evidently at the basis of the discussion of the 'circuit flow of money' in the various works of Messrs. Foster and Catchings. But they neither made it clear that the argument applied only in so far and to the extent that savings were used to employ formerly unemployed factors, nor do they appear to have been aware in what way this innocuous increase in money incomes was limited by the future rate of savings. My criticism of their views expressed in the article on "The 'Paradox' of Saving" ought, however, to be supplemented by the considerations developed here.

So long as the increase of money incomes does not increase the demand for consumers' goods by more than the amount by which, at the time this new demand reaches the market, other people will be willing to increase their saving, total demand for consumers' goods will not increase. The increase of money incomes in this case really means that future savings are anticipated (in the literal sense of the word, i.e., they are not merely foreseen, but the possibilities of increasing investment which are created by the future saving are made use of before these savings are actually made).

But, as we have already seen, it is not merely the increase in net savings following the increase in incomes which in the course of the revival will allow an increase of employment in the investment goods industries without this leading to a rise in the prices of consumers' goods and in profits. There is also the increase in the output of consumers' goods in excess of the cost of working existing equipment which can be used to sustain additional people producing capital goods. And as the revival proceeds some of the new investment made in the course of it will begin to contribute to the current flow of consumers' goods. All these sources contribute to the fund out of which the new demand for consumers' goods from those producing investment goods can be satisfied.

We can now make somewhat more precise our former statement about the limits within which the expansion of investment must keep if the rate of profit is not to rise: the increase of money incomes resulting from an increase of investment will not bring about a rise in prices and profits in the consumers' goods industries if by the time part or all of this new income is spent on consumers' goods, either savings, or the value of the output of consumers' goods (in terms of replacement costs), or the sum of these two magnitudes, increase by a total amount equal to that new demand. Is the rate of expansion, once the revival has set in, likely to keep within these limits if the supply of credit is highly elastic and the rate of interest kept at the initial figure?[49]

14. Different Forms of Investment Distinguished According to the Rate at Which They Will Contribute to the Flow of Consumers' Goods. The answer to the last question depends largely on the form the new investment will take. We have seen before that total investment will be determined as the product of two factors: the volume of investment per unit of expected demand (the 'multiplier')—

---

[49] These considerations also appear to provide the answer to a difficulty which has much puzzled me on earlier occasion, namely, the question of what constitutes 'neutral money' in a progressive society where the quantity of 'original' factors and particularly population increases. The conclusion which then seemed to me to be inescapable and which I drew reluctantly, that even in this case aggregate money incomes ought to be kept constant (*Prices and Production*, 1st ed., p. 90, 2nd ed., p. 107 [reprinted, pp. 267–68—Ed.]), was therefore erroneous. The cases of an increase of productivity of a given supply of factors and of an increase in the supply of these factors are not, as I then thought, similar but fundamentally different.

which varies inversely with the rate of profit—*times* the number of such units which demand is expected to reach (the 'multiplicand'). Various combinations of rates of profit and expected volumes of demand may therefore lead to the same amount of investment; but equal amounts of investment which will generate the same additional money income will therefore differ in one very important respect according as they are the result of a high expected demand *plus* a high rate of profit or the result of a low expected demand *plus* a low rate of profits. If a given amount of investment has been guided by a comparatively low rate of profit, the rate at which this investment will contribute to the output of consumers' goods will be slow; after investing in that form at a given rate for a period of, say, one year, the rate at which at the end of that year we shall have contributed to the current output of consumers' goods may be only a small fraction of the rate at which we have been investing during the year; £5,000 invested in the course of a year in a very durable building may yield only services of a value of £300 p.a. If the investment had been guided by a higher rate of profit this rate at which a given amount of investment will contribute to the stream of consumers' goods would be higher.

Without entering here deeper than is necessary into the intricacies of the theory of capital it will be useful somewhat further to elaborate this proposition that the lower the rate of profit and the more 'capitalistic' therefore the type of investment undertaken, the slower will be the rate at which after any given interval a given expenditure of investment will contribute to the output of consumers' goods. If a building is made more durable, the rate of flow of services from it will, during any given period, bear a smaller proportion to the cost of constructing it than would be the case if it were less durable. If more expensive and more labour-saving machines are introduced in the manufacture of any commodity, the value of the output during any given period will also bear a smaller proportion to the initial expenditure on starting the new process. The same will be true if industries requiring comparatively more capital expand more than others, or if in any other sense more roundabout methods are introduced. It will be convenient to call for our present purpose this proportion of the current contribution to the flow of consumers' goods after, say, one year, to the amount of investment during that year to which it is due, the Quotient or simply Q—although this simple concept would hardly be adequate for any more systematic treatment of the theory of capital.[50] It will at once be obvious that Q is simply the inverse of the 'multiplier' of the accel-

[50] The defects of this concept are essentially the same as those of the concept of the 'average period of production' to which it is indeed related in a very simple manner; like the latter it can be used in most connections only if we assume that the results of the investments made at any moment are spread evenly over a definite period of time; and it disregards various complications introduced by the rate of interest. But it has probably the advantage over the latter concept of referring to more concrete facts.

eration principle, so that, if Q is $1/10$, a given increase in final demand will tend to increase investment by ten times this amount and so on.

Less obvious but equally important is the fact that Q also tells us how long any new investment at a given rate will have to continue before the resulting addition to the capitalistic structure of production will be 'complete' and self-maintaining, i.e., till the mere maintenance of the existing structure without any further net investment will require continued production of capital goods at a constant rate.[51] If, e.g., Q is $1/10$ and investment of this kind at a constant rate continues for ten years the contributions to current output of consumers' goods due to this investment will grow year by year from $1/10$ to $2/10$, $3/10$, and so forth, of the amount of annual (gross) investment, and the part of the investment that is net will correspondingly decrease, till in the tenth year the output of consumers' goods will have become equal to current gross investment; and this latter will have ceased to be net investment in any part, as it will have to continue at a constant rate merely to maintain current final output.[52]

The last point is of special interest to us as it is *net* investment, and net investment only, that creates incomes in excess of the value of the current final output, and in connection with which a problem of the relation between it and (net) saving arises.[53] An increase merely of gross investment without a si-

---

[51] See on this point the well-known discussion between Professor R. Frisch and Professor J. M. Clark on "Capital Production and Consumers' Taking" in the *Journal of Political Economy* for 1931 and 1932. [Cf. Ragnar Frisch, "The Interrelation between Capital Production and Consumer-Taking", vol. 39, October 1931, pp. 646–54, and John Maurice Clark, "Capital Production and Consumer-Taking", vol. 39, December 1931, pp. 814–16, followed by Frisch, "A Rejoinder", vol. 40, April 1932, pp. 253–55, Clark's "A Further Word" and Frisch's "A Final Word", vol. 40, October 1932, pp. 691–93 and p. 694, respectively.—Ed.]

[52] [Hayek's argument in this paragraph appears somewhat confused. Obviously, "investment . . . at a constant rate" cannot refer to a rate of *net* investment, because net investment cannot be positive in (stationary) equilibrium. Yet if it is the rate of *gross* investment that is constant, then—as Hayek points out—"the part of the investment that is net will correspondingly decrease" from year to year, and after ten years the net addition to the capital stock must be less than ten times the constant yearly rate of (gross) investment. Consequently, after ten years the increase in output will be less than the constant rate of gross investment, too, and thus the restructuring of production will not have been completed. In fact, under these assumptions the new structure of production will be completed only asymptotically. However, Hayek is right in emphasising that after an increase in the constant rate of gross investment (e.g., brought about by an increase in the constant rate of gross saving) during the transition to the new structure of production, as the capital stock grows, net investment will decrease just to the extent required for the increase in reinvestment until, in the end, gross investment "will have to continue at a constant rate merely to maintain current final output".—Ed.]

[53] The definition of net saving and net investment is undeniably difficult, and still more so is the measurement of their magnitude since the distinction must inevitably be based on subjective criteria; but I cannot see that this is an argument for substituting for these 'net' concepts the quite irrelevant 'gross' concepts. The mere fact that when one uses the gross concepts the definition of what is and what is not investment is necessarily purely arbitrary and that it does not

multaneous increase in net investment must mean that the output of consumers' goods has increased by the same amount (or merely that some commodities change hands more often than before, which under the 'gross' approach would have to be treated as an increase of output).[54] And similarly, an increase merely of gross incomes will as a rule[55] mean that gross saving and gross investment have simultaneously changed by identical amounts. It is only in connection with changes in net investment and consequently of net income that the problem arises whether this will be matched with a corresponding change in net saving, or what the marginal propensity to consume will be.[56] While changes merely in gross investment, without a change in net investment, as it were 'finance' themselves (because ex definitione there must be a corresponding change in the production of consumers' goods or in gross savings), it is only in connection with net investment that the problem arises whether or not they will be equalled by independent decisions to perform net saving.

15. The Demand for, and the Supply of, Consumers' Goods During the Upswing. We have seen that a low rate of profits will tend to make incomes grow relatively fast and the output of consumers' goods grow relatively slowly, while a high rate of profit will tend to make incomes grow relatively slowly and the output of consumers' goods grow relatively fast. And it follows from this that if the initial rate of profit were too low it must lead to an increase in incomes and in the demand for consumers' goods which sooner or later would exceed the supply, and therefore to a rise of profits; and that if the initial rate of profits were too high it would sooner or later lead to an increase of output in excess of the increase in demand and therefore to a fall in the rate of profit. And there will be one rate at which net investment will grow at the same rate as net saving and the output of consumers' goods will grow so that the rate of profit will remain stable. Is the initial rate likely to be that equilibrium rate, or is it likely to be above or below it?

The first point to be noted here is that the initial rate of profit will be low, not because the rate of saving at this stage will be high, but because total in-

---

matter where we draw the line shows that it is an altogether irrelevant, if not meaningless magnitude. That the definition of what is net income, net saving, and net investment must be based on subjective factors these concepts have in common with all other concepts of economic theory. On the whole question see my article on "The Maintenance of Capital".

[54] [According to the framework adopted for national income accounting today such an increase in *gross*, but not *net*, investment could come about by a rise in the amortisation quotas required for the maintenance of capital.—Ed.]

[55] An exception of considerable importance for trade cycle theory is the treatment of capital gains, particularly of speculative profits on the stock exchange, as net income.

[56] To speak of a given marginal propensity to consume with respect to gross incomes and irrespective of its composition of net income and mere amortisation quotas appears to me an altogether unjustifiable procedure.

comes will be low: the income available for expenditure on consumers' goods will be small] compared with their total cost because only part of the equipment used in their production will be currently replaced. But this provides no reason to expect that when incomes grow the part of them which is spent on consumers' goods will grow no faster than the output of consumers' goods. To prevent this it would by no means be sufficient that savings should grow in proportion with incomes;[57] because the proportional share of the total income which is derived from net investment will increase; and to prevent the rate of profits from rising it would be necessary that total net saving should increase *pari passu* with net investment.

At first, and for some time after the beginning of the revival, the rate at which the output of consumers' goods increases will be comparatively fast, the amount of net investment comparatively small, and Q for the *total* new employment comparatively high: while the new investment will generate much more income than it contributes to the output of consumers' goods, it will be possible, by taking idle machinery in the consumers' goods industries into operation, to add to the current output of consumers' goods while at the same time disbursing less in costs than their current value. But since the amount of unused capacity in the consumers' goods industries is even in the depth of a depression usually fairly limited, and since the fact that equipment is currently replaced by more capitalistic, more labour-saving, kinds will tend at first to decrease rather than to increase total capacity,[58] this tendency will continue only for a comparatively short period. And as the rate of investment contin-

---

[57] As it has been seriously suggested that until comparatively recently most economists were unaware of the fact that a rise in incomes will lead to a rise in saving I may perhaps be permitted to refer to the closing sentence of my article on "Saving" in the *Encyclopedia of the Social Sciences*, ed. Edwin Seligman, vol. 13 (New York: Macmillan, 1934), pp. 548–52 (reprinted, partly for this reason, later in this volume [that is, as chapter 5 in *Profits, Interest and Investment*, to be reprinted in *Capital and Interest*, ed. Lawrence White, vol. 11 (forthcoming) of *The Collected Works of F. A. Hayek*—Ed.]), which treats this fact, in conformity with the views generally held at the time of its publication, as a self-evident commonplace. It was indeed so much taken for granted that in the German discussions of this sort of problem ten years ago the only point at dispute was whether the increase of voluntary savings following a credit expansion would or would not equal the 'forced savings' brought about by that expansion. [This refers to the debate initiated by Albert Hahn's theory of credit creation, see p. 138 above. In the closing sentence of "Saving", reprinted, p. 170, Hayek had stated, "A transfer of income from classes with a smaller to classes with a greater income . . . is therefore likely to increase the supply of savings. And a rise in aggregate incomes, which might be brought about by the same cause, will, of course, have the same effect."—Ed.]

[58] While this more expensive kind of machinery will, of course, produce more per unit of collaborating labour, it will produce less during any unit of time per unit of its own costs—at any rate if the introduction of the new machinery is not the result of a new invention but of a rise in real wages and a fall in profits. The result of such a conversion of a given amount of existing capital into more 'capitalistic' forms will therefore be that it will now be capable of turning out consumers' goods only at a smaller rate than before. (The potential gain consists in that in consequence labour is released for other purposes.)

ues to increase the proportion of total income that is earned from net investment will likewise increase, and therefore, if profits on the production of consumers' goods are not to rise, the *proportion* of incomes that is saved will have to increase parallel with the proportion of total income that is earned from net investment. (This will at least be true if, as is likely to be the case, the rate at which investment increases is greater than Q, i.e., greater than the rate at which current investment will contribute to the output of consumers' goods.[59] Or, in other words, if Q is smaller than the marginal propensity to consume, the point is bound to come when the demand for consumers' goods will rise more rapidly than the supply of consumers' goods, and profits in the consumers' goods industries will begin to rise.)

16. The Anomaly of the Cumulative Process. The rise of the rate of profit in the consumers' goods industries above the initial low level is probably inevitable if investment revives at all fast. But at first this increase of profits may not matter. Profits may not have been expected to remain at the very low initial level. Since such a rise of profits, even if it only confirms expectations, is, however, likely to stimulate investment further, they will continue to rise, and sooner or later increase beyond the level that was foreseen when investment began to revive.

Even when profits begin to rise beyond expectations this will for a considerable period serve to increase further the total amount of investment. At first the rise in the rate of profit will be confined to the consumers' goods industries. If this led immediately to a similar rise in the rate of interest, marginal rates of profit would everywhere have to be adjusted to this higher rate of interest and activity in the investment goods industries would have to be reduced till this was the case. But if the rate of interest does not rise at this stage the increase of profits in the consumers' goods industries will, as we have seen, for some time stimulate investment further (the reduction of the 'multiplier' will at first be less effective than the increase of the 'multiplicand'). We get then the anomalous position that an increase in the demand for consumers' goods will further increase the proportion (and the absolute amount) of incomes earned from net investment so that the discrepancy between the demand for consumers' goods and the supply of consumers' goods must get larger and larger. It is this anomaly that the increase in the demand for consumers' goods will for some time increase the output of investment goods more than the output of consumers' goods, and that every further increase in investment will increase profits on consumers' goods still further, that makes the position inherently unstable. It is a cumulative process, indeed an explosive process, leading fur-

---

[59] If the proportion by which investment increases during any given period, say a year, is greater than the proportion by which this investment at the end of this period will have contributed to the output of consumers' goods (i.e., greater than Q), this will necessarily lead to a cumulative increase of net investment. If investment increases at a rate smaller than Q, however, net investment will tend to decrease.

ther and further away from an equilibrium position till the stresses become so strong that it collapses.

The popular idea that an increase of investment will necessarily lower the rate of profit to be earned is true only of equilibrium conditions where no more income is derived from investment activity than will be saved. But once investment exceeds the amounts that will be saved out of the income thus increased, this can bring only a further rise and never a fall in profits; and since, so long as a rise in profits still further stimulates investment, this can only lead to a further gain of investment over saving and a further rise of profits, the process can only come to an end when the rise of profits begins to operate as a curb to investment in the way explained before. Once the cumulative process has been entered upon the end must always come through a rise in profits in the late stages and can never come from a fall in profits or an exhaustion of investment opportunities.[60]

17. The Short Run Ceiling of Stable Employment. We have seen that once the rate of profit in the consumers' goods industries rises beyond a certain point the system enters into an inherently unstable position: the rise of the rate of profit may for some time further stimulate investment and employment, but the effect of this must be to raise profits further till this very rise of profits leads to a curtailment of investment. This development could only be prevented if from the beginning the rate of interest rose with the rate of profit.[61] But the point at which the rate of interest might have to rise in order to prevent a further growth of investment that would lead to such an unstable position might be a phase in the recovery where there is still very considerable unemployment. Where the point of maximum stable employment which can be maintained will lie, will depend largely on what has happened during the early stages of the recovery. The 'critical point' to which we have referred earlier is not a fixed point in the sense that a certain rate of investment must never be

---

[60] An exhaustion of investment opportunities and over-investment in this sense may, of course, occur in particular industries, as for instance in the building or the motor-car industry. It means that most of the additional income generated by the investment in these industries is not spent on the product of these industries but on the products of other industries. In this case, however, while profits fall and investment declines in the industries where the over-investment has taken place, the reason why it will not pay immediately to increase investment in the other industries will probably be that there the rate of profit will be too high to make the introduction of more labour-saving methods profitable. This is therefore not a case where a discontinuity in the schedule of the marginal productivity of capital leads to a sudden fall in the returns to be expected on further investment, but a case where a (horizontal) misdirection of investment has tied up so much capital in a few industries as to create a scarcity of capital in the other industries.

[61] It should be remembered here that in this phase of the boom a general rise in money wages will only tend to raise prices and profits further and will scarcely affect real wages. A rise of money wages in the consumers' goods industries (or the late stages generally) might, however, partly counteract the rise of profits.

exceeded. The stage at which the expansion enters into the unstable phase will depend on a number of factors, particularly the form investment has taken during the early stages of the recovery, the rate at which investment has increased, and the rate of saving.

If the rate of profit by which investment was guided at the beginning of the recovery was very low, i.e., if real wages were then comparatively high, and if in consequence investment took a form so that Q was very low and income from investment grew fast compared with the output of consumers' goods, and if in addition the rate of saving were low (or the marginal propensity to consume high), the critical point would evidently be reached sooner and the maximum of stable employment that could be attained would be comparatively low. We should have a situation where in consequence of the high real wages (or the low rate of profit) in the beginning of the recovery the limits set by the available 'supply of capital' would have been exhausted by equipping fewer workmen with much capital per head: the available supply of capital would have been given such forms as if only a smaller number of men were to be permanently employed.

The maximum level of stable employment that can be reached in the short run (i.e., without redistributing resources between industries) will accordingly be higher at least up to a certain point, according as:

(a) the initial rate of profit is high (or real wages low) and Q accordingly high;

(b) the speed at which investment increases is small (which will partly be influenced by (a), because the amount of investment that will be undertaken in view of any given demand will be small, and partly by psychological factors); and

(c) the rate of saving is high (or the marginal propensity to consume low).

But while the ceiling of stable employment that can be reached in the short run will vary with the rate of profit ruling during the revival, this does not mean that there must be a rate of profit or a level of real wages which will lead to a stable position of *full* employment with the existing distribution of labour between industries. There is in fact every reason to doubt whether full employment with the given distribution of labour between industries can be a stable position.[62] This distribution is the legacy of former booms, the result of the capital goods industries operating in periodical spurts and supplying the

---

[62] See on this Dennis H. Robertson, "A Survey of Modern Monetary Controversy", a paper read to the Manchester Statistical Society, 1937, p. 13 [as published in *The Manchester School*, vol. 9, no. 1, 1938, pp. 13–14, reprinted in his *Essays in Monetary Theory*, pp. 146–47, in *Essays in Money and Interest*, p. 118, and in *Business Cycle Theory: Selected Texts 1860–1939*, vol. 3: *Monetary Theories of the Business Cycle*, ed. Harald Hagemann (London: Pickering and Chatto, 2002), pp. 351–52—Ed.].

consumers' goods industries by this intermittent working with all, or rather more than the equipment, which at the rate of profit that will rule under full employment it is profitable for the latter to use. If we find that, as appears to be approximately the case, average unemployment over a whole trade cycle is in the neighbourhood of 25 per cent in the earlier stages of the capital goods industries and somewhere about 10 per cent in the consumers' goods industries,[63] this would mean that continuous full employment of all the available labour in these industries would increase the output of capital goods belonging to relatively early stages by one-third and the total output of consumers' goods by only one-ninth. And it seems clear that the consumers' goods industries could absorb such an increase in the output of capital goods only if the labour supply there were considerably increased. But so long as the capacity for producing consumers' goods is not much increased by a transfer of labour from the capital goods industries to the consumers' goods industries and an increased output of equipment capable of producing consumers' goods as against further increase of capacity for producing capital goods, all attempts to create full employment with the existing distribution of labour between industries will come up against the difficulty that with full employment people will want a larger share of the total output in the form of consumers' goods than is being produced in that form. In other words, if the last boom has come to an end because savings proved to be insufficient to maintain the rate of accumulation which full employment with the existing distribution of resources between industries implies, it is very probable that any attempt to reach full employment with the same distribution would lead to the same result.

18. The 'Equilibrium' Rate of Profit and Interest. If too low a rate of profit during the upswing, while rapidly increasing employment in the capital goods industries where unemployment is greatest (and perhaps even further increasing the already excessive number of people attached to these industries), will make another crisis inevitable, too high a rate of profit might equally have the effect

[63] These figures are given merely as an illustration of a general tendency and make no claim to accuracy, being based on a general impression rather than a systematic study which this question would well deserve. But they are rather remarkably well borne out by figures of the mean unemployment rate (i.e., the percentage of the insured males unemployed) for the period 1927–36, which have been kindly supplied by Sir William Beveridge to the author since he used the above figures in an earlier draft of this essay. According to Sir William's calculations the mean unemployment rate during this period was 25.6 per cent for the six metal manufacture industries of the *Labour Gazette* classification, 24.1 per cent in the six extractive industries other than coal mining, 24.6 per cent in coal mining, 20 per cent in the eight instrumental industries, and 20.2 per cent in the extractive, instrumental and constructional industries generally, compared with 10.1 per cent in the food, clothing, and consumers' service industries. [Cf. on this, e.g., William H. Beveridge, "Unemployment in the Trade Cycle", *Economic Journal*, vol. 49, March 1939, pp. 52–65.—Ed.]

of reducing the maximum level at which employment can be lastingly maintained. While a rate that is too low may create employment in the consumers' goods industries and the capital goods industries in a proportion which corresponds to the existing distribution of labour between these industries, but will lead with full employment to a total amount of investment that cannot be maintained with the available savings, a rate that is too high might stop investment before the maximum of stable employment had been obtained.

It should be clear, then, that the dangerous misdirections of investment will occur, that the seeds of future trouble will be sown, long before the actual 'critical point' is reached, that it is the form that investment takes right from the beginning of the recovery which decides how far the expansion may be carried without making an ultimate breakdown inevitable. A policy designed to mitigate fluctuations will therefore have to watch the recovery from its very beginning. The problem is to find a middle path between the Scylla of keeping the rate of profits too low and the Charybdis of keeping it too high. The former would have the effect that profits would later rise steeply and, if expansion is allowed to continue, would lead to a crash after a period of high employment in the investment goods industries; while the latter would mean that not even that maximum level of employment will be reached which can be attained in the short run and maintained afterwards without a redistribution of resources—a further increase beyond this point being only possible as savings gradually accumulate and a redistribution of labour between industries proceeds. The question is, therefore, how to find from the beginning a level of the rate of profit (and real wages) which as far as possible makes further changes in this rate unnecessary (at least changes beyond the point at which they would seriously disappoint the expectations of many people).

This 'equilibrium' rate will in almost all cases be higher than the rate which will increase employment as quickly as possible, and it will also be higher than any rate which will make it possible temporarily to reach full employment with the existing distribution of labour between industries. The only way in which this short run ceiling of employment can be raised (and the 'equilibrium' rate of profit lowered), it appears, is an increase in the rate of saving to a level which would allow us to accumulate capital continuously at the rate to which the existing distribution of labour between industries is adapted.

19. Possibilities of Mitigating Fluctuations. Apart from the possibility last mentioned, which is probably of importance only in the long run, our considerations suggest two ways in which the violence of industrial fluctuations might be mitigated.

In the first instance everything seems to point to the desirability of preventing the rate of profit from falling too low, and real wages from rising too high, in the later stages of the depression. While some fall of the rate of profit in the consumers' goods industries, and therefore (failing some compulsory transfer of income from consumption to investment) some reduction of incomes, seems to be necessary after the crisis, there appears to be a strong case for measures designed to prevent demand for consumers' goods and prices of consumers' goods from falling too far. Since some movement in this direction is necessary, it would delay readjustment if such measures were taken too early. And as investment and incomes begin to increase again, such extra expenditure should clearly be curtailed at the same rate. But during the later half of the decline a policy of supplementing demand by public expenditure may well be justified.

Once the rate of profit in the consumers' goods industries has already fallen too far and real wages risen too high, however, the proper remedy appears to be a reduction of wages. While, unfortunately, in the later stages of the boom a rise in money wages is not likely to have favourable effects, because it will not raise real wages, I see no reason why in the depression a reduction of money wages should not lead to a fall in real wages. And a reduction of real wages, by raising the rate of profit, will have the desired effect of preventing investments of a too capitalistic type. It will be clear on the other hand that in this situation any attempt to stimulate recovery by lowering the rate of interest below the already low rate of profit could only accentuate the later difficulties.[64]

[64] It may perhaps be pointed out here that it has, of course, never been denied that employment can be rapidly increased, and a position of 'full employment' achieved in the shortest possible time by means of monetary expansion—least of all by those economists whose outlook has been influenced by the experience of a major inflation. All that has been contended is that the kind of full employment which can be created in this way is inherently unstable, and that to create employment by these means is to perpetuate fluctuations. There may be desperate situations in which it may indeed be necessary to increase employment at all costs, even if it be only for a short period—perhaps the situation in which Dr. Brüning found himself in Germany in 1932 was such a situation in which desperate means would have been justified. But the economist should not conceal the fact that to aim at the maximum of employment which can be achieved in the short run by means of monetary policy is essentially the policy of the desperado who has nothing to lose and everything to gain from a short breathing space. [Heinrich Brüning (1885–1970), German politician, as chancellor of the German *Reich* from March 1930 to May 1932 presided over the final phase of the Weimar Republic. Facing the twin problems of German reparation payments and the Great Depression, he pursued a deflationist policy, not only because of his liberal economic convictions but also to demonstrate Germany's impossibility to fulfil the demands of the creditor countries—the ultimate success of this policy being the abolition of reparations in the treaty of Lausanne in summer 1932, when Brüning had already been dismissed. In any case, Brüning's 'non-expansionist' policies towards the depression were much contested by contemporaries. The most outspoken liberal critic was probably Wilhelm Röpke; cf., e.g., his "Trends in German Business Cycle Policy", *Economic Journal*, vol. 43, September 1933, pp. 427–41. On Hayek's view on this matter cf. his letter to Röpke, reprinted in F. A. Hayek, *New Studies in Philosophy, Politics, Economics and the History of Ideas* (Chicago: University of Chicago Press; London: Routledge, 1978), p. 211.—Ed.]

20. The Negative Role of the Rate of Interest. The remarks of the last section on questions of trade cycle policy have inevitably been cursory and incomplete. There arises, however, in this connection one point which is closely connected with our main problem and therefore needs more systematic consideration, namely the precise role played by the rate of interest. So far our main conclusion with respect to the rate of interest, rather borne out by recent experience, is that we might get the trade cycle even without changes in the rate of interest. We have seen that if the rate of interest fails to keep investment within the bounds determined by people's willingness to save, a rise in the rate of profit in the industries near consumption will in the end act in a way very similar to that in which the rate of interest is supposed to act, because a rise in the rate of profit beyond a certain point will bring about a decrease in investment just as an increase in the rate of interest might do. This, of course, does not contradict the truism that a high rate of profit, if general, makes for prosperity. There is in every situation a rate of profit which can be the same for all industries,[65] and such a uniform rate of profit throughout the system is the condition of a stable equilibrium. It is the function which the rate of interest is supposed to perform, but actually performs but very imperfectly, that if anywhere in the system changes in the rate of profit occur, the rates of profit are equalised at a new level by the appropriate expansions and contractions of investment in the various industries. We have seen that the operation of the rate of profit in the place of the rate of interest applies not only to the phase of expansion but also to the phase of contraction, and that it is probably the fall in the rate of profits rather than the fall in the rate of interest which in the end stimulates the introduction of more labour-saving machinery, etc., and thus revives investment. Must we conclude from this that the rate of interest is of little significance?

This is by no means the case, although we shall probably have to conclude that its main influence is more of a negative than a positive kind; it fails to do what in equilibrium theory it is supposed to do, and what it would have to do if equilibrium were to be preserved or rapidly to be restored after a disturbance. But failing the action of the rate of interest, other and more complicated forces come into play at a later stage and act as in pure theory the rate of interest is supposed to act. In real life the importance of the rate of interest is probably considerably greater than we have assumed here, since, while the link which connects the rate of profit and the rate of interest is very elastic, it does exist and, however tardily, the rate of interest does ultimately follow the movements of the rate of profit. For our purpose it was, however, conve-

---

[65] The 'same rate of profit' for the various industries means here such a position of their profit schedules that with normal employment marginal rates of profit will be the same. The statement in the text is, however, subject to the qualifications of section 17 above.

nient to assume that the rate of interest remained constant (or at least did not rise), in order to show that the changes which the rate of interest is supposed to bring about are not due to monetary causes but will come about even in the absence of changes in the rate of interest. The rise of the rate of profit would by itself bring the boom to an end. But in real life the rise in the rate of interest will usually bring this effect about before the rate of profit rises sufficiently.

But if in real life the rate of interest is not quite as immovable as we have assumed, its movements may yet be too tardy or too small to be effective and the rate of profit may therefore be the decisive factor. Since we know from general theoretical considerations that in order to preserve or restore equilibrium changes in the rate of interest will from time to time be necessary, all that we need to confirm the practical relevance of our argument is evidence that in real life changes in the money rate of interest are not of major significance to business men. If it can be shown that compared with the changes in the rate of profit the changes in the rate of interest are small, and that investments are actually guided, at least in many fields, much more by the rate of profit or the level of wages than by the rate of interest, this would be the best verification of our argument that we could expect.

The familiar doubts of men of business experience about the efficacy of the rate of interest, well brought out by the recent Oxford inquiry,[66] provide considerable evidence that such is the real situation. If in fact movements of the rate of interest follow only at a distance behind the movements of the rate of profit, and if in addition the total amplitude of fluctuations in interest rates is much smaller than the amplitude of fluctuations in the rate of profit, the rate of interest would indeed in many fields cease to be a major consideration in deciding investment policy. But if the rate of interest fails to adjust the rate of investment to that volume which can be maintained with the available supply of 'real capital' (the output of consumers' goods not consumed by its producers), the other forces which we have considered must come into play and restore the balance.

It has, of course, never been doubted, at least in more recent times, that the money rate of interest depends largely on accidental and arbitrary factors. But if, when the rate of interest fails to follow the movements of the rate of profit, it is the rate of profit which earlier or later takes command of the situation, the factors which determine where the rate of interest actually is become much less important than the factors which determine where it ought to be. And not only would it seem as if the importance which attaches to the

[66] Cf. Hubert D. Henderson, "The Significance of the Rate of Interest", and James E. Meade and Philipp W. S. Andrews, "Summary of Replies to Questions on Effects of Interest Rates", in *Oxford Economic Papers*, no. 1, October 1938, pp. 1–13 and 14–31, respectively.

question what determines the actual money rate of interest would be much smaller than is suggested by the great amount of effort and ingenuity which has recently been devoted to this question; it also appears that manipulations of the rate of interest are of much more limited value than is often supposed because, if we try to fix it below or above its 'natural level',[67] it soon ceases to be effective.

21. Can the Rate of Interest Be Made Effective? It seems then that the idea that investment is guided by the rate of interest is to a large extent an ideal rather than a fact. But if it is true that under existing conditions the rate of interest does not perform this function, or performs it only to a very limited extent, this does not mean that it cannot or that it ought not to be made to do so. And it does not even necessarily mean that in order to make the rate of interest more effective its movements would have to be bigger than they are to-day. Even if there are many considerations which make it plausible that the initiating power of spontaneous changes in the rate of interest is comparatively small, these considerations do not necessarily apply to its power to offset changes in the rate of profit. If it is mainly changes which affect his current business which make an entrepreneur look round and revise his plans, it may well be that he is fairly indifferent to much spontaneous changes in the rate of interest, but quite sensitive at the moment when changes in his profits make him think of altering his investment policy.

We must not forget that the rise (and similarly the fall) of the rate of profit only becomes so big as it actually does because, failing a parallel movement of the rate of interest, a rise of profits will for a considerable period further stimulate investment of all kinds. And while, once this process has gone some distance, the rise in the rate of interest required to check it might indeed be very considerable, a prompt adjustment of the rate of interest as soon as profits begin to rise (or fall), although not involving a great change, might well be effective.[68] While changes in the rate of interest within the customary range may be quite powerless at the date at which, because of the delay action of our credit mechanism, they now take place, their effect might be quite sufficient to preserve a reasonable equilibrium if they were made promptly. It is even probable that the total amplitude of the changes in the rate of interest

[67] [The 'natural level' of interest is that unaffected by inflation or deflation as explained above, section 13.—Ed.]

[68] It is no contradiction to argue that investments in the individual firm are guided not so much by the rate of interest as by the rate of profit, and at the same time to advocate the use of the rate of interest as a means to control investment. Although a rise of the rate of interest may have little effect on the proportional amount of capital used by particular firms, it will, by reducing the total amount of production in the early stages where profits have not risen, reduce the amount of investment for industry as a whole.

required would be smaller than the fluctuations observed in the past if only they followed more promptly upon changes in the rate of profit.

What amount of changes in the rate of interest would be necessary to prevent the recurrence of cumulative processes in either direction we do not know because such a policy has never been tried.[69] And it is, of course, true that in the absence of an automatic mechanism making rates of interest move with rates of profits it would require superhuman wisdom to adjust them perfectly by deliberate policy. But this by no means proves that we might not get much nearer to the ideal than we have ever done. It is, e.g., evidently an anomaly which indicates inflationary developments that in almost all past booms the prices of fixed interest securities have been allowed to rise (i.e., the long term rate of interest has been allowed to fall) for some time after industrial profits have already begun to move upwards. It seems clear that such a development ought to be prevented by a timely increase of the money rate of interest. Actual developments of policy, particularly in recent times, have, however, been in the opposite direction; the tendency to keep the rates of interest stable, and especially to keep them low as long as possible, must appear as the arch-enemy of stability, causing in the end much greater fluctuations, probably even of the rate of interest, than are really necessary.[70] Perhaps it should be repeated that this applies especially to the doctrine, now so widely accepted, that interest rates should be kept low till 'full employment' in general is reached.[71] While it appears that we can have the trade cycle without changes in the rate

---

[69] An exception should probably be made for the action of the Federal Reserve Board in the spring of 1923, when by raising the rates of interest they brought an incipient boom to an end and caused a merely slight and short recession, soon followed by a rapid revival. But this policy was unfortunately abandoned and actually reversed on the next occasion in 1927, with the fatal consequences we all know.

[70] This has, of course, been argued again and again by economists ever since the beginning of last century. To mention only one author who has been rather neglected in the recent historical surveys of these discussions, H. D. Macleod, *The Theory and Practice of Banking*, vol. 2, 1st ed. (London: Longman, Brown, Green, and Longmans, 1856), pp. 371–72, 3rd ed. (London: Longmans, Green, Reader, and Dyer, 1879 [1876]), p. 273, wrote: "We may feel quite certain that if during the various crises this country has passed through, there had been more attention paid to observe the natural rate of discount, instead of thwarting the course of nature, though [the] variations would have been more frequent, they would have been less violent and extreme. . . . Such, however, is the perversity of men, that many think that a uniform and invariable rate of discount is the great thing to be preserved, no matter what nature may say to the contrary, and their ingenuity is racked to devise a plan for always keeping it so, just as if the governor of a [the] steam engine ought always to revolve with uniform velocity." [Henry Dunning Macleod (1821–1902), British banker, developed a credit theory of money and wealth, yet never succeeded in acquiring academic recognition as an economist.—Ed.]

[71] [For example, Keynes denoted the rate of interest that preserved the equality between the rate of saving and of investment consistent with full employment as the 'neutral' rate of interest and considered it as the 'optimum rate'; cf. *General Theory*, pp. 242–43.—Ed.]

of interest we shall probably never have a reasonable degree of stability without such changes.

If we have to steer a car along a narrow road between two walls, we can either keep it in the middle of the road by fairly frequent but small movements of the steering wheel; or we can wait longer when the car deviates to one side and then bring it back by more or less violent jerks, probably overshooting the mark and risking collision with the other wall; or we can try to keep the steering wheel stiff and let the car bang alternately into either wall with a good chance of leading the car and ourselves to ultimate destruction.

NINE

THE RICARDO EFFECT[1]

Machinery and labour are in constant competition, and the former can frequently not be employed until labour rises. —D. Ricardo[2]

1.

When in a recent essay on industrial fluctuations the author introduced "the
familiar Ricardian proposition that a rise in wages will encourage capitalists
to substitute machinery for labour",[3] this was done under the illusion that thus
an argument he had long employed could be stated in a more readily acceptable form.[4] That illusion has been dispelled by the various comments on that
essay;[5] and a re-examination of the earlier literature on the subject has revealed a rather peculiar situation: while the proposition has been supported

---

[1] [First published in *Economica*, n.s., vol. 9, May 1942, pp. 127–52, and reprinted in slightly revised form in F. A. Hayek, *Individualism and Economic Order* (Chicago: University of Chicago Press,
1948; London: Routledge and Kegan Paul, 1949), pp. 220–54. The text is that of the first version (1942).—Ed.]

[2] [From chapter 31, "On Machinery", of David Ricardo, *On the Principles of Political Economy
and Taxation* [1817], 3rd ed. (1821); cf. *The Works and Correspondence of David Ricardo*, ed. Piero
Sraffa, vol. 1 (Cambridge: Cambridge University Press, 1951; reprinted, Indianapolis: Liberty
Press, 2004), p. 395.—Ed.]

[3] "Profits, Interest and Investment", in *Profits, Interest and Investment. And Other Essays on the Theory
of Industrial Fluctuations* (London: Routledge, 1939), p. 8 [this volume, p. 215—Ed.]; cf. also *The
Pure Theory of Capital* (London: Macmillan, 1941), chapter 17 [reprinted, ed. Lawrence White,
as vol. 12 (2007) of *The Collected Works of F. A. Hayek* (Chicago: University of Chicago Press; London: Routledge)—Ed.].

[4] [In the 1949 reprint Hayek added, "a more familiar and readily acceptable form".—Ed.]

[5] Cf. particularly the review of *Profits, Interest and Investment* by Hugh Townsend in the *Economic
Journal*, vol. 50, March 1940, pp. 99–103, and Tom Wilson, "Capital Theory and the Trade
Cycle", *Review of Economic Studies*, vol. 7, June 1940, pp. 169–79. I have not been able to see
Carsten Welinder, "Hayek och 'Ricardoeffekten'", *Ekonomisk Tidskrift*, March 1940. [The article
appeared in vol. 42, pp. 33–39.—Ed.]

and used by numerous writers ever since it was first enounced by Ricardo,[6] it seems never to have been adequately expounded. In particular, although it is fundamental to the discussions of interest in the works of Böhm-Bawerk, Wicksell, and Mises, none of these authors develops it at any length. The frequent brief references to it in other general theoretical works in modern times,[7] which seemed to confirm the impression that it was widely accepted, prove on examination to be not only inadequate but often to be based on faulty reasoning. And although it used to be treated as a commonplace in realistic studies of the influence of high wages on the use of machinery, there, too, we search in vain for a reasoned argument.[8] The relatively fullest discussion in recent times is to be found in some German publications.[9] But when in

[6] The relevant passages of Ricardo's *Principles* will be found mainly in *The Works of David Ricardo*, ed. John Ramsey McCulloch (London: Murray, 1846), pp. 26 and 241 [cf. *Works and Correspondence*, ed. Sraffa, vol. 1, pp. 39–40 and 395—Ed.].

[7] E.g., Nikolaas Gerard Pierson, *Principles of Economics*, trans. A. A. Wotzel, vol. 1 (London: Macmillan, 1902), pp. 219 [pp. 219–220], 308; Gustav Cassel, *The Nature and Necessity of Interest* (London and New York: Macmillan, 1903 [reprinted, New York: Kelley, 1971]), p. 116: "Supposing the rate of interest to be constant, the more expensive labour becomes, the greater will be the substitution of waiting for it"; Frank A. Fetter, *Economic Principles* (New York: Century, 1915), p. 340; Henry Rogers Seager, *Principles of Economics*, 2nd ed. (New York: Holt, 1917), pp. 278, 289; Ralph George Hawtrey, *The Economic Problem* (London: Longmans and Co., 1926), pp. 324 et seq. [pp. 324–27]; see also H. Gordon Hayes, "The Rate of Wages and the Use of Machinery", and Clyde Olin Fisher, "An Issue in Economic Theory: 'The Rate of Wages and the Use of Machinery'", in *American Economic Review*, vol. 13, September 1923, pp. 461–65, and December 1923, pp. 654–55, respectively, a particularly characteristic discussion in which a faulty presentation of the argument by the first author was easily demolished by the second.

[8] E.g., Gerhart von Schulze-Gaevernitz, *Der Großbetrieb—ein wirtschaftlicher und sozialer Fortschritt: Eine Studie auf dem Gebiete der Baumwollindustrie* (Leipzig: Duncker and Humblot, 1892); Jacob Schoenhof, *The Economy of High Wages* (New York: Putnam, 1893 [1892]), pp. 33 [pp. 33–34], 279; Lujo Brentano, *Hours and Wages in Relation to Production* (London: Sonnenschein; New York: Scribner's Sons, 1894) [the translation of *Über das Verhältnis von Arbeitslohn und Arbeitszeit zur Arbeitsleistung* (Leipzig: Duncker and Humblot, 1876); Hayek cites the title inaccurately as, "*in Their Relation*"—Ed.]; and John Atkinson Hobson, *The Evolution of Modern Capitalism: A Study in Machine Production* (London: Walter Scott; New York: Scribner's Sons 1894 [reprinted, London: Allen and Unwin, 1965]), p. 81.

[9] See particularly Hans Neisser, "Lohnhöhe und Beschäftigungsgrad im Marktgleichgewicht", *Weltwirtschaftliches Archiv*, vol. 36, October 1932, pp. 415–55 [cf. an abridged version translated by Christian Gehrke as "The Wage Rate and Employment in Market Equilibrium", *Structural Change and Economic Dynamics*, vol. 1, June 1990, pp. 141–63—Ed.]; and Alfred Kähler, *Die Theorie der Arbeiterfreisetzung durch die Maschine: Eine gesamtwirtschaftliche Abhandlung des modernen Technisierungsprozesses* (Leipzig: Buske, 1933), pp. 75 et seq. [pp. 75–80]. I should perhaps add that it is partly due to Professor Neisser that I was confirmed in the belief that the proposition was generally accepted; since when, about the same time as his article appeared, I got (in an article in the same journal) badly mixed up on the point, and it was he who promptly caught me out and orally pointed out to me the confusion. [The article in question is F. A. Hayek, "Kapitalaufzehrung", *Weltwirtschaftliches Archiv*, vol. 36, July 1932, pp. 86–108, translated as "Capital Consump-

this country[10] a few years ago Professor Hicks made use of the proposition in a chapter of his *Theory of Wages*, Mr. Shove in his review[11] of that work produced what has become the standard reply, that so long as the rate of interest is unchanged a general change in wages will affect the cost of production of the different methods of production in the same proportion (which is undeniable), and that therefore it cannot alter their relative advantages (which does not follow); and Professor Hicks's later withdrawal[12] of the whole chapter in which occurred the passage criticised seemed to imply that he abandoned the contention. Still more recently Mr. Kaldor,[13] in an article to which we shall have to refer later, while admitting the principle, seemed to restrict its significance to rather special conditions.

The proposition in question is of importance far beyond the special context in which it has been used in recent discussions. It is not surprising that those who completely reject it seem at the same time to be unable to attach any meaning to the conception of a given and limited supply of real capital[14]:

---

tion", in *Money, Capital and Fluctuations: Early Essays by F. A. Hayek*, ed. Roy McCloughry (London: Routledge and Kegan Paul; Chicago: University of Chicago Press, 1984), a new translation to appear in *Capital and Interest*, ed. Lawrence White, vol. 11 (forthcoming) of *The Collected Works of F. A. Hayek.*—Ed.]

[10] [That is, as added in the 1949 edition, "in England".—Ed.]

[11] John R. Hicks, *The Theory of Wages* (London: Macmillan, 1932 [2nd ed., 1963]), chapter 9, and Gerald Frank Shove's review in *Economic Journal*, vol. 43, September 1933, p. 471. [John Richard (later Sir John) Hicks (1904–89), British economist and Nobel Prize winner in 1972, contributed significantly both to neoclassical and Keynesian economics. In the 1930s he had been a lecturer at LSE until 1935, then left for Cambridge, taught as professor at Manchester, and eventually, 1950–65, at Oxford.—Ed.]

[12] John R. Hicks, "Wages and Interest: The Dynamic Problem", *Economic Journal*, vol. 45, September 1935 [cf. in particular, p. 467n.1, reprinted in John Hicks, *The Collected Essays on Economic Theory*, vol. 2: *Money, Interest and Wages* (Oxford: Basil Blackwell, 1982), p. 78n.15; see also the Prefatory Note, ibid., pp. 64–67—Ed.].

[13] Nicholas Kaldor, "Capital Intensity and the Trade Cycle", *Economica*, n.s., vol. 6, February 1939, pp. 40–66 [reprinted as chapter 6 of *Essays on Economic Stability and Growth*, vol. 2 of his *Collected Economic Essays* (London: Duckworth, 1960, 2nd ed., 1980)—Ed.]; cf. also his "Annual Survey of Economic Theory: The Recent Controversy on the Theory of Capital", *Econometrica*, vol. 5, July 1937, pp. 201–33 [reprinted, under the title "The Controversy on the Theory of Capital", as chapter 9 of *Essays on Value and Distribution*, vol. 1 of *Collected Economic Essays*. Nicholas Kaldor (1908–86), born in Hungary, studied at the University of Berlin and then at LSE. After a short spell under the influence of Robbins and Hayek, he became a leading figure within the Keynesian movement, and his relations with Hayek turned notoriously inimical. For a closer account see the editor's introduction, this volume, pp. 3–5. At LSE Kaldor supervised Wilson's thesis, published as *Fluctuations in Income and Empoyment* (London: Pitman, 1942; 3rd ed., 1949, reprinted, Nendeln: Kraus, 1970), with Wilson's article cited above reprinted as chapter 6. Tom (Thomas) Wilson (1916–2001) became the Adam Smith Professor for Political Economy at Glasgow University, 1958–82.—Ed.].

[14] As I have attempted to show elsewhere (*The Pure Theory of Capital*, particularly p. 147 [reprinted, pp. 154–55—Ed.]) the only adequate description of this 'supply of capital' is a com-

because it is through this effect that the scarcity of real capital will make itself ultimately felt, however much the rate of interest may be affected by purely monetary factors, and that the volume of investment must ultimately be adjusted to a level compatible with the demand for consumers' goods. The proposition thus is an essential part of the elementary theory of production. If this is true, the lack of agreement on it would go far to explain the sharp and apparently irreconcilable conflict of economists on the more complex problems of industrial fluctuations, and an attempt at a fuller statement of the argument on which the proposition is based seems to be urgently needed.

Such a statement will be attempted here in terms which should make it as far as possible independent of disputed points of the theory of capital, and without direct application to the problems of industrial fluctuations beyond (1) a general stress on short run rather than long run effects, and (2) concentration on the effect of a fall rather than a rise of wages relatively to product prices, because it is in this form that the principle seems to be particularly relevant for the exploration of industrial crises. In order to separate the various parts of the argument the problem will be approached in stages. The next section will be devoted to an explanation of the concepts used and an exposition of the general principle on assumptions which will enable us to disregard the money rate of interest. After the general principle has thus been established,

---

plete enumeration of the range of possible output streams of different time shapes that can be produced from the existing resources. Which of these different output streams will be produced depends in the first instance on what may be called the 'rate of employment' (i.e., the rate at which people will be employed at successive moments of time during the period in question) and on the form that employment will take, factors which in turn depend on final demand, the level of money wages, and the result of these, the relation of money wages to the prices of the products. There will, as a rule, be only one output stream which in its production will generate an income stream of such size and time shape that the part of that income which at any time will be spent on consumers' goods will just equal the cost of the current output of consumers' goods, inclusive of that rate of return on capital in the expectation of which the method of production actually employed has been decided upon.

It was the fatal mistake of Böhm-Bawerk (and to much less an extent of Wicksell) that, although he was quite aware that the existing stock of capital goods was capable of producing more than one single output stream, he attempted to simplify his exposition by identifying the stock of capital goods with a definite quantity of consumers' goods and to represent this in his illustrations by a fixed amount of available money capital. The analysis of the famous final chapter on "The Market for Capital in its Full Development" of *The Positive Theory of Capital* makes perfect sense if we remember this simplification but must seem to have no relevance to anything in the real world to anyone who takes the representation of the supply of capital by a sum of money literally. [Hayek's reference is to Eugen von Böhm-Bawerk, *The Positive Theory of Capital*, translated by William Smart (London: Macmillan, 1891) from the first edition of *Positive Theorie des Kapitales* (Innsbruck: Wagner, 1884 and 1889; reprinted, Düsseldorf: Verlag Wirtschaft und Finanzen, 1994 and 1991); in the more recent translation of the fourth edition by George D. Huncke, vol. 2 of *Capital and Interest* (South Holland, IL: Libertarian Press, 1959), the chapter is titled "The Rate of Interest Under the Fully Developed Market for Capital".—Ed.]

the concrete ways in which it is likely to affect investment demand will be discussed in Section 3. The interplay between the Ricardo Effect and the rate of interest on money loans will be taken up in Section 4 and will be discussed first on assumptions concerning the supply of credit which are approximately true of the real world. In Sections 5 and 6 the same problem will be considered on the assumption of a 'perfectly elastic supply of credit', which, though highly unrealistic, raises theoretical problems of considerable interest. In a final section will be added a few considerations which have to be taken into account in any attempt at statistical verification of the theorem.

2.

The proposition here described as the Ricardo Effect asserts that a general change in wages relatively to the prices of the products will alter the relative profitability of different industries or methods of production which employ labour and capital ('indirect labour') in different proportions. In its original form it asserts that a general rise in wages relatively to the prices of the products will reduce the profitability of the industries or methods employing relatively more capital to a lesser extent than those employing relatively less capital.[15] We are here more particularly concerned with the inverse of this, namely, with the proposition that a general fall in wages relatively to product prices will have the opposite effect.[16]

A general change in the relationships between wages and product prices may be caused by a general change in product prices, by a general change in wages, or by a change in technical knowledge or the physical quantities of other factors available which change the productivity of labour.[17] While any of these changes may serve for our purpose as the independent variable, we must, of course, not treat in the same way changes in the productivity of labour

---

[15] [In the 1949 reprint Hayek modified this passage to read, "In its original form it asserts that a general rise in wages relative to the prices of the products will not reduce the profitability of the industries or methods employing relatively more capital to the same extent as those employing relatively less capital."—Ed.]

[16] As a result of a criticism of this article in the proof-stage by Mr. G. F. Shove, I am no longer so sure that the establishment of the truth of the proposition in the inverse form also proves the correctness of the original proposition. [Gerald Frank Shove (1887–1947) was a British economist in the Marshallian tradition, a Fellow of King's College, Cambridge.—Ed.]

[17] [Note, however, that there is a crucial difference between a rise in product prices with the money wage constant and a fall in the money wage with product prices constant. In the former case, as long as the rate of interest and the prices of capital goods remain unchanged, the relative price of labour in terms of capital goods will remain unchanged, too, while in the latter case this relative price will fall.—Ed.]

which are the consequence of variations in the proportion between capital and labour employed, since this is the dependent variable of our problem.

The particular kind of change on which we shall here illustrate the proposition will be a general rise in the prices of final products (or consumers' goods, henceforth briefly referred to as 'commodities') while money wages are assumed to remain constant (and thus to fall *relatively* to commodity prices). We shall assume this rise of prices to be due to an increase of demand, caused by a growth of incomes earned from producing investment goods, and exceeding the amount beyond which the output of commodities can be readily increased. We shall further assume that entrepreneurs expect commodity prices to remain at least for some considerable time at the new higher level. No assumption will be made concerning any change in the price of capital goods, this being part of our problem.

The assumption of a general rise in the prices of commodities while wages remain unchanged means, of course, that *all* wages fall relatively to commodity prices. It is important to emphasise this because the theorem has often been misunderstood to refer to a situation where only the wages of labour co-operating with machinery change relatively to prices, while the wages used in the production of machinery remain unaffected.[18] And it should be at once admitted that with such a general change in the wage level relatively to final prices, the costs of producing final goods by different methods must, if we assume a uniform rate of interest, be changed in the same proportion. Our contention is that nevertheless the attractiveness of investing in different industries or methods of production will be affected differently.

In order to exclude, for the purpose of the present section, any influence exercised by the money rate of interest, we shall assume for the time being that there is no lending of money of any kind during the period with which we are concerned: entrepreneurs either owning all the capital they employ and being effectively prevented from lending any of it, or being limited by a strict rationing of credit. We shall assume, however, that before the rise in commodity prices occurred, the rates of return on capital had been the same in all the firms. By excluding any consideration of the rate of interest in discussing the effects of the changes in commodity prices we are, for the moment, deliberately avoiding what will later become our main problem. This temporary shelving of the central issue will, however, help us to isolate the more elementary parts of the argument which seem still to need explicit statement.

Our present problem thus is how, with unchanged wages, the rise in com-

[18] While many later authors were confused on this point, Ricardo clearly assumed a general change in wages; the starting point of his brief discussion of the whole problem is the question whether, if wages rose by 10 per cent, "will not machinery [the machine] rise in price" to the same extent? See Ricardo, *Principles of Political Economy*, ed. McCulloch, *Works*, p. 26 [*Works and Correspondence*, ed. Sraffa, vol. 1, p. 40—Ed.].

modity prices will affect the current distribution of the funds at the command of the entrepreneurs between expenditure on wages (or investment in 'circulating capital') and expenditure on machinery (investment in 'fixed capital'). To avoid complications arising from changes in the prices of raw materials, etc., which I have discussed elsewhere,[19] we can assume that the firms with which we are concerned are all of the type represented by a brickyard on marginal land where the labour employed produces not only all the raw material but also the fuel.

It remains to introduce an unambiguous and, so far as possible, uncontroversial measure of the proportions in which capital and labour are combined in the various firms and possible methods of production. For the purpose in hand, the most convenient measure which has also the advantage of being familiar to business men, is the concept of the 'rate of turnover', applied either to the whole or to any part of the capital of a firm. That some firms can expect to 'turn over' their capital (i.e., to re-invest out of current receipts an amount equal to their capital) once in two months, while others can expect to do so only once in five or even ten years, and that this rate of turnover depends, at least in part,[20] on the nature of the business and the character of the methods adopted is a familiar fact. Similarly, it will also be true that within any given firm some parts of its assets will be 'turned over', or wholly turned into cash and re-invested, twelve times a year, while others may be thus completely amortised and replaced only once in twenty years. The 'rate of turnover' expresses (as an integer or fraction) the number of times the capital is turned over in the course of one year. As it will be convenient to have an adjective describing firms or methods with a relatively high or relatively low rate of turnover, we shall, for reasons which will be obvious, occasionally employ the technical term 'more capitalistic' for firms or methods with a relatively low rate of turnover, and 'less capitalistic' for firms or methods with a relatively high method of turnover.[21]

The concept of the rate of turnover of capital provides a specially use-

---

[19] "Profits, Interest and Investment", pp. 29 et seq. [this volume, pp. 228–30—Ed.].

[20] The rate of turnover depends, of course, not only on the nature of the business and on the technical methods adopted, but also (apart from the 'state of trade') on the skill and success of the entrepreneur. The entrepreneur who in the same trade and with the same technical methods can make a given amount of capital go further than his marginal colleague will unquestionably derive from this skill a differential profit; but this does not alter the fact, to be discussed presently, that entrepreneurs of the same skill, in different trades and with different technical methods, will have to earn different profit margins on each turnover in order to earn the same rate of return on their capital. It is well known, e.g., that a second-hand bookseller, because his rate of turnover is very much smaller than that of a dealer in new books, will have to earn a much larger percentage on each book sold than the latter.

[21] [Apparently, this should read, "high rate of turnover" instead of "high method of turnover".—Ed.]

ful starting point for our discussion, because changes in the wage-price relationship will evidently in the first instance affect the gain made each time the
product of a given expenditure can be sold. So long as the prices of commodities remain high relatively to costs, the difference will be a source of a given
proportional profit on the capital every time the capital is turned over. And
any given rise in product prices relatively to costs will enable entrepreneurs to
make higher profits *per unit of time* from their given capital according as they
are able to turn over their capital more frequently.

In the situation of long period equilibrium which we assume to have existed
before prices rose, a situation in which the rate of return on capital will be
the same for all firms, the relation between the rate of turnover and the proportional gain on each turnover is very simple. In order to avoid the ambiguous term profit, we shall henceforth employ the following terms: (1) The per
annum net percentage return on the whole capital of a firm (or on any part
of it for which we find it necessary to compute it separately), net of 'wages of
management'[22] and of risk premium, we shall designate as the 'internal rate
of return'.[23] In the position of long term equilibrium to which we have just
referred, these internal rates of return will be the same for all firms and each
part of the capital of any firm. (2) The proportional gain on each sale, and
therefore on the capital on each turnover, expressed per cent, we shall designate as the 'profit margin'. When it is remembered that the rate of turnover
expresses the number of times total sales (or rather the costs of the products
sold in a year) exceed the value of the capital of the firm, it is clear that, if the
internal rate of return is to be uniform for all firms, profit margins will have to
vary inversely with the rates of turnover. Thus, if we call the internal rate of
return I, the rate of turnover T, and the profit margin M, the relationship will
be represented by $I = TM$ or $M = I/T$. If, e.g., the internal rate is 6 per cent,
the profit margin of a firm turning over its capital six times a year will have to
be 1 per cent, while a firm turning over its capital only once in two years will
have to earn 12 per cent on all sales, and a firm turning over its capital only
once in every ten years will have to earn a profit margin of 60 per cent.[24]

How will these internal rates of return of the different firms be affected by
a general rise of prices of, say, 5 per cent? As such a rise means a proportional
increase of the receipts from the sale of any quantity of commodities, the

[22] ['Wages of management' as remuneration for the supervision of business, from the classical
economists onwards, have been distinguished from pure profits.—Ed.]

[23] The term 'internal rate of return' is borrowed from Mr. Kenneth E. Boulding, "The Theory
of a Single Investment", *Quarterly Journal of Economics*, vol. 49, May 1935, pp. 478 et seq. [pp.
478–83]. Its German equivalent (more precisely the term 'innerer Zinssatz') has been used earlier, I believe, in discussions of the effects of credit rationing, but I cannot now recollect when
or by whom.

[24] To simplify calculations, compound interest is disregarded throughout.

cost of production of which is unchanged, it will mean a clear addition to the profit margins earned on each turnover equal to the amount of the rise. For the three firms which we have just considered by way of illustration, the first (with an annual rate of turnover $T = 6$) will find its profit margin increased from 1 to 6 per cent; the second (with $T = 1$) from 6 to 11 per cent; and the third (with $T = 1/10$) from 60 to 65 per cent. Multiplying these profit margins by the corresponding rates of turnover we obtain the new internal rates of return of $6 \times 6 = 36$ per cent for the first, $1 \times 11 = 11$ per cent for the second, and $1/10 \times 65 = 6.5$ per cent for the third firm.[25]

In the circumstances assumed these differences of the internal rates of return of the different firms cannot, in the short run, bring about any change in the capital at their disposal (beyond any reinvestment of profits)—although the effect these differences would have in the real world on the distribution of capital between the firms will be readily seen. Let us therefore turn from the differences between the effects on the return of the different firms to the differences between the effects of the same change on the rate of return on the different parts of the capital of any one firm. The concept of separate and ascertainable rates of turnover of, and rates of return on, different parts of the capital of any firm (certainly known, although probably never precisely determined in practice) depends on the possibility of ascertaining the marginal contribution to the product of the different parts of the capital; and this, in turn, depends in the familiar manner on the possibility of varying the proportions in which the different forms of capital are combined. We shall in the next section explain why we think that in the relevant sense this variability is fairly high, even in the short run. For the present we shall proceed on the assumption that this is so and that we are consequently in a position to determine the rate of turnover as well as the marginal product of, and therefore the profit margin earned on, any part of the capital of the firms.[26]

---

[25] These figures show, of course, the impact effect of the rise of prices on the profits of the different firms, and will be changed by the adjustments in the composition of their capital, which we are going to discuss.

[Indeed, if in accordance with the preceding example the rate of turnover of the second firm were $T = 1/2$ (instead of $T = 1$), the profit margin would increase from 12 per cent to 17 per cent, and the internal rate of return would be $1/2 \times 17 = 8.5$ per cent.—Ed.]

[26] Dr. Hawtrey, in his review of my *Pure Theory of Capital* (*Economic Journal*, vol. 51, June–September 1941, p. 286) attempts to draw a distinction between the measurement of the yield of any investment in terms of "net cost[-]saving capacity" and in terms of its marginal contribution to final output and asserts that while the former will be regularly possible, the latter will be possible only in exceptional cases. But these two approaches are surely merely different aspects of the same thing and neither seems to be more likely to be useful than the other: the difference between them is merely that in the first instance we assume the proportions between the different factors to be so adjusted as to leave output constant, while in the second we assume the quantity of all the resources except one to be constant and observe the effects of the change in the one on the quantity of output. Or, in other words, the first approach is in terms of movements along an equi-product curve and changes in the marginal rates of substitution between the factors, while

We can use for the purpose of this analysis the same numerical illustration which we have just used in connection with different firms: i.e., we can assume that for the major component parts of the capital of the particular firm which we now consider the rates of turnover are 6 for the sums invested in current wages, 1 for the operating parts of the machine tools, etc., and 1/10 for the heavier machinery, buildings, etc. We shall again assume that after a uniform internal rate of return of 6 per cent had been established, product prices rise by 5 per cent, and that in consequence the internal rates of return earned on the different kinds of capital rise as before to 36 per cent, 11 per cent, and 6.5 per cent, respectively. This can clearly be only a temporary position if the proportions between the forms of capital with different rates of turnover can be varied. It will now pay to redistribute current outlay so as to increase investment in capital with a high rate of turnover and to reduce investment in capital with a low rate of turnover. And this change will be continued till the expected rates of return are once more the same on all forms of investment, and current investment will continue in this new form so long as the same conditions prevail, till ultimately all the capital of the firm has been adapted to the new conditions. As a result a new and once more uniform internal rate of return for the firm will be established somewhere between the extremes of 6.5 and 36 per cent, and at this new rate of return the total yield that can be earned from the limited resources of the firm (augmented only by any reinvested extra profits) will have reached its maximum.

Although once more uniform for any one firm, the internal rates of return will however remain different for different industries and (to a lesser extent) different firms in the same industry. Where the internal rate will be fixed for any one firm will depend on the original composition of the capital of the firm and on the degree to which costs will be raised by any transition to less capitalistic methods. But, generally speaking, the rates of return will remain higher in the industries which, because of the nature of their product, need relatively less capital, and lower in the industries which need relatively more capital, although both kinds of industries will tend to change so far as possible to less capitalistic methods of production.[27]

---

the second is in terms of movements parallel to the axes of the same diagram and of the consequent changes in the marginal product. [In this argument Hayek appears to follow the device of a neoclassical production function along the lines of chapters 5 and 6 of John R. Hicks, *Value and Capital* (Oxford: Clarendon Press, 1939; 2nd ed. rev., 1946).—Ed.]

[27] It has been argued (by Mr. T. Wilson in the article quoted before ["Capital Theory and the Trade Cycle", pp. 170–71—Ed.]) that the numerical illustrations I have again employed in the preceding argument are misleading because under modern conditions the practical choice is not between capital lasting a few months and other capital lasting one or two years, but between various kinds of machinery all lasting many years, and that as between them the difference in the rates of return caused by changes in product prices is so small as to be negligible. It is perfectly true that, e.g., in our illustration, where the return on capital with a rate of turnover of 1/10 is

3.

Before going further it will be advisable to consider briefly the probable quantitative significance in the short run of the phenomenon considered. The belief has been expressed, and appears to be widely held, that, although the argument may be correct, the practical importance of the effect in question could only be small.[28] And although it would be convenient to postpone these considerations of a more concrete kind till the theoretical argument is complete, it is probably as well to forestall a feeling of impatience on the part of the reader who may feel that all this lengthy argument is wasted on a point the practical significance of which, even if proved, would be negligible.

This widely-held belief seems, however, to be based on a misconception.

---

raised from 6 to 6.5 per cent, the rate of return on capital with a rate of turnover of 1/12 would be raised from 6 to 6.417 per cent, a difference which is indeed insignificant. But this objection entirely misses the point of the argument. It is based on a confusion, due, presumably, to the verbal similarity of two different statements. It is true that the new, more durable (or more labour-saving) machine will replace a less durable or less labour-saving machine. But it does so in a sense different from that in which it can be said that the additional capital displaces other factors. The extra capital, the extra amount that is invested in the new, more expensive (because more durable or more labour-saving) machine, above what would be necessary to replace the old machine by an identical one, is not destined to replace the old machine. There would be no point in this. It is destined to save further costs, to reduce the amount of other factors required, and it is with the return on capital invested in these other factors for which the extra capital is substituted, with which its return must be compared. Slightly simplifying we can say that the extra capital invested in the machine is used to displace more *labour* by making the machine more durable, with the result that the additional investment in the machine will displace more labour than would have been true of the amounts invested in less durable machinery (because, at any positive rate of interest, it will be profitable to make machines more durable only if their life is increased more than in proportion to the extra expenditure); or that it is used to make the machine more labour-saving in which case it is even more evident that the additional capital is substituted not for other machines but for current labour. By comparing (in the illustration to which Mr. Wilson objected) the effects of a price rise on a two years' investment with that on investments for a few months, I was understating my case, and what appeared to be true on these assumptions must be *a fortiori* true of the more realistic situations where machinery that will last ten or even twenty years is introduced to save current labour.

It remains true, of course, that if we compute the rate of turnover (or the 'average period of investment') and the rate of return for the whole of the capital of a firm, the changes in either will be small. But the point is precisely that at any moment the decision has *not* to be made for the whole of the capital and that the alternative gains to be made on the sums currently to be reinvested will differ very considerably, absolutely, as well as expressed as percentages of these amounts currently to be reinvested.

[28] [For an example of such criticism cf. Gottfried Haberler, *Prosperity and Depression: A Theoretical Analysis of Cyclical Movements*, 3rd ed. (Geneva: League of Nations, 1941), p. 488: "It seems to the present writer that Professor Hayek tremendously overestimates the short-run possibility of substituting labour for capital and vice versa in response to changes in the rate of profit (or the rate of interest)."—Ed.]

Of course the proportion in which fixed capital and circulating capital (or more and less durable or labour-saving machinery) are used in production can only be changed gradually and slowly over a long period of time. But this is not the point. We are not interested in the proportions between the existing *stocks* of fixed capital and circulating capital, but in the relative rates at which firms will spend their current outlay on renewing (or adding to) the two kinds of capital assets. And here both common experience and general considerations suggest that this proportion is highly variable in the short run.

The mistaken impression is probably caused by the kind of illustrations of the transition from less to more capitalistic methods commonly used in textbooks and describing alternative positions of long-term equilibrium. The familiar instances of 'changes in the method of production' through replacement of all machines by those of another kind, of less durable by more durable, of less labour-saving by more labour-saving machinery, or of processes which are altogether shorter by processes which are altogether longer, stress an aspect which would indeed seem to be relatively unimportant in the short run. To realise how the same tendency operates no less strongly in the short run we must overcome our prepossession with the 'comparative statics' of the textbook and try to think more realistically of the concrete decision which entrepreneurs will continuously have to make.

Within limited space we can illustrate this only by selected examples. But they will, I hope, show the width of the range of variations possible in the very short run.

We have to think of entrepreneurs equipped at any given moment with a given stock of durable machinery of which only a small part needs replacement during any short period of time. If conditions had remained what they had been, they would have continued period after period to invest their earned amortisation quotas in machinery of the same kind. But they will do so merely because this would be the most profitable method of using their funds, and we must not assume that they will continue to do so after conditions have changed. Particularly when demand increases there will be any number of possible ways of increasing output other than by multiplying machinery of the kind they have been using before. And if they cannot borrow so as to bring their internal rate down to the former level, some of these will appear more profitable than those used before.

There will be mainly two kinds of changes which will now appear advantageous: an entrepreneur may use his existing machinery more intensively (i.e., with more labour)—employing for this purpose part of the funds which would have otherwise been invested to replace the machinery by new machines of the same kind—or he may replace those machines that wear out by a larger number of cheaper ones. Both of these methods will probably be resorted to, although the first is probably the more important one.

The obvious methods of quickly increasing output as commodity prices rise is to work overtime, to introduce double or treble shifts, to provide extra assistance to relieve the workers on the existing machines from ancillary operations, etc. This will normally raise labour costs per unit of output and this fact will have prevented these devices from being used before prices had risen. But if the adoption of any of these methods increases marginal labour cost per unit of output by, say, 4 per cent,[29] this would, with a 5 per cent rise in prices, still leave an extra profit of 1 per cent which, with a rate of turnover of 6, would make the internal rate of return on this form of investment still 12 per cent compared with the 6.5 per cent on the machine with a rate of turnover of 1/10. This more expensive method of production will therefore now become the one through which, with the limited resources at the disposal of the entrepreneur, the largest profits can be realised; and the labour co-operating with the machinery will be increased till the fall of the return on funds invested in more labour and the rise of returns on funds invested in machines make the two rates of return once more equal at an intermediate figure.

The kinds of changes in the machinery used which have to be taken into account even in the short run will be equally numerous and will also all have the effect of raising marginal costs. There will, in the first instance, be the possibility of less perfect maintenance and attention, makeshift instead of thorough repairs, shorter or fewer periods of laying off for inspection and overhaul, which will reduce the efficiency and shorten the life of the existing machinery but may well be worth while if current output can thus be increased. There will be, secondly, the possibility of outright non-renewal, not, of course, of essential parts of the equipment, but of the many auxiliary labour-saving devices such as automatic feeders and other gadgets performing operations which can also be done by hand. Thirdly, there will be the possibility of using obsolete or second-hand machines instead of new ones. Many older factories have a certain amount of such old machinery for temporary use to meet peak-time demands or in an emergency, for which it would not pay to keep a new machine in reserve. And there exists in many branches a supply of second-hand machinery which can be used in the same way. Fourthly, and lastly, there will be the possibility of replacing those machines that wear out by new but cheaper and less efficient ones. So long as the internal rate of return of any firm remains above what it has been before, it may well be profitable to buy two less efficient machines at the price of one more efficient one, if the two less efficient machines enable the firm, though with the co-operation of much more labour, to increase output more than with the more efficient one.

---

[29] If it be objected that the increase of costs which we assumed to be caused by the adoption of overtime or similar devices is improbably small, this would merely mean that the very small rise of prices of five per cent, which we have assumed, would not have this particular effect and that it would require a rise of, say, 20 or 25 per cent, to bring it about.

If we consider the effect of all these possible changes, *not* on the proportion in which the stock of capital of any firm is composed of different parts, but on the *rates* at which its current outlay is *spent* on different kinds of resources, or on the *proportion* in which total outlay is *distributed* between fixed and circulating capital, it seems to be clear that in consequence of a general change in commodity prices, very large changes[30] in the latter magnitudes may be brought about in a comparatively short time. In extreme cases it may even be profitable for entrepreneurs temporarily to discontinue all demand for machinery and yet for a considerable period greatly to increase output. But while this extreme result may not be probable, it does not seem unlikely that the demand for certain kinds of new equipment will be absolutely reduced. This would seem to be likely particularly where, as is true in the case of buildings and most heavy machinery, the equipment has to be made to order and large sums will have to be locked up in it by the buyer during the period of production without bringing any current yield; the same would seem to be true wherever a gradual transition to some new (e.g., more labour-saving) but more expensive kind of machinery has been under way, which will now be stopped; and generally wherever the change in the methods of production adopted will involve a change from equipment made by one group of people to that made by another group of people.[31] In so far as any labour is specific to the production of the kind of equipment, the demand for which now decreases or ceases entirely, the consequence of the rise in final demand will thus be unemployment in the capital goods industries.

4.

We have now to introduce the possibility of borrowing money at rates of interest determined by the market and not necessarily changed in response to an increase in the demand for funds. In the present section we shall consider how far this modifies the conclusions so far arrived at if we make assumptions which in the most important respects approximately correspond to conditions in the real world and which will therefore enable us to judge what the practi-

---

[30] [The reprinted version of 1949 deletes the word "very".—Ed.]

[31] It seems that the term 'structure of production', which I introduced in *Prices and Production* to describe the distribution of *current* labour between the different 'stages of production' has sometimes been interpreted in a materialistic sense which supported the misunderstanding that the 'changes in the methods of production' I was discussing implied an instantaneous change in the machines actually used. But the 'structure of production', in the sense in which I used the term, can, of course, change fundamentally without any change in the equipment actually used; this latter change will come about only gradually as a consequence of the change in the former; and the most radical change of this sort would indeed be the entire cessation of the production of machines, although the people might yet go on for a long time using the same machines in the production of consumers' goods.

cal significance of our conclusions is likely to be. The theoretically very interesting but practically irrelevant case of a 'perfectly elastic supply of credit' will be deferred till the next section.

The sharp distinction between the two cases and the order of treatment is indicated by the frequent but misleading application to this problem of the category of 'perfect competition'; this concept is quite inappropriate to it, simply because successive (additional) loans to the same borrower will never represent the 'same commodity' in the sense in which the term is used in the theory of competition. While in a commodity market 'perfect competition' means that any single buyer can buy at the given market price any quantity he likes, it would, of course, be absurd to assume that even in the most perfectly competitive money market every borrower (or, for that matter, any borrower) can at the given rate of interest borrow any amount he likes. This is precluded by the fact that in given circumstances the security a borrower has to offer is not as good for a large amount as for a small one. In consequence, every prospective borrower will have to face an upward sloping supply curve of credit—or, rather, not a continuous supply curve, but an upward stepped 'curve', showing that the rate of interest, while constant within certain limits, will go up by distinct steps whenever one of the limits is reached up to which he can borrow at a given rate.

The most important, though not the sole, factor limiting the borrowing capacity of a firm at any given rate of interest will be the size of the capital owned by it. Bankers, as a rule, will not be willing to lend to any one firm more than a given proportion of its own capital and take very good care that no firm borrows at the same time from more than one bank; and beyond this limit the firm will be able to obtain funds only at a higher rate of interest, or, what comes to the same thing, on more onerous conditions of some other kind. This limitation of the amount of funds any firm can raise to increase its output will be further strengthened where banks provide loans only for investment in circulating capital and effectively refuse to provide funds for the investment in fixed capital. The general fact we have to remember in this connection is that, in the existing institutional framework, lending (in the strict sense of the word), and particularly short-term lending, will secure mobility of capital only to a limited extent, and that, in a world where risk is ever present, it will by itself not be sufficient to bring about an equalisation of the rates of return on capital invested in different firms or completely to adjust these rates to a given market rate of interest. For this, in addition to lending, transfers of capital by way of full participation in the risk of the business, i.e., changes in the share capital or what we may quite generally describe as the 'own capital'[32] (as distinguished from the borrowed capital) of the firms will be necessary. But this latter process is necessarily much slower than the provi-

---

[32] [That is, 'equity capital'.—Ed.]

sion of additional bank loans, and it will therefore frequently be true that in the short run most firms will not be able to raise as much capital as they could profitably use, or that they will be able to do so only at rates much higher than the 'market rate'.

This is not to say that the maximum a firm will be able to borrow at a given rate of interest will be rigidly fixed in proportion to its own capital. The director of a firm who can convince his bank manager that he has an exceptional opportunity of making large profits on additional capital and thus can provide a large margin of safety in case his optimism should prove not to be quite justified, will be able to borrow proportionally more than another. And in general when prospects are good all firms may be able to borrow more in proportion to their own capital than when prospects are poor.[33] The stepped supply 'curves' of credit which all firms face will be shifted to the right as general prospects get better (and to the left when prospects get worse) and such sideways shifts of the supply curves will frequently act, and often be deliberately used, in exactly the same way as an outright change in the rate of interest (i.e., as a raising or lowering of the whole curve).

But although any general increase in expected profits is likely to increase the amounts firms can borrow, it will in many instances increase the amounts they would like to borrow at the current rates of interest still more and thus bring firms up to the limit beyond which they can raise capital only at higher costs. Though there will be, at the ruling rate of interest, an unsatisfied demand, this demand will not be 'effective' demand, because it will not fall within the categories to which the ruling rates apply and these rates will therefore remain unchanged. The situation is similar to that caused by credit rationing, although it will arise, without the intervention of authority or a monopolist, merely as a result of the views the banks hold about the 'credit-worthiness' of the borrowers.

There is no need to explain at any length that whenever the amounts people would like to borrow at the current rate of interest are larger than the amounts they can obtain at that rate, it will be these *amounts* and not the ruling market rate which will determine the internal rates of return of the different firms. As in the situation discussed in the last section these internal rates will be different for different firms according to the circumstances then enumerated (to which we must now add the limitations on the borrowing facilities of any particular firm), and the investment of each firm will be governed by

---

[33] It should be noted that the limit thus imposed on the borrowing capacity of the firms will be a sliding limit, fixed only in the short run, but rising gradually as, in consequence of each addition to the volume of credits already granted, incomes and final demand and thereby the prospects of profits rise. In other words, it will limit merely the rate of expansion of credit, but may not prevent a continuous, progressive and (if for the purpose of estimating the security of the borrower the value of his assets is written up with rising prices) even limitless expansion of credit.

its own internal rate, which may be very much higher than the market rate, which may not have changed at all. And the rise in internal rates would lead to a general change to less capitalistic methods of production, different in extent according as the internal rate has changed in the different firms.

There remains, however, the question whether to the extent that the firms are able to procure additional credits this will reduce the degree to which their internal rates will rise, and therefore the degree to which they will change to less capitalistic methods of production, compared with the case where no additional credit at all was available. The problem which arises here is the same as that which we intend to consider in its more general form in the next section, since, if our proposition holds true even when the supply of credit is completely elastic, it must apply still more in the present case. We can, therefore, immediately proceed to this 'stronger' case.

5.

The assumption that the supply of credit at a given rate of interest is perfectly elastic is not only unrealistic but, when we contemplate its implications, perfectly fantastic; and it makes the analysis rather complicated. But, as it brings us face to face with a fundamental theoretical problem, this is well worth undertaking. It raises in its purest form the question of the relationship between the monetary and the real factors affecting the relative profitability of different methods of production.

The contention that if the supply of credit is perfectly elastic it must be the money rate of interest which will determine which forms of investment are most profitable may be based on either of two assertions which ought to be clearly distinguished: it may be asserted that in this case the cost price relations (or the relation between wages and commodity prices) must necessarily be so adjusted by either a change in wages or a change in commodity prices as to make the difference correspond to the money rate of interest; or it may be asserted that even when this does not happen and wages remain, e.g., too low relatively to commodity prices, it will still be the money rate of interest and not the cost price relationship that will govern the form of investment.

With regard to both these arguments, but particularly with regard to the first, it is important to remember that the situation which we consider is eminently *not* one of equilibrium but one in which the causes of continuous and cumulative change are inherent. It is indeed the classical instance of a cumulative process[34] with which we are dealing: the perfectly elastic supply of credit

---

[34] [The notion of the 'cumulative process' derives from Wicksell's analysis of the 'indirect mechanism' that links money and prices, such that a market rate of interest below the natural

at a rate of interest lower than the internal rate of all or most of the firms will be the cause of continuous changes of prices and money incomes where each change makes further changes necessary. There is no point in saying with respect to such a situation that 'in equilibrium there must' exist such and such a relationship, because it necessarily follows from the assumptions that the relationship between at least some prices must be out of equilibrium. This is important particularly with reference to the two propositions: first, that prices must be equal to marginal costs, and, second, that the prices of the factors must be equal to the expected price of their marginal product discounted at the rate of interest at which credit can be freely obtained. All we need to say with respect to the first proposition is that, except in a very special and for our purpose irrelevant sense,[35] it is just not true in the very short run, although a dogmatic belief that prices must always be equal to marginal costs in the relevant sense is probably responsible for a great many confusions in this field. The second proposition is the one with which we are here more directly concerned.

The belief that, if the supply of money at a given rate of interest is perfectly elastic while investment demand is inelastic,[36] the former will uniquely determine the rate of return at which supply and demand will be equal, is derived by analogy from the general rule that if either the quantity demanded or the quantity supplied of anything is completely elastic at a given price, it follows necessarily that this will be the price. But while this statement is true enough when we discuss demand and supply in 'real' terms, it neglects an essential difference of the present case where the 'price' in question is the relationship between the prices of two groups of goods (labour and commodities), while the supply which is infinitely elastic is not that of one of the two goods but merely of the money that is in the first instance to be spent on one of the two goods; it neglects that any increase of money expenditure on the one kind of good is bound to cause an increase of money expenditure on the other kind of good.

When it was said before that we are dealing with a position of disequilibrium, this meant precisely that we had to deal with two sets of forces tending

---

(or equilibrium) rate will bring about price inflation. Cf., e.g., his *Interest and Prices* (London: Macmillan, 1936; reprinted, New York: Kelley, 1965, and Auburn, AL: Ludwig von Mises Institute, 2007), the translation of *Geldzins und Güterpreise* (Jena: Fischer, 1898; reprinted, Aalen: Scientia, 1968).—Ed.]

[35] The proposition can be made true in the shortest of short runs if we include in marginal costs all costs (including the personal effort of the entrepreneur) of increasing output during the short period in question—i.e., if we include in marginal costs the costs of increasing output at a certain rate. But if we do so, marginal costs are no longer uniquely correlated with the volume of output and we have to consider separate marginal cost curves for each rate at which output is increased, becoming steeper as we assume a faster rate of increase till, for a strictly instantaneous increase of output, the marginal cost curve becomes perpendicular.

[36] [Presumably, what Hayek means is "while investment demand is not perfectly elastic".—Ed.]

to fix the same price (or rather the same relationship between two groups of prices) at different figures. On the one hand we have a given output of consumers' goods (only slowly variable) and a given propensity of the people to spend a certain proportion of their income on consumers' goods, which together would for each volume of employment (and therefore of total income) determine a definite ratio between the prices of commodities and the prices of all factors; and, on the other hand, we have an infinitely elastic supply of money which tends to determine the prices of factors in a certain fixed relation to the prices of the products which is different from that determined by the first set of factors.

It is not to be denied, of course, that through changes in the money stream the relation between the prices of goods as determined by the real factors can be very considerably modified. The problem is merely whether there is no limit to the extent to which, and the period of time for which, the price structure as determined by the 'real' factors can be thus distorted, or whether the fact that the extra money which has first raised one group of prices will soon work round to affect the other group of prices in the same direction does not set a limit to the possible degree of distortion. The question is rather similar to that whether by pouring a liquid fast enough into one side of a vessel we can raise the level at that side above that of the rest to any extent we desire. How far we shall be able to raise the level of one part above that of the rest will clearly depend on how fluid or viscid the liquid is: we shall be able to raise it more if the liquid is syrup or glue than when it is water. But in no case shall we be at liberty to raise the surface in one part of the vessel above the rest to any extent we like.

Just as the viscosity of the liquid determines the extent to which any part of its surface can be raised above the rest, so the speed at which an increase of incomes leads to an increase in the demand for consumers' goods limits the extent to which by spending more money on the factors of production we can raise their prices relatively to those of the products.[37] The problem arises most sharply when we assume that the money rate is arbitrarily lowered to a very low figure in a new country with little capital and a very high 'marginal efficiency of capital'. If the proposition we are considering were true at all, it would have to hold in this case also, i.e., the availability of an unlimited

---

[37] The economic equilibrium differs, of course, from our hydrostatic simile by the fact that the equilibrium position between the prices is not constant but will be affected by changes in the real quantities of goods available. These real changes, however, will only strengthen the tendency, because they will necessarily work in a direction opposite from the monetary factors: in our case their effect will be to increase the proportion of people engaged in producing things other than consumers' goods to the available output of consumers' goods and thus to increase the difference between wages and commodity prices which will establish itself as soon as the flow of new money ceases.

quantity of money at the low rate of interest would bring it about that wages would be driven up to the discounted value—not merely of the present marginal product of labour, but of the marginal product[38] labour could be expected to produce after the machinery had been installed which it would be profitable to install at the low rate of interest. The aggregate value of the services of labour at that real wage might be very considerably larger than the total current output of consumers' goods and certainly very much larger than the whole current output of labour. The effect of this must be that the demand for consumers' goods and their prices would rise accordingly. If this rise of prices stimulated entrepreneurs to borrow and invest still more, this would only make prices rise still further, and the faster entrepreneurs expected prices to rise, the more they would necessarily speed up this price rise beyond their expectations. Although they might succeed at times in driving wages up to the discounted value of the *expected* price of the marginal product of labour, they could not possibly, whatever their effort, actually raise real wages to the figure corresponding to the low rate of interest, because the stuff to provide this real income would just not be there.

In the situation to which we have to apply these considerations, such as will exist in a modern society in the late stages of a boom, the position will be different only in degree. It still remains true that entrepreneurs, by offering higher money wages, cannot effectively raise real wages to the level which would correspond to the low money rate of interest, because the more they raise money wages, the more the prices of commodities will rise.[39] And in this case, too, the limiting factor is simply that the consumers' goods are not there and that, so long as all investment takes highly capitalistic forms, every increase in employment adds only a fraction of its value to the output of consumers' goods. This brings us to the second hard fact which dominates the situation we are considering: that in this situation there will not be labour enough available to increase at the same time the current output of consum-

---

[38] [The word "which" was added after "marginal product" in the 1949 reprint.—Ed.]

[39] This is, of course, not to say that the share of labour as a whole in the real income of society is rigidly fixed. An increase in the sum of money wages will enable labour to encroach on the real income of the rentier class. But the rise in money wages necessary to give an increased number of people the same real income per head at the expense of the people with fixed money incomes would have to be very large indeed—so large that it is not likely to be offered by entrepreneurs till they have come to expect a galloping inflation. In other words, we do, of course, not wish to deny that there will be some forced saving largely at the expense of the rentier class; what we deny is merely that it is likely that by forced saving it will be possible to give an ever increasing number of men employed in producing investment goods a constant wage in terms of consumers' goods. Perhaps it should also be added that the argument of the text does *not* imply that *all* the additional money income paid out in wages is promptly spent on consumers' goods, but only that this is true of a substantial part of it. See on this "Profits, Interest and Investment", pp. 52 et seq. [this volume, pp. 243–45—Ed.].

ers' goods and to push investment to the limit indicated by the rate of interest. So long as unused reserves of labour are available there is, as we shall presently see, indeed no reason why the entrepreneurs should not use the unlimited funds to do both: to increase the output of consumption goods for the near future by the expensive but quick methods, and provide for cheaper production by investing on a large scale. And this is the reason why in the early stage of a boom the money rate of interest will control the situation. But although this would mean that in these circumstances the low rate of interest was effective so far as the volume of investment was concerned, it would still not mean that once consumers' goods prices began to rise, real wages could be maintained by proportional adjustments in the money wages.

6.

That in the circumstances considered it will sooner or later become inevitable that real wages should fall, and investment expenditure be reduced, will be evident if we consider for a moment the paradoxical results that would follow if things worked as appears to be assumed by the contrary view. The increase in the prices of commodities, with unlimited amounts of money available at a fixed rate of interest, would lead to an increase of investment expenditure and of real investment, which, since no reserves of labour are available, could take place only at the expense of the output of consumers' goods in the near future. The consequent increase of money incomes and of final demand, coupled with the decrease in the output of consumers' goods, would cause a further rise in their prices relatively to wages. This further rise in the prices of consumers' goods would, according to that view, bring about a further increase of investment at the expense of the output of consumers' goods, and so on, presumably till there are no people left producing consumers' goods and everybody is engaged in providing machinery destined to produce consumers' goods in some distant future when the men will all have died of starvation in the interval. While some tendency in this direction probably exists during the earlier part of a boom, it hardly needs any superstitious belief in the self-righting forces of the economic system to suspect that, some time before that extreme result is produced, counter-forces will operate to check such a development. This brings us to the second version of the argument according to which it must be the money rate of interest which rules the roost.

This version, which admits that wages may remain relatively too low compared with the rate of interest, but insists that in spite of this, if the supply of money is perfectly elastic, it will be the rate of interest and not the level of wages which will govern the form of investment, is represented mainly by Mr.

N. Kaldor and Mr. T. Wilson.[40] These two writers, however, as we shall try to show, so much simplify their task that they do not prove what they mean to demonstrate. All they do prove, in a quite unnecessarily elaborate manner, is that, so long as an unlimited amount of money can be obtained at the given rate of interest, it will depend solely on the rate of interest which method will bring the highest *current* profit above *current* costs *after* the equipment appropriate to that method has been procured. This is no more than another version of the truism[41] which we have emphasised from the beginning that, so long as the rate of interest remains constant, a change in real wages cannot alter the relative costs of the different methods of production. What Mr. Kaldor and Mr. Wilson completely disregard is that in comparing the profits obtained from producing with different methods they are comparing methods employing different amounts of capital without counting in any way the cost of creating the extra real capital required for the one of the two methods. They do this by omitting to give any attention to what will happen during the period of transition before the new equipment is available. Whether this equipment will be ever available will depend, however, precisely on what happens during this interval. The problem is not answered by the statement that, if we adopt a certain course, the excess of current receipts over current outlay will be largest from a certain future date onwards, if we are not also told what happens between now and that future date. In choosing between the two alternative methods we cannot decide merely on the basis of what the position would be after *some* new long term equilibrium has been established, but we must also consider what will happen between now and then, because it will depend on this *which* long term equilibrium will be established. What the procedure of Mr. Kaldor and Mr. Wilson amounts to is to leave out from their data the real factors which determine the supply of capital, and to assume that the quantity of capital will in the long run necessarily adjust itself so as to bring its 'marginal efficiency' to the level of a rate of interest determined solely by monetary factors.

Speaking more concretely, Mr. Kaldor and Mr. Wilson assume that, if only the funds are available, it will, in the circumstances assumed, necessarily be most profitable to meet an increased demand for the product by increasing equipment in proportion to the increase in the amount of the product that can be sold at any given price,[42] although in this way it will as a rule be pos-

[40] Kaldor, "Capital Intensity and the Trade Cycle", and Wilson, "Capital Theory and the Trade Cycle".

[41] [A truism is a self-evident truth.—Ed.]

[42] [This accords with the usual formulation of the 'accelerator principle', which relates the *increase* in consumption demand to the (desired) *increase* in equipment and thus to the *level* of (desired) investment.—Ed.]

sible to catch up with increased demand only after some considerable interval. Only if (and to the extent that) we can assume the extra equipment needed to be waiting in the shops ready to be bought and instantaneously to be installed would no such interval occur. This assumption (which amounts to presupposing that all the real capital required for an expansion is already in existence) is evidently one which might be true for any one firm, but which will not be true when all firms are simultaneously in the same position. In the situation with which we are concerned the additional equipment and still more the output produced by it will be available only after considerable delay. And in the interval till this output is available profits which might have been made by quicker methods will be lost and ought to be counted as part of the cost of the production for the more distant future.

To this it will no doubt be answered that there is no reason why the entrepreneurs should not do both: provide for the output in the near future by the quick but expensive methods *and* provide for the more distant future by ordering more machinery. But this brings us up to the fundamental issue whether the amount of real resources, and particularly of labour, will be sufficient to make both possible at the same time. Or, in other words, the question arises which it is now fashionable to disregard in discussion of these problems, whether an unlimited supply of funds secures an equally unlimited supply of real resources. We have already seen that, in the kind of situation with which we are concerned, this is not likely to be the case.

It is instructive, however, to examine a little more closely how some economists manage to gloss over this difficulty and thereby apparently succeed in eliminating the given supply of capital from the relevant data of the problem. Mr. Kaldor's treatment of the question in the article referred to is in this respect most illuminating. He explicitly claims to deal with all the cases where the output of individual firms is limited by "falling demand curves for the products *and/or rising supply curves for its factors*"[43] as the only possible alternative to a limitation by an inelastic supply of credit.[44] But when he comes to discuss the case he assumes, and finally even introduces in a footnote, the explicit assumption that "*the elasticity of supply of factors, to the individual firm, is infinite*".[45]

---

[43] Kaldor, "Capital Intensity and the Trade Cycle", p. 46 [reprinted, p. 127—Ed.] (Our italics.)

[44] [Again, this should read, consistently, "an imperfectly elastic supply of credit.—Ed.]

[45] Ibid., p. 50n.4 [reprinted, ibid., p. 131n.2. The italics are Hayek's.—Ed.]. The assumption is implied in the whole discussion on this and the preceding page, since only if unlimited amounts of labour are available at the given price is the "supply curve of capital horizontal" in the real sense in which the term capital is there used. [Responding to this criticism, Kaldor ("Professor Hayek and the Concertina-Effect", *Economica*, n.s., vol. 9, November 1942, reprinted in this volume, p. 307n.70) points out that an infinite elasticity of supply of factors to the individual firms is just the defining assumption of perfect competition and does in no way preclude a less than infinite elasticity of supply of factors at the aggregate, economy-wide level.—Ed.]

But although he has thus in fact confined his proof to only part of the group of cases for which he has originally undertaken to provide it, he proceeds as if he had proved it for all and continues to treat his original alternative (inelastic supply of credit *or* falling demand curves for the product and/or rising supply curves for the factors) as corresponding to the distinction between situations where either only the rate of wages or only the rate of interest determines the methods of production that will be profitable.

Mr. Kaldor's omission to face the effects of limitation in the supply of labour is so significant because it is through the rise in the supply price of labour that the shortage of real resources available for investment (caused by the competing demand of the producers of consumers' goods) makes itself felt. His conclusion follows solely from the assumption that, and is true only if, the elasticity of the supply of labour (and other factors) is infinite. When this is true there is indeed no reason why entrepreneurs should not succeed in using the unlimited money funds to increase output quickly by costly methods and at the same time to make arrangements for a more economical production of a larger output at a later date. So long as unused reserves of labour are available at an unchanged price, unlimited funds mean unlimited control over resources. But this is not the condition which is relevant for the position of full employment that will prevail near the top of a boom.

We shall see the problem involved more clearly if for a moment we assume that each firm represents a completely integrated process of production, that is, that not only the production of the final commodity and of all the various raw materials, etc., used, but also that of all machinery required for the production of that output is produced within the firm. In the circumstances we are considering each of these integrated firms would be able to attract additional labour only by offering higher wages; and although the relatively less capitalistic industries might find it profitable to increase their labour in this way at the expense of the more capitalistic industries, this will, if there are no unemployed available, not be possible for all firms or for industries or firms of average 'capital intensity'.

For each of these firms, which for our purpose may serve as representatives of a general trend, the problem will therefore be how to distribute its given labour force between the production of commodities and the production of machinery. The way to maximise the excess of current receipts over current outlay for all periods after the change had been completed would be temporarily to transfer labour from the production of commodities to the production of machinery. This would involve a reduction of the current output of commodities, and therefore of current profits, not only below what they would be if the past volume of output had been maintained, but still more below the level which could be achieved if current output were increased, by adopting quick and more costly methods till marginal costs just equalled price. These profits, which would have to be forgone if the additional machinery is to be provided, would have to be regarded as costs of, and would therefore have to be offset against, the larger profits which in consequence could be continuously earned from some future date onwards. It is this item which represents the costs of the extra waiting which the more capitalistic methods involve and which nowhere enters the calculations of Mr. Kaldor and Mr. Wilson. And since these profits which will be earned during this interval are, as we have seen, likely to be very considerable, it is more than likely that they will turn the scales against the more capitalistic process. In other words: profits will be higher on the method with the higher rate of turnover, *not* because they would accrue at a higher rate *after* the new equilibrium envisaged by Mr. Kaldor had been established (which they would not do), but because the profits on the less capitalistic method will *begin to accrue earlier* than those on the more capitalistic method. And it is the profits from now onwards, not merely profits after the additional equipment has been created, which must be considered in deciding whether that additional equipment is to be created at all. It is for this reason that our integrated firms, if their internal rates of return only rise high enough, will certainly not transfer labour from the production of commodities to the production of machinery, but, on the contrary, will transfer labour from the production of machinery to the production of commodities. And this change will not be merely temporary, but will evidently have to be maintained so long as the conditions continue which made it appear profitable in the first instance, i.e., so long as the prices of consumers' goods remain high relatively to wages.

Before leaving the integrated firms it is worth while to consider a little more closely exactly what will happen in their machine shops. These machine shops will have to give up some of their labour that can also be used indirectly to produce consumers' goods. And they will have to turn to the production of less elaborate, less costly machinery. Both of these changes will have the effect of making superfluous other kinds of labour which are specific to the production of the more elaborate kind of machinery or to jobs (such as the extraction of certain raw materials used in the production of machinery) which are wanted in a rigid quantitative proportion to the total output of machinery. In other words, the result of the shortage of the more generally employable labour will be unemployment of certain particular kinds of labour—that which is highly specific to the production of some kinds of machinery.

While it seems fairly evident that the results must be the same if we abandon the assumption of complete integration of the different industries, I must admit that I find it difficult to visualise precisely how it will be brought about. The physical conditions of the problem are of course the same: it will still be true that there will not be enough labour available at the same time to increase the output of consumers' goods quickly and to provide more machinery to produce a still larger output by more efficient methods at a later date. And it will also still be true that if entrepreneurs decide for the costlier but speedier methods this will bring them the larger profits. The problem is what will enable them to foresee this result; because, so long as they believe that at the ruling price they will be able both to get the labour to increase the output immediately and to get the manufacturers of machines to produce machines for them, it will appear profitable to try and do both; the individual entrepreneur will no longer be directly faced with the problem of using the same labour either to produce more commodities or to produce more machinery; and it will be only when he and all the other entrepreneurs who are in the same position try to do so that they will find out that it cannot be done.

The answer, I think, is to be sought *firstly* in the fact that the provision for the near future will necessarily have the first attention of the entrepreneur, because if the profits which might be made in the near future are not obtained, they (and perhaps a certain amount of permanent business) will be lost for good to a competitor, while delay in obtaining the more efficient machinery will affect the volume of output less and merely postpone the date when its costs will be lower. Closely connected with this will be the effect of the increasing uncertainty concerning the more distant future. Although the entrepreneur may expect the higher prices to continue indefinitely, he will be less certain that this will be so in the more distant future than in the near future. And on the principle of 'making hay while the sun shines', provision for the profits to be made in the near future will take the precedence.

Secondly, there is the fact that, since *in the short run* the more capitalistic methods will require *more* labour for any given increase of output than the less capitalistic methods, the rising supply price of labour will make itself felt more with the former than with the latter, i.e., the attempt to procure the machinery necessary for a given increase of output will meet with a rise in the price of the machinery comparatively greater than the rise in wages which would be caused by employing the number of men required to produce the same amount by less capitalistic methods.

Thirdly, there is the point that in so far as the producers of commodities increase their output in the first instance, not without any additional machinery but by the use of a cheaper kind of machinery, the need for the more elaborate machinery will arise only after the machinery provisionally installed wears out, and that therefore the demand for the more elaborate kind of machinery may for a time cease completely.

Finally, and perhaps most important, there will be the fact that so long as the producers of commodities do not succeed in actually increasing output quickly to the extent necessary to bring marginal returns down to a level they can expect to prevail in the long run, they will be uncertain which of the various elements in the picture will change so as to create a new equilibrium position. In other words, so long as profits on the quick methods do not actually fall and further endeavour appears to be needed to gather all the high profits that can be made immediately, the more elaborate preparations for future profits at a lower rate (though higher in the aggregate) and involving greater risk will not appear very attractive. But so long as people try to do both, to increase output quickly and to order more machinery, incomes and final demand will continue to run ahead of the expectations of the producers of consumers' goods. It will be only after investment has been considerably reduced that the cost of the expensive methods will catch up with prices and that thus the more capitalistic methods will once more appear attractive.

I am fully aware that all this is not very satisfactory and that a clearer picture of the precise process by which competition brings about this result would be very desirable. But I am not sure whether this is possible. We are dealing with a position of disequilibrium in which developments depend on the precise order in which the various changes follow each other in time and where the situation at any moment is likely to be, as we have learnt to say,[46] 'confused'. We cannot say precisely when entrepreneurs will abandon the self-defeating attempts at the same time to build up elaborate equipment and to increase production quickly. All we can say is that the longer the effect with which we are concerned is delayed, the stronger must become the forces tending to bring it about (i.e., the longer increases in final demand are allowed to bring about proportionally larger increases in investment, the greater must become the rise of prices of final goods relatively to costs), and that therefore they are bound sooner or later to become the dominating element in the picture.

7.

Any attempt to discover from the available statistical information whether the Ricardo Effect does in fact operate as these considerations suggest encounters considerable difficulties. We can do no more here than show what are these difficulties of an attempt at verification and why the evidence so far available does not seem to allow any definite conclusions.

In the first instance it must be pointed out that, although the phrase 'real wages' is sometimes used in this connection, the relation between wages and product prices with which we are concerned has no close connection with 'real wages' in the sense in which this term is commonly used. While in most contexts when real wages are discussed what is meant is the relation between wages as received by the worker and the prices of the commodities on which he spends these wages, we are concerned with the costs of labour to the entrepre-

---

[46] [The 1949 edition explicates, "as we have learnt to say during the war".—Ed.]

neur and their relation to the prices of the products he produces. We shall only just mention that even the wages paid to the workers and the cost of labour to the entrepreneur may sometimes move differently.[47] The more important difference is, however, that between the prices of the goods on which the workers spend their wages and the prices of the goods in the production of which the labour is used. The following are the main sources of this difference:

1. While the 'cost of living' is affected largely by the prices of agricultural products, it is for our purpose mainly the prices of manufactured articles that are of importance. More generally, the importance for our purpose of the change in price of any particular product varies with the relative amount of capital used in its production (which is relatively low in agriculture and relatively high in manufacture). The significance of this will be seen when it is remembered that for our purposes a mere shift in demand from articles requiring comparatively little capital in their production to articles requiring a great deal would have the same effect as an increase in total demand. Any statistical investigation would probably do well to confine itself in the first instance to the effect of changes in the relation between the prices of the product and wages in any given industry on investment in that industry. In so far as a more general investigation is attempted, prices ought probably to be weighted according to the proportional amount of capital used in the production of the different goods. And where we have to deal with an 'open system', as will regularly be the case in statistical investigations, we shall have further to distinguish between prices of home produced and of imported commodities.

2. While from the 'cost of living' point of view it will be retail prices that will be relevant, for our purpose it will be prices received by the manufacturers that will count; and it is in general true that, for reasons into which we need not go here, the latter (or at least wholesale prices) fluctuate more than retail prices.

3. While from the 'cost of living' point of view it is the relation between wages and the price of a fixed quantity of commodities which is relevant, we are here concerned with the relations between the costs of labour and the marginal product of that labour. This marginal product, however, is itself not a constant but a variable and either may vary as a consequence of the effect with which we are concerned or may by its change become the cause of this effect. In other words, changes in the marginal product may appear either as dependent variables, when they are the consequence of a change in the proportional combination of capital and labour, or as independent variables,

---

[47] In consequence of changes in taxation, social insurance charges, and legislative or trade union regulations affecting conditions of work. I remember having once seen detailed comparative statistics of the 'real wages' of linotype operators in Sweden and Austria, which seemed to show conclusively that while the purchasing power of the wages to the workers was much lower in Austria, they meant a much larger real cost of labour to the manufacturer.

when they are brought about by changes in the 'data', particularly by changes in technological knowledge. Technological change, at least when it is rapid and general, may here cause serious difficulties.

So long as technological knowledge remains constant the relations between the cost of labour and the price of its product which are relevant for our purpose will generally be the same as the relations between the costs of a fixed amount of labour and the price of a fixed amount of the product—although when we have to deal with an 'open' system changes in the price of an important raw material may disturb even this simple relationship. But once changes in technical knowledge have to be taken into account, the problem becomes very much more complex. It is evident, to take an extreme case, that if an advance in knowledge enabled us to produce with exactly the same machinery and other outlay 20 per cent more than before, the immediate effect would be very similar to that of a rise in the price of the product. So long as such a change occurs in isolation, there is no special difficulty about it. But when it is combined with price changes, a problem arises for which it is difficult to see a practicable solution. To judge the significance of any price change occurring together with technological change we should have to know which price relationship now 'corresponds' to the price relationship which existed before, i.e., which relation between the cost of labour and the price of the product will now make investment no more and no less attractive than the price relationship which existed before the technological change. At the moment I have no solution of this difficulty to offer.

TEN

PROFESSOR HAYEK AND THE
CONCERTINA-EFFECT[1]
by Nicholas Kaldor

1.

It was more than ten years ago that Professor Hayek first fascinated the academic world of economists by a new theory of industrial fluctuations which in theoretical conception, and perhaps even more in its practical implications, was diametrically opposed to the current trend of monetary thought. The term 'fascination', though perhaps slightly unacademic, aptly describes the effect of the *first impact* of Professor Hayek's ideas on economists trained in the Anglo-Saxon tradition (and the present writer has no wish to conceal that he was among the fascinees) to whom it suggested aspects of the nature of capitalistic production they were never taught to think of. It suggested those 'deep-seated underlying maladjustments'[2] in the structure of capitalist production, which may have been ultimately caused by, but which could not be adequately described in terms of, those purely monetary processes with which most of the then current speculation was concerned. In comparison with Professor Hayek's 'triangles', 'distorted price-margins', and unduly-elongated production periods, the prevailing concern with price-levels, and with the banks doing this or that, must have appeared facile and superficial.

This was the first impact. On second thoughts the theory was by no means so intellectually satisfying as it appeared at first. There were admitted gaps here and there in the first published account which was merely intended as rudimentary,[3] and when one attempted to fill these gaps, they became larger, instead of smaller, and new and unsuspected gaps appeared—until one was

---

[1] [First published in *Economica*, n.s., vol. 9, November 1942, pp. 359–82, a slightly revised version reprinted as chapter 7 of Nicholas Kaldor, *Essays on Economic Stability and Growth*, vol. 2 of *Collected Economic Essays* (London: Duckworth, 1960; 2nd ed., 1980). The text is that of the first version (1942).—Ed.]

[2] [F. A. Hayek, "Capital and Industrial Fluctuations", *Econometrica*, vol. 2, April 1934, p. 163, reprinted in this volume, p. 200, speaks of the "underlying real maladjustments" as the primary cause of crisis; cf. also Dennis H. Robertson, *Money*, 1st ed. (London: Nisbet, 1922), p. 161, for the phrase "deep-seated maladjustments".—Ed.]

[3] *Prices and Production* (London: Routledge, 1931) [2nd ed. rev., 1935; reprinted in *Business Cycles, Part I*, ed. Hansjoerg Klausinger, vol. 7 (2012) of *The Collected Works of F. A. Hayek* (Chicago: University of Chicago Press)—Ed.].

driven to the conclusion that the basic hypothesis of the theory, that scarcity of capital causes crises, must be wrong. These 'second thoughts' produced a remarkable crop of critics of *Prices and Production* in the pages of English and American journals the number of which could rarely have been equalled in the economic controversies of the past.[4] Professor Hayek himself took an active part in this controversy and some eight years later produced a new version of his theory which in many ways radically departed from, and contradicted, the first.[5] It is with this second version, and in particular with the 'Ricardo effect', around which it is built, that the present article is chiefly concerned.

2. Professor Hayek in 1931 and 1939

In order to enable readers who are not well versed in the literature of the subject to understand what the issues are, it will be necessary to begin by recapitulating briefly, and without entering into criticisms, the main features of the two versions of Professor Hayek's theory.

The first version is mainly concerned with the effect of monetary credit expansion on the structure of production via its effect on interest rates. The banking system, owing to the elasticity of credit, keeps the rate of interest unduly low (i.e., it either actually reduces it, or prevents it from rising as it should) and thereby encourages entrepreneurs to embark on capital investments in excess of those for which current savings are available. This takes the form of entrepreneurs adopting more capitalistic methods of production (i.e., methods using more capital per unit of output) which are profitable only so long as interest rates remain at their artificially low level. But since this involves a cumulative inflation (a progressive rate of increase of the volume of bank credit) it must be brought to a halt sooner or later; when it is, interest rates rise and the longer processes become unprofitable; while the return to shorter pro-

---

[4] [To cite only the most significant pieces, cf. John Maynard Keynes, "The Pure Theory of Money: A Reply to Dr. Hayek", *Economica*, no. 34, November 1931, pp. 387–97; Piero Sraffa, "Dr. Hayek on Money and Capital", *Economic Journal*, vol. 42, March 1932, pp. 42–53; both reprinted as chapters 4 and 7 of *Contra Keynes and Cambridge: Essays, Correspondence*, ed. Bruce Caldwell, vol. 9 (1995) of *The Collected Works of F. A. Hayek*; and Alvin H. Hansen and Herbert Tout, "Annual Survey of Business Cycle Theory: Investment and Saving in Business Cycle Theory", *Econometrica*, vol. 1, April 1933, pp. 119–47. Kaldor had voiced his criticism before in "Capital Intensity and the Trade Cycle", *Economica*, n.s., vol. 6, February 1939, pp. 40–66, reprinted as chapter 6 of *Essays on Economic Stability and Growth*.—Ed.]

[5] "Profits, Interest and Investment", chapter 1 of *Profits, Interest and Investment. And Other Essays on the Theory of Industrial Fluctuations* (London: Routledge, 1939) [reprinted as chapter 8 of this volume—Ed.]. Also, *The Pure Theory of Capital* (London: Macmillan, 1941), Part IV [reprinted, ed. Lawrence White, as vol. 12 (2007) of *The Collected Works of F. A. Hayek*—Ed.]. For a succinct account of the two versions, cf. Gottfried Haberler, *Prosperity and Depression: A Theoretical Analysis of Cyclical Movements*, 3rd ed. (Geneva: League of Nations, 1941), pp. 48–57 and 481–91.

cesses involves a painful process of readjustment, during which some of the resources become unemployable.[6]

In the second version, Professor Hayek concentrates on the effect of a rise in the demand for consumers' goods (brought about by an expansion of credit, or some other cause) and the consequent rise in the rates of profits earned in the consumers' goods industries. He explicitly assumes, for the purposes of the argument, interest rates and also rates of money wages to remain unchanged during the whole cycle, and the existence of unemployment in both the consumers' goods and capital goods trades. As the demand for consumers' goods increases, the *prices* of consumers' goods increase (owing to short-period diminishing returns in these industries) and *real wages* (i.e., wages in terms of product-prices) fall. This has two consequences. One is that there will be an increase in investment demand in order to increase output capacity (there will be 'widening'). The other is that owing to the fall in real wages, *less* capitalistic methods of production will be adopted (there will be 'enshallowing'),[7] so that the amount of capital required per unit of output capacity will be reduced. (It is this latter which is called the 'Ricardo effect'.) In Professor Hayek's view, this second tendency must, ultimately if not immediately, overshadow the effects of the first and bring about a fall in the *total* demand for loanable funds, and hence spell depression in the capital goods industries This, he believes, must be the case, because so long as investment rises the rate of profit will continue to rise, and the more the rate of profit rises, the stronger will be the second tendency as compared with the first. "So long as investment continues to increase, the discrepancy between prices and costs of consumers' goods must become progressively larger till the rise in the rate of profit becomes strong enough to make the tendency to change[8] to less durable and expensive types of machinery dominant over the tendency to provide capacity for a larger output. Or, in other words, in the end the 'acceleration principle of derived

---

[6] "The situation would be similar to that of a people of an isolated island, if, after having partially constructed an enormous machine which was to provide them with all necessities, they found out that they had exhausted all their savings and available free capital before the new machine could turn out its product. They would then have no choice but to abandon temporarily the work on the new process and to devote all their labour to producing their daily food without any capital. Only after they had put themselves in a position in which new supplies of food were available could they proceed to attempt to get the new machinery into operation. In the actual world, however, where the accumulation of capital has permitted a growth of population far beyond the number which could find employment without capital, *as a general rule the single workman will not be able to produce enough for a living without the help of capital and he may, therefore, temporarily become unemployable*" (*Prices and Production*, 1st ed., p. 84 [reprinted, p. 257—Ed.]). (Italics mine.)

[7] [That is, the opposite of 'capital deepening'. As noted above (pp. 235–36), the terms 'deepening' and 'widening' are due to Ralph G. Hawtrey, *Capital and Employment* (London: Longmans, 1937), p. 36.—Ed.]

[8] [In the 1942 version the quotation is inaccurate, with the word "to" missing; this has been corrected in the reprint, p. 150.—Ed.]

demand' becomes inverted into a 'deceleration principle'—and the classical maxims that a scarcity of capital means a scarcity of consumers' goods, and that demand for commodities (= consumers' goods) is not demand for labour assert their fundamental truth."[9] Moreover, there is no question of an investment boom coming to an end in any other way except the one described (such as, e.g., through a *fall* in the rate of profit). "Once the cumulative process has been entered upon the end must always come through a *rise* in profits in the late stages and can *never come* from a fall in profits or an exhaustion of investment opportunities."[10]

It is clear from this brief summary that Professor Hayek's new version radically differs both from his own earlier theory and also from all other current theories on the subject. Most writers on capital theory and trade cycle theory (in fact *all* of those known to the present writer, with the exception of Professor Hayek) regard the level of investment demand as a function of the relation between profits and interest rates, in such a way that the *higher* is the rate of profit relatively to the rate of interest, the *greater* will be the demand for investment, and vice versa. They differ only as regards the causes which narrow the gap between profits and interest, and thus cause a fall in investment. One school, the under-consumptionists, believe that the gap narrows through the gradual fall in the rate of profit, brought about through the accumulation of real capital. The other school, the over-consumptionists, believe that the gap is narrowed through the inevitable rise in interest rates relative to the rates of profit which comes about when credit expansion is brought to an end. One believes that the fundamental trouble is that savings are too large, the other that they are too small. But both agree that it is the *relation* between profits and interest which determines how large the level of investment, and of industrial activity in general, is going to be. Professor Hayek, in his earlier days, himself belonged to the 'other school'. It was the basic tenet of *Prices and Production* that the level of investment[11] depends on the height of profits relative to the height of interest.[12] If he now succeeded in overthrowing this principle, its ramifications would be far wider than the theory of the trade cycle. Few branches of economic theory would escape unscathed this "more than Jevonian" revolution.[13]

[9] "Profits, Interest and Investment", p. 33 [this volume, p. 231—Ed.].

[10] Ibid., p. 56 [this volume, p. 246—Ed.]. (Italics mine.)

[11] [The phrase "level of investments" of the 1942 version has been corrected to "investment" in the reprint, p. 151.—Ed.]

[12] By no means all writers who believe in this doctrine subscribe to the 'acceleration principle of derived demand'. The two propositions are not identical. The accelerationists assert not only that a rise in profits raises investment demand, but that the magnitude of the rise depends on the *rate of change* of profits. This latter proposition seems to be invalid; but this is a matter that cannot be gone into here.

[13] [Cf. John R. Hicks, who in his review of Keynes's *General Theory* (*Economic Journal*, vol. 46, June 1936, p. 238) spoke of "this alleged more than Jevonian revolution". The Jevonian revo-

The rise in the rate of profit taking up the role of the rise in the rate of interest is not, of course, the only difference in the two versions of Professor Hayek's theory. The earlier concern with methods of production becoming unduly 'roundabout' is now replaced with the opposite fear that they become unduly 'direct'.[14] This shift is not merely in the nature of a correction in *sign*, a minus replacing a plus, as sometimes happens in mathematical calculations, as a result of the detection of an error in one of the equations. The whole character of the phenomenon has changed. In *Prices and Production*, as we have seen, the trouble was that during the boom the capitalist system engaged in the building of superior capital goods, for the completion of which the available resources were insufficient. It was likened to the case of the islanders who had to abandon the construction of an enormous machine because they ran out of food before the machine was ready to produce it. There is nothing similar to this in the "Profits, Interest and Investment" version. When the demand for their products goes up, entrepreneurs make higher profits. They then discover that by turning over their capital more quickly they can make still higher profits. They therefore proceed to do so, and this ultimately involves a fall in investment. If they had curbed their greed, and contented themselves with the profits they could get on the usual methods, or if this choice of still-higher-profits through the use of 'inferior machinery' had not been open to them, then, as far as Professor Hayek's present analysis goes, the boom would have been made permanent: high profits, high investment, high employment, could have gone on indefinitely. Thus, on this theory, a 100 per cent excess profits tax is sufficient to eliminate the trade cycle and stabilise prosperity. For it would suspend the operation of the 'Ricardo effect'—there would be no point in trying to make profits still higher by making production less roundabout, if none of these profits could be retained.

There are two important respects, however, in which Professor Hayek's new theory is faithful to the old. One is the fundamental importance he still attaches, in the explanation of the trade cycle, to what may be termed the 'concertina-effect'[15]: to the production periods becoming alternatively longer and shorter, in the successive phases of the cycle. In the first version they become unduly

---

lution refers to the marginal revolution against classical economics, usually associated with the writings of William Stanley Jevons, Alfred Marshall, Carl Menger, and Léon Walras. In particular, William Stanley Jevons (1835–82) emphasised the time dimension of production, similarly to the Austrian capital theory put forward later on by Böhm-Bawerk and developed by Wicksell.—Ed.]

[14] [As noted above, p. 221n.18, 'roundabout' or 'direct' denote 'more or less capitalistic' methods of production.—Ed.]

[15] [Kaldor took the comparison of the cyclical movements of the capital structure to a 'concertina' from Hayek himself; cf. F. A. Hayek, *Preise und Produktion* (Vienna: Springer, 1931; reprinted, 1976), p. 92n. (reproduced in F. A. Hayek, *Business Cycles, Part I*, p. 258n.39).—Ed.]

long during the boom and had to be shortened in the depression; in the new version they become progressively shorter as the boom progresses, and gradually lengthen as real wages rise with the fall in employment. But in both cases it is these variations in the *technique* of production, rather than the changes in the total stock of capital, and in total output of consumption goods, which are causally significant. The other respect in which Professor Hayek remained faithful to his original doctrine is in regarding excessive consumption, and not a deficiency of consumption, as the sole cause of the breakdown of a high level of prosperity. In the first version, this excessive consumption, via a process of cumulative inflation, forced interest rates to rise and the more capitalistic processes to be abandoned. In the new version, the rise in consumption caused product prices to rise relative to wages and thus to set in motion the fateful train of consequences of the 'Ricardo effect'. In both cases, it is because the level of consumption rises too much, and not because it does not rise fast enough, that periods of relatively high activity come to an end.

In my view, the 'concertina-effect' as a phenomenon of the trade cycle is non-existent or insignificant, while the supposition that a scarcity of savings causes booms to collapse is fallacious. The first is one of those blind alleys of economic speculation which appear very suggestive for a time, but whose significance evaporates as soon as one tries to fit the theoretical conclusions more closely to the observed phenomena. The second, I am now convinced, must be altogether abandoned as a supposition before any reasonably consistent explanation of the trade cycle can be reached.

Our present task, however, is not to suggest alternative explanations of the trade cycle but to show why the particular explanation offered by Professor Hayek is wrong. This, in its new version, all centres around the supposed operation of the 'Ricardo effect', and it is therefore to this question that the remaining parts of this paper must be largely devoted. It will be a 'roundabout' and arduous journey; and the only apology I can offer in asking the reader to undertake it is that apart from the more specialised task of unravelling particular errors in Professor Hayek's argument, it may also clear up some obscure points of capital theory.

In the following sections we shall attempt to prove (1) that the operation of the 'Ricardo effect' presupposes certain special conditions as to the position of individual firms which are clearly inapplicable to the major field of modern industry; (2) that even in those cases where the 'effect' does operate, its quantitative importance must be small, and is not likely to exceed the equivalent effect of a small change in the interest rate; (3) that quite apart from (1) and (2), the operation of this 'Ricardo effect' is wholly irrelevant to Professor Hayek's central thesis—i.e., that a rise in the demand for consumers' goods will lead to a fall in the demand for capital goods—since *under no circumstances* can total investment demand become smaller in consequence of a rise in the rate of profit.

3. Ricardo and the 'Ricardo Effect'

Before, however, we can enter into the substance of his argument, it is necessary to clear up a matter of '*Dogmengeschichte*';[16] the relation of Ricardo to what Professor Hayek calls the 'Ricardo effect'. Since Professor Hayek so generously acclaims Ricardo as the true originator of his theorem, it is necessary to make it clear that the proposition of Ricardo and that attributed to him by Professor Hayek are not the same—the assumptions are different, the mode of operation is different, and the conditions of validity are quite different—so that any criticism made against Professor Hayek's 'Ricardo effect' would not necessarily apply to Ricardo. This should be apparent as soon as one compares the passage in Ricardo's *Principles* to which Professor Hayek refers[17] with Professor Hayek's exposition of it.[18]

What is Ricardo's argument? He supposes a case where a machine costing £5,000 can do the work of one hundred men, whose wages also cost £5,000. Initially, therefore, the manufacturer would be indifferent between employing the men or buying the machine instead. "But suppose labour to rise, and consequently the wages of one hundred men for a year to amount to £5,500, it is obvious that the manufacturer would now no longer hesitate; it would be for his interest to buy the machine and get his work done for £5,000. But will not the machine rise in price, will not that also be worth £5,500 in consequence of the rise in labour? It would rise in price if there were no stock employed on its construction, and no profits to be paid to the maker of it. If, for example, the machine were the produce of . . . one hundred men, working one year upon it, with wages of £50 each, and its price were consequently £5,000; should those wages rise to £55, its price would be £5,500, but this cannot be the case; less than one hundred men are employed or it could not be sold for £5,000, for out of the £5,000 must be paid the profits of stock which employed the men. . . . *If therefore the maker of the machine should raise the price of it in consequence of a rise of wages, an unusual quantity of capital would be employed in the construction of such machines[19] till their price afforded only the common rate of*

[16] [That is, the slightly old-fashioned German term for the 'history of economic ideas'.—Ed.]

[17] David Ricardo, *On the Principles of Political Economy and Taxation* [1817], 3rd ed. (1821), reprinted in *The Works of David Ricardo*, ed. John Ramsey McCulloch (London: Murray, 1846), chapter 1, section 5, pp. 26–28 [cf. *The Works and Correspondence of David Ricardo*, ed. Piero Sraffa, vol. 1 (Cambridge: Cambridge University Press, 1951; reprinted, Indianapolis: Liberty Press, 2004), pp. 39–43—Ed.]. This is the only passage known to me where the principle is expounded, apart from a brief reference to it in chapter 31 (ibid., p. 241 [cf. ibid., ed. Sraffa, p. 395—Ed.]).

[18] "Profits, Interest and Investment", pp. 8–10 [this volume, pp. 215–17—Ed.]. The argument is reproduced in an article entitled "The Ricardo Effect", *Economica*, n.s., vol. 9, May 1942, pp. 129–34 [reprinted in this volume, pp. 260–65—Ed.].

[19] This is one of those Ricardian passages which are difficult through excessive brevity. The passage means, in modern terminology: "an unusual amount of profit would be earned in the

profits. We see then that machines would not rise in price, in consequence of a rise of wages."[20]

It is perfectly clear from the above that Ricardo's argument depends on (a) machines *falling* in price relatively to labour; (b) the rate of profit in different industries being kept at equality through competition, so that, when there is a general fall in the rate of profit, there must ensue a relative fall in the price of machines,[21] otherwise this equality in the rates of profit earned in different industries cannot be maintained. If Ricardo had dealt with Professor Hayek's case (a rise in product prices, instead of a rise in wages), his argument would have run as follows: When the prices of the products of the machine-using industries rise, there will be a rise in the rate of profit in these industries, but not in the machine-making industries. Therefore capital will flow from the latter to the former, the output of machines will be reduced and their prices rise. With the rise in machine prices the rate of profit in the two industries will be gradually restored to equality. As the price of the machines rises, in consequence of the reduction in their output, the machine-using industries will be tempted to substitute labour for machinery.

It is clear that Ricardo's argument (as distinct from the 'Ricardo effect') is really exactly the same as the familiar 'Austrian' proposition that when the rate of interest rises, the costs of production, and hence the prices, of goods containing more capital will rise relatively to those containing less capital, and this will cause a substitution of the latter for the former, all along the line.[22] For a general fall in wages, for Ricardo and the classics generally, meant a rise in the general rate of profit, while the general rate of profit and the rate of interest were regarded as the same thing: the supply price of capital for any one industry was simply the rate of profit earned in other industries. This assumed, of course, that the rate of interest on money loans is entirely governed by the rate of profit ruling in industry generally.

Professor Hayek, in his *Prices and Production* days, has subscribed, of course, to this 'Austrian' proposition. He was, moreover, aware also that, in so far as the rate of interest is *not* governed by the rate of profit, it is the rate of interest, and not the rate of profit, which determines what the relative prices of goods of differing 'roundaboutness' were going to be. For if the rate of

---

making of these machines, and therefore additional capital would enter the industry, expand production, and drive the price down, etc."

[20] Ricardo, *Principles of Political Economy*, ed. McCulloch, *Works*, pp. 26–27 [cf. *Works and Correspondence*, ed. Sraffa, vol. 1, pp. 40–41. Kaldor's quotation is slightly inaccurate as the second sentence ends: "in consequence of the rise of labour?"—Ed.]. (Italics mine.)

[21] [That is, as pointed out in the reprint, p. 155, "a fall in the price of machines, in terms of labour".—Ed.]

[22] This interpretation is reinforced (if further proof were needed) by a subsequent sentence, Ricardo, *Principles of Political Economy*, ed. McCulloch, *Works*, pp. 27–28 [cf. *Works and Correspondence*, ed. Sraffa, vol. 1, pp. 41–42—Ed.].

interest is held constant, then (keeping to our example) the capital employed in the machine-making industry, and hence the output of machines, will *not* be reduced, and the supply price of machines to the consumption industries will *not* rise, however much the profits of the consumption industries might increase,[23] and the tendency towards substitution of less capitalistic methods will not arise. Indeed, it was one of the main contentions of *Prices and Production* that so long as the rate of interest does not rise, the use of the 'more capitalistic processes' will continue.

And what is Professor Hayek's present argument? He does *not* assume any change in the relative prices of labour and machinery, or any change in the rate of interest, or any necessary tendency for equality in the rates of profit earned in different industries.[24] The substitution of labour for machinery, consequent upon the rise of product prices (all other prices, and the rate of interest, remaining the same) will be independent of all this and will come about because (a) producers will adopt that method of production which maximises the rate of profit per unit of capital; (b) the relation between the rates of profit earned on investments of differing degrees of roundaboutness will be altered by the change in product prices. This second proposition might be illustrated in terms of Ricardo's own example. Let us suppose that the labour is invested for one year, while the machine lasts for ever,[25] so that the investment period of the machine is infinite. Let us suppose, further, that the rate of profit is initially 10 per cent, both on labour and on machinery, which implies that the value of the product of the 100 labourers costing £5,000 will be £5,500, while the value of the annual product of the machine, also costing £5,000, will be £500. Let us suppose that product prices rise by 10 per cent. Then the value of the annual product will rise to £6,050 and £550, respectively, which implies that the rate of profit on labour will rise to 21 per cent, but the rate of profit on machinery only to 11 per cent. If the rate of profit per unit of capital were the governing consideration (and Professor Hayek assumes that this is always the case, without any further examination), then clearly it would 'pay' to replace machinery by labour, *independently* of any change in the relative prices of labour and ma-

---

[23] Because (a) it is the relation between the profits earned in an industry and the rate of interest (i.e., the relation between the demand price and the supply price of capital) and not the profits earned elsewhere, which determines the scale of investment in that industry; (b) and quite apart from this, because the profits in the machine-making industries will not fall, relatively to the profits in the consumption goods industries, except under conditions implicit in Ricardo's, but not in Professor Hayek's theory, that the total demand for the products of both industries must be constant.

[24] He explicitly states in a footnote ("Profits, Interest and Investments", p. 14 [this volume, p. 219n.15—Ed.]) that he does not intend to say that the rise in the rates of profit will be uniform in the different industries.

[25] This is an extreme case, chosen for the sake of simplicity. This simplification does not affect the principle in question though it maximises the numerical effect on relative profit rates of the change in product prices.

chinery (whereas, as we have seen, Ricardo's argument entirely depends on this change in relative prices of machinery and labour).

Now, whatever the truth in this latter argument (and we shall consider this question at some length below), it is certainly not Ricardo's. The term 'Ricardo effect' is clearly a misnomer. The real author of Professor Hayek's proposition, as we shall see below, is Knut Wicksell. I should not like to rechristen it the 'Wicksell effect', however, for I doubt if Wicksell would have shared Professor Hayek's views as to the manner of its operation.

Before, however, we can come to Wicksell, we must examine how the capital intensity of investments is in fact determined.

4. The Rate of Interest and the 'Marginal Productivity of Waiting'

It was, I believe, first demonstrated by Jevons that the optimum amount of capital employed in production (the amount of capital which minimises the cost of producing any given output) is the one which makes the rate of interest equal to the "marginal productivity of waiting" where the latter is defined as "the rate of increase in the produce [of a given amount of labour] divided by the whole produce".[26, 27] Since this "marginal productivity of waiting" is en-

---

[26] Since the meaning of this formula still presents difficulties to many people, it may be elucidated by a simple numerical example. Suppose that the produce of 100 labourers is £5,000 when invested for 1 year, £6,000 when invested for two years, £6,600 when invested for three years, and £6,930 when invested for four years. Then the 'marginal product' of two-year investment, as compared with one year, will be £1,000/£5,000, or 20 per cent; that of three-year investment £600/£6,000, or 10 per cent; that of four years £330/£6,600, or 5 per cent. If the rate of interest is below 5 per cent, four years' investment will be most profitable; if it is between 5 and 10 per cent, investment for three years, and so on.

It is clear that these marginal products are entirely independent of the wages of the labourers, since both the numerator and denominator of the expression refer to the *produce* of labour, and not the cost of labour. [This property is due to the process in question being of the 'point-input-point-output' type; it does not apply to more complicated processes, e.g., of the 'flow-input-point-output' type, where capital intensity would be determined by the ratio of factor prices, that is, the ratio of wages to the rate of interest. This does not mean, however, that a change in output prices, with the ratio of factor prices constant, would under the assumptions in question give rise to a change in capital intensity. On the various types of processes cf. F. A. Hayek, *The Pure Theory of Capital*, reprinted, pp. 85–86.—Ed.]

[The quotation is from William Stanley Jevons, *The Theory of Political Economy*, 4th ed. (London: Macmillan, 1911), reprinted as vol. 3 of Jevons, *Writings on Economics* (Basingstoke: Palgrave, 2001), p. 246.—Ed.]

[27] If less capital is employed, profits can be increased by employing more (since the additional cost will be less than the additional gain) and vice versa. "Every trade will employ capital up to the point at which it just yields the current interest. If any manufacturer or trader employs so much capital in supporting a certain amount of labour that the return is less than in other

tirely independent of the level of wages—for only the *produce* of labour and not the *cost* of labour figures in this expression—changes in the level of wages, relative to product prices, cannot affect the optimum amount of capital to be used per unit of output. The latter depends therefore solely on the cost of capital, i.e., the rate of interest.

Now Jevons' formula measures the amount of capital per unit of labour (or per unit of output) in terms of the 'investment period'[28]—a concept that has been rightly criticised, on numerous grounds. Fortunately, as I have shown elsewhere,[29] the marginal productivity of capital[30] can be defined in a way that is free from the difficulties inherent in the investment-period approach. It is simply the saving in annual cost, per unit of output, brought about by the employment of additional capital, divided by the initial cost of the additional capital.[31] (This expression is also independent of the relation of wages to output prices, since only the cost of labour figures in the expression, and not the produce of labour.)

Thus, in the case of the example we have adopted from Ricardo,[32] the Jevonian formula would be useless; for the change in the investment period in-

---

trades, he will lose; for he might have obtained the current rate by lending it to other traders" (Jevons, *The Theory of Political Economy*, 4th ed., p. 244 [p. 245]).

[28] Professor Hayek now calls it the 'turnover period'. [In "The Ricardo Effect", this volume, p. 262, Hayek uses the concept of the "rate of turnover", which is the reciprocal of the turnover period, to which Hayek refers as the "average period of investment" (ibid., this volume, p. 266).—Ed.]

[29] Cf. "Annual Survey of Economic Theory: The Recent Controversy on the Theory of Capital", *Econometrica*, vol. 5, July 1937, p. 213 [reprinted as "The Controversy on the Theory of Capital", in *Essays on Value and Distribution*, vol. 1 of *Collected Economic Essays*, pp. 165–66—Ed.], and "Capital Intensity and the Trade Cycle", p. 43 [reprinted, p. 123—Ed.].

[30] In an earlier article ("Capital Intensity and the Trade Cycle", p. 50 [reprinted, p. 131—Ed.]) I called this "the marginal productivity of capital intensification", to distinguish it from Keynes's "marginal efficiency of capital" (of which more later). The "marginal productivity of waiting", which has the merit that it is unambiguous, has other unfortunate connotations.

[31] This formula will yield identical results with Jevons's in those particular cases where the 'investment period', and the lengthening of it which is involved in any particular change, can be determined. As a formula, it is really older than Jevons and the whole time-period theory of capital, as it comes to the same as Mountifort Longfield's definition of the marginal productivity of capital: "the labour saving efficiency of the least efficient machinery use" (*Lectures on Political Economy* (Dublin: Milliken, 1834), pp. 187–88). [Cf. the reprint in The London School of Economics Scarce Tracts in Economics Series, vol. 1 (London: London School of Economics and Political Science, 1963; Routledge and Thoemmes Press, 1996). Kaldor's is more a paraphrase than a quotation. In full Longfield's definition is, "The sum which can be paid for the use of any machine has its greatest limit determined by its efficiency in assisting the operations of the labourer, while its lesser limit is determined by the efficiency of that capital which without imprudence is employed in the least efficient manner" (p. 188). Cf. also: "The profits of capital will be regulated by that portion of it which is obliged to be employed with the least efficiency in assisting labour" (p. 193).—Ed.]

[32] See p. 293 above.

volved when labour is replaced by machinery which lasts for ever[33] cannot be calculated. Yet the marginal productivity of the additional capital required when the labour is replaced by the machinery can be easily determined. Since the annual product of 100 men is £5,500, while that of a machine is £500, it requires 11 machines to produce the same output as 100 men. The additional capital required is therefore £55,000 − 5,000 = £50,000. The saving in annual cost is £5,000 (the annual wages of the 100 men), therefore the marginal productivity 5,000/50,000 = 10 per cent. So long as the relative prices of labour and machinery remain unchanged, this expression remains the same, whatever happens to the price of the output; and so long as the cost of capital is less than 10 per cent it will be more profitable to employ machinery than to use labour. Thus, assuming a rate of interest of 9 per cent, the profits on producing the output by labour will be £50 per annum, while the profits on producing the same output by machinery will be £550. If the price of the product rises by 10 per cent, the profits will be £600 and £1,100. If it falls by 10 per cent, they will be −£500 and zero. If we assume a rate of interest of 10 per cent, the profits on the two methods will be equal in all cases. At a rate of interest of 11 per cent the employment of labour will yield a higher profit, irrespective of the price of the product. Clearly, the choice of methods depends on the rate of interest and nothing else.

What is wrong then with the argument reproduced above,[34] which purports to establish the opposite conclusion, by showing that the *rate* of profit on capital moves differently, with a change in product prices, in the two cases? In that example, the amount of *capital invested* was taken to be the same in the two cases (£5,000 in each case), while the output produced was very different (£5,500 and £500 per annum). This argument therefore proves nothing as to what is the optimum method of producing a given output, while for a competitive industry, or for an entrepreneur who can vary the amount of capital employed in his business by borrowing or lending (and this is clearly involved when we talk about a 'rate of interest') the relevant consideration is not the maximum profit on a given sum of capital, but the maximum profit on a given rate of output. When the price of the product rises (or strictly: the *expected* price of the product rises) it becomes profitable to increase output, and to extend output-capacity, until the expected price, or the marginal revenue, is back again to conformity with cost. As Ricardo said, "an unusual quantity of capital would be employed till their price afforded only the common rate of profits".[35] Or, as Lord Keynes would say, until the marginal efficiency of

---

[33] It was assumed that labour, which is invested for one year, works without the cooperation of machinery; and machinery without the cooperation of labour.

[34] See p. 293.

[35] [Ricardo, *Principles of Political Economy*, ed. McCulloch, *Works*, p. 27; *Works and Corrspondence*, ed. Sraffa, vol. 1, p. 41; as already quoted above, pp. 291–92.—Ed.]

capital is again equal to the rate of interest. There will be *more* output and *more* capital employed, but not *less* capital per unit of output.

In "Profits, Interest and Investment", Professor Hayek asserts that the rise of the rate of profit, due to the rise in product prices, will reduce capital intensity, even if the rate of interest is constant. The passage where he attempts to prove that it is so deserves to be quoted at length[36]:—"But, it might be objected, must not the rate of profit always become equal to the rate of interest, which we have assumed to remain constant? That is, will not production always be expanded to the point where the marginal rate of profit is equal to the rate of interest? Now this is probably quite true of the *marginal* rate of profit; but this in no way constitutes an objection to our argument. What we are concerned with are not marginal rates of profit but the *rates of profit on any given output*, and with any given method of production (or the profit schedules or profit curve for all possible outputs and all the various methods of production); and the *main point is exactly* that the only way to make the marginal rate of profit equal to any given rate of interest if real wages have fallen is to use a larger proportion of labour and a smaller proportion of capital. . . . If, by keeping the rate of interest at the initial low figure, marginal profits are also kept low, this will only have the effect of a reduction in cost, that is, it will raise the figure at which the supply of and the demand for capital[37] will be equal; but it *will not affect the tendency to produce that output with comparatively less capital, a tendency which is caused, not by any change in the rate of interest, but by the shift in the position of the profit schedule.*"

The fallacy here is in the sentence beginning "the main point is exactly". The main point is exactly the opposite. When the rate of interest is given, the marginal rate of profit can only be brought to equality with the rate of interest by extending output capacity until 'marginal real wages' are raised to the previous level—until, that is to say, the previous cost-price relationship is restored as regards the marginal unit of planned output.[38] When the rate of interest is given, the rise in the demand for the product will only involve 'widening'.[39, 40]

If the increased demand for capital, resulting from the extension of capacity, causes a rise in the rate of interest, then, and only then, will there be a ten-

---

[36] "Profits, Interest and Investment", p. 15 [pp. 15–16; this volume, pp. 220–21—Ed.]. (Italics mine, except the word "marginal".)

[37] [Here Kaldor's quotation is misleadingly inaccurate: it should read, "demand for final output" instead of "demand for capital".—Ed.]

[38] Although the *average* rates of profit can, of course, remain higher in the new equilibrium.

[39] I have analysed this problem more fully in "Capital Intensity and the Trade Cycle", pp. 48–57 [reprinted, pp. 128–33—Ed.].

[40] Professor Haberler, who otherwise maintains a healthy scepticism about Professor Hayek's new theories, is himself misled by Professor Hayek on this point. Cf. his attempted refutation of Mr. T. Wilson [cf. Tom Wilson, "Capital Theory and the Trade Cycle", *Review of Economic Studies*, vol. 7, June 1940, pp. 169–79—Ed.] in Haberler, *Prosperity and Depression*, 3rd ed., p. 485n.2.

dency for the capital intensity of new investments (of fresh extensions of capacity) to be reduced; and *the strength of the tendency will depend on the magnitude of the change in interest* (on the elasticity of supply of capital) and not on the magnitude of the change in product prices, which indirectly caused it.

In his most recent article, Professor Hayek appears to have conceded this, since he says at one place[41] that it is a "truism which we have emphasised from the beginning that, so long as the rate of interest remains constant, a change in real wages cannot alter the relative costs of different methods of production". (It is a little surprising that he should now call this proposition a "truism", considering that he so strongly asserted the opposite in his previous essay!) Before, however, we can deal with Professor Hayek's latest views on this question, we must make another *détour*, and examine how Wicksell came to advocate the views which Professor Hayek attributes to Ricardo.

5. Wicksell's Difficulty and His Way Out

Ricardo, and the classical economists generally, did not bother much about the implications of the assumption of competition which they made the basis for their theories. The meaning of 'perfect' and 'imperfect' competition was unknown to them;[42] they did not realise that particular conditions must be satisfied as regards the position of any particular individual in the market, in order that the competitive mechanism should work in the way they assumed it works—in order that prices should be governed by marginal costs, that the rate of profit in industry should be equal to the rate of interest on loans, etc. It was only with the emergence of the 'mathematical school', after the path-breaking work of Cournot and Walras,[43] that economists familiar with the

[41] Hayek, "The Ricardo Effect", p. 145 [this volume, p. 277. The quotation is inaccurate as Hayek's formulation is "of the different methods of production".—Ed.].

[42] With the exception, perhaps, of John Stuart Mill. [The notion of 'imperfect competition' had been introduced into economic discourse just recently; cf. Joan Robinson, *The Economics of Imperfect Competition* (London: Macmillan, 1933), and Edward Chamberlin, *The Theory of Monopolistic Competition* (Cambridge, MA: Harvard University Press, 1933). Kaldor himself contributed to the ensuing discussion and in "Capital Intensity and the Trade Cycle" had examined the relevance of imperfect product and factor markets.—Ed.]

[43] [On this issue cf. George J. Stigler, *Essays in the History of Economics* (Chicago and London: University of Chicago Press, 1965), chapter 8: "Perfect Competition Historically Contemplated", with references to Antoine Cournot, *Recherches sur les principes mathématiques de la théorie des richesses* (Paris: Hachette, 1838), reprinted in *Oeuvres complètes*, ed. André Robinet, vol. 8 (Paris: Vrin, 1980); translated as *Researches into the Mathematic Principles of the Theory of Wealth* (New York: Macmillan, 1927; reprinted, Kelley, 1960), and, as of lesser importance in this regard, Léon Walras, *Éléments d'économie politique pure* (Lausanne: Corbaz, 1877; edition définitive, Rouge, 1926), reprinted as a variorum edition in vol. 8 (1988) of *Oeuvres économiques complètes*; the edition définitive translated as *Elements of Pure Economics*, trans. William Jaffé (London: Allen and Unwin, 1954; reprinted, New York: Kelley, 1977). Antoine Augustin Cournot (1801–77), a French math-

mathematical method realised the existence of these conditions,[44] and explicitly introduced the assumption of the general rule of 'perfect competition':
that any individual, whether in his capacity as producer or consumer, is confronted with given prices in the markets (since he is such a small fraction of
any market that he cannot individually influence price formation in any way),
which it is now fashionable to express by saying that he is confronted with 'infinitely elastic' demand and supply curves.

As soon as this assumption was explicitly made, however, a new problem
emerged in the theory of production: the problem of how the scale of operations of the individual producing unit is determined. The output of an *industry*
is determined by the conditions of supply and demand ruling in the market;
but the division of the output among the individual firms (and it is necessary
that this output should be divided among a large number of firms, otherwise the industry's output cannot be determined either from the conditions of
supply and demand) is not so determined; on the contrary, since the unit, by
hypothesis, can buy and sell anything in unlimited quantities, and since there
are 'constant returns to scale'—"small scale and large scale production must
be equally profitable", an assumption which was also a prerequisite of a state
of perfect competition, and of the theory of distribution as well[45]—it was apparently not determined by anything at all. Yet it was necessary that there
should be some factor limiting the size of operations of the individual firm,
otherwise the state of perfect competition could not be stable.

The most eminent of the late nineteenth century economists, Marshall and
Wicksell, both realised the existence of this problem, but instead of drawing the obvious conclusion (the abandonment of their general view as to the
working of competition) they dealt with it in two characteristically different
ways. Marshall's solution was the elevation of 'organisation' or 'entrepreneur-
ship' to the status of a separate factor of production, on equal footing with

---

ematician and economist, was the first to present the theory of demand and monopoly in mathematical terms. On Walras see above, p. 168.—Ed.]

[44] Menger and the succeeding Austrians, who were not trained in the mathematical school
(with the exception of Auspitz and Lieben) never did realise it. [The Austrian economist Carl
Menger (1840–1921) is here referred to as the founder of the Austrian school of economics. Rudolf Auspitz (1837–1906) was a politician and businessman, the owner of a sugar refinery and
jointly with Richard Lieben (1842–1919) of a family bank. Their *Untersuchungen über die Theorie
des Preises* (Leipzig: Duncker and Humblot, 1889) was an outstanding nineteenth-century contribution to mathematical economics, without however being duly recognised within the Austrian
economics community.—Ed.]

[45] Cf. Knut Wicksell, *Lectures on Political Economy*, vol. 1: *General Theory*, trans. Ernest Classen (London: Routledge, 1934 [reprinted, New York: Kelley, 1967, and Auburn, AL: Ludwig
von Mises Institute, 2007]), p. 126. [Kaldor's quotation is inaccurate. Wicksell assumes "that
large-scale and small-scale operations are equally productive". Technically, 'constant returns to
scale' imply that an equi-proportional change in all inputs used in production leads to an equal
proportional change in output.—Ed.]

land, labour and capital, but with the peculiarity that it cannot be hired in the market, so that each firm can only possess a certain amount of it, which in turn fixes an 'optimum size' to the firm's scale of operation, owing to the diminishing returns which arise when entrepreneurs are overworked. I analysed the difficulties inherent in the Marshallian solution some years ago[46] and have little to add to it. Wicksell adopted a different solution. He assumed, purely as an analytical device, that the owner of one of the factors required in production becomes 'entrepreneur' and hires the other factors; but that *each entrepreneur is only allowed to hire factors dissimilar to his own, and not factors of the same type which he himself owns.* Thus, if the labourers are entrepreneurs they are only allowed to hire land and capital, but *not* labour. If the landowners are entrepreneurs they are not allowed to hire land, and so on. On this assumption each entrepreneur can only produce a limited output, the limit being given by the amount of that factor which he owns himself.[47] Since he[48] restricted himself to describing the conditions of stationary equilibrium under perfect competition it did not matter which factor was 'entrepreneurial'—the earnings of the factors, and their allocation between different uses, were the same, whether labourers, landowners, or capitalists were entrepreneurs.

When he came to deal with capitalistic production he assumed that the capitalists are the entrepreneurs—though he also toyed with the assumption that the labourers are entrepreneurs[49]—and therefore, in accordance with this analytical device, he assumed that the capital each entrepreneur employs in his business is constant—he can neither hire capital nor lend his own capital to outsiders—so that the determining condition of equilibrium became the maximisation of the *rate* of profit on capital. Since he also assumed, however, that in equilibrium, the rate of profit, for each entrepreneur, must be equal—because if certain entrepreneurs earned more than others they would move from one industry to another—the results were no different from the case where entrepreneurs hire capital.

But the reaction-mechanism of the system is different. When each entrepreneur possesses a constant amount of capital there is no supply price of

---

[46] "The Equilibrium of the Firm", *Economic Journal*, vol. 44, March 1934, pp. 60–76 [reprinted as chapter 2 of *Essays on Value and Distribution*—Ed.]. I was not aware at the time that Wicksell had similar doubts about the validity of the Marshallian construction.

[47] We must remember that Wicksell's construction, unlike Marshall's, was not meant to be 'realistic'—it was purely an auxiliary construction designed to get his problem out of the way. (When Wicksell analysed the 'conditions of equilibrium' he always had his tongue in his cheek a little bit—which was certainly not true of Marshall.)

[48] [That is, Wicksell.—Ed.]

[49] Cf. *Über Wert, Kapital und Rente* (Jena: Fischer, 1893 [reprinted, Aalen: Scientia, 1969], pp. 95ff. [pp. 95–105; cf. the translation *Value, Capital, and Rent*, trans. Stephen H. Frowein (London: Allen and Unwin, 1954; reprinted, New York: Kelley, 1970, and Auburn, AL: Ludwig von Mises Institute, 2007), pp. 120–30—Ed.], and, *Lectures*, vol. 1, pp. 172ff. [pp. 172–84].

capital for the business; there is no 'rate of interest'; and since the only alternative form of employment of capital is to invest it in a different method of production (in producing a larger or smaller stream of output), a rise in the rate of profit under these conditions produces exactly the same effects as a rise in the rate of interest. A rise in the rate of profit from, say, 5 to 6 per cent will have exactly the same effect on the optimum use of capital as a rise in the interest rate from 5 to 6 per cent. And since, under conditions of perfect competition and constant returns to scale, the average and the marginal rates of profit are necessarily equal, the only circumstance capable of changing the rate of profit will be a change in wages, relative to output prices; the optimal output per unit of capital will, therefore, depend only on 'real wages'.

Wicksell, however, unlike Professor Hayek, was aware of the limitations which this device imposed on his analysis, as becomes abundantly clear from the following passage:—[50] "Naturally, the entrepreneur strives to attain the maximum absolute and not relative profit; we must therefore necessarily start from something fixed and given, or else the whole edifice will vanish into thin air.[51] We must assume that the entrepreneur disposes of *either* a given amount of capital (his own or borrowed), or else a given area of land, or finally a given amount of labour (as in co-operative agriculture). *But in this case the Principle of Substitution only comes into operation for the factors of production demanded by him and not for those he already possesses.* Only in a general equilibrium resulting from competition between entrepreneurs, *where their profits are theoretically forced down to zero,* does the Principle of Substitution or marginal principle hold universally."[52]

As we shall see below, this is precisely what Professor Hayek is trying to do: to examine the problem of the substitution between capital and labour by postulating conditions under which the Principle of Substitution does not apply.

6. The Wicksell-Firms and their 'Ricardo Effect'

Professor Hayek, in his latest essay,[53] while he re-emphasises the fundamental importance of the 'Ricardo effect' in the causation of economic crises,

---

[50] "Cassel's System of Economics", reprinted in *Lectures*, vol. 1, p. 244. Italics mine, except the word "either". [Kaldor's quotation is inaccurate as in the second sentence it should read, "disposes over".—Ed.]

[51] By the "whole edifice" he presumably means the competitive equilibrium theory of economics.

[52] [The 'Principle of Substitution'—the term is that of Cassel, whom Wicksell is criticising—establishes that, given substitutability, factor prices will be proportional to marginal productivities; cf. ibid., p. 230.—Ed.]

[53] "The Ricardo Effect", p. 145 [this volume, p. 277—Ed.].

and goes to great lengths to prove that credit expansion makes it "sooner or later inevitable that real wages should fall and investment expenditure be reduced",[54] now appears to realise that the operation of this 'effect' depends on the assumption that scarcity of funds sets the effective limit to a firm's scale of operations. At any rate, the re-statement of the Ricardo effect is now explicitly done under the assumption that "there is no lending of money of any kind during the period with which we are concerned: entrepreneurs either owning all the capital they employ and *being effectively prevented from lending any of it*, or being limited by a strict rationing of credit".[55] He apparently forgets that these assumptions make his model completely unsuited for an examination of the problem he is interested in, i.e., whether a rise in the rate of profit will be followed by a rise or fall in investment expenditure; since such firms by hypothesis cannot either increase or decrease their investment, being strictly limited to the steady re-investment of their amortisation quotas. We obviously cannot assume that the whole economic system consists of such 'Wicksell-firms'; if we did, there would be a constant rate of investment, and no trade cycle. The mere fact that there are wide fluctuations in the level of investment (which is after all the basic phenomenon Professor Hayek is trying to explain) is sufficient to show that, in a considerable section of the economy at any rate, the supply of funds must be elastic—the scale of operations of individual firms must be determined by some factor other than the scarcity of funds at their disposal.[56]

---

[54] Ibid., p. 144 [this volume, p. 276. The quotation is inaccurate as there should be an ellipsis after "sooner or later" and a comma after "fall".—Ed.].

[55] Ibid., p. 130 [this volume, p. 261—Ed.]. (My italics.) [Note that Hayek states that this assumption is just "for the time being", that is, preliminary (ibid.).—Ed.]

[56] Professor Hayek regards the case where the firm is faced with an infinitely elastic supply of credit as "theoretically very interesting but practically irrelevant" (ibid., p.138 [this volume, p. 270—Ed.]), and in one sweeping passage he condemns its assumption as "not only unrealistic but, when we contemplate its implications, perfectly fantastic" (ibid., p. 140 [this volume, p. 272—Ed.]). But this must be due to a confusion between the concept of 'infinite elasticity' and 'infinity'. All that his own argument demonstrates is that no firm can borrow *infinite* amounts—that the borrowing power of any firm must ultimately be limited. But this is quite consistent with the elasticity of the curve being infinite in the neighbourhood of equilibrium; indeed, it follows from his own assumption of the 'stepped up' supply curve of credit that this elasticity *will* be infinite—unless borrowing power is the effective limiting factor, in which case it will be zero. What he should have argued, therefore, is *not* that there are ultimate limits to borrowing power, but that borrowing power is necessarily the *effective* limiting factor of the firm's scale of operations; that other limiting factors—such as internal diseconomies of scale to the firm, or imperfect competition (limitation of selling power)—are inoperative. No doubt, he can set up a model, like Wicksell, where other limiting factors are ruled out (by assuming perfect competition and constant returns to scale); a world where each firm must always invest up to the limit of its borrowing power. But this model, though it may be necessary for the dem-

Let us concentrate, however, on these 'Wicksell-firms'—ignoring, for the moment, whether they exist in reality or not, or whether they could play an important role in the trade cycle. Will the behaviour of these firms really exhibit the characteristics Professor Hayek attributes to them? Professor Hayek insists, in both of his essays on the subject, that the effect of even a small change in product prices relatively to wages will be very far-reaching on the kind of investment adopted—it will cause widespread substitution of 'shorter' for 'longer' processes, of 'labour' for 'machinery'. We have already seen above that the magnitude of this reaction in response to a given rise of the rate of profit[57] will be the same as that of an equivalent rise in the rate of interest. But the magnitude of the rise in the rate of profit, resulting from a given rise in product prices, will depend on the period of turnover (in other words, on the amount of capital used per unit of output). If *very short* investment periods are assumed, the effect will be large. Professor Hayek's firms are assumed to have investment periods of one month, three months, six months, etc.—the longest being two years.[58] On this basis he is able to show that even in response to such a small rise in product prices as 2 per cent the rates of profit will be raised from 6 to 30 per cent (for the one-month firm), 6 to 14 per cent (for the three months firm), and so on.[59]

But what is the point of such examples? We are not concerned with the economics of the Trobriand Islanders, but of the industrial communities of a Western world, and here the average period of turnover of capital should be measured in years and not in months. If the amount of capital used per unit of output is five times the annual value of that output—and this is surely not an unreasonable figure[60]—the rise in the rate of profit will be only from

---

onstration of the 'Ricardo effect', could hardly be suitable for dealing with problems of the trade cycle.

In another place [ibid., this volume, pp. 272–73—Ed.] he links up the assumption of an infinitely elastic supply of capital to the *firm* with there being an infinitely elastic supply of *money*, to the economic system as a whole. The two are clearly not the same, all that the former assumption presupposes is the existence of a capital market, where capitalists can lend to each other.

[57] Strictly speaking, the *marginal* rate of profit. But we may assume for simplicity that there is perfect competition and constant returns to scale, so that the marginal and average rates of profits are equal.

[58] "Profits, Interest and Investment", pp. 8–9 [this volume, pp. 215–16—Ed.].

[59] This assumes, of course, a kind of perfectly competitive pricing system where the profit margin is entirely governed by the period of turnover of capital, i.e., for the firm with the one-month turnover period it will only be 1/2 per cent of price. In this case, a 2 per cent rise in prices will raise the profit margin, and thus the rate of profit on capital, to five times the former figure.

[60] [In present-day terminology Kaldor's average 'period of turnover of capital' corresponds to the 'capital-output ratio'. Today a typical estimate of the (incremental) capital-output ratio will be about three and thus somewhat lower than Kaldor's conjecture. The Trobriand Islands,

6 to 6.4 per cent. The 'enshallowing' effect in this case will be negligible; and since—in reality, as distinct from theory—the 'investment period' cannot be varied continuously but only in discrete intervals (for there are only a limited number of alternative methods available) it might well be non-existent.

To put the same thing in another way: the strength of the 'Ricardo effect' of the Wicksell-firms depends on the magnitude of the proportionate change in profit margins (i.e., the percentage excess of price over prime costs). A given change in prices will cause an appreciable change in profit margins only if these profit margins are small or if the change in prices is large. Thus, if the profit margin is only 3 per cent, a 3 per cent rise in price will double it. But if the profit margin is 30 per cent, a 30 per cent increase in price is needed to double it. Since it needs no prolonged empirical research to discover that profit margins in the real world are more of the order of 30–40 per cent than 3–4 per cent, it is clear that fairly large changes in product prices (relatively to wage-levels) would be required in order to make the 'Ricardo effect' quantitatively significant—changes for which there is no statistical evidence whatever.[61]

Professor Hayek, in answer to Mr. Wilson, who already put forward this argument,[62] denies its validity, and says it is due to a confusion. He re-asserts the view that the 'Ricardo effect' will be important, and goes even further, and says it will be all the *more* important the longer is the investment period. "By comparing the effects of a price rise on a two years' investment with that on investments for a few months, I was understating my case, and what appeared to be true on these assumptions must be *a fortiori* true of the more realistic situations where machinery that will last ten or even twenty years is introduced to save current labour" (or, rather, he should have said, since he is considering the effects of a price rise, "where current labour is introduced in order to save machinery that lasts ten or twenty years").[63] If our own reasoning is correct, then this last statement must be the opposite of the truth.

7. The Irrelevance of the 'Ricardo Effect'

So far we were merely concerned in showing the particular assumptions required in order that the 'Ricardo effect' should operate, and the additional

---

by the way, are an archipelago of several low-lying coral islands to the northeast of New Guinea.—Ed.]

[61] On this cf. section 8, pp. 309–10 below. [In the reprint, p. 168, Kaldor speaks of "changes far greater than those which the available evidence warrants".—Ed.]

[62] "Capital Theory and the Trade Cycle", pp. 170–71.

[63] "The Ricardo Effect", p. 134n.1 [p. 135n.1; this volume, p. 266n.27. In Kaldor's quotation there should be an ellipsis after "By comparing".—Ed.].

conditions necessary in order that it should be quantitatively important. All these were preliminaries. We now come to the main point of the story: how far is this whole business relevant to Professor Hayek's main thesis, which is that a rise in demand for consumers' goods leads to a fall in investment expenditure, thereby causing unemployment and general depression?

Professor Hayek asserts that owing to the 'Ricardo effect' sooner or later this must *inevitably* happen—the question is, can it happen at all?

Let us assume conditions most favourable to Professor Hayek: let us suppose that the economic system consists of firms each of which is faced with an 'upward sloping' supply curve of capital. If we assumed, like Wicksell, that the supply curves are vertical, there could be no reactions on investment expenditure, positive or negative. If we assumed horizontal supply curves, then, as Professor Hayek now himself admits,[64] the 'Ricardo effect' would be inoperative. But with the upward sloping supply curve we have a case where investment expenditure is variable and at the same time the 'Ricardo effect' works— in the sense that a rise in the demand for the products of the firms will tend to be followed by a reduction of the capital intensity of their investments.

The capital intensity will be reduced, in this case, because the rate of interest has risen, and the rate of interest will have risen because the rate of investment has gone up; if the rate of investment had *not* gone up, the rate of interest would not have risen. But in that case the capital intensity of their investments would not be reduced. However hard we try, we cannot construct a case where as a result of a rise in the rate of profit the capital intensity falls *and* as a result of this fall in capital intensity, investment expenditure will be less than it was before.[65] To argue in this way, involves the same fallacy as saying that because a rise in demand for a commodity will cause a rise in its price, and the rise in price causes a restriction in demand (because less is bought at a

---

[64] Cf. p. 298 above.

[65] This proposition may be made clearer perhaps if set out in mathematical terms. In the situation contemplated, the rate of investment expenditure, I, is a product of the level of planned output, x, and the amount of capital per unit of output, k. The marginal rate of interest, r, will be an increasing function of I; k, as shown in section 4 above, will be a diminishing and single-valued function of r, while x will be an inverse [that is, a decreasing—Ed.] function of the rate of *real* wages, w (which is treated as a datum).

We have therefore a system of four equations

$I = kx$

$r = f(I)$

$k = \phi(r)$

$x = \psi(w)$

to determine the four variables, k, x, r and I. Since r depends only on I, and k on r, df/dI and $\partial I/\partial x$ are positive, dI/dx must be positive, and dI/dw negative—a fall in real wages must be followed by a rise in investment expenditure. [The solution of the system of equations is $dI/dw = k\phi'/(1 - x\phi'f') < 0$, confirming Kaldor's result.—Ed.]

higher price than a lower price), the increase in demand will lead to a reduction in the amount bought. No doubt the rise in price will make the increase in purchases (following upon the increase in demand) less than it would have been if the price had not risen. But it cannot make it less than before, since the price has only risen because the amount bought has gone up. In the same way, the reduction in capital intensity will make the rise in investment expenditure less than it would have been if capital intensity had remained constant. But it cannot eliminate it altogether because capital intensity would not have fallen if investment expenditure had not risen.

This is the fundamental point, which knocks the bottom out of Professor Hayek's new theory of the trade cycle, quite apart from any arbitrariness or unreality of the assumptions on which it is based.

Professor Hayek makes really no attempt to prove this proposition, on which his whole theory of the trade cycle turns. But he brings forward three different arguments in connection with it—none of which affords the slightest support to his proposition. We shall attempt to deal with them briefly.

(1) In "Profits, Interest and Investment" there is a long and involved argument,[66] the gist of which is this. Suppose there are two kinds of machines, produced by two different industries, and that the labour in the two industries is not interchangeable. When the rate of profit goes up in the machine-using industries, and capital intensity falls, the demand will be switched from machine A to machine B.[67] The A-machine industry will get depressed. For a time the growing unemployment there will be offset (from the point of view of society as a whole) by the rise in employment of the B-machine industry; but this can happen only so long as the B-machine industry has a reserve of labour. Once this is exhausted, further increases in the rate of profit will *further* reduce employment in the A-industry, without a compensating increase in the B-industry. So it comes about that "there will be an increase in the demand for kinds of labour of which no more is available, while at the same time the demand for other kinds of labour will fall and total employment will consequently decrease".[68]

The fallacy here is that with the rise in profits in the machine-using industries, the employment of A-machines did not become *absolutely* unprofitable, but only *relatively* unprofitable. In fact, the profits to be made by using A-machines increase all the time; demand is switched to B-machines solely because the profits to be made on these are even greater. As soon as the B-machine industry gets fully employed, in response to further rises of demand B-machines will

[66] "Profits, Interest and Investment", pp. 20–29 [this volume, pp. 223–29—Ed.].

[67] Machine A is assumed to require more labour to construct but to be more labour-saving in use than machine B.

[68] Ibid., p. 28 [p. 26; this volume, pp. 226–27. The opening quotation mark should be after "there".—Ed.].

rise in price, or simply become unobtainable. In either case it will again become more profitable to use A-machines. When employment in the B-industry ceases to rise, then, on Professor Hayek's own assumptions, the demand for A-machines will begin to rise.

(2) In the "Ricardo Effect" there is another argument,[69] based on the 'limitation of real resources', which, as far as I understand it, is as follows. Professor Hayek supposes that the boom has reached a stage where there is full employment in the machine-making industries (while presumably, although this is not explicitly stated, there is still a reserve of labour available in the machine-using industries). Hence the price of machines will rise, relatively to the price of labour in the machine-using industry, and this will cause a tendency to install less costly machinery.

Now it is quite true that when the price of machines rises, relatively to the price of labour in the machine-using industry, this does affect the productivity of different kinds of machines. But what is Professor Hayek trying to prove? Again he confuses influences coming from the side of demand with influences coming from the side of supply. If the price of machinery rises, the demand for machines will be less than if it did not rise. But the price of machinery has only risen, on his assumptions, *because* demand has risen; how does this explain then the emergence of unemployment? His business is to prove that demand will fall; not that a rise in demand will be checked by a rise in price.[70]

But quite apart from this, why assume a situation where the labour in the

---

[69] "The Ricardo Effect", pp. 146–47 [this volume, pp. 278–79—Ed.].

[70] In connection with this argument, Professor Hayek takes me to task for having failed in an earlier article to deal with the problem of what determines capital intensity under conditions of monopsony in the labour market. (This refers to "Capital Intensity and the Trade Cycle", pp. 45ff. [pp. 45–50; reprinted, pp. 125–30—Ed.].) According to him, in this way I have "apparently succeeded in eliminating the given supply of capital from the relevant data of the problem" ("The Ricardo Effect", p. 146 [this volume, p. 278—Ed.]). I cannot pretend to see the connection between the problem of the "given supply of capital" (does Professor Hayek mean by the "supply of capital" the supply of savings or the supply of labour?) and monopsony in the labour market; but the reason for my failure to deal with this case is easily explained. When there is monopsony in the labour market, the relevant concept is not 'marginal real wages', but 'marginal real labour cost', which depends also on the elasticity of supply of labour to the entrepreneur. When, however, the 'labour' in question is situated in different industries (in the machine-making and machine-using industries) the assumption of a given elasticity of supply, for all labour, has no meaning, and the concept of 'marginal real wages' breaks down. I fail to see, however, how the assumption of monopsony adds anything to Professor Hayek's argument. The problem of a scarcity of labour can be dealt with quite easily without assuming monopsony. [Indeed, Hayek's criticism did not assume monopsony in the labour market, that is, an upward sloping supply curve of labour to the individual firm, but a limitation to the economy-wide ('aggregate') supply of labour. It is, however, central for the model of 'perfect competition' to combine such an upward sloping supply curve in the aggregate with a horizontal ('infinitely elastic') supply curve faced by the individual firms.—Ed.]

machine-making industries becomes scarce *relatively* to the labour in the consumption goods industries? Surely it is more in keeping with Professor Hayek's own assumption as to the 'shortage of savings', and more in accordance with what might happen in the course of a boom, that the labour in the consumption goods industries becomes scarce, relatively to the labour in the machine-making industries. In that case, however, the scarcity of labour will have the *opposite effect* to that contemplated by Professor Hayek: it will give an extra stimulus to deepening, and not to enshallowing.

(3) Also in the "Ricardo Effect" Professor Hayek argues that, although it may pay the entrepreneur best to install the more expensive machinery, in the sense that it will give him higher profits once it is installed, the less expensive type of machinery can be installed more quickly, it will begin to earn profits sooner and therefore the entrepreneurs will prefer it.[71] There are three comments to be made on this argument. First, he does not show why the less expensive machinery should necessarily be obtainable more quickly. The more expensive machinery requires more labour to make it, but not necessarily a longer construction period. Second, if it does, the extra interest cost during construction is already taken into account in determining its marginal productivity; in determining, that is to say, at what rate of interest its installation becomes profitable. It is only if the entrepreneur expects higher prices for his products in the near future than in the more distant future that it might become profitable to install the machine with the shorter construction period, even though the rate of interest is the same. Third, assuming that the latter is the case, what does it prove? Nobody wishes to deny that the capital intensity of investments under boom conditions might be less than under depression conditions—either for this or that or some other reason.[72] But Professor Hayek has taken on himself to prove that this will cause a fall in demand for capital goods, and thus unemployment in the capital goods trades; and to the latter contention this argument contributes nothing at all.

8. The Truth About the Concertina-Effect

We have now seen that the concertina-effect, even in its new version, fails to live up to expectations: it cannot be advanced as the causally significant factor in the trade cycle. But the question still remains whether it exists at all as an accompanying phenomenon of the cycle. Is it true that the fluctuations in

---

[71] [Cf. "The Ricardo Effect", pp. 147–48; this volume, pp. 279–80.—Ed.]

[72] Cf. my articles "Stability and Full Employment", *Economic Journal*, vol. 48, December 1938, pp. 642–57 [reprinted as chapter 5 of *Essays on Economic Stability and Growth*—Ed.], and "Capital Intensity and the Trade Cycle".

the rate of investment are accompanied by fluctuations in the capital intensity and, if so, does the concertina move cyclically or counter-cyclically? Professor Hayek, as we have seen, was an adherent at one time or another of both these views.

In the new version, the concertina-effect is all based on the alleged cyclical fluctuation of real wages and profit margins. According to him, it is "one of the best established empirical generalisations about cyclical fluctuations" that "somewhere half-way through the cyclical upswing"[73] real wages begin to fall and profit margins rise, while during the downswing the opposite happens. Moreover, he suggests, throughout these essays, that these variations are fairly considerable.[74]

Now reliable evidence on this matter cannot be gained merely by comparing wage-series and cost-of-living indices; since the relevant price-relation is not, as Professor Hayek himself insists, wages in terms of cost-of-living goods, but wages in terms of the prices of their own products. To obtain this evidence we must turn therefore to Census of Production statistics, which give information on profit margins (the difference between the value added by manufacture and wages cost). The following figures, relating to the percentage of gross profit margins in the value of the net output of manufacturing industry, of the United States and Germany, were calculated by Dr. L. Rostas (see table 10.1).[75]

The figures suggest, if anything, that cyclical movements of profit margins are neither significant nor do they follow a regular pattern. Thus in Germany, in the boom year of 1929, profit margins were considerably *lower* than in the depression year 1932; in the United States they are practically the same in 1929 and 1931—at the top of the boom and the middle of the depression—while they gradually fall during the revival years, 1933–37. The evidence,

---

[73] Hayek, "Profits, Interest and Investment", p. 11 [this volume, p. 217. Kaldor's quotation of the passage is inaccurate. It should read "industrial fluctuations" for "cyclical fluctuations" and "a cyclical upswing" for "the cyclical upswing".—Ed.]

[74] [The version of 1960 reprints the next paragraphs in revised form "in the light of more recent statistical material" (Kaldor, *Essays on Economic Stability and Growth*, p. 173n.) and deletes the final paragraph.—Ed.]

[75] British Censuses of Production are unfortunately too infrequent to afford evidence of cyclical movements. [These calculations were part of the "Profits Margin Inquiry", started 1938 in Cambridge and continued 1940–46 under the direction of Michal Kalecki in Oxford. As a result Laszlo Rostas published a monograph, *Productivity, Prices and Distribution in Selected British Industries* (Cambridge: Cambridge University Press, 1948), which contained detailed information on costs and pricing in eight British industries. Cf. J. E. King, "Introduction to an Unpublished Note by Nicholas Kaldor and Joan Robinson", *Review of Political Economy*, vol. 12, July 2000, pp. 261–65. In the reprint (Kaldor, *Essays on Economic Stability and Growth*, p. 174) this table has been replaced by more recent data from the U.S. drawing on John W. Kendrick, *Productivity Trends in the United States*, eventually published, New York: National Bureau of Economic Research, 1961.—Ed.]

Table 10.1
Share of Gross Profit in the Net Output of Manufacturing Industry

	United States	Germany
1919	59.3	—
1921	56.8	—
1923	58.7	—
1925	61.2	—
1927	61.7	—
1929	64.5	61.8
1931	64.0	—
1932	—	69.9
1933	64.7	67.5
1935	60.5	68.8
1937	59.8	69.5

such as it is, suggests rather the opposite of Professor Hayek's "best established empirical generalisation".

Does this mean that we should go back to Professor Hayek's original position, and assume that the concertina works the other way?[76] Capital intensity, as we have seen, is much more a matter of interest rates than of profit margins; and the rate of interest on the whole tends to be higher in boom periods than depression periods, although the differences are not large. This would suggest 'deepening' in the depression and 'enshallowing' during the boom. But there is another factor to be taken into account. New technical inventions are constantly occurring, and since they are mainly of a labour-saving character, they create a trend of constant deepening (quite independently of movements of interest rates or profit margins) which probably swamps any cyclical fluctuation between 'deepening' and 'enshallowing'.

The investment cycle, as Mr. Hawtrey has said, is essentially a matter of widening and not of deepening.[77] Some deepening always goes on, and though the extent of deepening might vary between booms and depressions, it is by no means certain which way the variation goes. The adoption of new techni-

---

[76] [Cf. Kaldor's judgment of 1960: "I think the evidence rather suggests that the concertina, whichever way it goes, makes a relatively small noise—it is drowned by the cymbals of technical progress" (*Essays on Economic Stability and Growth*, p. 175).—Ed.]

[77] [A source could not be identified; in particular, Hawtrey in *Capital and Employment* is equivocal on this issue.—Ed.]

cal processes largely depends on a general atmosphere of optimism, and this is more likely to be present during booms.

But in any case the variation is more likely to be one between greater and lesser deepening, and not, as the 'concertina-effect' suggests, between deepening and enshallowing.[78]

9.

The presence of so many contradictory arguments is not accidental: it is due to the desire to demonstrate, at all costs, that the scarcity of capital is the great cause of economic crises and a direct cause of unemployment. Professor Hayek has been trying to prove this proposition ever since he first wrote on the subject. In the course of time the arguments became more ingenious and more complicated, but they brought him no nearer to proving it than he was at first. Since that time it has been shown over and over again that the only sense in which the concept of the 'scarcity of capital' has a definite meaning is an insufficiency of saving; and the only way an insufficiency of saving can manifest itself is in causing hyper-inflation in a state of full employment, and not in depression-unemployment.

Professor Hayek, as far as I know, has never answered these arguments; nor has he troubled to explain why a trade boom cannot come to an end through a *fall* in the rate of profit. There is the dogmatic assertion that the end of the boom can "*never* come from a fall in profits or an exhaustion of investment opportunities",[79] but it is not supported by any analysis or argument; and although he analyses certain features of the investment process with great detail and subtlety, other and more important features (such as the effects of past investment in increasing output capacity and thus reducing the need for further investment) are completely passed over. Nor is there, in any of his recent essays on the trade cycle, any mention of the numerous recent theories

---

[78] Professor Alvin H. Hansen, in his book on *Fiscal Policy and Business Cycles* (New York: Norton, 1941 [reprinted, London: Routledge, 2003]), emphasises how unimportant deepening is, as a form of investment (let alone its cyclical variation!) as compared to widening. Both in the United States and in England, the rate of growth of real capital, since the last quarter of the nineteenth century, was no greater than the rate of growth of output. "Thus during the last fifty years or more, capital formation for each economy as a whole has apparently consisted mainly of a widening of capital. Surprising as it may seem, as far as we may judge from such data as are available, there has been little, if any, deepening of capital" and "our system of production is little more capitalistic now than fifty or seventy-five years ago" (ibid., p. 355). There can be little doubt that as far as the trade cycle is concerned, the analysis of the cyclical process would not be altered in any significant particular, if one excluded the consideration of the deepening process altogether.

[79] [Hayek, "Profits, Interest and Investment", this volume, p. 246.—Ed.]

311

of the trade cycle (Kalecki, Harrod, Schumpeter, Hansen[80]—to mention only a few) which all reach the opposite conclusion. The economic journals of the world have been buzzing with theories of this type in the last few years, but as far as Professor Hayek's writings are concerned they simply don't exist. If on some future occasion he would start 'at the other end', and would show why all these other theories are wrong, instead of giving yet another version of his own views, it might be easier to arrive at the truth.

[80] [Cf., e.g., Michal Kalecki, *Essays in the Theory of Economic Fluctuations* (London: Allen and Unwin; New York: Farrar and Rinehart, 1939; reprinted, New York: Russell and Russell, 1972), reprinted in *Collected Works*, ed. Jerzy Osiatynski, vol. 1 (Oxford: Clarendon Press, 1990); Roy F. Harrod, *The Trade Cycle: An Essay* (Oxford: Clarendon Press, 1936); Joseph A. Schumpeter, *Business Cycles: A Theoretical, Historical, and Statistical Analysis of the Capitalist Process* (New York: McGraw-Hill, 1939); and Hansen, *Fiscal Policy and Business Cycles*. Michal Kalecki (1899–1970), a Polish economist, influential in what was to become the post-Keynesian tradition, worked at the Oxford Institute of Statistics 1940–55. Roy Forbes Harrod (1900–1978) spent his academic life at Oxford University; his major accomplishment was to add a dynamic dimension to Keynesian macroeconomics. On Schumpeter and Hansen see above, pp. 169 and 186.—Ed.]

A Comment[1]

As it is impossible for me to foresee at present when I shall be able to answer more fully Mr. Kaldor's criticism, I am anxious to add here at least as much as is necessary to prevent a misunderstanding from spreading. Mr. Kaldor considers that a fundamental conflict and even a contradiction exists between my views as expounded in *Prices and Production* and those developed in the later 'versions' of my theory with which he is more directly concerned. Though I hope that in the dozen years since I wrote *Prices and Production* my understanding of the problems involved has somewhat increased, I find it impossible, hard as I try, to find any irreconcilable conflict between the earlier and the later version. Whatever may be the merits of Mr. Kaldor's criticism of either version, I cannot help feeling that in so far as he stresses the contrast between them he is labouring under a misapprehension.

In this brief note I must confine myself to the two main points on which I am represented as having changed my views. The first is connected with the admitted shift of emphasis from changes in the money rate of interest to changes in the relation between factor prices and product prices as the element governing the choice of the methods of production. If Mr. Kaldor will re-read my discussion of the changes in the 'price margins' (as I then called them) on pp. 68–83 of the first edition of *Prices and Production* (pp. 72–92 of the second edition),[2] he will find that they played then precisely the same role as they do now, and particularly that it always was these 'price margins' and not changes in the money rate of interest which I treated as the cause of changes to more or less 'capitalistic' methods of production. It is true that (after explicitly pointing out that these price margins may move independently of the money rate of interest) I did not further consider the possibility of such a divergence between the price margins and the rate of interest continuing for very long. But then I was at that time not concerned with the case of a major inflation (or deflation) but assumed (I still think reasonably) that a change in price margins would sooner or later bring about a change in the money rates of interest in the same direction. Since this naturally raised the question whether all the unpleasant consequences I discussed could not be avoided by preventing the money rate of interest from rising, I was led later to investigate the same mechanism on the assumption that money rates of interest were deliberately kept constant. The essential argument is still the same, but the assumptions under which I describe the operation of the mechanism in question are different.

The second point is the alleged shift of emphasis from the phase in which the 'period of production' is unduly lengthened to the phase in which it is

---

[1] [First published in *Economica*, n.s., vol. 9, November 1942, pp. 383–85.—Ed.]
[2] [Reprinted, pp. 244–56.—Ed.]

shortened and the connected assertion that in my 'new' theory the 'lengthening' and the 'shortening' of the capital structure are assigned to other phases of the cycle than those in which they were originally supposed to take place. Though Mr. Kaldor's references to this point hardly suggest this, he must surely be aware that these are both necessary phases in that process of alternate 'lengthenings' and 'shortenings' of the investment period which I still believe to be characteristic features of industrial fluctuations. I am afraid I cannot see the difference between fearing the necessity of having to abandon investments because it has been attempted to make the capital equipment more 'capitalistic' than is compatible with the size of that part of the people's income which they want to take out in the form of consumers' goods, and fearing that the methods of production may be made unduly capitalistic because that will later make the abandonment of these methods necessary. We can prevent such waste either by preventing the misdirected investment in the first stage or, if it has already occurred, by keeping down consumption in the second to the level which is compatible with the completion of the investments.

When Mr. Kaldor asserts of the role of the changes of the production period in the successive phases of the cycle that "in the first version they become unduly long during the boom and had to be shortened in the depression; in the new version they become progressively shorter as the boom progresses, and gradually lengthen as real wages rise with the fall of employment",[3] this statement is inconsistent with the more correct interpretation of the first version which he gives elsewhere. As he rightly emphasises, the lengthening was then supposed to be the effect of low interest rates. But low interest rates prevailed during the characteristic cycle of the past only during the early stages of the upswing and to those the lengthening process was, and is, therefore confined. In the old scheme this lengthening process would come to an end as interest rates begin to rise, just as this happens under the different assumptions underlying the new scheme when profit margins begin to rise. And under both schemes this would lead to a reduction of the volume of investment only when the effect of the shortening was strong enough to outweigh the effect of what we have since learnt to call the 'widening' of capital—though this interaction of the two different effects was not explicitly discussed in the earlier version.[4]

Finally, the apparent paradox that a high level of profits compared with the rate of interest should bring about a reduction of investment appears a paradox only because Mr. Kaldor fails to distinguish clearly between the aggregate volume of profits and the 'profit margins' in the technical sense in which I

---

[3] [Kaldor, "Concertina-Effect", this volume, pp. 289–90.—Ed.]

[4] I had already tried to make this point clear against a similar earlier statement by Mr. Kaldor in "Profits, Interest and Investment", pp. 38–39n. [this volume, pp. 234–35n.40—Ed.]

have defined the term, i.e., the ratio between factor prices and product prices. I have not denied, of course—and it forms, in fact, an essential part of my argument—that high profits in the ordinary sense are the strongest stimulus for the entrepreneurs to increase *output* and that the higher profits are the more anxious entrepreneurs will be to expand output quickly. And it is equally obvious that the larger the *amount* of profits entrepreneurs can gain by increasing investment the more ready they will be to borrow at any given rate of interest. But the whole point is that expanding final output and expanding the volume of investment are not necessarily the same thing, and that the endeavour to provide a large output quickly, such as may be caused by a large 'profit *margin*', may be the cause of a decrease in the volume of investment—in other words, that an increase of the 'profit margins' may create a situation where each entrepreneur aiming to maximise his aggregate profits may result in a smaller volume of total investment.

The 'island' illustration which Mr. Kaldor is good enough to quote at length[5] from *Prices and Production* fits as well into my present views as it fitted into those expounded in that book. It seems to me obvious that in the situation depicted in that example, and assuming a price system to operate on the island, it would be the rise in the prices of consumers' goods which would bring about the abandonment of the investments undertaken when consumers' goods were cheaper. The question with which I have been concerned more recently was whether the difficulties of the unfortunate islanders could be overcome by giving them merely enough money to keep the money rate of interest from rising. Mr. Kaldor, with the now fashionable opinion, seems to believe that this would solve their problems. I rather doubt it.

---

[5] See above, Kaldor, "Concertina-Effect", p. 360n. [this volume, p. 287n.6—Ed.] The italicising of the last phrase in this passage by Mr. Kaldor seems however to suggest an interpretation of the passage which I do not quite understand and which has clearly nothing to do with anything I had in mind when I wrote it.

Postscript[1]
By Nicholas Kaldor

With regard to the "Comment", I should like to remind Professor Hayek that in his *Prices and Production* theory, the increase in the level of investment and the 'lengthening of the productive period' were regarded as different aspects of the same thing; whereas on his recent theory, the 'period of production' varies *inversely* with the level of investment. He can either argue (as he did then) that the investment boom generated by credit creation is a foredoomed attempt to force the use of more productive methods on a reluctant community; or (as he did more recently) that credit expansion, on the contrary, involves the progressive sacrifice of productivity, in the desire to obtain ever larger streams of consumption output. But he cannot maintain both of these propositions at the same time; nor can he assert—without depriving words of the last vestige of meaning—that an 'undue lengthening' of the period of production is the same thing as an 'undue shortening' of it.

---

[1] [First published as a postscript to Kaldor, "Concertina-Effect", *Economica*, n.s., vol. 9, November 1942, p. 382, in response to Hayek's "Comment" above.—Ed.]

Postscript[1]

I am sorry that in the "Postscript" Mr. Kaldor has added in reply to the above, he should have misinterpreted me even worse than before. It is certainly not my view, or compatible with my views, to say that "the 'period of production' varies *inversely* with the level of investment".[2] The growth of the volume of investment during the early stages of the boom is, on the contrary, entirely the result of the 'lengthening' of the period of production. But while on the assumption of full employment this was the *only* cause of the growth in the volume of investment, the latter can evidently continue for some time after the former has ceased, if 'widening' is possible.

[1] [First published as a postscript to Hayek, "A Comment", *Economica*, n.s., vol. 9, November 1942, p. 385, in response to Kaldor's "Postscript" above.—Ed.]

[2] [Kaldor, "Postscript", this volume, p. 316.—Ed.]

ELEVEN

THREE ELUCIDATIONS OF
THE RICARDO EFFECT[1]

The immediate aim of this paper is to clear up a point on which Sir John Hicks in his recent review[2] of my earlier discussions[3] of the relation between

[1] [First published in *Journal of Political Economy*, vol. 77, March/April 1969, pp. 274–85, and reprinted as chapter 11 of F. A. Hayek, *New Studies in Philosophy, Politics, Economics and the History of Ideas* (London: Routledge and Kegan Paul, 1978). The text is that of the reprint.

This essay originated from correspondence between F. A. Hayek and John Hicks, which started when Hicks decided to include a reappraisal of Hayek's early work in a collection of essays (which eventually became "The Hayek Story", in John Hicks, *Critical Essays in Monetary Theory* (Oxford: Clarendon Press, 1967), pp. 203–15), and circulated a preliminary draft to Hayek. The ensuing correspondence comprehends up to a dozen letters, extending from May 1966 to December 1967, and has been preserved in the Friedrich A. von Hayek Papers, box 24, folder 32, Hoover Institution Archives, Stanford University. It has been partly reprinted as an addendum in *Good Money, Part II: The Standard*, ed. Stephen Kresge, vol. 6 (1999) of *The Collected Works of F. A. Hayek* (Chicago: University of Chicago Press; London: Routledge), pp. 100–105.

In the "Preface" (p. ix) to his *Critical Essays* Hicks gives the following account:
> One of the chief contributors to that blaze [that is, the blaze of controversy of the 1930s] was Professor Hayek (*Prices and Production*). To one who like myself felt the full impact of that work on its first appearance, it has long appeared as one of the mysteries of economics. Something, one has long realized, had gone wrong with it; but just what? The question has been nagging at me; so I decided, a couple of years ago, to write out what I thought to be the solution. Wisely, as it turned out, I submitted it to Professor Hayek . . . He told me, and he convinced me, that I had got him quite wrong. So I made another attempt . . . It is still something of an indictment, and do not expect that Professor Hayek will plead guilty to it. But I think it is now clear of any straightforward misunderstanding.

Hicks was, of course, right that Hayek did not concur with his account, and Hayek tried to set the record straight in "Three Elucidations".—Ed.]

[2] Hicks, "The Hayek Story".

[3] *Prices and Production* (London: Routledge, 1931) [2nd ed. rev. (1935); reprinted in *Business Cycles, Part I*, ed. Hansjoerg Klausinger, vol. 7 (2012) of *The Collected Works of F. A. Hayek*—Ed.]; *Profits, Interest and Investment. And Other Essays on the Theory of Industrial Fluctuations* (London: Routledge, 1939) [cf. in particular chapter 1, "Profits, Interest and Investment", reprinted in this volume—Ed.]; and "The Ricardo Effect", *Economica*, n.s., vol. 9, May 1942, pp. 127–52, reprinted in F. A. Hayek, *Individualism and Economic Order* (Chicago: University of Chicago Press, 1948; London: Routledge and Kegan Paul, 1949) [also reprinted in this volume—Ed.]. Since a rightly esteemed recent study of the development of economic doctrines asserts that my discussion of the Ricardo

the demand for consumer goods and investment, is in error. It deserves careful analysis, as I believe he has been misled into this error by an erroneous assumption characteristic of much contemporary reasoning on this and similar subjects. I will attempt such an analysis in part 2 of this paper. But, as the general thesis of what I have called the 'Ricardo Effect'[4] may not now be familiar to all readers, I shall first restate it in a manner which, though not wholly unobjectionable, I have often found to be more readily intelligible than the more precise statement I have given on earlier occasions. In part 3 I shall answer another objection to my analysis. It was frequently raised during the earlier discussions, and I was not then able to supply a satisfactory answer. Now, however, it appears to me comparatively easy to refute.

1.

The theorem called the Ricardo Effect asserts that in conditions of full employment an increase in the demand for consumer goods will produce a decrease of investment, and vice versa.[5] The manner in which this result is produced can be conveniently represented in a diagram corresponding to the familiar representations of the production function. In this diagram, however, the total *stock* (fixed *and* circulating) of capital is measured, on the abscissa; and the total *stream* of input, including all that is required to maintain the stock of capital at the level most profitable in the circumstances, is measured on the ordinate. We shall assume for the present purposes that this production function is linear and homogeneous.[6] Since the magnitudes represented along the two co-ordinates both consist of variable combinations of hetero-

---

Effect in two of my publications ("Profits, Interest and Investment" and "The Ricardo Effect") involves a reversal of the position taken in *Prices and Production*, it should be said that they are, of course, different statements of the same basic contention. Sir John's criticism refers mainly to the earlier version. [The "recent study" to which Hayek refers is Mark Blaug, *Economic Theory in Retrospect*, 1st ed. (Homewood, IL: Irwin, 1962), cf. p. 519: "The reader is warned that Hayek's Ricardo Effect is a reversal of his earlier position in *Prices and Production* (1931) . . ." This passage was deleted from the book's later editions. See also Hayek's letter to Blaug (January 26, 1963), in Hayek Papers, box 12, folder 15.—Ed.]

[4] I chose this name because Joseph A. Schumpeter, *Business Cycles: A Theoretical, Historical, and Statistical Analysis of the Capitalist Process* (New York and London: McGraw Hill, 1939), pp. 345, 812, 814, had referred to a more general and even less original aspect of my theory as the 'Hayek Effect', and I did not wish what I regarded as an old-established doctrine to be regarded as an innovation.

[5] [Note that the assumption of full employment is part of the earlier, but not of the later version of the 'Ricardo effect'.—Ed.]

[6] [A linear homogeneous production function exhibits constant returns to scale, that is, a proportional increase in all inputs leads to an equi-proportional increase in output.—Ed.]

geneous goods and services, these can of course be represented only in value terms. This would be strictly legitimate only if we could assume that the prices of the various goods and services involved remain constant. In fact, however, the changes which we will consider necessarily involve some changes in the relation between these prices. Hence the slightly unsatisfactory nature of this technique, to which I have referred before, derives. It seems to me, however, that this defect is of comparatively minor significance and does not seriously detract from the validity of the conclusions which can be derived in a comparatively simple manner by these methods. Readers who wish to see a more exact demonstration will have to refer to my 1942 article. But for the present purposes, I trust that this simplified exposition will suffice. I have long found it effective in teaching, but because of this defect, have refrained from putting it into print.

The effect I want to consider is that of a change in the prices of the product relative to the prices of the factors, and I shall primarily consider the case in which the former rise while the latter remain unchanged. I shall at first assume that the intention of the producer is to produce a given quantity of output and to maximise the percentage return on the capital employed. On these assumptions, we will ask which of the various possible combinations of stock of capital and current input the producer will find most advantageous to use in producing this particular quantity of output. Let us consider for this purpose the lower isoquant drawn in fig. 11.1 and assume that, before the price of the product rises, it stands at a figure which would bring an amount of receipts for the total output which, since it is also accruing at a time rate, we can measure along the ordinate on which we measure current input. Assume these receipts at the initial price to be OF.

What will then be the most profitable combination of stock of capital and current input to produce this given output? Evidently this will be the point on the isoquant at which a straight line drawn from F just touches it, that is, the point P. Here the slope of the line connecting F with a point on the isoquant is steeper than for any other point on this curve; this means that the proportional profits EF/OC are higher than at any other point.

Assume now that the price of the product rises from F to F'. The result must be that the point of tangency of a line drawn from F' will lie to the left and above P and that this point P' will correspond to a combination of a smaller stock of capital, C', and a larger amount of current input, E', than were used before.

This is the chief conclusion for the case in which the aim is to produce a constant output. We will examine what this conclusion implies before we extend it to the case in which the producer intends to use all his capital in the production of the commodity in question and tries to produce from it as much as he most profitably can with all his available capital (and assuming, as we

320

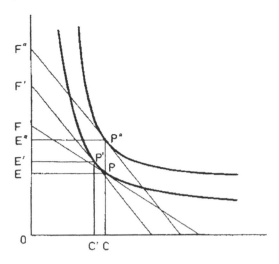

Figure 11.1

shall throughout, that he faces a horizontal demand curve for his product). The conclusion means, in the first instance, that, though the total outlay in production will have increased, it will increase proportionally less than receipts: the share of profits in the total will grow. In addition to this, the distribution of current outlay between current cost of production and the maintenance of capital stock will also change: a larger proportion will go to the former and a smaller proportion to the latter. Precisely where we draw the line between the part of this total outlay we call current costs and that which we call (gross) investment is always to some degree arbitrary. But wherever we draw this line, it is clear that the share of investment in the total must fall and that, if we define investment sufficiently narrowly, the absolute amount of investment must also fall: the demand for certain kinds of highly labour-saving or very durable equipment will be reduced. This is necessarily implied by the transition from a more to a less capital-intensive method of production. The chief point, that an increase in the demand for consumer goods will lead (in conditions of full employment) to a decrease in the demand for the kind of investment goods appropriate only to more highly capital-intensive methods of production, is thus established.

The same conclusion follows if, after the rise in the prices of consumer goods, we assume that the producer, instead of aiming at producing the same quantity of output as before, will aim at producing as much as will bring him the highest return on the amount of capital employed before. This is readily seen if we continue the line CP upward until it intersects a higher isoquant at a point P'' where its tangent is parallel to that at P'. The price for this quan-

321

tity of output will be *OF"*. The current input required for producing *OF"* will be *OE"*, with *E"F"* representing the maximum amount of profit obtainable at this price by combining a larger input with the given total quantity of capital. But this unchanged total quantity of capital will again have to consist of less labour-saving or less durable equipment than before; the demand for the more labour-saving or more durable kinds of equipment will therefore fall.

It is not necessary to show explicitly that in the opposite case, of a fall in the price of the product with factor prices remaining constant, a corresponding transition from more to less capital-intensive methods will take place.[7]

2.

This basic proposition of the Ricardo Effect is, of course, as much a part of the elementary theory of capital as it is important for the understanding of industrial fluctuations. It shows how changes in the demand for consumer goods will affect the rate of investment through a change in the relative prices of products and factors of production (or, more simply, through a change in 'real wages') and will lead to such a change in the rate of investment even if there is no lending of money and therefore no market rate of interest for money loans. The 'scarcity of capital' will in this case express itself only in the relation among the prices of the goods belonging to the different stages of production (or what in *Prices and Production*[8] I called the 'price margins' between stages of production).

The chief significance of the proposition arises, however, in connection with a money economy in which the equilibrium structure of prices determined solely by the 'real' factors may be distorted for prolonged periods by continuing changes in the quantity of money, producing a difference between what is saved out of current income and what is spent on investment. If some of the money that is received as income and not spent on consumer goods is not invested but hoarded or otherwise withdrawn from circulation, or if investment is fed in excess of the amount of saving, by additional money created for the purpose, or is released from cash balances, a persistent alteration of the price structure will be produced which will continue to exist and to determine the rate of investment, as long as the *change* in the volume of the money stream persists.

It is at this point that Sir John Hicks's criticism comes in. He maintains that such a distortion of the price structure can only be of a very transient char-

---

[7] [This is an obvious slip of the pen. It should read, "from less to more capital-intensive methods".—Ed.]

[8] Second edition (1939 [1935]), pp. 72–80 [reprinted, pp. 244–50—Ed.].

acter and that, even though the change in the volume of the money stream continues, there must be a determined time interval, or 'lag', after which relative prices will return to the equilibrium position determined solely by the real factors. This contention appears to me wholly unfounded and erroneous. It seems to me that it can be shown that there can be no such determined lag after which the price structure will resume the equilibrium position depending only on the real factors. On the contrary, as long as the change in the volume of the money stream continues, there will persist a different position, a sort of steady state (as the biologists call such a 'fluid equilibrium'), determined by the continuing inflow or outflow of money into the system.

The crucial contentions are stated by Sir John in a single paragraph of his exposition.[9] For the convenience of the reader, I will reproduce here most of this paragraph, with Sir John's own italics rendered in small capitals and the parts to which I specially want to draw attention in italics:

> When the market rate of interest is reduced below the natural rate, what will happen to the QUANTITIES of inputs and outputs? The correct answer, on these assumptions, is very simple: The effect will be nil. *Prices will rise uniformly*; and that is that. When the Wicksell model is taken strictly (as it was taken strictly), it is in NEUTRAL EQUILIBRIUM. The whole REAL system, of quantities and of RELATIVE prices, is completely determined by the supply and demand equations in the particular markets; in this REAL system THE rate of interest is included. There can only be one rate of interest when the markets are in equilibrium; a market rate that is equal to the natural rate. The 'reduction' of the market rate below the natural rate must therefore be regarded as a disequilibrium phenomenon; *a phenomenon that can only persist while the markets are out of equilibrium.* As soon as equilibrium is restored, equality between the market rate and natural rate must be restored. Thus there is *no room for a discrepancy* between market rate and natural rate *if there is instantaneous adjustment of prices* [to what?—the 'real' data only?]. Money prices will simply rise UNIFORMLY; and that is that.[10]

The conception of equilibrium implied in this passage is that of a structure of relative prices determined only by the real factors (that is, excluding the effects of any continuing monetary change), a structure which will restore itself promptly after being disturbed by the first impact of a monetary change, even while the change itself (inflow or outflow of money into or out of the sys-

[9] "The Hayek Story", p. 206.

[10] [Hayek's quotation is slightly inaccurate. In the first sentence, "When the market rate is reduced", he amended "of interest", below he added "the" in the passage, "equality between market rate and natural rate", and in the penultimate sentence deleted "prolonged" from the original "no room for a prolonged discrepancy".—Ed.]

tem) still continues. That is, even if part of the investment is continuously financed by money created for the purpose (or in the reverse case), the price structure is presumed to return to the position it had before this happened. In other words, the continuing inflow or outflow of money is not considered part of the data to which the price structure will remain adapted as long as this condition persists, but apparently as affecting the price structure only temporarily when the change first occurs and as rapidly disappearing although the changed condition persists. My contention is that this 'disequilibrium' is an adjustment to a new datum, the inflow of new money, and must continue as long as these additions to the money stream continue to enter the system at a given point and at a constant percentage rate.

Sir John does not say explicitly whether he is arguing in terms of a single addition to the quantity of money taking place during a short period or of a protracted process of this kind extending over many months or even years. It will be useful to analyse these cases in turn. We will assume first that a single dose of additional money is spent in the course of a single month on a part of the investment activities which amounts to 1 per cent of all expenditure on goods and services, and that this doubles the amount spent on those particular goods and services on which it is spent in the first instance. This will mean that the total money stream also increases by 1 per cent. It will simplify the exposition if we further assume that the transaction velocity of money is twelve times per year (cash balances equal to monthly expenditure), in which case the increase of the expenditure by 1 per cent in the course of one month will also mean a 1 per cent increase in the quantity of money.

What will, in consequence, happen to prices? The aim of the extra expenditure is to attract more factors to the production of the investment goods in question; this, in conditions of full employment, can be achieved only by driving up their prices. How much their prices will rise will depend on the elasticity of their supply. The particular figures we assume for the purposes of illustration do not matter. To keep the figures as simple as possible, we shall assume that a doubling of the demand brings forth a 60 per cent increase of the supply at a price raised by 25 per cent.

This rise of some (and a very small part of all) prices by 25 per cent will have been produced by an increase in the money stream (and, on our assumptions, also of the stock of money) of 1 per cent. Of course, if the expenditure of the additional money on investment were a single nonrecurrent event, confined to a single month, the effects would be of a transient character. The money received by the producers of the investment goods would in turn be spent by them on other goods and gradually spread throughout the system. In the end, the old structure of relative prices would be restored at a level roughly 1 per cent higher than it was originally. (We can here disregard any changes in the price structure due to a redistribution of assets and consequently of the personal distribution of incomes and the resulting changes in the direction of demand which may occur in the course of the process.) The main point is that the 25 per cent initial rise of some prices necessary to bring about the addition to real investment by 60 per cent will be of a wholly temporary nature and will ultimately produce a rise of all prices of only 1 per cent.

What happens, however, if the increase in the quantity of money entering through additional investment continues for a much longer period? We shall now assume that it does so, not at a constant, absolute rate, but at such a rate as is necessary to maintain the increased volume of real investment. This will mean a constant percentage increase in the total flow (and quantity) of money, because, if before it needed a 1 per cent addition to attract the additional resources to investment, after the total money stream (and general prices) will have risen by 1 per cent, it will need an increase of 1.01 per cent to produce the same effect, and so on.[11]

This process can evidently go on indefinitely, at least as long as we neglect changes in the manner in which expectations concerning future prices are formed. Whatever the lag between the impact effect of the new expenditure on a few prices affected immediately and the spreading of this effect to any other prices, the distortion of the 'equilibrium' price structure corresponding to the 'real' data only must continue to exist. The extra demand which continually enters in the form of newly created money remains one of the constant data determining a price structure adjusted to this demand. However short the lag between one price change and the effect of the expenditure of the increased receipts on other prices, and as long as the process of change in the total money stream continues, the changed relationship between particular prices will also be preserved.

In other words, the order in which the additional money expenditure reaches the different goods will determine a gradient in the whole price structure which must continue to exist as long as the total money stream continues to increase. Indeed, the prices affected later never will catch up with those affected first. When the influx of money, which is the cause of the rise in prices, stops, the prices which have risen first must actually fall—of course not to the original level, but to somewhere near the new average level that will establish itself after the whole additional money has distributed itself throughout the system. But some prices must continue to run ahead of the rest as long as part of the demand for them does not spring from the receipts for some previous

[11] [According to this illustration in order to sustain the distortion of the price structure the absolute amounts of money injected into the economy must rise progressively, from 1 per cent of the initial quantity of money to 1.01 per cent and so on; this corresponds to a constant proportional rise in the quantity of money, that is, to a *constant* rate of growth of money of 1 per cent. Taking into account the formation of inflationary expectations—as Hayek is suggesting—would then necessitate an accelerating rate of growth of money.—Ed.]

sale of other goods or services but from money created (or released from cash balances) for that purpose. As long as the general process of a rise (or fall) of prices continues, it is impossible for the structure of relative prices to be the same as that which would exist if the forces causing the general change of prices were absent, for the simple reason that the same cause (the change in the quantity of money) can affect the different prices only successively and not simultaneously. More investment than will take place in the state of equilibrium determined only by the real factors can take place only as long as, compared with other prices, the prices of investment goods are higher than they would be in that equilibrium. "And that is that."

I find it useful to illustrate the general relationship by an analogy which seems worth stating here, though Sir John (in correspondence) did not find it helpful.[12] The effect we are discussing is rather similar to that which appears when we pour a viscous liquid, such as honey, into a vessel. There will, of course, be a tendency for it to spread to an even surface. But if the stream hits the surface at one point, a little mound will form there from which the additional matter will slowly spread outward. Even after we have stopped pouring in more, it will take some time until the even surface will be fully restored. It will, of course, not reach the height which the top of the mound had reached when the inflow stopped. But as long as we pour at a constant rate, the mound will preserve its height relative to the surrounding pool—providing a very literal illustration of what I called before a fluid equilibrium.[13]

In connection with such phenomena, the conception of a 'lag' does not seem to be very useful. There is certainly no assignable interval of time between the first change of a price due to changes in the quantity of money and the moment when all prices have changed in the same proportion, because, unless the monetary change (the inflow or outflow of money into the system) continues, the first price change will have been partly reversed before most of the other prices are affected. Nor is the relevant change in the price structure dependent on a rapid change in the general price level. In our example, the increase in the prices of the relevant investment goods by 25 per cent was brought about by a 1 per cent increase in the quantity of money. Such an increase is

[12] [Indeed, after Hayek had brought forward a similar example in a letter from October 30, 1966, Hicks responded belatedly in a letter, dated January 3, 1967, where he admitted that he did not "find it a convincing analogy". Hicks fully agreed "that if there is continuous inflation, and if there is any lag, it will act on the relative price-system . . . like an increase in genuine saving". Yet, "surely there must be a relation between the length of the lag, the rate of inflation and the amount of price-distortion", so that—Hicks attributing this very assumption to Hayek—if "there is only a short lag . . . , then there can only be a serious distortion if the rate of inflation is very rapid".—Ed.]

[13] [Hayek used an analogous simile already in "The Ricardo Effect", this volume, p. 274.—Ed.]

surely not unlikely to occur in the course of a boom. And since it might well take many months before this effect spreads through the whole price system, it would also be some time before it becomes necessary to increase the absolute rate of increase of the money stream in order to maintain the given volume of real investment in the face of the gradual rise of the competing demand for consumer goods.

When, however, the inflow of money through investment ceases, the spreading of its effects will continue and will tend to restore something similar to the initial position. It is at this point that the Ricardo Effect operates in a manner in which it is least understood. Prices of investment goods at this stage will fall; prices of consumer goods will, for some time, continue to rise. This will make some of the investment which has been taking place less profitable than it was before, at the same time that the flow of investable funds is reduced. The controlling factor will thus be that, after the inflow of new money has ceased and, in consequence, smaller funds are available for investment, the prices of consumer goods will continue to rise for some time. The result will be that some of the factors which during the boom will have become committed to producing very capital-intensive equipment will become unemployed.

This is the mechanism by which I conceive that, unless credit expansion is continued progressively, an inflation-fed boom must sooner or later be reversed by a decline in investment. This theory never claimed to do more than account for the upper turning point of the typical nineteenth-century business cycle. The cumulative process of contraction likely to set in once unemployment appears in the capital-good industries is another matter which must be analysed by conventional means. It has always been an open question to me as to how long a process of continued inflation, not checked by a built-in limit on the supply of money and credit, could effectively maintain investment above the volume justified by the voluntary rate of savings. It may well be that this inevitable check only comes when inflation becomes so rampant—as the progressively higher rate of inflation required to maintain a given volume of investment must make it sooner or later—that money ceases to be an adequate accounting basis. But this cannot be further discussed without raising the problem of the effect of such changes on expectations—a problem which I do not wish to discuss here.

3.

An objection which in the past has frequently been raised against my analysis of the Ricardo Effect is that, if money can be borrowed in any desired amount at the current market rate of interest, the character of the investment will be determined by this market rate, and the internal rate of return of the enterprises will be adjusted to it. It seems to me now that this conclusion is the result of an illegitimate extension of an assumption that is reasonable enough concerning the supply of a commodity, but which cannot apply to the supply of credit or loans.

This objection against the operation of the Ricardo Effect in a money economy rests on the tacit assumption that competitive conditions require that the individual enterprises face a horizontal supply curve of loan capital and therefore can borrow, at the current market rate of interest, as much as they desire. This assumption seems to me neither to follow from the concept of perfect competition nor to be true of any real circumstances. It rests on the belief that successive loans to a given borrower can and ought to be regarded as the 'same' commodity and therefore to be available at the same price. This, however, is evidently not the case, since the risk to the lender increases with the amount of the loan to any one borrower possessing a given amount of capital or equity.

For our purposes, we may greatly oversimplify and assume that the proportion of the total indebtedness of a borrower to his equity is the only factor determining the risk to the lender. There would then exist a uniform market rate of interest at which every borrower could borrow up to say, 25 per cent of his equity. For an additional 10 per cent, he would have to pay more; for yet another 10 per cent, still more; and so on. The reason for this will be that to the lender a loan to somebody already in debt to an amount equal to 25 per cent of his equity is a different commodity from a loan to somebody who has much smaller debts. There may thus exist a perfect market for loans of each class, and every borrower who wants to increase his borrowing within this range may be able to do so at the same rate of interest; but he will, if he wants to borrow beyond this range, have to pay a higher rate.

In other words, although for every class of loan there may prevail a perfectly elastic supply at the given rate of interest, *every borrower will, after a while, be faced with a rapidly rising supply curve of loans,* because additional amounts which he may borrow must be regarded not as the same but as a different kind of commodity compared with his earlier loans. This clearly is the realistic way of looking at the position, and only the inappropriate habit of treating successive loans of a given borrower as homogeneous commodities could lead to a neglect of this obvious fact.

But if, even in a perfect credit market, we must assume that every individual borrower is faced with a supply curve of loans which, beyond a certain point, begins to rise more and more rapidly (and probably at some point becomes almost perpendicular), we can no longer assume that the given market rate will determine the internal rates of return of the existing enterprises. There will be a long-run tendency to adjust the internal rates of return to the market rate for loans, but this will operate very slowly and largely via changes in the equity capital of the enterprises concerned and the entry of new enterprises into the industries in which the internal rates of return have changed. But in the short run, including the sort of periods with which we are concerned in the analysis of industrial fluctuations, no such adaptation of the internal rate of the return on capital to the market rate for loans can be assumed to take place generally. What will then be the position of an enterprise that finds that the price of its product has risen relative to the price of the factors (or that, as I have expressed it on earlier occasions, 'real' wages have fallen)? If it could borrow, at the unchanged market rate of interest, as much as it liked, the enterprise would, of course, wish to increase all its equipment proportionally, that is, to produce more by methods as capital-intensive as those employed before. But it will find that, at the market rate of interest, it cannot borrow anything like the amount that would be necessary for that purpose. In addition, what it can borrow at the market rate it will probably obtain only for increasing its circulating capital but not for increasing its fixed capital. The firm's internal rate of return will have greatly risen, but what it can borrow at a rate corresponding to this increased rate of internal return will be only a fraction of what it could profitably employ at that rate—certainly not enough to bring its internal rate of return down to anywhere near *the* market rate. The use it will make of the limited capital at its disposal will therefore be determined by its internal rate of return, which will be equal to the *marginal* rate at which *it* can borrow but which is likely to be considerably above what is regarded as *the* market rate. So far as it can borrow a little, its internal rate of return will of course be somewhat under the figure it would reach if the firm could not raise any additional funds at all. But the rate which will govern the nature of its investments will still be its individual internal rate, considerably above the market rate, and possibly very different for different enterprises.

Since the firm can raise little or no additional funds to increase its total investments, and since it encounters particular difficulties in obtaining additional funds for long-term investment, and since, at the same time the returns it can obtain from circulating capital have risen relative to those of fixed capital, it will be driven to what formerly was called a 'conversion of fixed into circulating capital';[14] the firm will put as little as possible of what becomes available for investment into durable equipment, or will put it into less durable or less labour-saving equipment and as much as possible into labour and raw materials.

I will not enter here into another question about which doubt has often

---

[14] [In *Prices and Production*, reprinted, pp. 262–63, Hayek presented examples of the prevalence in the second half of the nineteenth century of the reverse notion of 'a conversion of circulating into fixed capital' as a characteristic of a credit-fuelled boom. Cf. also *The Pure Theory of Capital* (London: Macmillan, 1941), reprinted, ed. Lawrence White, as vol. 12 (2007) of *The Collected Works of F. A. Hayek*, Appendix 2.—Ed.]

been expressed in this connection, namely, the question of the extent to which we can assume realistically that such changes are technologically feasible in the short run. The single instance of the possibility of a change from one shift to two or three, which is only one of a very large number of similar possibilities, seems to me to be a sufficient answer. At a relatively higher rate of 'real wages', and at the corresponding lower internal rate of return, the higher costs of labour in a second or third shift may have made the change appear unprofitable. But with the fall in 'real wages' and the consequent rise of the rate of return on short-term investment compared with that on long-term investment, the change will become profitable, and at the same time part of the existing equipment will become abundant. And what is saved on the replacement of that equipment becomes available for paying more labour. Total outlay may remain the same (or, insofar as the firm can borrow, increase a little), but more of it will be spent on labour and less on equipment.

It should be obvious from a rather elementary consideration, that there must exist some such mechanism through which, sooner or later, an increase in the demand for consumer goods leads not to an increase but to a decrease in the demand for investment goods. If it were true that an increase in the demand for consumer goods *always* leads to an increase in investment, even in a state of full employment, the consequence would be that the more urgently consumer goods are demanded the more their supply would fall off. More and more factors would be shifted to producing investment goods until, in the end, because the demand for consumer goods would have become so very urgent, no consumer goods at all would be produced. This clearly points to an absurdity in the reasoning which leads to such a conclusion.[15] The mechanism which prevents such a result is the Ricardo Effect. And though its operation may not be obvious for a long time because of more apparent monetary complications, and may even be altogether suspended as long as there is general unemployment, sooner or later it must reassert itself. Sir John Hicks is right to the extent that the relationships determined by the real data only must assert themselves sooner or later. But this does not happen as instantaneously as he assumes. There may be a prolonged period during which the relations corresponding to the 'real equilibrium' are greatly distorted by monetary changes. It still seems to me that this has much to do with the phenomenon of industrial fluctuations.

[15] [See on this the editor's introduction above, p. 20.—Ed.]

TWELVE

THE FLOW OF GOODS AND SERVICES[1]

Foreword

I have asked the director's permission to speak here, to the day exactly fifty years after I delivered from the same platform the first of four lectures that led to my appointment to a professorship at this school, which I then held for the following nineteen years.[2] I believe I owed this invitation wholly to Lionel Robbins, who then, as today, was in the chair, my senior by a few months and himself only two years before appointed to his professorship. He indeed has, I believe except for the war years, continuously taught here for fifty-two years, so there is nothing very spectacular about my returning after all this time, except that to me the event meant the decisive step in my career. It was a stroke of improbable luck, and decisive for all my future development, that I received such an invitation at that particular moment. It was unlikely enough that a lecture I had delivered two years earlier, as a test for a readership at the University of Vienna, on "The 'Paradox' of Saving",[3] should attract the attention of an English professor who knew enough German to understand what he did

---

[1] [F. A. Hayek read this paper on the occasion of the fiftieth anniversary of his *Prices and Production* lectures at LSE on January 27, 1981. It has since then been translated into German as *Der Strom der Güter und Leistungen*, trans. Claudia Loy, Walter Eucken Institute, *Vorträge und Aufsätze*, no. 101 (Tübingen: Mohr-Siebeck, 1984). Originally, the essay (except the foreword) was intended as chapter 10 of F. A. Hayek's *The Fatal Conceit*, yet was not included in the published version, edited by W. W. Bartley III, as vol. 1 (1989) of *The Collected Works of F. A. Hayek* (Chicago: University of Chicago Press; London: Routledge). The text reprinted here consists of the original typescript prepared for the lecture as edited by Hayek for the intended publication in *The Fatal Conceit*. (Cf. also Ulrich Witt, "Bibliographic Note on F. A. Hayek, 'The Flow of Goods and Services'", appended to the typescript prepared for the 1999 Liberty Fund Symposium "The Legacy of F. A. Hayek Today".)—Ed.]

[2] [The reference is to the 1931 lectures at LSE that ultimately turned into *Prices and Production* (London: Routledge, 1931; 2nd ed. rev., 1935), reprinted in *Business Cycles, Part I*, ed. Hansjoerg Klausinger, vol. 7 (2012) of *The Collected Works of F. A. Hayek.*—Ed.]

[3] ["Gibt es einen 'Widersinn des Sparens'?" *Zeitschrift für Nationalökonomie*, vol. 1, November 1929, pp. 387–429, translated as "The 'Paradox' of Saving", *Economica*, no. 32, May 1931, pp. 125–69, reprinted as chapter 2 of *Contra Keynes and Cambridge: Essays, Correspondence*, ed. Bruce Caldwell, vol. 9 (1995) of *The Collected Works of F. A. Hayek.*—Ed.]

not know already: A. C. Pigou had earlier reviewed Knut Wicksell,[4] and J. M. Keynes Ludwig von Mises for the *Economic Journal*,[5] both, as Keynes later admitted, able to understand in German only what they knew already.[6] It was also an extraordinary coincidence that I had at that moment for the first time clearly perceived the outlines of an argument which I still think important, but had not yet become aware of all the difficulties its full elaboration would encounter. I was thus able to give a relatively simple overall sketch without being too concerned about the details. Indeed, *Prices and Production* is the only book of mine which I ever wrote out in a few weeks, in the excitement about a new insight gained, and not from notes accumulated over years. Moreover, I had also a few years before been able to spend a little over a year at New York where, before the time of the Rockefeller fellowships, I had gone at my own risk and with a minimum of money in my pockets, and thus acquired some ability to express myself in English—quite intelligibly, as I was told after the lectures, as soon as I diverted from my carefully prepared manuscript, which Lionel Robbins afterwards turned into readable English. But I had also, for a historical introduction to a textbook on money which I never completed,[7] devoted much of the immediately preceding years to a thorough study of the development of English monetary theory and institutions, and as a result could impress my audience with a familiarity with the relevant English literature which among them probably only the late Sir Theodore Gregory shared.[8] These are the

[4] [Arthur Cecil Pigou, "Review of Knut Wicksell, *Vorlesungen über Nationalökonomie auf der Grundlage des Marginalprinzips*", *Economic Journal*, vol. 23, December 1913, pp. 605–6. Wicksell's *Vorlesungen* were later on translated as *Lectures on Political Economy*, vol. 1: *General Theory*, trans. Ernest Classen (London: Routledge, 1934; reprinted New York: Kelley, 1967; Auburn, AL: Ludwig von Mises Institute, 2007).—Ed.]

[5] [John Maynard Keynes, "Review of Ludwig Mises, *Theorie des Geldes und der Umlaufsmittel*", *Economic Journal*, vol. 24, September 1914, pp. 417–19. For an English translation of the revised second edition (1924) see *The Theory of Money and Credit*, trans. H. E. Batson (London: Cape, 1934; reprinted, Indianapolis: Liberty Press, 1981).—Ed.]

[6] [Cf. John Maynard Keynes, *A Treatise on Money*, vol. 1 (London: Macmillan, 1930), reprinted as vol. 5 (1971) of *The Collected Writings of John Maynard Keynes*, ed. Austin Robinson and Donald Moggridge (London: Macmillan; Cambridge: Cambridge University Press), p. 178n.2: "In German I only clearly understand what I know already!—so that *new* ideas are apt to be veiled from me by the difficulties of language."—Ed.]

[7] [*Geld und Kredit als Grundlagen der Verkehrswirtschaft* (that is, *Money and Credit as the Basis of a Market Economy*), planned as volume 4, part 2 of the famous series *Grundriß der Sozialökonomik* (Tübingen: Mohr, 1914 and later); cf. the Friedrich A. von Hayek Papers, Incremental Material, box 104, folder 11, Hoover Institution Archives, Stanford University, for the plan of the book. The chapters on the history of British monetary policy have now been translated and reprinted as chapters 9–12 of *The Trend of Economic Thinking: Essays on Political Economists and Economic History*, ed. W. W. Bartley III and Stephen Kresge, vol. 3 (1999) of *The Collected Works of F. A. Hayek*.—Ed.]

[8] [The British economist Theodore E. Gregory (1890–1970), Cassel Professor of Economics 1927–37, was Hayek's colleague at LSE.—Ed.]

sorts of accidents by which a successful academic career is launched, and I cannot be grateful enough for this decisive opportunity at its beginning.

Those lectures were also the first occasion at which I made use of what became the leading theme of most of my later work, an analysis of the signal function of prices in guiding production, a conception which I first expounded systematically a few years later in my presidential address to the London Economic Club on "Economics and Knowledge".[9] It has ever since been growing more central to my thinking on economic theory.

What I am going to read to you today is essentially a chapter of a book on a much wider subject which I am preparing.[10] For the argument of that book the contention is of critical importance that the coordination of economic activities, to which we owe our ability to maintain the present population of the world, is due to our relying for guidance on prices formed on competitive markets which generate the indispensable signals which tell us what to do. This chapter will be preceded in the book by a more general statement of the process of extension of the economic order into the unknown, and what I am going to select is the discussion of those more complex events that occupied me already fifty years ago, and which, I believe, explain why we allow this process of ordering to perform its potential capacities so much less effectively than it could. Parts of this reasoning are today fairly widely accepted.

What I shall thus speak about is the general subject of my lecture of fifty years ago: the relations between prices and production, but without entering into details of the monetary problems involved. Yet I cannot resist the temptation first to quote just one sentence from that earlier lecture which may be even more topical today than it was then. Speaking of what I called "the more mechanistic forms of the quantity theory of money" (now called 'monetarism') I said then that I was "even ready to concede that so far it goes it is true, and that, from a practical point of view, it would be one of the worst things that could befall us if the general public should ever again cease to believe in the elementary proposition of the quantity theory"[11] (as John Maynard Keynes soon after would succeed in making it)—only to devote all the rest of my lectures to show what a gross over-simplification of the real processes that theory constituted.

The motto which, according to my old habit, I have placed at the head of this chapter, should be familiar to you.

---

[9] [The presidential address of November 10, 1936, printed in *Economica*, n.s., vol. 4, February 1937, pp. 33–54, reprinted as chapter 2 of *Individualism and Economic Order* (Chicago: University of Chicago Press, 1948; London: Routledge and Kegan Paul, 1949).—Ed.]

[10] [Which was to become F. A. Hayek, *The Fatal Conceit*.—Ed.]

[11] [*Prices and Production*, reprinted, pp. 194–95. Note the minor inaccuracies in the quotation, which should read, "even ready to concede that so far as it goes it is true" and "the elementary propositions of the quantity theory".—Ed.]

The Flow of Goods and Services

And you all know security is mortals' chiefest enemy.

—William Shakespeare[12]

Most productive efforts nowadays serve consumption only for much later and often at very distant dates. All production takes time, and when and how men's current efforts will serve consumers is mostly unknown to the producers. Yet how large a part of the products of current efforts we can wait for and for how long will depend on the provisions we have already made for our needs in the nearer future. And because the total amount of potential present income which we are willing to shift to the more distant future is always smaller than that which would still increase its return,[13] we must, in order to achieve the best results, select among the various time-consuming possibilities of transformation ('methods of production') those for which the time-rate of increase of what we invest is largest.

This distribution of resources among the different manners of serving the needs of wide ranges of future dates will be guided by price signals in the same manner as that in which the distribution of resources between different kinds of needs is effected. It will be convenient to refer to this distribution of resources along that time-dimension as the longitudinal (or vertical) distribution in contrast to the cross-sectional or horizontal distribution between the production of the different kinds of goods and services for any one future date. I shall similarly distinguish by already established terms between a 'lengthening and a widening' of the streams of production[14] according to whether the changes aim at devoting more resources to production for a more distant date or at equipping with more capital a larger amount of primary resources without extending the waiting period.

The structure of production must thus be seen as a multi-dimensional affair in which at any one moment men work for the output of a wide range of future dates, and the output of any one date is correspondingly the effect of the application of resources during a wide range of earlier dates. The several parallel streams of maturing products can, of course, be only distinguished conceptually—they appear as a continuum not only side by side but also longitudinally—and for most of the constituent parts their ultimate destination

---

[12] [*Macbeth*, act 3, scene 5.—Ed.]

[13] [That is, the rate of return on investment as determined by the volume of voluntary saving will be positive, indicating a positive rate of time preference.—Ed.]

[14] [In the terminology of Ralph G. Hawtrey the equivalent terms are 'capital deepening' and 'widening', the former being identical to the Austrian notion of the 'lengthening' of the structure of production. Hayek used Hawtrey's terms, e.g., in "Profits, Interest and Investment", chapter 1 of *Profits, Interest and Investment. And Other Essays on the Theory of Industrial Fluctuations* (London: Routledge and Sons, 1939), reprinted in this volume, p. 235.—Ed.]

will not yet be discernible. The elements bear no marks of their destination and at each successive step it will be price gradients[15] which will determine what parts of the total of any kind of output will move in the different possible directions. For many intermediate goods the date at which, and the form in which, they will serve the consumer, is as little determined at the beginning as in the case of the primary factors of production used. How one of millions of nails or steel balls, cotton thread or lumps of rubber, glass bulbs or tons of coal will serve the needs of the consumers will be as indeterminate as the destination of the efforts of their makers. A part of the stream of available supplies, the proportion of any aggregate which will go the different ways, may change at each successive phase, some probably still waiting for uncertain distant uses while others have already been consumed.

The amount and variety of things on which we can draw to serve the needs of the near future are necessarily always more restricted than those of which we can avail ourselves in providing for more distant dates. Present goods will for this reason (even apart from seasonal fluctuations) be generally scarcer and dearer than those expected to be available only in the future: the former[16] represent a larger range of opportunities. Taking time, or 'waiting', makes possible an increase of the results of our efforts. But since we can do only a limited amount of waiting, we must choose *those* possibilities in which, in proportion to the length of the time we have to wait for the result, the relative increase of value is greatest.

The second aspect of the problem of resource allocation which this raises is seen most clearly if we conceive of the whole process of production as a continuous stream or flow which at its mouth yields a continuous output, emerging after having passed through various transformations since the first resources had been applied. At any one moment a great number of such streams, or rather complex ramified river systems, will be proceeding concurrently, each a little more advanced than the next one. The finished products of all these streams will emerge at more or less distant future dates. This condition is sometimes described by saying that an analogue of the stream through which the current output has already passed, or of any of the now proceeding streams which will mature in the future, is always simultaneously present in a kind of synchronised state—representing all the phases through which the current output has already passed, or of any of the future streams through which the current input will have to pass before the final output will reach consumption. But, helpful as this fiction may be in some respects, it becomes misleading if it is interpreted to mean that the corresponding phases of the successive streams

---

[15] [Cf. for a similar use of this term F. A. Hayek, "Three Elucidations of the Ricardo Effect", *Journal of Political Economy*, vol. 77, March/April 1969, reprinted in this volume, p. 325.—Ed.]

[16] [Apparently, this is a slip of the pen and should refer to "the latter", that is, to future goods.—Ed.]

are wholly alike. This can never be the case: it was the flows of the past which prepared the channels for the present stream. Even if the external circumstances remained unchanged, it would be a stream which would change all the time because in each passage it would tend somewhat to alter the conditions for each succeeding one.[17]

Most important, however, there will rarely exist a close correspondence between the volume of aggregate input and aggregate output. In consequence, the volume of the stream will tend to swell or shrink in some degree because *final demand, and demand for primary factors, will change at different rates, and at times even in opposite directions.* The conventional picture on which the whole of Keynesian analysis is based which represents the connection of final demand and employment as analogous to the relation between the suction applied at one end of a pipe and its intake at the other end, is thus very misleading. Between the two lies an elastic or variable reservoir, the size of which is determined by a set of circumstances largely neglected in the Keynesian analysis.

Lord Keynes showed his failure to comprehend this by his derisory reference to Leslie Stephen's true remark that "the doctrine is so rarely understood that its complete apprehension is, perhaps, the best test of an economist— that demand for commodities is not demand for labour".[18] Keynes certainly

---

[17] [Perfect synchronisation is only possible in a stationary state of the economy, where past, present, and future are all alike. In this sense, in such a synchronised state capital is steadily reproduced, which led some capital theorists, e.g., John Bates Clark, to speak of the permanency of capital as a fund. This type of "synchronization economics" stands in stark contrast to the "advance economics" propagated by Austrian capital theory. Whereas the latter is aware "that what society lives on at any given moment is the result of past production", the former points out that in a stationary state, due to synchronisation, "the process works *as if* society did live on current production" (as formulated by Joseph A. Schumpeter, *History of Economic Analysis* (London: Allen and Unwin, 1954; reprinted, Routledge, 1994), p. 565). Cf. also Hayek on the limitations of the analysis of stationary states: "In actual life the existing stock of capital goods is always the result of an accidental historical process, consisting of a succession of unforeseen changes, and they will never be reproduced in exactly the same form." (*The Pure Theory of Capital* (London: Macmillan, 1941), reprinted, ed. Lawrence White, as vol. 12 (2007) of *The Collected Works of F. A. Hayek*, p. 102.)—Ed.]

[18] Leslie Stephen, *History of English Thought in the Eighteenth Century*, vol. 2 (London: Smith, Elder, 1876), p. 297; cf. John Maynard Keynes, *The General Theory of Employment, Interest and Money* (London: Macmillan 1936) [reprinted as vol. 7 (1971) of *The Collected Writings of John Maynard Keynes*— Ed.], p. 359n. [Hayek himself quoted Stephen in *The Pure Theory of Capital*, reprinted, p. 389. The doctrine in question originates from John Stuart Mill, *Principles of Political Economy*, ed. William James Ashley (London: Longmans, Green, 1909; reprinted, New York: Kelley, 1976), book 1, chapter 5, paragraph 9, p. 79; cf. *Principles of Political Economy, Part 1*, ed. John M. Robson, vol. 2 (1965) of the *Collected Works of John Stuart Mill* (Toronto: University of Toronto Press; London: Routledge and Kegan Paul; reprinted, Indianapolis: Liberty Fund, 2006), p. 78; see also Hayek, "Profits, Interest and Investment", this volume, p. 231. The English author and critic Leslie Stephen (1832–1904) was the father of Virginia Woolf and Vanessa Bell of Bloomsbury group fame.—Ed.]

did not pass that test, and his oversimplified one-dimensional picture of the relation between final demand and employment is the result of this failure to understand the factors which guide the successive steps in the stream of production so as to alternatingly bringing about changing rates of accumulation and decumulation of capital.

The necessity of maintaining the stream of unfinished goods and stocks, of tools and equipment, or of increasing their volume if we wish to bring about a later growth of output, is what is the only appropriately called capitalistic method of production. In this sense *all* production that takes advantage of the available technological possibilities is of necessity 'capitalistic'. The conception is disliked because people resent the fact that nobody has power to determine how the total available capital is to be used. This must, however, be left to be decided by the only process by which it can be effectively done, the impersonal market process, while the methods suggested as alternatives to 'capitalism' require that the use of all capital resources be placed in the hand of government which would have no means of deciding how to do so efficiently: it is by guiding from moment to moment the changes in the composition of this stream in adaptation to the continuously changing circumstances by persons aware of their particular local circumstances only but necessarily ignorant of the overall scheme into which their activities must fit, so that an orderly flow of the whole is secured. The theoretical models of which the millions knowing and deciding individuals make up the parts, can therefore never provide an effective basis for a central direction of these activities.

Once we have comprehended the basic but rarely understood fact that it is not technologically determined fixed combinations of resources, but economically determined variable combinations on which both the size and the continuity of the flow depends, it is in two respects that an awareness of this complexity of the process that produces a fairly steady stream of goods assumes great importance. On the one hand the relative steadiness of the stream can be secured only by constant adjustments to the details by the individual actors obeying signals which tell them what to do, and, secondly, the transmission of demand from the consumers' end to the primary factors is not taking place at a constant rate, but is effected by a process which makes the two magnitudes move not only at different rates but occasionally even in opposite directions.

At one stage of the development of economics the emphasis on the demand for intermediate products, tools, raw materials and primary factors being a *derived* demand, transferred from the demand for consumers' goods, was an important advance. But it can lead, and has led, to very erroneous conclusions. The idea that this demand is transmitted at a constant rate, as is the suction through a tube of constant diameter from the end of which a fixed intake is drawn, is simply false. The volume of the stream which lies between the beginning and the end can vary very much, and for so many different reasons, that the assumption that the demand for labour will normally change in proportion, or even in the same direction as the final demand, leads to wholly false recommendations for policy. This applies both to the relation between final demand and the demand for labour in general, and even more to the structure of relative prices which guides the use of the various kinds of resources.[19]

It is the neglect of these problems of ordering the structure of production by relative prices which was the cause of the general failure of macro-economic theory adequately to account for the problems of unemployment. The variable volume of the stream between the input of labour and the output of consumers' goods is of course what we call the capital of society—an extremely complex and constantly varying aggregate of things, the continuous reordering of which is one of the chief functions of the market process. Nowhere is the guiding function of prices more indispensable than in the constant adaptation of this structure of capital—both to the concrete objects that emerged from past efforts and that are awaiting further use, and the potentialities of new investment determined by the extent to which the expected demand for consumers' goods is already provided for and leaves some fraction of the available resources available for production for the future.

The relation between supply and demand, or the push and pull, is of course much more complex than the operation of the gradients of the branches or tributaries of a river. I wish I had time to describe more fully the complexity of this structure and the reasons which will make its constant change necessary to keep the stream moving. But of the ramifications of this flow, or rather countless interlocking and intertwined flows, requiring confluences at determined but variable rates, and each spreading like a tree as well as each branch combining with branches of other streams into a multiplicity of river systems, it is scarcely possible to form more than a grossly simplified abstract picture.

It is tempting to describe as an 'equilibrium' an ideal state of affairs in which the intentions of all participants precisely match and each will find a partner willing to enter into the intended transaction. But for all capitalistic production there must exist a considerable interval of time between the beginning of a process and its various later stages. The achievement of an equilibrium is strictly impossible. Indeed, in a literal sense, *a stream can never be in equilibrium*, because it is disequilibrium which keeps it flowing and determines its directions. Even an apparent momentary state of balance in which everybody succeeds in selling or buying what he intended, may be *inherently* unrepeatable, irrespective of any change in the external data, because some of the constituents of the stream will be the results of past conditions which have changed

---

[19] [In the edited typescript the last sentence is put in square brackets, probably indicating that it should be deleted.—Ed.]

long ago; or, to put it differently, part of the so-called 'data' will always be an effect of earlier adaptations to different data which no longer exist. The stream is maintained by constant adaptation to passing local conditions—the use of passing chances which have no systematic connections with the rest of the structure.

The price 'gradients', as I have called them, which keep the stream moving, are signals indicating momentary and passing conditions largely determined by events of the past; and how many of the potential productive forces the stream will be able to absorb will depend both on whether enough of these price signals or constellations of signals, stand at clear, indicating that in certain directions prices of output exceed prices of input, *and* whether the whole system of signals favours an increase or a decrease of *the volume of the whole stream*, and not merely the rate of flow at its mouth. Every price which is slow in adjusting itself to changes in local conditions may choke a particular streamlet and thereby impede the continuous movement of the whole. The *degree* to which the order will ever approach the unattainable ideal of equilibrium will depend on the speed of adaptation and of the communication process which brings it about. This is much more important than the degree of perfection towards which it may tend: since the process of adaptation never ends, the average closeness to the ideal will be determined by the speed of the response to changes in the data. The fluctuations which are inevitable in an order brought about by feedback processes, which social structures share with biological ones, will always cause divergences from stability and it will be the speed, not the ultimate perfectness of adaptation which will determine the steadiness of the flow.[20] Prompt movements in the right direction will do more to keep the stream flowing than any precise calculations of equilibrium conditions could do whose results would probably come too late to improve the flow. Inflexibility of prices, particularly of the prices of labour, can block many of the arteries on which the nourishment of society, and especially of the very people who endeavour to maintain their relative position, depend. Unemployment is not so much a function of 'aggregate demand' as of the elasticity of the price structure which, of course, all striving for a 'just' distribution obstructs.

Steadiness of the whole structure can be achieved solely by constant minor adaptations which will take place only if those in charge of the special activities are promptly informed of their necessity. *Changes of relative prices are the stabilisers of the whole system without which the coordination of the several activities would be soon disrupted.* But what the individuals are most likely to demand from government are stable prices, and what is called economic policy generally attempts to meet this wish. Yet those most pressing demands for 'security' or protection

---

[20] [In the edited typescript this sentence is in square brackets.—Ed.]

against unforeseen changes, and particularly against the effects of competition, are in the strict sense anti-social demands, disruptive of an order which can never continue in an unchanged state but can be preserved only by constant change—changes made necessary not only by events in the surrounding world which we either cannot or (in the case of growth of knowledge) do not wish to prevent, but also because the stream must draw on past provisions which were made in adaptation to conditions which no longer exist. Though stability of the prevailing prices may be desired by the producers and the users of most commodities, it is most likely to become the cause of instability of the system as a whole. If it is true, as is now often asserted, that price changes have largely been replaced by changes in the quantities bought and sold at unchanged prices, this may well be the cause of the growing inability to make full use of the available resources even when there is evident scarcity of many others. And while we may reasonably wish for a monetary order under which the changes of money prices do not actually misdirect production, and under which the inevitable uncertainty of future prices is so reduced that unforeseen changes of individual prices in one direction are likely to be offset by equal probabilities of unforeseen changes of other prices in an opposite direction, all use of the power to fix particular prices at figures different from those which would be arrived at on a competitive market can merely impede the spontaneous coordination of productive efforts.

Demand[21] will in general tend to favour production with less capital-intensive methods of production. An increase of the prices of consumers' goods is more likely to decrease than to increase the demand for more labour-saving machinery to make them. Whether the contents of the whole stream will grow or shrink, how they must be rearranged to secure as large a total product as possible, and the consequent differences between changes in final demand and the demand for primary factors, can be determined only by relative prices, but will be concealed by an analysis stressing exclusively the aggregate demand for final products.

Some of these problems have more recently been rediscovered. But through a neglect of the role which changes in relative prices play in this connection, and forcing the whole issue into a general equilibrium mode, were rather mishandled under the names of 'switching' and 'capital reversing'.[22] What seems to have been overlooked in these discussions is that the rate of return on in-

---

[21] [That is, final demand, demand for consumers' goods. In fact, Hayek is here reasserting the validity of the Ricardo effect.—Ed.]

[22] [Here Hayek refers to the so-called 'Cambridge capital controversy'; cf. the editor's introduction, p. 35. Although Hayek is right in emphasising that all the paradoxes examined are those present in comparisons among steady state equilibria, it is not true that the analyses involved neglect the role of relative prices and their intimate relationships with the rate of interest.—Ed.]

vested capital and the overall gradient of prices are not two different things but one and the same.

All these circumstances determining the smoothness of the overall flow have indeed very little to do with those changes in aggregate final demand to which Lord Keynes attached the central role in his theory of employment.[23] The great success of this theory is evidently due to its direct appeal to the daily experience of the corner grocer who rightly believes that his prosperity depends first of all on the volume of demand. But to the functioning of the variable, echeloned and interlaced arterial system which today yields our product, this has little relevance: the suction at the end is not uniformly transmitted through all the channels, and the constantly arising local discrepancies between demand and supply can be corrected only by a promptly responding direction mechanism.

To free ourselves from the perspectives of the corner grocer, to whom strong consumers' demand is the evident requirement for prosperity—the view which has ever been the source of inflationist ideas—we should really replace the simplified one-dimensional model of final demand sucking at varying strengths at the orifice of a pipe which at the other end lifts up corresponding quantities of matter, by the picture of a conical container of an expansible substance, with holes along all its length through which it can absorb material, and the size of which is determined by other circumstances, so that, as its volume increases or decreases, the intake may not only be different from, but possibly move in opposite direction to the rate of its outflow. Perhaps an expansible bladder or bag will provide a better simile if we imagine that the producers of consumers' goods pull after them, as it were, a pack of tools and supplies, becoming more efficient as they are better equipped. Their demand for replenishing the contents of this bag will not change in strict proportion with their sales and we should not expect anything but an always pulsating demand by them for what they require.

The whole phenomenon of the cyclic expansion and contraction of this supporting structure in imperfect correspondence to the rate of their sales— the alternate swelling and shrinking of the contents of their bag—is in some measure probably an inseparable consequence of the longitudinal division of labour. But so long as the self-correcting response of the market is kept intact, the swings are likely to keep within moderate dimensions. But men's ingenuity has discovered a way to escape for a time the unwelcome necessity of such corrections: faking a non-existing supply of investable capital by manufacturing additional credit-money—making it thereby possible for a disproportion-

---

[23] [It should be noted that while Hayek identifies 'final demand' with the demand for consumers' goods, in Keynesian theory 'aggregate demand' also comprises the demand for capital goods.—Ed.]

ate volume of investment to continue for a long time. The extent of misdirection of resources which this produces will sooner or later have to be corrected may become very substantial.[24]

It is thus the guide function of relative prices in bringing about longitudinal shifts of resources to earlier or later segments of the stream of production which determines both changes in the contents of the capital stock and of the kind and amount of resources that a given final demand will evoke. I shall as a matter of convenience speak in this connection of actual changes in prices where perhaps a more precise analysis would speak of changes in the demand schedules for the same kinds of primary factors at different points of the stream which sometimes will result in changes of their prices. And since we are mainly interested in the effects of the employment of labour I shall also speak about wages to describe what applies to the prices of all primary factors.

What is so rarely understood is that a shortage of capital ultimately always means that the demand for consumers' goods is too intense to leave over enough labour to supply the demands of those who do not themselves turn out consumable products. This may be temporarily disguised by providing those wishing to produce capital goods with extra money at sufficiently low rates of interest to make this appear attractive. But because the consumers' goods which these amounts of money are meant to buy are not available, the increasing pull out of the growing incomes for those[25] will catch up the increased demand for capital goods as soon as this grows at an accelerating rate. This will happen even if there is not full employment so long as there exist no surpluses of any critical factors, i.e., if not all supplies of factors are perfectly elastic.

High real wages make advantageous comparatively long intervals between the application of a large proportion of labour and the emergence of its products in consumable form; and wages kept high by union monopolies force the entrepreneurs to use the available capital in such capital-intensive forms. But the result will be that the available capital will be sufficient to equip only part of the labour force with disproportionally much capital per head. If this obstacle is at first overcome by providing more fictitious money capital for the purpose, the increasing money income will soon lead to an increase in the demand for consumers' goods, raise their prices and thus again bring down real wages. As an increase in demand fed by an increase in the quantity of money always does, this additional money works round and by raising prices of prod-

---

[24] [This sentence is corrupted in the edited typescript. A plausible conjecture might be, "The extent of misdirection of resources which this produces and which will sooner or later have to be corrected may become very substantial."—Ed.]

[25] [Apparently, "those" refers to the "consumers' goods" mentioned at the beginning of the sentence.—Ed.]

ucts and reducing real wages again eliminates the faked greater productivity of the more capitalistic processes. Unlike goods, which are used up, such money comes back, as it were, in its circular course and leads to those characteristic self-reversing effects of a fictitious demand. In the hands of those who have earned it, it is directed towards what they want to obtain and returns as demand for precisely what a step earlier has been snatched away[26] for other purposes, leading to that reassertion of the lack of capital which had been temporarily disguised by the creation of credit.

When forty-two years ago J. A. Schumpeter generously called this effect of real wages on employment the 'Hayek-Effect'[27] I tried to fend off this honour which suggested that it was a new invention. I suggested that it had better be called the 'Ricardo Effect'[28] since the basic conception had clearly already been stated by David Ricardo. I will no longer resist my name being coupled with that of Ricardo in this connection, but I still believe that he saw the crucial point first.

I will not enter here into any further discussion of how well the market today performs the function of keeping the flow of goods and services going. "It is not done well; but you are surprised to find it done at all."[29] Though the adaptation to constantly changing circumstances will scarcely ever have time to become perfect, its effectiveness depends on how fast it operates. Economics is a problem of taking advantage of unforeseen contingencies and no previously laid down plan can ever solve this problem. It is the speed with which the communication of information through the signalling system of the market spreads which prevents constant stoppages by prompt redirection of the flows. When price changes are not allowed to do this, nonavailability or nonsaleability take their place and the local manager no longer has the opportunity to judge what extra outlay is justified to keep the stream flowing. A centrally directed system will in this respect evidently be slow and clumsy, since it can only periodically recalculate and reissue the overall plan. The planning authority will have to feed into a computer what has been reported to it, while demand and supply feed directly into the market.

I have no doubt that the functioning of the market can still be improved by improving the framework of those rules of law within which it operates. And

[26] [The edited typescript corrected the original version, "what a step earlier it has snatched away", by deleting the word "it". The text has been restored by adding "been".—Ed.]

[27] [Joseph A. Schumpeter, *Business Cycles: A Theoretical, Historical, and Statistical Analysis of the Capitalist Process* (New York: McGraw-Hill, 1939), pp. 345, 812, 814; cf. also the reference in Hayek, "Three Elucidations", this volume, p. 319.—Ed.]

[28] [Cf. Hayek, "Profits, Interest and Investment", this volume, especially pp. 215–17.—Ed.]

[29] [The quotation is from James Boswell, *The Life of Samuel Johnson, LL.D.*, vol. 1 (London: Dilly, 1793), p. 428. In full it reads, "Sir, a woman's preaching is like a dog's walking on his hinder legs: It is not done well; but you are surprised to find it done at all."—Ed.]

we certainly have still ahead of us the major task of giving the monetary system the chance to develop into a mechanism which will give correct signals to the market. Its present imperfection is largely the result of positive interference by government, or at least the toleration of such by privileged or coercive agencies. It appears to me that at the present time priority must be given to removing the obstacles which, because of lack of understanding of the function of the market, governments have erected or are allowing private agencies to erect. We owe it to the folly of our predecessors that this negative task has become more urgent than positive ones have. Once we have again cleared the road for the more powerful spontaneous forces, we shall be able to return to the slower and more delicate efforts of improving the framework within which the market will function more effectively and beneficially.

I am afraid I must also deny myself any further pursuit of the monetary causes which can bring about those distortions of the real structure of production, that misdirection of efforts produced by the swellings and shrinkings of the flow of goods. That is another story to which I still hope to devote a separate study. I will merely repeat that those shifts in demand between different segments of this flow of real goods will alter the real structure by altering the relative prices (or demand schedules) at these stages. We must not forget that all investment involves taking away some resources from the satisfaction of present needs and that this must be done by the outbidding of the demand for them for making consumers' goods in the near future. This implies that a rise in the current prices of consumers' goods will normally lead to less investment.

Though there was some justification for Keynes' objection against proceeding on such an analysis from the assumption of full employment,[30] his going to the other extreme and proceeding on the assumption of full *un*employment, i.e., on the availability of unused resources of all kinds, wholly eliminated the crucial effect of the changes of relative prices from his account of events. He did, in effect, assume away scarcity and with it the economic problem. It was an approach guided by the illusion of the impending abundance to which many thinkers of his generation were prone. (See his essay on the "economic possibilities for our grandchildren" of 1930!)[31] Today's reformers seem still to alternate between the mirage of potential abundance and the fear of immi-

---

[30] [As Hayek did, e.g., in *Prices and Production*, reprinted, pp. 218–19. Cf. also his earlier stipulation in "The 'Paradox' of Saving", reprinted, p. 91n.49, that the assumption of the existence of unused resources "is theoretically inadmissible as a starting point for a theory which attempts . . . to show the causes of crises, and thus of unemployment, on the basis of the modern 'equilibrium' theory of price determination".—Ed.]

[31] [John Maynard Keynes, "Economic Possibilities for our Grandchildren", *The Nation and Atheneum*, vol. 48, October 11 and 18, 1930, pp. 36–37 and 96–98, reprinted in *Essays in Persuasion*, vol. 9 (1972) of *The Collected Writings of John Maynard Keynes*, pp. 321–32.—Ed.]

nent famine. It is an illusion[32] that there is no real scarcity, and that, if we only used our intelligence properly, we could satisfy all our reasonable desires. In fact we owe what we have achieved to a process which enables us to use more information than any individual or agency can possess, and which uses knowledge which otherwise would not exist as a whole.

It is not the size of aggregate demand which keeps the stream flowing, but that prompt redirection of the streamlets of which it is composed, which is made possible by the play of prices—those unwelcome signals which tell people that they must do something different from what they used to. It is the changing prospects of profit which operate like gravity directing each streamlet to the steepest gradient through which it will contribute most effectively to the main stream. If we remember that this must happen in the countless points of contact of what is best conceived as a superimposition of literally thousands of distinct arterial systems, each contributing its distinct nourishing substance, with their flows joining at thousands of junctions and combining at variable rates in what becomes stems of further tree-like structures, it becomes obvious that it is madness to believe that this can be ordered by a surveyor of it all and that the continuance of the flow depends on its self-regulating character.[33] There is no other way of releasing this stream in all its potential than by freeing it of all arbitrary interference with the competitive determination of prices, whether it be called price-fixing, monopolistic wage determination or incomes policy.

It is not much better to imagine that we can control this flow according to the oversimplified one-dimensional picture by managing the volume of final demand. There are at least two further chief dimensions of demand which no deliberate central direction but only the free play of prices on a competitive market can adequately guide: the horizontal distribution between different goods and the longitudinal (vertical or temporal) one between the different segments of the stream. It was the neglect of these aspects in his persuasive exposition which invalidates the theory of Lord Keynes, that ornament of a civilisation that would be in much better shape if he had never written on economics. When *The General Theory* appeared I felt indeed that I had refuted its presuppositions before it even came out and could not bring myself to devote as much time and effort to analysing it as I had shortly before devoted to his *Treatise*,[34] only to be told by Keynes, when the second part of my review ap-

---

[32] ["It is an illusion" is a conjecture instead of the original text, which reads, "The illusion that . . ." In the edited typescript the sentence is followed by a passage, put in square brackets, "that the knowledge which it is now in our power to acquire would enable us to do so, while . . ."—Ed.]

[33] [In the edited typescript the passage beginning with "and that the continuance" is in square brackets.—Ed.]

[34] [Here Hayek refers to Keynes's *General Theory* (1936) and his earlier *Treatise on Money* (1930).—Ed.]

peared, that he no longer believed in all that.[35] I have ever since blamed myself for not having then returned to the charge, but I certainly did not believe that what to me seemed to be so obviously wrong and simply reviving long-refuted errors, should for a whole generation again govern opinion and policy.[36] In this field we will have to start anew and for this purpose we have to discard not only his particular theories but the whole approach which he made fashionable: macro-economics.

[35] [The second part of Hayek's review was published as "Reflections on the Pure Theory of Money of Mr. J. M. Keynes (continued)", *Economica*, no. 35, February 1932, pp. 22–44, reprinted as chapter 6 of F. A. Hayek, *Contra Keynes and Cambridge*. For Keynes's response cf. his letter to Hayek, March 29, 1932 (reprinted, ibid., p. 173): "I doubt if I shall return to the charge in *Economica*. I am trying to re-shape and improve my central position, and that is probably a better way to spend one's time than in controversy."—Ed.]

[36] [For these and other reasons Hayek gave for not reviewing Keynes cf. Bruce Caldwell, "Why Didn't Hayek Review Keynes's *General Theory*?", *History of Political Economy*, vol. 30, Winter 1998, pp. 545–69, and Susan Howson, "Why Didn't Hayek Review Keynes's *General Theory*? A Partial Answer", *History of Political Economy*, vol. 33, Summer 2001, pp. 369–74. However, one should be aware of the 'unreliability of memory' before taking Hayek's own explanations at face value (cf. Bruce Caldwell, "Life Writings: On-the-Job Training with F. A. Hayek", in *Economists' Lives: Biography and Autobiography in the History of Economics*, ed. E. Roy Weintraub and Evelyn L. Forget (Durham, NC: Duke University Press), pp. 344–47.—Ed.]

INDEX

acceleration principle of derived demand, 222–23

Åkerman, Johan Henryk, 171, 171n.4

Anderson, Benjamin McAlester, Jr., 171, 171n.4

Bentham, Jeremy, 156–60, 156n.3

bimetallic currencies, 139, 139n.19

Birck, Laurits Vilhelm, 73n.15

Böhm-Bawerk, Eugen von, 147n.10

Bresciani-Turroni, Costatino, 171, 172n.4

Budge, Siefried, 171, 172n.4

Cannan, Edwin, 58n.9

capital: investment raising demand for, 206–11; rate of turnover of, 262–63

capital goods, demand for different kinds of, 226–29

capitalistic production, structure of, 223–26

Cassel, Carl Gustav, 63n.19

Catchings, Wadill, 143, 143n.4

Chamberlin, Edward, 3

circuit of money, 107–8

Clark, John Bates, 147n.10

closed circuit of money, 107–8

completing investments: causes of urgent demand for funds for, 210–11; rate of interest and, 208–9

concertina-effect, 21n.79; Hayek and, 285–317; truth about, 308–11

consumers, purchasing power of, and Great Depression, 141–55

consumers' goods, demand for and supply of, during upswings, 243–45

cumulative process, anomaly of, 245–46

deflation, 176; Hayek and, 5–15, 5n.20; induced, 176n.14

depression, revival and, 232–34. *See also* Great Depression

direct exchange, 74–75

Durbin, Evan F. M., 15–16, 16n.60, 23

employment, stable, short run ceiling of, 246–48

Eucken, Walter, 171, 172n.4

exchange, 74–89; direct, 74–75

exchange value of money, review of, 136–40

expectations, role of, 221–22

Fannon, Marco, 171, 172n.4

Fasiani, Mauro, 171, 172n.4

Fisher, Irving, 62–63

"Flow of Goods and Services, The" (Hayek), 41–43

fluctuations, industrial, 171–79; possibilities of mitigating, 249–50; reply to criticism of, 186–205

forced saving, 187; development of doctrine of, 156–70

Ford, Henry, 143, 143n.4

Foster, William Truffant, 143, 143n.4

goods and services, flow of, lecture on, 331–46

347